The Doctors (Hans Burgkmair, German, 1473-1531)
Reproduced from Medicine and the Artist (Ars Medica) by permission of the Philadelphia Museum of Art.

Ex Libris:

On Private Madness

On Private Madness

ANDRÉ GREEN

INTERNATIONAL UNIVERSITIES PRESS, INC.

Madison   Connecticut

Published by
International Universities Press,
Madison, Connecticut

Library of Congress Cataloging-in-Publication Data

Green, André.
    On private madness.

    Articles reprinted from various sources.
    Bibliography: p.
    Includes index.
    1. Psychoanalysis. I. Title. [DNLM: 1. Psycho-
analysis—collected works. 2. Psychoanalytic Theory—
collected works. WM 460 G7950]
RC509.G69 1986   616.89'17   86-27641
ISBN 0-8236-3853-7

Manufactured in the United States of America

Contents

ACKNOWLEDGEMENTS

This book owes much to Christopher Bollas's constant support and incessant encouragements.

I wish to express my thanks in particular to Katherine Aubertin for her translations of three chapters in this volume.

Introduction

One day, a former analysand asked me: 'Why do you write?' The question took me by surprise: it was not one I had ever asked myself. Without thinking, I answered: 'As a testimony.' To be sure, I was aware of the less avowable reasons that I had learned from my analysis: the need to be admired, exhibitionism, oedipal rivalry, and so on. But there were other reasons, too, on a more evolved level: the wish to organize experience into theory, and, last but not least, the expression of my search for truth in the filiation of Freud. However, all this would not have constituted the right reply. I should have said: 'I write because I cannot do otherwise' – which does not contradict the interpretations I have just given, but rather includes them all. For, this persisting wish (which belongs to the unconscious) to satisfy, in a sublimated form, the instincts of one's infantile sexuality does not disappear with time, but endures, though transformed, ever endowed with the same imperiousness. And it is a necessity no less imperious which seizes the elements of a complex experience, often obscure and sometimes elusive, to organize it into a coherent vision which ensures that it does not completely escape our understanding. The aims of both the unconscious and the ego come together in the compulsion to write. They are founded on a third element, which takes into account the imperatives of the superego and the ego ideal. I feel hardly free to write or not to write: I must write to contribute to the increase of knowledge and to maintain a self-image which I can recognize. In each instance, the agencies which compose my psychical personality, as Freud says, converge towards the same goal, which is imposed upon me rather than freely chosen.

Nevertheless it is also true that my writing, however one may judge it, is also a testimony. It is, I think, a fairly representative sample, a derivative, of the French psychoanalytic movement of the second half of the twentieth century. And this is what I would like to impart to the Anglo-Saxon reader on the threshold of this translation.

One may query the fact that I designate myself thus, by nationality. Does not psychoanalysis, in its endeavour to shed light on that which is most universal, tend to abolish frontiers? Perhaps this is just an illustra-

tion of the narcissism of minor differences, of which Freud spoke.
Whatever the ideal wish may be to arrive at formulations that may be
embraced by all, as was the case with Freud, the fact remains that
psychoanalysts today seem to stand out more particularly in terms of
their divergences, resulting from different conceptions about the mind,
but also because of differences stemming from their cultural traditions.
Lacan's work could only have evolved in France, and I believe that
Winnicott's work is intimately related to what he owes to his native land.
In spite of this, nothing prevents these works from crossing the frontiers
of the countries where they first came to light. It may, however, explain
certain misunderstandings which have arisen when they were subjected
to criticism.

It seems to me that the best way of introducing this collection of papers
to the reader is to recount briefly my own psychoanalytic history; the
more so because French psychoanalysts have the reputation with their
foreign colleagues of having a complicated form of thought – too
theoretical, it is said, often hard to grasp, and too far removed from
clinical experience and daily practice. The explanation is simple: French
psychoanalysts belong to a different cultural tradition from that of the
Anglo-Saxon world, where empiricism and pragmatism are considered
to be qualities; where intellectualism and abstraction count as vices
rather than as virtues. This type of judgement has never really convinced
me, for I have thought, when reading certain well-known Anglo-Saxon
authors, that their literature seemed extremely abstract; which is
another way of saying that their theorisation did not get through to me.
On the other hand, the work of Bion and that of Winnicott have always
seemed to me to be highly intellectual; which means that to categorize
thought as intellectual is, for me, laudatory.

One generally believes that an analyst who presents clinical material
in a paper shields himself from the reproach of being abstract. The
reader will not find much 'case material' in this collection. This is a
deliberate choice, for a number of reasons. The first is discretion towards
my patients, many of whom may read my work, psychoanalytic literature being read in France by a public which extends well beyond
professional circles; not to mention the fact that many of my analysands
belong more or less to this milieu. Secondly, I do not think that
presenting clinical observations constitutes proof of what an analyst
advances from a theoretical point of view. Presentation of material can
obviously be modulated to fit one's demonstration, and the same
material can be used to illustrate different if not opposing views,
depending on the circumstances. No clinical observation has the validity

to settle a theoretical debate. In psychoanalytical congresses, participants whose opinions differ on theoretical grounds will one by one demonstrate the 'proof' of the correctness of their reasoning with clinical examples to back them up, which only convince those who were convinced beforehand. The third and last reason is that a 'theoretical' paper is also clinical inasmuch as it stimulates associations in an analyst reader, in connection with his own experience or that of his patients. I strive to attain this goal in my writing without using explicit references to clinical material. Once again, what is theoretical, that is to say intellectual, is at the antipodes of abstraction.

Abstraction versus intellectuality; this needs explaining. A structured psychoanalytic theory, which is coherent, is the product of psychical activity, a *'Durcharbeitung'*, which is a progress in intellectuality, to cite a late work of Freud, *Moses and Monotheism* (1939a). But for all that, it is not an abstract product; not only because it is enriched by clinical experience, but because all working-through – by the analysand as well as by the analyst – consists of the interplay of representations and affects in the exchange of transference and countertransference. To distinguish between abstraction and intellectuality is no easy task, the first being easily able to pass for the second. This is what my psychoanalytic autobiography has taught me.

I started my psychoanalytic training in 1956, but only after three years' specialization in psychiatry and neurology when I had the good fortune to study with prestigious teachers, who were exceptionally talented and who combined remarkable clinical understanding with a strong taste for reflection, debate and discussion with their younger colleagues. I began by believing that the key to mental disorders was to be sought within the brain. It was only when I began seriously to care for patients in psychiatry who were entrusted to me that I realized that I was on the wrong track. Understanding these patients' discourse gave me the obscure feeling that the mechanisms I was observing had a different causality from those revealed by the study of the brain. Besides, far from being merely a witness, as I had supposed, I very soon became conscious that I was the object of transference, in spite of myself. I soon felt overwhelmed by the emotional reactions which I had provoked and which escaped my control.

1953 was an important year for three reasons. First, a personal factor, it represented the beginning of my psychiatric training. Secondly, it was the year of a therapeutic revolution; that of the introduction of psychotropic medication in psychiatry. Thirdly, it was the date of a split in the Paris Psychoanalytic Society which saw the departure of Jacques Lacan,

Daniel Lagache and others. At the Hôpital Sainte Anne, in 1954, I had heard Jacques Lacan give a conference which made an enormous impact on me, and I also had the opportunity of seeing him interview patients, which he did with great talent. I had read his text 'The function and field of speech and language in psychoanalysis' (Lacan, 1956a) when it was published – and which has now become famous, under the title of the Rome Report. It had been read to an audience of dissidents in 1953: a violent criticism of current psychoanalytic trends, which he held responsible for causing psychoanalysis to stray from the paths that Freud had opened up; stigmatizing the latent behaviourism of the North American concepts, the pre-eminence given to phantasy – the imaginary – (more specifically unconscious phantasy) in the work of Melanie Klein, and finally the replacement of the reference to transference with the reference to countertransference. Standing up against the entire psychoanalytic community, Lacan proposed to return to the spirit and the letter of Freud's thinking by giving speech and language precedence again. Influenced by the rediscovery of the linguist Ferdinand de Saussure, by the philosopher Merleau-Ponty and the anthropologist Lévi-Strauss, he inaugurated a structuralist conception of psychoanalysis by giving priority to the symbolic as opposed to the imaginary and the real. The symbolic stood for the unconscious organization, such as dream-work allows one to apprehend it, for example. In other words, the unconscious was not a matter of contents, but an organizing and organized system.

The newness of Lacan's point of view impressed me, and struck a chord within me. However, when I decided to undertake psychoanalytic training, I chose the other camp. In 1956 M. Bouvet had just published a work of clinical interest which seemed important to me, on 'object relations'; so I decided that he should be my analyst.

One must draw attention here to the difference between the two perspectives. Lacan's proposition was that the world of words created the world of things: in other words, that psychoanalysis could be nothing but the analysis of the patient's speech. Bouvet implicitly opted for the opposite thesis: namely, that it is object relations which direct the patient's discourse. For Lacan, the unconscious was structured like a language. For Bouvet, the unconscious was formed, as Freud had indicated, of object representations structured in a different fashion from that which governs language. However, it is clear that the theory of object relations is somewhat different from the Freudian conception of object representations; the more so as Bouvet's theory diverged distinctly from what was generally understood by this expression at that time, whether by Fairbairn or by Melanie Klein.

From 1956 to 1960 I trained at the Paris Institute of Psychoanalysis, occasionally going to meetings held by Lacan, but without attending his public seminars. I only started to attend these in 1961. In November 1960, a few months after the death of M. Bouvet, an important conference on the unconscious was organized by Henri Ey, bringing together psychiatrists, philosophers and psychoanalysts. It was the first time since the split of 1953 that the antagonists of both groups had confronted each other in public. J. Laplanche and S. Leclaire presented a paper which was inspired by Lacan's theses, illustrating his proposition: 'the unconscious is structured like a language'. Although I recognized the interest and merit of this work, I criticized it in detail, already at this period, by pointing out the lack of attention to, even the occultation of, the place and function of affects in Lacan's theory. This seemed to me to be contrary both to clinical experience and to Freud's thinking.

Nevertheless, in 1961 I decided to accept Lacan's invitation to follow his teaching, while still remaining a member of the Paris Psychoanalytic Society. The impact of his thinking – and his personal charisma – drew me into his wake, as a fellow traveller. Neither more nor less.

I took an active part in Lacan's seminars from 1961 to 1967. I entered as far as I was able into the intricacies of his thought. I even belonged to a small working group, where seven or eight participants presented clinical material to him, in order to secure a better grasp on how his theory could be applied in practice. If my curiosity was not satisfied on this point, I retain the memory of interesting work in my exchanges with him. I think that the years between 1961–67 were among the best of Lacan's teaching; those in which his ideas came to maturity and when the man seemed to me to be at the peak of his form. Still, however attractive these seminars were, they never won me over completely.

I must truthfully say that, for all those who followed him, Lacan was a tremendous intellectual stimulant. He awakened in me, as in others, the ardent wish to work and think. He urged us not to content ourselves with an overview of Freud's texts, but to try to elicit from them the way in which his thought was articulated, and the impetus of his speculative work. To be sure, it was Lacan's hope that the result of such an examination would be an ever firmer acceptance of his own interpretation. Re-reading Freud was meant to lead to the conclusion that Lacan was his authentic continuator, his legitimate heir. The power of Lacanian thought was presumed to excuse all the rest, that is to say, the liberties taken in practice, the manipulation of transference and unconditional allegiance to his person. In my own case, by effecting a split, which I later realized was of a defensive nature, I had decided to make a distinction between the theoretician and the practitioner. I agreed to listen to the first while turning a deaf ear to the second.[1] This split allowed me to work intensely, however, with results whose outcome I had glimpsed from the start, but which I had to demonstrate in detail.

Hence Lacan advocated a return to Freud, for he believed that post-Freudian psychoanalysis had gone astray. He gave birth to what subsequently became known as the 'French Freud'. It is true that Freud's thought is polysemic and that one could also speak of an 'American Freud', Hartmann's Freud, for instance, having nothing in common with Lacan's. I followed Lacan's advice to study Freud thoroughly, almost exegetically. But the more progress I made in understanding Freud's works, the more I became aware that the 'return to Freud', as I understood it, did not accord with the interpretation provided by the spokesman of the 'French Freud'. Lacan made the handsome gesture of giving me the chance to express my criticism publicly, at his seminar. Being an outsider, it was easier for me than for his disciples.

I began with the examination of a Lacanian concept (such as, the object 'a' [Green, 1966], or his grammatical interpretation of the id); I endeavoured to examine its implications as completely as possible; I drew attention to the differences between Lacan and Freud; and I put forward notions of my own which seemed to me to be more profitable. Thus, for example, I proposed the concept of negative hallucination in opposition to the concept of the structure of the signifier, and the interpretation of absolute primary narcissism as the expression of the psychical apparatus to reduce excitation to nought; a manifestation of the death instinct.

In 1965 a second split took place which led to the separation of Lacan and Lagache. Many of Lacan's students left him for good on this occasion. For my part, I continued to follow his teaching in the same way, notwithstanding various pressures designed to make me give it up. Meanwhile, ever since 1961, during the Pre-congress in London and the Congress in Edinburgh, I had been in touch with psychoanalysts from the British Society. That was when I made the acquaintance of D. W. Winnicott, Herbert Rosenfeld, Hanna Segal and J. Klauber, whose clinical presentations greatly impressed me.

Thus I discovered another manner of understanding psychoanalytic

---

[1] It took me years to realize the interdependence of these two aspects (theoretical and practical) of Lacan's activity. I have recently developed this viewpoint in 'Le langage dans la psychanalyse' (Green, 1984), a continuation of my work on affect, *Le discours vivant*, to which I shall refer further on.

practice, and of interpreting what was to be heard. The more familiar I became with their frame of mind, the more I had the feeling that this was where I could find what was missing in Lacan's approach, which seemed to me unsatisfactory, even misguided, with its excessive abstraction. I gave up attending Lacan's seminar in 1967, after the publication of a paper on primary narcissism (Green, 1967b), in which Lacan considered that I had not taken his own ideas sufficiently into account.

I had followed Lacan in the name of freedom of thought, and now he was upbraiding me for thinking for myself. It was the end of our collaboration. On the other hand, I was turning more and more towards the work of members of the British Psycho-Analytical Society, which enriched my psychoanalytic experience. From this date I became a fervent defender of entente cordiale in psychoanalysis.

In 1970 I presented a report to the Congress of French-speaking psychoanalysts, on affect, which was published in book form under the title *Le discours vivant: la conception psychanalytique de l'affect* (Green, 1973). This work allowed me to clarify my thoughts. In the first place, it enabled me to analyse the concept as completely as I could, drawing both on Freud's work and on post-Freudian psychoanalysis, and also considering it from a clinical point of view; with a personal interpretation of it as well.[1] Secondly, it provided the opportunity of a much wider hearing for the criticism of Lacan's theory which I had been formulating ever since 1960.

It is a fact that Freud's theory favours representation rather than affects, at least until 1923, the date of the second topographical model of the psychical apparatus. If reference to representation is less marked after this date, on the other hand the replacement of the unconscious by the id leads Freud to allude more and more frequently to instinctual impulses rather than to affect itself. Of course, *Inhibitions, Symptoms and Anxiety* (Freud, 1926d) refers to the affect of anxiety. But apart from this, it is recognized that the Freudian conception of affects remains incomplete and often obscure to this day. Besides, a notable psychoanalytic trend, starting with Fairbairn, Melanie Klein and Marjorie Brierley and extending today to Kernberg, includes the question of representation and affects in the framework of object relations. This evolution is not a purely speculative undertaking. It is also the consequence of an evolution in practice, which has never foregone its interest in the analysis of non-neurotic structures. One can also note that, in the final period of his work, Freud opposes neurosis to psychosis rather than to perversion.

---

[1] For a shorter discussion of affect, see chapter 8 below (p. 174).

In 1972 J.-B. Pontalis invited me to serve on the editorial committee of the *Nouvelle Revue de Psychanalyse*. Here I encountered colleagues of my own generation; we had all followed Lacan, and we had all subsequently left him. The general orientation of the *Nouvelle Revue de Psychanalyse* was situated in the post-Lacanian filiation on the one hand, and on the other it manifested a growing interest in the works of analysts of the British Society. Masud Khan, who served on the committee as foreign co-editor, guided us with suggestions for the translation and diffusion of Winnicott's work, in particular, but also certain American authors such as Searles. In France the impact of Winnicott's work, thanks to the translation of his books, marked a veritable turning-point in French psychoanalysis. I consider *Playing and Reality* (Winnicott, 1971*b*) to be one of the fundamental works of contemporary psychoanalysis. Also, the work of Melanie Klein, already known in France, became the object of renewed interest as a result of the work of her successors, namely H. Segal, H. Rosenfeld and especially W. Bion. It is this last author who most attracted my attention, and I studied his work from 1970 onwards.

The writings of Winnicott (and of his followers, especially Masud Khan and Marion Milner) had an incomparably true ring, clinically: one was struck by the originality of his concepts, their newness and, I would add, their freshness. They gave an airing to psychoanalytic space, stripping classical technique of its rigidity and giving renewed freedom to the analyst-analysand pairing. Such freedom had already existed in the last period of Ferenczi's work (1928–33) and was expressed by his successors – particularly M. Balint. But I believe that it is with Winnicott, who had taken a different course, through paediatrics to psychoanalysis (cf. Winnicott, 1975), that it reached its full development. One knows how Winnicott's work was influenced by Melanie Klein, though not without sustaining a keen need to escape from the dilemma posed by external object (Freud and A. Freud)–internal object (M. Klein), and thus creating the intermediary space and transitional phenomena which were essential to the understanding of non-neurotic structures.

W. Bion gave orthodox Kleinianism – if I may put it that way – new impetus by linking her work with that of Freud. Completely absorbed with exploring the most unconscious phantasies and the most archaic anxieties in psychotic structures, Melanie Klein did not seem to realize fully that each had an incidence on thought processes. This is what Bion understood. His considerable theoretical acumen permitted him to blend Freudian and Kleinian thought. His endeavour to link knowledge gained through psychoanalysis to other modes of learning (philosophy, logic, mathematics, physics, biology) found its accomplishment in the work of his mature years, from *Learning from Experience* to *Attention and Interpretation*; after which, as though he were disappointed with his own elaboration in the face of the immensity of the unknown, which his theorisation could not reach, his work took a tangent which disconcerted even his most fervent admirers. In my own case, I found in Bion an author who could measure up to Lacan. I think that each, from his own angle, had a common project, with completely different clinical and theoretical references: the hope of reformulating psychoanalytic theory within a contemporary epistemological framework which would allow one to overcome that which, in Freud's work, was hampered by the thinking of his time, which is no longer ours. However, while Lacan took his stand on the side of language and structural linguistics, banishing affect from his theory, Bion started with the most primitive emotional experiences and lead up to the most intellectual concepts. Today, I would say Lacan made the error of excessive abstraction, whereas Bion, with his constant reference to affect and the process of transformation, is the more authentically intellectual, in the best sense of the term.

In 1974, the Committee for the London Congress of the International Psychoanalytical Association of the following year, entrusted me with a report on changes in psychoanalytic theory and practice (see chapter 2 below). This gave me the opportunity of gathering together the threads that bound a number of contemporary works into a comprehensive picture, and to propose a theoretico-clinical model stemming from experience with borderline patients. Beside the model of neurosis (as the negative of perversion) that Freud left us, it seemed to me there was room for another model arising from a new perspective on neurosis and psychosis, revealed by psychoanalytic literature in the preceding twenty years. This work was dedicated to the memory of D. W. Winnicott.

I believed that what had changed since Freud was probably less the population of analysands than the analysts' way of listening to them. Certainly one must not rule out the fact that one encounters fewer neurotics than in Freud's day, if only for the reason that this population is more diluted because of the greater number of analysts. But above all, it was the ear of the analyst that was no longer the same. Nowadays one's hearing is more sensitive to picking up conflicts that are laden with archaic potential, which perhaps passed unnoticed in the past. Today – even if we do not all formulate it in the same way – we are sensitive to the process of symbolization, which I understand less within a Lacanian or Kleinian perspective than a Winnicottian. Finally, the problem of the absence of the object and its repercussions on the function of representation, which reflects back to the analyst and to symbolization, seems to me to be fundamental. On this point, what I had learned from Lacan and his ideas on language as a presence-absence were very useful.

After 1976 I had regular personal encounters with Bion, whom I met for the first time at the Symposium on 'Borderline Personality Disorders', which was organized by the Menninger Foundation at Topeka. The English-speaking reader may get the impression that my personal affinities drew me closer to the far side of the Channel than to the far side of the Atlantic. Yet, if my psychoanalytic culture is incomplete and rather limited concerning the world of Anglo-Saxon authors, I have often expressed the deep regret that these same authors make very few mentions of the work of their French or French-speaking colleagues in their writing; at least until very recently.[1]

After 1966, my work followed two main directions: the clinical and theoretical study of narcissism, and the study of borderline pathology. My preoccupation with narcissism was from an angle somewhat different from the usual approach. I was struck by the fact that after proposing his final theory of the instincts, Freud lost interest in narcissism. He did not even manifest the need to explain how the opposition of life and death instincts modified his previous views on narcissism, and how one should reinterpret this concept in the light of his new ideas. The success of Kohut's work clearly shows, however, that this same concept continues to be useful, theoretically and clinically, even though one may not agree with the interpretation he gives, nor the clinical application which stems from it. A mistake frequently made is to oppose narcissism to instincts. Now, narcissism is an expression of ego libido, itself attached to the theory of the instincts. In my opinion, there is a positive narcissism, a unifying factor from the ego, where its libido – as opposed to object libido – endeavours to achieve ego cohesion: this narcissism tends towards Oneness. My hypothesis is that this tendency towards Oneness is counteracted by negative narcissism, arising from the destructive instincts, which acts in the reverse direction, and is only manifest in the tendency to reduce ego cathexes to Nought. Clinically this is evident in all narcissistic pathology that confronts us with states of a psychical void

[1] It is to be hoped that, in the future, translations will remove linguistic barriers for all psychoanalysts who wish to keep themselves informed of the different trends of thought which nourish the psychoanalytic world. Up to now, these barriers have been lifted for English-language authors vis-à-vis French-speaking readers, but not vice versa – at least, not in the same proportion. This is why it is especially agreeable to me to have this book published in English, in this prestigious collection.

I am also glad to have had the opportunity of presenting some representative aspects of French psychoanalytic thinking when I was lecturing at the Freud Memorial Chair at University College, London, in 1978–79 (see chapter 1 below, p. 17).

and decathexis of the ego. It is in this manner that object libido and object cathexes are doubly attacked: by positive narcissism, which favours ego libido, as well as by negative narcissism, which decathects ego libido, without returning it to the object. The resulting indifference does not even serve egoism by means of a lack of empathy for the object. In many cases it appears that the ego becomes as disinterested in itself as in the object, leaving only a yearning to vanish: to be drawn towards death and Nothingness. For me, this is the true expression of the death instinct, which is in no way comparable to aggressivity or even to primary masochism. Freud's expression, absolute primary narcissism, seems to be an equivalent of this absolute barrier against any exchange, not only with the object, but within the centre of the ego itself, which is subject to the process of unbinding, with the depletion of the capacity to project. I concede that this is a speculative proposition, but it is one which conforms to observation and which can be found in certain oriental philosophies, which encourage their adepts to absolute detachment at the cost of their own ego, inasmuch as it remains the prisoner of its own and its object's desires.

Every psychoanalyst knows that clinical experience is the source of our knowledge, but it only takes on true meaning if it is illustrated by the theory that takes it into account. Now, since Freud's death, and doubtless even before that, one can no longer refer to psychoanalytic theory in the singular. As is demonstrated above, the psychoanalyst today must find his way through the forest of contemporary theories, with Freud's heritage alone to guide him. Each of us makes his choice at the theoretical crossroads, and opts for the path that seems the best to him, to find his own way forward. For, even if the work of Freud remains beyond question the greatest, there is more than one way of reading it and interpreting it. Besides, the psychoanalytic practice is no longer the same, and today's analyst is confronted with problematic cases whose nature is such that Freud's work may be of little help. I do not see this as something to lament, but rather as a challenge to continue the work that Freud initiated and to open up new perspectives of research. This is what makes psychoanalysis a living and advancing discipline.

I myself have not escaped the common lot. After a thorough study of Freud, my theoretical elaboration was influenced by Lacan, Winnicott and Bion. I am, however, neither Lacanian, Winnicottian nor Bionian, and I do not think that I have fallen into the trap of eclecticism either. I have tried to enrich my thinking with these three authors, without foregoing my own individuality. They attracted me more than others because their work gave me more cause for thought than others'. I do not claim that it should be so for every analyst, and I recognize the right of other people to make other choices and to arrive at different conclusions. Our analysands confide such rich and complex material to us, which constitutes a fund for constant reflection, that no theoretical interpretation can claim to give an exact, still less an exhaustive, rendering of it.

To put the emphasis on interpretation, whether it concerns patients or reading Freud, does not mean, for all that, that I share the views of some who see psychoanalysis as a branch of hermeneutics. The papers that take this line nowadays are frequently quite radically sceptical. I do not believe that all interpretations have the same value, or that their relation to the truth depends solely on one's point of view. The wish to minimize the importance of the discoveries of psychoanalysis underlies this attitude which relativizes our psychoanalytic knowledge, perhaps excessively so. The area of our certitudes is limited, for sure; however, one should not confuse critical debate with theologians' quarrels. Nor do I believe those who speak, in my opinion lightly, of the science of psychoanalysis; or one should state clearly, at any rate, that the official criteria of science considerably limit its interest, from the point of view of the study of the human psyche. I am convinced that contemporary psychoanalysis has to find its own tongue, which is neither that of religious theology nor that of scientific positivism; neither that of the irrational nor that of narrow reason. There is a logic, or rather logics, of the unconscious which we have begun to understand better and better since Freud, perhaps to an extent that he never suspected. Winnicott showed us the heuristic interest of paradoxes within the theory: such as the paradox which opposes the subjective object and the object objectively perceived.

For many years I tried to oppose Freud's work to that of his successors, just as I saw neurotic structures as being opposed to non-neurotic structures. Today I am inclined to believe that these oppositions, which appear to be valid, are not so clearcut as I thought. More precisely, a parallel arises when one confronts them. I shall take one example to illustrate what I mean. The study of non-neurotic structures has brought to light two types of anxiety, which most authors seem to agree upon, even though they use different terms; namely, separation anxiety and intrusion anxiety, which manifest a weakness of the boundaries between the ego and the object. Now, if one adds to castration anxiety (described by Freud) penetration anxiety – more specific to female sexuality, in my opinion – one is confronted with the pair castration-penetration which finds its corresponding pair in separation-intrusion. Without doubt, these two pairs of opposites refer to different clinical entities, and are concerned with developmental levels that are not the same; but, fundamentally they refer to the common question of binding-unbinding which is found in Freud, of separation-reunion in Winnicott's terms, or of container-contained in Bion. Quite some time ago M. Bouvet already proposed the concept of distance from the object in a similar perspective.

These remarks refer to psychical space, but one could also demonstrate analogous correspondences in the order of time. Freud saw the tendency to discharge of the primary process as being opposed to the possibility of the secondary process to defer action. Bion situated the fundamental dilemma of the psyche in the alternative: either flight from frustration by evacuation, or tolerance of it by elaborating it through thought. He said of the psychotic that he carries out projective identification with interstellar speed. Winnicott, finally, sought to define the optimal time of waiting for the infant. When this time is reduced to nothing by the mother who immediately replies to the baby's wants (or anticipates them), she deprives him of the ability to elaborate. If on the contrary, her response exceeds a certain threshold, it engenders catastrophic reactions in the infant with experiences of disintegration. Here the right distance becomes the right timing. The good enough mother is also the bad enough mother.

It could be that, on an elevated theoretical level, the questions with which we psychoanalysts are confronted are also those which face all thinkers: the true and the false (I think of the false-self); the real and the illusory (I think of the intermediary space); good and bad (I think of the Kleinian breast); good and evil (that is the ethical question of the superego); the order of language and the order of the world (here is Lacan and his signifier); sense and non-sense (Freud's unconscious); reason and unreason (madness or psychosis?). Unlike philosophers, we try to reply to these questions, not within the isolation of our own thoughts, but through the endeavours of the analyst-analysand couple, within the psychoanalytic setting. Certainly, our answers are not always satisfactory. We must content ourselves with approximations (Bion), compared with an absolute truth which remains inaccessible. Experience and reflection convince us, however, that we do wring a not negligible parcel of knowledge from the unknowable of the human mind.

Freud already knew that the boundaries between neurosis and normality are barely discernible. Following him, we have learned that many persons who are well adapted to social and external reality harbour what I have termed private madness. Psychoanalysts themselves are far from being immune from it. One learns this when certain of them, like H. Searles, break the law of silence. And Winnicott also said that for us to be able to understand psychotics, we must necessarily have something in common with them. Those who keep away from borderline patients, to devote themselves only to the analysis of neurotics, no doubt have the good fortune of benefitting from stronger or more efficient repressions. But what analyst can practice his profession today by turning away from his couch all patients who do not present a classic neurosis, or supposedly so? It is not certain that we have the choice. Private madness will be there to meet us more often than we would either foresee or hope for. One may as well recognize it and reckon with it.

When an analyst assembles a number of his papers into book form, he becomes aware of a curious phenomenon. This collection, which gathers together papers that stretch over more than a decade, reveals that ideas which seemed at the time to be developing in a new way, when compared with earlier works, had in fact already been germinating many years before in a previous article. Of course the idea, when first formulated, existed only in a rudimentary form, and one would not have thought it would finally take on such importance. It could even be that an idea for which one claims authorship was borrowed from a colleague; a cryptomnesia carried out in silence.

I have already had the opportunity of making this observation when the publication of another collection led me to a deduction. Every analyst is aware of the psychoanalytic process within the cure. It could be that, for the analyst who writes, a psychoanalytic process exists which does not reveal itself through his self-analysis alone. I propose to call it the theoretical psychoanalytic process. One owes one's personal style of thinking to this process.

Our psychoanalytic training includes our personal analysis, supervisions, the study of theory. Nowhere does it train one how to write, thank goodness. An analyst's written work is probably another way of continuing his self-analysis in a form by which others may profit. There is no doubt that this is an exercise that falls within the realm of sublimation. To define what is being sublimated goes beyond the purpose of this introduction. Perhaps one should attribute more to the analyst's masochism than is normally done. He uses his leisure time in which to write, for writing does not necessarily form part of his work. He sacrifices to writing, with whatever pleasure he may derive from it, the pleasures that he obtains from other less intellectual pursuits. When colleagues get together, they agree: 'What a mad profession!' Perhaps writing is also part of the analyst's private madness. He can rid himself of it, in part, only by writing of others' private madness: that of his analysands, to whom the psychoanalyst consecrates one of the most precious parts of himself in the inter-subjective exchange of the unconscious.

I

Psychoanalysis and Ordinary Modes of Thought

In an unfinished work written in London during the autumn of 1938, Freud wrote: 'Psychoanalysis has little prospect of becoming liked or popular. It is not merely that much of what it has to say offends people's feelings. Almost as much difficulty is created by the fact that our science involves a number of hypotheses – it is hard to say whether they should be regarded as postulates or as products of our researches – which are bound to seem very strange to ordinary modes of thought and which fundamentally contradict current views. But there is no help for it' (Freud 1940b, p. 282). Freud is alluding here to the unconscious. He explains that the resistances to the unconscious are not only due to a moral censorship but to an intellectual one as well, as if its existence threatened reason and logic. In this opening chapter I will try to show that the progression of Freud's work compelled him to recognize the existence of modes of thought even more extraordinary then he could have expected when he proposed his first hypothesis on the unconscious.

When we advise the analysand to avoid censuring his thoughts and to say all that comes to mind, the censure pertains to both moral and intellectual categories. The analysand's use of free associations implies that he has accepted the surrender of all claim to the rational connection of thoughts, so that another type of connection can be established by means of the analyst's freely floating attention. The relationships established by the analyst's mind between different parts of the material communicated by the analysand's free association, including some missing links which are implicitly active in silence, suggest that a certain form of logic is at work behind the scenes, which does not obey the rules of common reason. Would it not be the case that either there would be no latent content at all or, if such a content existed, it would not be intelligible?

I do not intend to resume the various stages which led to the

This is a slightly revised version of the Inaugural Lecture given on 15 October 1979, at the start of my year's appointment to the Freud Memorial Chair at University College, London. The translation is by Pamela Tyrell.

demonstration of this other logic. I will simply make the point that this double logic was theorized by Freud in his classical opposition between primary and secondary processes. Although it is well known that secondary processes are the processes of traditional logical thought and obey the reality principle, it has not always been made clear that primary processes, which obey the pleasure–displeasure principle, also have an implicit logic. Its main characteristics are that it ignores time; it does not take negation into account; it operates by condensation and displacement; and it does not tolerate any expectation or delay. It succeeds in expressing itself by turning around the obstacles which would attempt to prevent it from making itself known; in other words, it permits our unconscious desires to experience a certain form of realization.

This is the point to note. In spite of the censorship, the repressed wishes succeed in finding satisfaction through a special mode of thought to ensure the victory of the pleasure principle. My feeling is that we have underestimated the healthy aspect of that achievement and overemphasized its pathological aspect.

The opposition between the primary and secondary processes should not be described in terms of the primary processes being irrational and the secondary processes rational. Rather, they are competitive and complementary processes which obey different types of reason. We can draw two important conclusions from this. First, the psychical unity of man is fallacious. The validity of the equation psychical–conscious was contested by the idea of the unconscious. The subject was no longer One but Two; or, put another way, the unity was that of a couple living in tolerable conflict or relative harmony. The second idea, proceeding from the first, is that the existence of two conflicting terms tends towards the creation of compromise formations which endeavour to build a bridge between them.

I feel that if Freud was so strongly attached to maintaining a dualist point of view concerning instinct theory, for example, it is because he had understood intuitively that the duality at the outset was the condition necessary for the production of something else born from the relationship between the two generic terms.

What I mean to say is not that the duality is primitive, but that the duality is the limit of the greatest possible reduction as far as intelligibility is concerned. The necessary and adequate condition for establishing a relationship is that there be two terms. This simple declaration has many implications. It sets up the pair as a theoretical reference which is more fruitful than all those which use unity as a base. If we reflect even further on the implications of this fundamental duality as the condition for the production of a third part, we find the basis of symbolic activity. In fact the creation of a symbol demands that two separate elements be reunited in order to form a third element which borrows its characteristics from the two others, but which will be different from the sum of these characters nonetheless.

All of this brings us to the analytic situation. In this situation the two parts which are its very essence are both brought together and kept apart. There is no physical contact between them. Contact can be established through the emotional climate of the silent session, but we know that silence can be experienced differently by each of the partners. A form of contact is also established through speech, indicating which part of himself the analysand wishes to place into contact with the analyst. Still, can we say that the discourse of the analysand is the analysand? Clearly we cannot, for rationalization and negation are at work. Nevertheless, if we did not believe that the analysand's speech tries to tell us something about himself we would not have decided to prefer this particular form of relationship. Thus, we must say that the analysand's discourse is and is not the analysand, and that it is produced by his symbolic activity which attempts to bring together that which is separated. Separation in fact becomes a new opportunity for another form of reunion.

That which is separated calls for a double separation. First of all, there is a separation between the analysand and the analyst. But this separation is reiterated by each of the partners, for each has an unconscious separated from his own conscious. The analysand's discourse will result then from a double compromise. It will be the expression of a compromise between the unconscious and the conscious, as well as the expression of a compromise between the desire to be in contact with the analyst and the desire to avoid this contact with him.

In much the same way the analyst's listening must work on all of these areas at the same time, for he must also acknowledge that what he hears is a compromise between what he deciphers with the help of his conscious and what he is able to understand by means of his unconscious. It would be wrong to say that the analyst does not share the desires of contact with the analysand, or is not similarly tempted to respond symmetrically to the movements by which the analysand attempts to break this contact. The interpretation strives to be the best possible compromise during these movements of come and go. The interpretation is expressed with paradoxical goals, for it must maintain the contact with the analysand while allowing the necessary distance so that this form of contact can lead to an insight. As for its content, the interpretation is also a compromise formation; it condenses the modes of reasoning which belong to both rational logical thought and to this form of logic which obeys another type of rationality. In fact our interpretations include statements which imply if, then, so, because, however, and so on. At the same time our interpretations also tell that this expressed hostility is a sign of love, this apparent love hides a lot of hate; that this indifference translates feelings of despair; that this wish to die actually wishes to have someone else die, or to merge with him eternally.

The situation I have just described implies that the ego can prove itself capable of recognizing the existence of the primary processes of subjective reason without withdrawing all claims to the secondary processes of objective reason. Above all it implies that the ego can go from one to the other without denying its psychic reality and without repudiating material reality. The ego must chiefly be able to establish flexible connections, which alternately are going to be done, forming temporary hypotheses and conclusions, and be undone, in order to leave room for others who give a better representation of the situation. I believe that it is useful to think that a third category of processes exists. I propose to call these instruments of liaison, or connections, *tertiary processes*. For, in opposition to what Freud thought, it is not so much a question of the secondary processes dominating the primary processes, but rather that the analysand can make the most creative use of their coexistence and do so in the most elaborate activities of the mind just as he does in everyday life. Perhaps this is asking a great deal.

As long as Freud had the feeling that he could call upon the ego to lead him towards an awareness of the unconscious through the return of the repressed, he could consider that he was in a position to solve the difficulties inherent in psychoanalytic treatment. But he came to the conclusion that a great part of the ego was itself unconscious, and this was, without doubt, a disappointing discovery for him. Until then, the unconscious gave itself away through the manifestations which proved its existence; slips of the tongue, parapraxes, fantasies, dreams, symptoms, transference, which, once analyzed, should have forced the ego to conclude that the unconscious was not a fiction. When Freud discovered that the ego is not only the seat of resistance but is unconscious of its resistances, and that its defence mechanisms remained opaque to himself, he relied upon signs that he could hear, but these signs remained silent for the analysand. Freud did not find the means at his disposal to analyze logically this non-repressed unconscious. He had made the ego's integrity into a preliminary condition for the possibility of undertaking an analysis. In 'Analysis terminable and interminable' he was forced to admit the hard truth: 'The ego, if we are to be able to make such a pact with it, must be a normal one. But a normal ego of this sort is, like normality in general, an ideal fiction. The abnormal ego, which is unserviceable for our purposes, is unfortunately no fiction. Every normal person, in fact, is only normal on the average. His ego approximates to that of the psychotic in some part or other and to a greater or lesser extent' (Freud, 1937c, p. 235).

We may observe that Freud refers here to psychosis and not to neurosis. This means that he is obliged to admit that the normal ego includes a number of distortions in his relationship to reality which call in question its capacity of integration or its power of synthesis. We may add that this alteration of the ego is also responsible for the defection of the second ally: transference. Positive or even ambivalent transference was based on the idea that, with the help of the analyst, a better compromise could be found between the demands made by the id and the ego which must also take into consideration both the superego and the reality principle. The negative therapeutic reaction contradicts this presupposition.

'No stronger impression arises from the resistances during the work of analysis than of there being a force which is defending itself by every possible means against recovery and which is absolutely resolved to hold on to illness and suffering. One portion of this force has been recognized by us, undoubtedly with justice, as the sense of guilt and need for punishment, and has been localized by us in the ego's relation to the superego. But this is only the portion of it which is, as it were, psychically bound by the superego, and thus becomes recognizable; other quotas of the same force, whether bound or free, may be at work in other, unspecified places. If we take into consideration the total picture made up of the phenomena of masochism immanent in so many people, the negative therapeutic reaction and the sense of guilt found in so many neurotics, we shall no longer be able to adhere to the belief that mental events are exclusively governed by the desire for pleasure. These phenomena are unmistakable indications of the presence of a power in mental life which we call the instinct of aggression or of destruction according to its aims, and which we trace back to the original death instinct of living matter' (ibid., pp. 242–3).

In this quotation Freud holds the destructive instincts responsible for this state of affairs. I shall not discuss here the concept of the death instinct, except to note that it is because the ego appears to have surrendered to this reversal of life values that the happy ending does not come about.

Two serious grounds pertaining to the ego and the instinct of aggression cause the analyst's action to fail. But if we try to understand what Freud says about these two situations according to the perspective I have chosen, that is the existence of a different logic, perhaps it would be possible to go beyond the stage of mere declarations.

Let us go back to Freud's quotation. What seems to take place with these analysands is that the pleasure-displeasure principle governing psychic activity has transposed the order of these terms. The search for pleasure has substituted itself for the search for displeasure, and the avoidance of displeasure has become avoidance of pleasure. It is as if the subject says 'Yes' to displeasure and 'No' to pleasure. In many cases the analyst thinks that the 'No' to pleasure is merely on the surface and that there are hidden satisfactions for this maintenance of suffering. But there are other cases where psychic pain is such that it appears difficult to believe that the subject receives any satisfaction from it at all. We can ask, what are the unconscious thoughts of these patients made out of? In short, what does their psychic reality look like, if we do not give up considering their manifest discourse as a cover-up discourse?

The psychic reality of these patients is not less complicated than the psychic reality in those cases where the pleasure principle dominates. Disguises use condensation and displacement here as well. Doubtless, the difference lies in the fact that the logic presiding over these operations is a logic of despair. Freud said that psychic reality is the only true reality. This applies in the case we are dealing with too. Melanie Klein showed us the importance of reparation processes in depression, and I believe that the cases Freud refers to are impregnated with depressive features. But there is even more. Winnicott showed that for certain patients the only reality is the reality of that which is not there, that which makes one suffer by its very absence. Absence leads not to hope but to despair. Here we can infer that the unconscious thought processes of the patients displaying the features described by Freud refer back to a psychic reality – the only true one for them – formed by objects which only exist through the disappointment or displeasure they create. The emptiness of the ego is more consistent than its achievements. All the self-hatred which dwells in these analysands reflects a compromise between the desire to carry out an unquenchable revenge and, co-existing with this, the desire to protect the object from these hostile wishes directed towards him. This revenge is born from a wound which hit their patients in their very being, which disabled their narcissism. Their failure to realize this stems in great part from the fact that their thoughts do not know how to distinguish between the harm they want to impose upon themselves – and of which they are often unconscious – and the harm they want to inflict upon their object. They do not forgive the object for its inability in valuing them, for its absence at the time when they most needed it, and the fact that this object has other sources of pleasure than themselves. This logic of despair has one constant goal: to produce evidence that the object is really bad, incomprehensive and rejecting because of the extent to which they entreat rejection by others. When they attain their goal they have proof not only that they are not able to instil love, but that the love of others is merely a superficial front behind which they hide their hatred. In short, love is always uncertain, hatred is always sure. Likewise, they make arrangements to perpetuate this form of sado-masochistic relationship which they have chosen for as long as possible, as long as they can find a partner who accepts the role they have assigned to him.

If analysis is based on the possibility of establishing new bonds in psychic activity with that which is separated by repression, we can declare that this ability to establish bonds is not destroyed here as in psychosis, but that these bonds always establish themselves in a way which confirms that the result of this bond is never positive. While the analytic work provides these patients with additional meaning, the result of an increase in meaning is always a reduction in being. Paradoxically these analysands only have the feeling of a 'more-being' (*plus-être*) in the lessening of their well-being (*bien-être*), which is always – in the end – an implicit accusation against those who brought them into the world, since they never asked to be born.

The answer to this situation tends to show the patient that his need to create despair in the analyst is necessary for him to be able to verify that the analyst can survive this hatred and continue to analyze what goes on in the patient's psychic world. This is the best proof of love that the analyst can give. That is to help him, the patient, in recognizing that this self-hatred is a sacrifice, and that this hatred directed towards the object is perhaps, as Winnicott believes, a ruthless love. For the extreme ambivalence of these patients goes hand in hand with their extraordinary intolerance of ambivalence, just as their unconscious guilt feelings reflect a refusal to feel guilty and an extreme idealization of the image they have of themselves, symmetrical to the image of the ideal object they look for in vain on this earth.

The logic explained earlier, that of primary processes, as Freud defined it, was – in a way – a logic based on the idea of a couple of opposites formed by desire, on the one hand, and prohibition on the other. If the prohibition were suspended, we could presume that nothing would prevent a happy union with the object. In short, it was not conceivable that the object could not love the subject, or hate it. In this perspective, the logic of primary processes is a logic of hope; a case opposite to what I have called the logic of despair. Here the object is in the forefront, not the wish, not the prohibition. If the happy union is experienced as being impossible, it is because the subject cannot feel loved by the object or cannot love the object. It is a different logic, over the conflict between the wish and the prohibition, because the conflict between the ego and the object about love and hate prevails. Of course, when I speak of the object I refer to the internal object which is so profoundly internal that it is a narcissistic object shaped on the subject's wounded narcissism.

The negative therapeutic action teaches us that the fixations on hatred are much more tenacious than the fixations on love. The first is the conviction of having been deprived of a love to which one has as much right as to the air one breathes. Under these conditions it is difficult to give up an object without wanting to obtain this love up until the end. The second reason is that hatred is accompanied by guilt. To give up the object is to give up hating; but to discover a possibility of love with another object not only means letting the primitive object of the fixation follow its own destiny, it also means making it literally disappear from the self and, in a way, abandoning it. There is guilt in hating the object, but there is just as much guilt if not more when the subject no longer hates the object in order to love another object. The solution then consists in perpetuating the internal bond with it, for it is better to have a bad internal object than to risk losing it forever. The correspondence between the relationship of the ego with the object and the ego with the superego is striking.

Let us return now to Freud's assertion concerning the psychotic distortions of the ego. Up to this point we only had to deal with hope and despair within a mirror-like system – with two terms – opposite to and symmetrical with each other. We can understand that, contrary to what we have said before, no third term is created, no symbolization occurs effectively. Tertiary processes are missing.

When Freud spoke of the repression of reality in psychosis and of its transformation, he wrote the following in his paper, 'The loss of reality in neurosis and psychosis': 'In a psychosis, the transforming of reality is carried out upon the psychical precipitates of former relations to it – that is, upon the memory-traces, ideas and judgements, which have been previously derived from reality and by which reality was represented in the mind' (Freud, 1924e, p. 185). In very severe forms of psychosis, such as the one he studies in the Schreber case, we can see the enormous development of this transformation which creates a feeling of strangeness for us. But usually we have to cope with patients less severely disturbed than Schreber, the so-called borderline cases.

In 'Neurosis and psychosis' Freud writes: 'It will be possible for the ego to avoid a rupture in any direction by deforming itself, by submitting to encroachments on its own unity and even perhaps by effecting a cleavage or division itself. In this way the inconsistencies, eccentricities and follies of men would appear in a similar light to their sexual perversions, through the acceptance of which they spare themselves repressions' (Freud, 1924*b*, pp. 152–3).

This quotation justifies the importance that splitting takes on in the last part of Freud's work. If during the course of an analysis it is necessary to depend on the cooperation of the ego, the analyst must know this ego is two-sided: split. In one of his last papers, 'Splitting of the ego in the process of defence', Freud describes the situation thus: between the demands made by an instinct and the prohibition by reality 'the child takes neither course, or rather he takes both simultaneously, which comes to the same thing' (1940*e*, p. 275). In other words, according to Freud, the child's ego does not decide; that is to say, it does not judge: it admits to two contradictory judgements *at the same time*. We can see how this operation is different from repression. In the latter a choice is made which apparently decides that reality must get the upper hand on the instinctive demands. Freud insists on this simultaneous co-existence, when splitting occurs: 'On the one hand, with the help of certain mechanisms he [the child] rejects reality and refuses to accept any prohibition; on the other hand, in the same breath he recognizes the danger of reality, takes over the fear of that danger as a pathological symptom and tries subsequently to divest himself of the fear. . . . The two contrary reactions to the conflict persist as the centre-point of a splitting of the ego' (*ibid.*, pp. 275–6).

In repression the relationship between the ego as representative of reality and the instinctive demands as representative of pleasure is vertical. Repression dominates the instinctive impulse by pushing it down towards the depth, while the instinctual impulse pushes in the opposite direction towards the top. The unconscious is underground in relationship to the conscious. In splitting the relationship is horizontal; the reason of the ego and the reason of the instinctive demands coexist in the same psychic space. A coexistence such as this constitutes a stagnation factor when it takes place during the analytic cure. It is as though the analysand only hears the analyst's interpretations with one ear. The other ear continues to let itself be rocked and cradled by the instinctual impulse mermaid song, completely ignoring the message received by the other ear. The two logics are in contradiction with one another. There is a refusal to choose any of the items. Prior to the discovery of the ego's unconsciousness, unconscious repression had to disguise itself in order to express itself. Behind the conscious 'No' we can reveal the unconscious 'Yes'. In the present case the ego's strategy changes. It says 'Yes' and 'No' at the same time. What is important is not so much the double game the ego plays by splitting, it is that the splitting is unconscious. We find a paradox here. In repression the unconscious is separate from the conscious, but the return of the repressed enables us to establish a bridge between the two. The repressed is hidden, but sometimes it shows itself through its disguises. While the two types of thoughts appear to the naked eye to coexist in splitting, the ego appears to misjudge totally its dual way of functioning. There is no communication between the split parts, no tertiary process. We find an extension of this situation in the analysand's associations. For the analyst these associations are significant, and the interpretation springing from them is conclusive. But the patient cannot establish the bonds which would allow him to arrive at the proper conclusion. It is as though the sequence of thoughts is made of independent pieces. In this case it would appear that the analyst's tertiary processes must be placed at the patient's disposal. After the logics of hope and despair we have described the logic of indifference.

All of these new concepts were born from the disappointments of Freud's (analytic) practice which lessened his therapeutic ambitions. Freud believed he had inflicted a terrible narcissistic wound upon mankind by showing that the rational ego is not the master in man. But time has shown that the ego's strange logic of the patient can also inflict a narcissistic wound on the analyst by opposing him with its extraordinary modes of thought.

In view of so many accumulated difficulties, what is the solution? For a long time the analyst's work consisted of thinking just like the unconscious wish in order to integrate this thought with that of the ego and teach it to recognize the other part of its mind which refuses to submit to common reason and reality. But now we are dealing with something else. It is a matter of reasoning, according to the processes of a deeply hidden madness of the ego. Consequently, the analyst must train hismelf to use kinds of thought further and further removed from rational logic. The logic of the pleasure principle as Freud found it in the primary processes appears much too simple in relation to the logic found in the difficult borderline cases. These cases reveal the existence of what I have called the analysand's private madness. This private madness is only revealed in the intimate transferential relationship. Outside this relationship the patient is more or less like many others, neither more nor less insane than anyone else. He is able to carry out the tasks he is set. He is far from lacking a sense of responsibility. But in the light of the transference he reveals an entirely different kind of psychic functioning in his inner world.

Transference has the power of revealing the extreme sensitivity of these patients to both loss and intrusion. They are always seeking to establish a psychic distance which will permit them to feel safe from the double threat of invasion by the other and its definitive loss. Thus a permanent contradiction evolves, causing them to desire what they are scared of losing and to reject what is already in their possession but whose invasion they fear.

In fact these attitudes hide something else. If there is a struggle against the invading intrusion it is because there is a secret desire to be completely invaded by the object; not only to be united with it but also to be reduced to total passivity, like a baby in his mother's womb. This wish can be counterbalanced by the desire to invade the mother and entirely occupy her body and thoughts. In the same way, if the relinquishment or the loss of the object is feared so much, it is also because there is a desire to kill the object in order to find shelter in a mythic self-sufficiency which will set the subject free from all the variations that the object imposes upon him and which deprive the subject of any constancy in his relationship with the object.

I believe we have not adequately taken into consideration the way in which the greatest contributions to modern psychoanalysis have added to our knowledge. They have taught us less in terms of the psychic contents, since we always deal with the same things but with varying outward appearances. They have contributed to our knowledge in terms of kinds or forms of thought. That which we call defence mechanisms are also ways of thinking.

When, for example, Winnicott describes transitional phenomena and transitional objects, he creates a class of objects and a type of space where the judgement of existence has no place. Such objects are and are not the breast or the mother. Despite what Freud thought, the suspension of judgement is not always prejudicial to the ego. All depends on the constructive or destructive value of these new types of objects.

The analysis of the 'Wolf Man' showed Freud the destructive effects of splitting. Freud's interpretations on the unconscious homosexuality of the patient were not able to resolve the case's riddle. Ruth Mack

2

The Analyst, Symbolization and Absence in the Analytic Setting

Tyger! Tyger! burning bright
In the forests of the night
What immortal hand or eye
Dare frame the fearful symmetry?

w. BLAKE *The Tyger*

but something
Drives me to this ancient and vague adventure,
Unreasonable, and still I keep on looking
Throughout the afternoon for the other tiger,
The other tiger which is not in this poem.

J. L. BORGES *The Other Tiger*

Every analyst knows that an essential condition in a patient's decision to undergo analysis is the unpleasure, the increasing discomfort and ultimately the suffering he experiences. What is true of the individual patient in this connection is equally true of the psychoanalytic group. Despite its appearance of flourishing, psychoanalysis is going through a crisis. It is suffering, so to speak, from a deep malaise. The causes of this malaise are both internal and external. For a long time we have defended ourselves against the internal causes by minimizing their importance. The discomfort to which the external causes subject us has now forced us to the point where we must attempt to analyse them. It is hoped that, as a psychoanalytic group, we carry within us what we look for in our patients: a desire for change.

Any analysis of the present situation within psychoanalysis must operate on three levels: (1) an analysis of the contradictions between psychoanalysis and the social environment; (2) an analysis of the contradictions at the heart of psychoanalytic institutions (those inter-

This paper, on changes in analytic practice and analytic experience, was first published in *The International Journal of Psycho-Analysis* (1975) 56, and was presented at the 29th International Psychoanalytical Congress, London, July 1975. It was written in memory of D. W. Winnicott. The translation is by Kim Lewison and Dr Dinora Pines.

mediaries between social reality on the one hand, and psychoanalytic theory and practice on the other); and (3) an analysis of the contradictions at the very heart of psychoanalysis (theory and practice) itself.

We face a difficulty in regard to the inter-connectedness of these three levels. To mix them leads to confusion; to separate them leads to splitting. If we were fully satisfied with the current state on the third level alone, we would be inclined to ignore the other two. That this does not always happen is undoubtedly linked with factors operating in the first two levels. However, I shall have to leave for the time being the ambitious aim of articulating the three levels. At present we have enough on our hands to try to examine certain contradictions in psychoanalytic theory and practice which give rise to the malaise previously mentioned. Anna Freud (1969), in her lucid and courageous analysis of 'Difficulties in the path of psychoanalysis' from various sources, has reminded us that psychoanalysis found the way into the knowledge of mankind through the negative experience of neurosis. Nowadays we have the opportunity to learn about ourselves through our own negative experience. Out of our present malaise may emerge both an elaboration and a transformation.

In this paper, devoted to recent changes brought about by psychoanalytic practice and experience, I should like to examine the following three topics:

(1) the role of the analyst, in a wider conception of countertransference, including his own imaginative elaboration; (2) the function of the analytic setting and its relation to mental functioning, as shown by the process of symbolization; and (3) the role of narcissism, which opposes and complements that of object relations, as much in theory as in practice.

CHANGES IN THE FIELD OF PSYCHOANALYSIS

The appreciation of change: an objective and a subjective view

Since I have chosen to confine myself to recent changes I must regretfully refrain from showing how psychoanalysis has always changed and developed from its very beginnings. This is true of Freud's work itself (one has only to re-read in chronological order Freud 1904a, 1905a, 1910k, 1910d, 1912b, 1912e, 1913c, 1914g, 1915a, 1919a, 1937c, the sequence of articles from 'Freud's psychoanalytic procedure' to 'Analysis terminable and interminable'), and of the work of his earliest colleagues. Among the latter Ferenczi (for whom we should certainly reserve a special place) had, in pathetic, contradictory and often clumsy efforts, adumbrated future trends in his later work (1928, 1929, 1930, 1931, 1933). But if insightful change is continuous the perception of it, just as in an analysis, is discontinuous. Frequently (and this is certainly the case today) a conception of change which had been formulated by isolated writers twenty years earlier may become a daily reality for every analyst. Thus a reading of psychoanalytic literature will show that as early as 1949 Balint entitled one of his papers 'Changing therapeutical aims and techniques in psychoanalysis' (Balint, 1950) and that in 1954 Winnicott in 'Metapsychological and clinical aspects of regression in the psychoanalytical set-up' formulated the bases of our current understanding of the problem (Winnicott, 1955).

As a first approach, this problem has been looked at from an 'objective' point of view because it makes us study the patient 'in himself' ('*en soi*'), in most cases without taking the analyst into consideration. Khan (1962) has drawn up an impressive list of instances which impose new demands on the analytical situation. He includes terms which are now familiar to every analyst and refers to borderline states, schizoid personalities (Fairbairn, 1940), 'as if' personalities (H. Deutsch, 1942), disorders of identity (Erikson, 1959), ego specific defects (Gitelson, 1958), the false personality (Winnicott, 1956) and the basic fault (Balint, 1960). The list grows if we also include some French contributions: pregenital structures (Bouvet, 1956), the operative thought of psychosomatic patients (Marty & de M'Uzan, 1963) and the anti-analysand (McDougall, 1972). Now the narcissistic personality (Kernberg, 1970, 1974; Kohut, 1971) occupies our attention. The fact that most of the descriptions rediscovered by recent diagnostic enquiries (Lazar, 1973) are of such long standing leads one to wonder whether the present change is due to no more than an increase in the frequency of such cases.

The change formulated twenty years ago has now become established. It is now our task to try to uncover the change which is being foreshadowed today. Rather than continue with the objective approach I would, at this point, prefer to turn towards the subjective approach. I shall take as a working hypothesis the proposition that the perception of the change which is beginning today is that of *a change within the analyst*. I do not intend to deal with the way in which the analyst may be affected by the society's attitude towards him, nor with the influence exerted upon him by our methods of selection, training or communication. Although all these factors play a part, I will confine myself to the theory and practice which emerges from the analytic situation; i.e. to the view of psychic reality as seen in the analytic situation, to the way that the patient enacts it and makes the analyst experience it. For, all things considered, there is change only to the extent that the analyst is able to understand such change and to report it. This does not necessarily mean that we must deny changes in the patient, but they are subordinated to changes of sensitivity and perception in the analyst himself. Just as the patient's view of external reality is dependent on his vision of his psychic reality, so our picture of *his* psychic reality is controlled by *our* view of our own psychic reality.

It seems to me that analysts are becoming more and more aware of the part they play, as much in their assessment of the patient in the first consultations as in the setting-up of the analytic situation and in the development of the analysis. The patient's material is not external to the analyst, as even through the reality of the transference experience the analyst becomes an integral part of the patient's material. The analyst even influences the communication of the patient's material (Balint, 1962; Viderman, 1970; Klauber, 1972; Giovacchini, 1973). Balint (1962) said at a congress in 1961: 'Because we analysts belong to different analytical tongues, patients speak differently to us and that is why our languages here are different.' A dialectical relationship is set up between patient and analyst. Inasmuch as the analyst strives to communicate with a patient in his language, the patient in return, if he wishes to be understood, can only reply in the language of the analyst. And the analyst cannot do anything in his effort to communicate, other than to show what he understands, through his own subjective experience, of the effect on him of what the patient tells him. He cannot claim an absolute objectivity in his listening. A Winnicott (see Winnicott, 1949) could show us how, confronted by a difficult patient, he has to go through a more or less critical personal experience, homologous or complementary to that of his patient, in order to reach material that had previously been hidden. More and more frequently we see analysts questioning their own reactions to what their patients communicate, using these in their interpretations along with (or in preference to) the analysis of the content of what is communicated, because the patient's aim is directed to the effect of his communication rather than to the transmission of its content. I think that one of the main contradictions which the analyst faces today is the necessity (and the difficulty) of making a body of interpretations (which derive from the work of Freud and of classical analysis) co-exist and harmonize with the clinical experience and the theory of the last twenty years. This problem is aggravated by the fact that the latter do not form a homogeneous body of thought. A fundamental change in contemporary analysis comes from what the analyst hears – and perhaps cannot help but hear – which has until now been inaudible. Not that I mean that analysts nowadays have a more highly trained ear than they used to – unfortunately one often finds the reverse – but rather that they hear different things which used not to cross the threshold of audibility.

This hypothesis covers a much vaster field than those views which propose an extension of the notion of countertransference (P. Heimann, 1950; Racker, 1968) in its traditional sense. I agree with Neyraut (1974) that countertransference is not limited to the positive or negative affects produced by transference, but includes the whole mental functioning of the analyst as it is influenced, not only by the patient's material, but also by his reading or his discussions with his colleagues. One can even speak of a swing from the transference to the countertransference without which no elaboration of what is transmitted by the patient could take place. This being so, I do not think that I have overstepped the limits which Winnicott (1960b) assigns to the countertransference in restricting it to the professional attitude. Furthermore, this enlarged view of the countertransference does not imply an enlarged view of the transference.

This way of seeing things seems to me to be justified by the fact that those difficult cases to which I alluded earlier are precisely those which, at the same time, test the analyst and invoke his countertransference in the strict sense, while also demanding a greater personal contribution from him. I also feel happier in adopting this point of view in that I can claim to speak only for myself. No single analyst can claim to present a complete picture of contemporary analysis as a whole. I hope not to exemplify Balint's remark (1950) that the confusion of tongues comes from the side of the analyst, each keeping to his own analytic language. In the multiplicity of dialects born out of the basic language of analysis (see Laplanche & Pontalis, 1973) we try to be polyglot, but our efforts are limited.

The debate on indications for psychoanalysis and the hazards of analyzability

For over twenty years we have seen the vicissitudes of an endless written and spoken debate between those analysts who want to restrict the scope of classical psychoanalytic technique (Eissler, 1953; Fenichel, 1941; A. Freud, 1954; Greenson, 1967; Lampl-de Groot, 1967; Loewenstein, 1958; Neyraut, 1974; Sandler *et al*, 1973; Zetzel, 1956) and those who support its extension (Balint, Bion, Fairbairn, Giovacchini, Kernberg, Khan, M. Klein, Little, Milner, Modell, Rosenfeld, Searles, Segal, Stone, Winnicott). The former oppose the introduction of distorting parameters, and go so far as to dispute the validity of using the term 'transference' to include all therapeutic reactions, such as in all those patients mentioned in the last section (see the discussion of the problem in Sandler *et al.*, 1973); or, if they accept the extended nomenclature of 'transference', call it 'intractable' (Greenson, 1967). The second group of analysts claims to preserve the basic methodology of psychoanalysis (refusal of active manipulation, maintenance of neutrality although of a more benevolent kind, major emphasis on transference, variously interpreted) while adapting to the needs of the patient and opening new avenues of research.

This split is more illusory than it seems. One can no longer validly regard as opposites those cases which are firmly rooted in classical analysis and those where the analyst wades through uncharted swamps. For today many surprises are possible in charted areas: the appearance of a disguised psychotic kernel, unexpected regressions, a difficulty in mobilizing certain deep layers, and the rigidity of character defences. All these features frequently lead to more or less interminable analyses. A recent paper by Limentani (1972) touches a sore point: namely, that our prognoses are shaky, as much with regard to our patients as with regard to our candidates. Fairly frequently, clinical material in a paper relies as much on the analysis of candidates as on that of patients. 'Suitable for analysis is not synonymous with analyzable.' This reinforces the scepticism of those who think that an evaluation before the setting-up of the analytic situation is illusory. Even the best of us fall into the trap. The definition of objective criteria, the suitability for analysis (Nacht & Lebovici, 1955) and the prognosis in borderline cases, for example (see Kernberg, 1971), are interesting but of limited value. Limentani observes that if a second opinion on analysability is taken, the final decision is significantly influenced by the theoretical conceptions, the affinities and the interaction of the second analyst with the patient. It seems difficult to lay down objective and general limits to analyzability which do not take into account the degree of experience of the analyst, or his specific gifts, or his theoretical orientation. Any limit will be overstepped by the interest formed in a patient, perhaps in collusion, but with the wish to embark on a new adventure. Furthermore, one often sees case material in the work of a supporter of the restriction of the field of psychoanalysis, which contradicts the very principles he propounds. Rather than be told what we should or should not do, it would be more profitable to be clear about what we are in fact doing. Because it may well be that, as Winnicott (1955) put it, we no longer have any choice. I personally do not think that all patients are analyzable, but I prefer to think that the patient about whom I have doubts is not analyzable by me. I am aware that our results do not measure up to our ambitions, and that failures are more common than we might hope. However, we cannot, as in medicine or psychiatry, be satisfied with an objective attitude to failure, when it can be reapproached and modified by the patience of the analyst, or by further analysis. We must also ask ourselves about its subjective significance for the patient. Winnicott showed us the need to repeat failures experienced in the environment, and we know the resultant omnipotent triumph felt by the patient, whether or not he gets better after termination or continues unchanged. Perhaps the only failure for which we are responsible is our inability to put the patient in contact with his psychic reality. The limits of analyzability can only be those of the analyst, the patient's alter ego. In conclusion I would say that the real problem in the indications for analysis is the evaluation by the analyst of the gap between his capacity for understanding and the material provided by a given patient, as well as gauging the possible effect, across this gap, of what he in return can communicate to the patient (which will be capable of mobilizing the latter's mental functioning in the sense of the elaboration within the analytical situation). It is no less serious for the analyst to be mistaken about his own capabilities than about the patient's. In this way, there could be a place for everyone in the analytic family, whether he devotes himself to classical analysis or to extending its scope; or indeed (which is more generally the case) to both.

Revision of the model of neurosis and the implicit model of borderline states

Is the heart of classical analysis, neurosis, therefore untouched? One may well ask. I am not going to deal with the causes of the growing infrequency of neurosis, which has been commented on many times but which would demand a lengthy study. Neurosis, which used to be seen as the domain of the irrational, is now seen rather as a consistent triad of infantile neurosis, adult neurosis and transference neurosis. In neurosis the analysis of the transference dominates. Through the analysis of resistances, its knots disentangle themselves almost on their own. The analysis of the countertransference may be limited to the acknowledgement of those elements of conflict within the analyst which are unfavourable to the development of the transference. In the extreme the role of the analyst as object is anonymous; another analyst could take his place. Just as the object of the drive is, of all its elements, that which is most easily substitutable, so in practice, as well as in theory, its role remains obscure. The resultant metapsychology reflects an individual with a capacity for unaided development, undoubtedly with the limited help of the object on which he relies, but without losing himself in it or losing the object itself.

Freud's implied model of neurosis is based on perversion (neurosis as negative of perversion). Today one may doubt whether psychoanalysts still hold that view. The implied model of neurosis *and* of perversion is nowadays based on psychosis. This evolution is present in outline even in the last part of Freud's work. As a result, today analysts are more attuned to psychosis rather than perversion, as lying behind neurosis. This is not to say that all neurosis is etched into an underlying psychosis, but that we are less interested in perverse fantasies of neurotics than in psychotic defence mechanisms, which we find here in a discreet form. In fact, we are asked to listen to a double code. That is what led me to say earlier that we hear different things nowadays, things which used to be inaudible. And this is also why some analysts (Bouvet, 1960) write that an analysis of a neurosis is not complete until the psychotic layer is reached, even in a superficial way. Nowadays the analyst is less deterred by the presence of a psychotic kernel within a neurosis, provided it appears accessible, than by fixed and rigid defences. That is what makes us question the authenticity of these patients even when strictly neurotic and even in the presence of apparent fluidity. When at last we reach the psychotic core we find what we may well call the patient's private madness, and this may be one reason why interest is now shifting towards borderline states.

From now on I will use the convention of referring to borderline states, not to denote certain clinical phenomena in contrast to others (e.g. false self, problems of identity or the basic fault) but as a generic clinical concept capable of division into a multiplicity of aspects. It might be better to consider them as 'borderline states of analyzability'. It may be that borderline states play the same role in modern clinical practice as the 'actual neurosis' played in Freudian theory, with the difference that borderline states are durable organizations capable of evolving in different ways. We know that what characterizes these clinical pictures is the lack of structure and organization – not only when compared with neuroses but also in comparison wth psychoses. Here, unlike in neurosis, we can observe the absence of infantile neurosis, the polymorphous character of the so-called adult 'neurosis' in such cases and the haziness of the transference neurosis.

The contemporary scope of analysis oscillates between two extremes. At one end lies social 'normality', of which McDougall (1972) has given a striking clinical description, referring to the 'anti-analysand'. She describes the failure to start the analytic process, albeit in an accepted analytic situation. The transference is stillborn, despite the analyst's efforts to help or even to provoke its appearance. The analyst feels caught in the patient's network of mummified objects, paralysed in his activity and unable to stimulate any curiosity in the patient about himself. The analyst is in a situation of 'object exclusion'. His attempts at interpretation are treated by the patient as his madness, which soon leads the analyst to decathect his patient and to a state of inertia characterized by an echo response. At the other end are those states which have in common a tendency towards fusional regression and object dependence. There are numerous varieties of this regression, from beatitude to terror and from omnipotence to total impotence. Their intensity varies from overt expression to subtle indications of their presence. We see it, e.g. in an extreme associative release, a haziness of thought, an ill-timed somatic display on the couch, as if the patient were trying to communicate through body language, or even more simply, when the analytic atmosphere becomes heavy and oppressive. Here the presence (Nacht, 1963) and the help of the object are essential. What is demanded of the analyst is more than his affective capacity and empathy. It is his mental functions which are demanded, for the patient's structures of meaning have been put out of action. It is here that the countertransference receives its most extensive meaning. The technique of the analysis of neuroses is deductive, that of analyzing borderline states inductive; hence its hazardous nature. Whatever the descriptive varieties, the causes invoked and the different techniques advocated, three facts emerge from the works of most of the writers who have described these states: (1) The experiences of primary fusion bear witness to a confusion between subject and object, with a blurring of the limits of the self. (2) The particular mode of symbolization is derived from a dual organization of patient and analyst. (3) There is present the need for structural integration through the object.

Between these two extremes ('normality' and fusional regression) there is a multiplicity of defence mechanisms against this regression. I shall regroup these into four fundamental categories. The first two constitute mechanisms of psychic short-circuiting while the last two are basic psychic mechanisms.

1. *Somatic exclusion.* Somatic defence is the polar opposite of conversion. Regression dissociates the conflict from the psychic sphere by restricting it to the soma (and not to the libidinal body) by a separation of the psyche and the soma. This results in an asymbolic formation through a transformation of libidinal into neutralized energy (I use the term in a different sense from Hartmann) which is purely somatic, and sometimes capable of putting the patient's life in danger. I refer here to the work of Marty, de M'Uzan & David (1963) and of M. Fain (1966). The ego

defends against possible disintegration in a fantasied confrontation which might destroy both the ego itself and the object, by an exclusion which resembles acting out, but is now directed towards the non-libidinal body ego.

2. *Expulsion via action.* Acting out is the external counterpart to psychosomatic acting in. It has the same value in expelling psychic reality. Both the function of transforming reality, and the function of communication contained in action, are overshadowed by its expulsive aim. Significantly, the act takes place in the anticipation of a type of relationship in which object and ego are alternatively consumed.

These two mechanisms have the remarkable effect of creating a psychic blindness. The patient blinds himself to his psychic reality, either to the somatic sources of his drive or to its point of entry into external reality, avoiding the intermediate processes of elaboration. In both these cases the analyst has the impression of being out of touch with his patient's psychic reality. He must make an imaginative construction of this, either from the depths of the soma or from a nexus of social actions which are over cathected to such a degree that they eclipse the internal world.

3. *Splitting.* The mechanism of (so-called) splitting remains in the psychic sphere. All the other defences described by Kleinian authors (the most accepted being projective and introjective identification, denial, idealization, omnipotence, manic defence, etc.) are secondary to it. The effects of splitting are numerous. They go from a protection of a secret zone of non-contact where the patient is completely alone (Fairbairn, 1940; Balint, 1968) and where his real self is protected (Winnicott, 1960a, 1963a) or again which hides part of his bisexuality (Winnicott, 1971), to attacks on linking in his thought processes (Bion, 1957, 1959, 1970; Donnet & Green, 1973) and the projection of the bad part of the self and of the object (M. Klein, 1946) with a marked denial of reality. When these mechanisms are used the analyst is in touch with psychic reality, but either he feels cut off from an inaccessible part of it or he sees his interventions crumble, being perceived as a persecutor and intruder.

4. *Decathexis.* I shall deal here with a primary depression, almost in the physical sense of the word, constituted by a radical decathexis on the part of the patient who seeks to attain a state of emptiness and aspires to non-being and nothingness. It is a question of a mechanism which is for me at the same level as splitting, but different from secondary depression with, according to Kleinian authors, its aim of reparation. The analyst feels himself identified here with a space devoid of objects, or finds himself outside it.

These two mechanisms suggest that the patient's fundamental dilemma, over and above all defensive manoeuvres, can be summed up in the alternative: *delusion or death*.

The implicit model of neurosis in the past led us back to castration anxiety. The implicit model of these borderline states leads us back to the contradiction formed by the duality of separation anxiety/intrusion anxiety. Hence the importance of the notion of distance (Bouvet, 1956, 1958). The effect of this double anxiety, which sometimes takes on torturing forms, seems to me to relate essentially not to the problem of the wish (as in neurosis) but to the formation of thought (Bion, 1957). Donnet and I have described (Donnet & Green, 1973) what we have called *blank psychosis* (*psychose blanche*), i.e. what we consider to be the fundamental psychotic kernel. This is characterized by blocking of thought processes, the inhibition of the functions of representation, and by 'bi-triangulation' where the difference of the sexes which separates two objects disguises the splitting of a single object, whether good or bad. The patient then suffers from the combined effects of a persecutory intrusive object and of depression consequent on loss of the object.

The presence of basic mechanisms belonging to the psychotic lineage and its derivatives is not enough to characterize borderline states. In fact, analysis shows us the superimposition of such mechanisms and their derivatives on the defence mechanisms described by Anna Freud (1936). Many writers point out in different terms the coexistence of the psychotic and neurotic parts of the personality (Bion, 1957; Gressot, 1960; Bergeret, 1970; Kernberg, 1972; Little & Flarsheim, 1972). This coexistence may be the result of a situation of sterile stalemate between the reality principle and sexual libido on the one hand, and the pleasure principle and aggressive libido, on the other. All pleasurable activity and all response to reality of the self are infiltrated by aggressive components. But, conversely, since all destruction is followed by a form of object recathexis, which is libidinal in the most primitive form, the two aspects of libido (sexuality and aggression) are not well separated. These patients show a great sensitivity to loss but also a possibility of object recovery through a fragile and dangerous substitute object (Green, 1973). This attitude is found in mental functioning through the alteration of linking and unlinking activity. Its consequence for the analyst is the permanent overvaluation or undervaluation both of his function as object and of the degree of development of the analytic process.

Let us pinpoint our observations on *blank psychosis* more precisely. In that psychotic kernel without apparent psychosis, the object relations which a patient shows us are not diadic but triadic; i.e. both the mother and the father are represented in the oedipal structure. However, the profound difference between these latter two objects is neither the distinction between their sexes nor their functions. The differentiation is effected by way of two criteria: the good and the bad on the one hand, and nothingness (or loss) and the dominating presence on the other. On the one side the good is inaccessible, as if out of reach, or never present in a sufficiently durable form. On the other, the bad is always intruding and never disappears, except for a momentary respite. Thus we are dealing with a triangle based on the relationship between the patient and two symmetrically opposed objects which are in fact one entity. Hence the term bi-triangulation. Generally we describe these relations solely in terms of love-hate relationships. This will not do. What we must add is the implication of these relationships for thought processes. In fact, the intrusive presence arouses a delusional feeling of influence and inaccessibility to depression. In both cases this has repercussions on thought. Why? Because in both cases it is impossible to constitute absence. The object which is always intrusively present, permanently occupying the personal psychic space, mobilizes a permanent countercathexis in order to combat this break-in, which exhausts the resources of the ego or forces it to get rid of its burden by expulsive projection. Never being absent, it cannot be thought. Conversely, the inaccessible object can never be brought into the personal space, or at least never in a sufficiently durable way. Thus it cannot be based on the model of an imaginary or metaphorical presence. Even if this would be possible for an instant, the bad object would drive the imaginary presence out. And again, if the bad object gave way, the psychic space which can only momentarily be occupied by the good object would find itself completely objectless. This conflict leads to divine idealization which conceives of an inaccessible good object (the resentment against this non-disposability being actively denied) and to diabolical persecution by the bad object (the attachment which this situation implies being equally denied). The consequence of this situation in the cases with which we are dealing is not manifest psychosis, where mechanisms of projection operate in a wide area, nor open depression where the work of mourning could take place. The final result is paralysis of thought which is expressed in a negative hypochondriasis, particularly with regard to the head, i.e. a feeling of empty-headedness, of a hole in mental activity, inability to concentrate, to remember, etc. The struggle against these feelings can bring in its wake an artificial thought process: ruminations, a kind of pseudo-obsessional compulsive thought, quasi-delirious wanderings, etc. (Segal, 1972). One is tempted to think that these are only the effects of repression. But this is not so. When a neurotic complains of similar phenomena we have good reason to think, when the context allows it, that he is struggling against representations of wishes which have been censored by the superego. When we are dealing with a psychotic, it is we who infer the existence of underlying fantasies. These are not, in my opinion, situated 'behind' the empty space, as in neurotics, but 'after' it, i.e. they are forms of recathexis. What I mean is that primitive drives, barely elaborated, force themselves forward, once again, into the empty space. The position of the analyst in the face of these phenomena is affected by the structure of the patient. The analyst will respond to the empty space with an intense effort of thought in order to try to think that which the patient cannot think, and which would find expression in an effort to achieve imaginal representation on the analyst's part, so that he will not be overtaken by this psychic death. Conversely, faced with secondary projection of a mad kind, he may feel confused, even amazed. The empty space must be filled and the overflow emptied. The search for a balanced exchange is difficult. If one fills the emptiness prematurely through interpretation, one is repeating the intrusion of the bad object. If, on the other hand, one leaves the emptiness as it is, one is repeating the inaccessibility of the good object. If the analyst feels confused or amazed he is no longer in a position to contain the overflow, which then expands without limit. And finally, if one responds to the overflow with verbal overactivity, then even with the best of intentions, one is doing no more than responding with an interpretative talion. The only solution is to give the patient the image of elaboration, situating what he gives us in a space which is neither the empty one nor one filled to overflowing, but a ventilated space, a space which is neither that of 'this is meaningless' nor that of 'this means that' but one of 'this may mean that'. It is the space of potential and of absence for, as Freud was the first to see, it is in the absence of the object that the representation of it is formed, the source of all thought. And I must add that language imposes limits on us here as, clearly, 'wanting to mean' does not simply signify using words, carrying content, but indicates the patient's search to transmit a communication in the most elementary forms, i.e. a hope directed to the object, where the aim is quite undefined. Perhaps this justifies Bion's recommendation (1970) that the analyst should attempt to achieve a state without memory or desire, doubtless in order to allow us to be permeated by the patient's state as fully as possible. The goal to strive for is to work with the patient in a double operation: to give a container to his content and a content to his container, always keeping in mind, however, the flexibility of boundaries and the multivalency of meanings, at least in the mind of the analyst.

Because analysis was born of the experience of neurosis it has taken the thought of the wish as its starting point. Today we can state that there are only wishes because there are thoughts, using this term in a wide sense which includes the most primitive forms. It is questionable that the attention devoted to thoughts today comes from intellectualization. For the originality of psychoanalytic theory, from Freud's first writings, is the connecting of thoughts with drives. One may even go further and state that a drive is an inchoate form of thought. Between drive and thought there is a whole series of intermediate and diversified chains which Bion has conceptualized in an original way. But it would not be enough simply to conceive of these as hierarchic relationships. Drives, affects, thing- and word-representations all communicate with one another and influence one another's structure. The unconscious is formed in the same way. But psychic space is contained within limits. Tensions remain tolerable there, and the most irrational fulfilments are successes of the psychic apparatus. To dream while fulfilling a wish is an accomplishment of the psychic apparatus, not only because the dream fulfils the wish, but because the dream itself is a fulfilment of the wish to dream. An analytic session has ofen been compared to a dream. However, if this comparison is justified, it is because, just as the dream is contained within certain limits (the abolition of the opposite poles of perception and motor activity), the session is also contained by the conditions of the analytic formalities. It is this containment which helps to maintain the specific functioning of the various elements of psychic reality. But all this is true in the classical analysis of neurosis and is subject to revision in difficult cases.

CURRENT PROBLEMS ARISING OUT OF THE PARALLEL DEVELOPMENT OF THEORY AND PRACTICE

Mental functioning and the analytic setting

Three tendencies can be distinguished in the parallel development of psychoanalytic theory and practice. For reasons of space I can only give an outline here which, like all outlines, is only relatively accurate, since reality, being more complex, ignores arbitrary limits, and different currents flow into each other.

1. In the first tendency analytic theory fastened on the historical reality of the patient. It uncovered the conflict, the unconscious, the fixations, etc. It moved towards the study of the ego and the mechanisms

of defence (Anna Freud, 1936), extended by psychoanalytic studies of the psychology of the ego (Hartmann, 1951). In practice it shows itself in the studies of the transference (Lagache, 1952) and resistances in the application of empirically established psychoanalytic rules, without introducing technical innovations.

2. In the second tendency interest moved towards object relations, understood in very different ways by, e.g. Balint (1950), Melanie Klein (1940, 1946), Fairbairn (1952), Bouvet (1956), Modell (1969), Spitz (1956, 1958) and Jacobson (1964). In a parallel movement the idea of the transference neurosis is gradually substituted by the notion of the psychoanalytic process. This is seen as a form of organization, during the analysis, of the internal development of the patient's psychic processes, or as exchanges between patient and analyst (Bouvet, 1954; Meltzer, 1967; Sauguet, 1969; Diatkine & Simon, 1972; Sandler *et al.*, 1973).

3. In the third tendency we can pinpoint a movement which concentrates on the mental functioning of the patient (Bion and the psychosomatic school of Paris), while in regard to clinical practice questions are asked about the function of the analytic setting (Winnicott, 1955; Little 1958; Milner, 1968; Khan, 1962, 1969; Stone, 1961; Lewin, 1954; Bleger, 1967; Donnet, 1973; and Giovacchini, 1972a). These questions relate to whether the analytic setting (frame) is not a precondition for defining the analytic object and the change which is the aim of the specific use of the analytic setting. The problem is both epistemological and practical.

To clarify things we can say that the analytic situation is the totality of the elements making up the analytic relationship, at the heart of which we can, in the course of time, observe a process whose knots are tied by the transference and the countertransference, due to the establishment and the limits of the analytic setting. (This definition completes that given by Bleger, 1967.)

Let us be more concrete. In a classical analysis the patient, after the surprises of the beginning, ends by assimilating all the elements of a situation which allows the analysis to proceed (regular appointments, fixed length of sessions, the respective positions of couch and armchair, limitation of communication to a verbal level, free association, the ending of the session, regular breaks, means of payment, etc.). Absorbed in the strangeness of what is going on inside him, he forgets the setting and soon allows the development of the transference in order to attach this strangeness to an object. The elements of the setting provide material for interpretation only when there are occasional modifications. As Bleger (1967) and others have seen, the setting constitutes a silent, mute base, a constant which allows the variables of the process a certain rein. It is a non-self (Milner, 1952) which reveals its existence only by its absence. One could compare it to the body, silent in health, if a better comparison had not been suggested by Winnicott, i.e. that of the facilitating environment.

Our experience has been enriched by the analysis of patients who cannot use the setting as a facilitating environment. It is not only that they fail to make use of it, it is as if somewhere inside them they leave it intact in the non-use they make of it (Donnet, 1973). One is therefore led from the analysis of the content to the analysis of the container, to an analysis of the setting itself. Equivalents can be found at other levels. Winnicott's 'holding' refers to the care of the external object, Bion's 'container' to internal psychic reality. It is no longer enough, even if analysis is considered as a 'two-body psychology', to study object relations. One has also to question oneself about the space in which these relations develop, its limits and its breaks as well as the temporal development in which they evolve, with its continuity and discontinuities.

We can establish two situations. The first is that already mentioned, where the silent setting, as though absent, becomes forgotten. It is at this level that the analysis takes place between persons, and allows us to enter their substructures and the intrapsychic conflicts between processes (Rangell, 1969) and even permits an analysis of the part object relations which are contained in a functional whole, to the extent to which the atmosphere of the session remains fluid and the processes remain relatively clear. Interpretation can afford the luxury of subtlety. The interaction of persons pushes the relation with the setting into the background.

The second situation is that in which the setting makes its presence felt. The feeling is that something is happening which acts against the setting. It is a feeling which can be found in the patient, but is above all present in the analyst. The latter feels the effect of a tension which acts like an internal pressure, which makes him aware of having to act through and within the analytic setting, as if to protect it from a threat. This tension forces him to enter a world which he can only glimpse and which requires efforts of imagination from him. This is the case where the analysis develops not between persons but between objects. It is as if persons have lost their reality and have given way to an ill-defined field of objects. The vivacity of certain representations can suddenly take on a shape emerging from a haze, but at the limits of imagination. It often happens that the analyst has even more ill-defined impressions which take on the shape neither of images nor of memories of earlier phases of the analysis. These impressions seem to reproduce certain drive-trajectories, through the expression of internal movement in the analyst, giving rise to feelings of envelopment and development. Intensive work takes place on these movements, which eventually succeeds in conveying them to the consciousness of the analyst before he can transform them, by an internal mutation, into sequences of words which will be used at the right moment to communicate with the patient by means of verbalization. When the analyst arrives at a sort of internal order, often before the verbalization, the affective disturbance changes to a feeling of satisfaction at having reached a coherent explanation, which plays the part of a theoretical construction (in the sense that Freud used the expression in his description of infantile sexual theories). For the moment it hardly matters whether this theory is true or false – there will always be time to correct it later in the light of further experience. What counts is the fact of having succeeded in binding the inchoate, and in containing it within a form. Everything takes place as if it were the analyst who has been able to reach a state analogous to an hallucinatory representation of the wish, as in a child or a neurotic. One frequently talks of a feeling of omnipotence which follows the realization of an hallucinatory wish. But omnipotence begins before that. It is associated with the success which consists in the transformation, through binding of the inchoate into a meaningful form, which can be used as a model for deciphering a situation still to come. However, if it is for the analyst to devote himself to the task of elaboration, it is certainly because the patient himself is only able to achieve a minimal degree of structure, insufficiently bound to make sense, but just enough to mobilize all the analyst's patterns of thought, from the most elementary ·to the most complex, and to give effect, albeit provisionally, to symbolization which is always begun and never finished.

The description I have just given can be applied either to certain critical moments in a classical analysis – when the deepest levels are reached – or to a wider comparison with the general atmosphere of the analysis of difficult cases, in contrast to those of classical analysis. But it must be remembered that such work is only possible through the function of the analytic setting and the guarantees given by its constancy, which relays the importance of the presence of the analyst as a person. This is necessary in order to maintain the isolation of the analytic situation, the impossibility of discharge, the closeness of contact which is restricted to the sphere of the psyche, and the certainty that the mad thoughts will not go beyond the four walls of the consulting room. It ensures that the language used as a vehicle for the thoughts will remain metaphorical; that the session will come to an end; that it will be followed by another session and that its weighty truth, truer than reality, will be dissipated once the door shuts behind the patient. Thus, rather than saying that the establishment of the setting reproduces an object relation, I find it more appropriate to say that it is this which allows the birth and development of an object relation. I have centred this description on mental functioning rather than on the expression of the drives and defences which lie at its root, because much has already been said about them, whereas mental functioning is still a vast uncharted area within the analytic setting.

When the theory of object relations was at the beginning of its development we were at first led to describe the interaction of the self and the object in terms of internal processes. Not enough attention was paid to the fact that in the phrase 'object relation' the word 'relation' was the more important. This is to say that our interest should have been directed at what lies between these terms, which are united by actions, or between the effects of the different actions. In other words, the study of relations is that of links rather than that of the terms united by them. It is the nature of the link which confers on the material its truly psychic character which is responsible for intellectual development. This work was postponed until Bion examined the links between internal processes and Winnicott studied the interaction between the internal and the external.

Let us take the latter case first. We only know what goes on inside the patient through what he tells us, while we lack knowledge of the source of the communication and of what is unfolding within these two limits. But we can overcome our ignorance of that internal space by observing the effect which the communication has on us, and what is produced between our affective (indeed bodily) impressions and our mental functioning. Of course we cannot claim that this is what is taking place inside the patient, but only that what happens to us provides an analogue or a homologue. And we displace the knowledge of what is happening in our own internal space into the space between him and us. The patient's communication – different from what he lives and feels – is situated in the transitional space between him and us, in the same way as our interpretation is carried by communication. Thanks to Winnicott we know the function of the transitional space, of the potential space which unites and separates mother and child, creator of a new category of objects. Language, in my view, is the heir to the first transitional objects.

I alluded earlier to the work of symbolization, and I would now like to explain why the analyst's internal processes have as their goal the construction of symbolization. The notion of symbol which I am using here goes beyond the limited meaning which it has in psychoanalysis, but follows its original definition very closely. The symbol is 'an object cut in two, constituting a sign of recognition when those who carry it can assemble the two pieces' (*Dictionaire Robert*). Is that not what happens in the analytic setting? Nothing in this definition suggests that the two parts of a symbol are equal. Thus even when the work of analysis compels the analyst to make great efforts, which lead him to form a picture in his mind of the patient's mental functioning, he supplies what is missing in the patient. I have said that he replaced the part which is missing in order to understand the relationship between the sources of the communication and its formation, through observing homologous processes in himself. But in the end the real analytic object is neither on the patient's side nor on the analyst's, but in the meeting of these two communications in the potential space which lies between them, limited by the setting which is broken at each separation and reconstituted at each new meeting. If we consider that each party present, the patient and the analyst, is composed of the union of two parts (what they live and what they communicate), one of which is the double of the other (I use the word double in the sense of a wide homologous connection while admitting the existence of differences), one can see that the analytic object is formed of two doubles, one belonging to the patient and the other to the analyst. One has only to listen to patients to realize that they continually refer to it. For, in order to have a formation of an analytic object, an essential condition is the establishment of homologous and complementary relations between the patient and the analyst. What determines our formulation of interpretations is not our appreciation of what we understand or feel. Whether formulated or withheld, it is always based on the measure of the distance between what the analyst is prepared to communicate, and how much of it the patient can receive in order to form the analytic object (what I call useful distance and efficacious difference). From this point of view the analyst does not only unveil a hidden meaning. He constructs a meaning which has never been created before the analytic relationship began (Viderman, 1970). I would say that the analyst forms an absent meaning (cf. chapter 15 below). Hope in analysis is founded on the notion of a potential meaning (Khan, 1978) which will allow the present meaning and the absent meaning to meet in the analytic object. But this construction is never free. If it cannot claim objectivity, it can claim a homologous connection with what escapes our understanding either in the present or in the past. It is its own double.

This conception, which evokes the notion of doubles (cf. chapter 15 below and Green, 1970), helps us to extricate ourselves from the deaf dialogue between those who believe that regression in treatment is, in its extreme forms, the reproduction of the initial infantile state, and that interpretation is the quasi-objective reproduction of the past (whether it aims at events or internal processes), and those who are sceptical about the possibility of reaching such states or of the objectivity of reconstructions. In fact, regression in treatment is always metaphorical. It is a miniature and modified model of the infantile state, but it is one which still has a homologous relationship to that state, just like interpretation which elucidates its meaning, but which would have no effect if the relationship of correspondence did not exist. It seems to me that the essential function of all these much-decried variants of classical analysis only aim, in varying the elasticity of the analytic setting, at searching for and preserving the minimum conditions for symbolization. Every paper on symbolization in psychotic or prepsychotic structures says the same thing couched in different terms. The patient equates but does not form symbols (the symbolic equation of H. Segal, 1957). He conceives of the other on the model of himself (the projective reduplication of Marty *et al.*, 1963). This also recalls Kohut's description (1971) of mirror transferences. For the patient the analyst does not represent the mother, he *is* himself the mother (Winnicott, 1955). The notion of 'as if' is missing (Little, 1958). We could also invoke the notion of 'direct acting out' (de M'Uzan, 1968). One can conclude from this that it is a question of the inherent shape of the dual relationship. On the other hand we must not forget the stress which has been placed on the lack of differentiation between self and object, on the blurring of boundaries to the extent of narcissistic fusion. The paradox is that this situation only rarely leads to a completely chaotic and unformed state, and that figures of duality emerge very quickly from the undifferentiated whole. One can add, to the dual relationships which characterize the interchanges with the object, what I shall call the dual relationship within the self itself, and which one finds in the importance of the mechanisms of double reversal (turning against himself, and reversal to the opposite) which Freud said were present before repression (Green, 1967*b*). Thus, to the idea of a mirror in the exchanges with the representative of the external object one can couple the idea of an internal mirroring of the self to oneself. All this seems to show that the capacity for reflection is a fundamental 'given' of the human. By this means one can explain the need for the object as an image of the 'similar' (see Winnicott's article on 'the mirror-role of the mother' in Winnicott, 1971*b*). For the most part symbolic structures are probably innate. However, we now know, as much through the study of animal communication as through psychological or psychoanalytic research, that they require the intervention of the object in order to move from potential to realization at a given point in time.

Without disputing the truth of clinical descriptions, we must now assess that duality in its context. Verbalization, however disorganized, introduces a distance between the self and the object. But we may already suppose that from the creation of what Winnicott calls the subjective object a very primitive triangulation between the self and the object is sketched out. If we now turn to the object which is the mother, we must admit that a third person is also present. While Winnicott tells us that 'there is no such thing as a baby', alluding to the couple that the baby forms together with maternal care, I am tempted to add that there is no such couple formed by mother and baby, without the father. For the child is the figure of the union between mother and father. The whole problem stems from the fact that, through a concern with reality, even in the boldest imaginative constructions, we seek to understand what goes on in the mind of the patient alone (i.e. with his mother) without thinking of what goes on between them. For between them we find the father who is always somewhere in the mother's unconscious (Lacan, 1966), whether he be hated or banished. It is true that the father is absent from this relationship. But to say that he is absent means that he is neither present nor non-existent but that he has a potential presence. Absence is an intermediary situation between presence (as far as intrusion) and loss (as far as annihilation). Analysts tend more and more to think that when they verbalize experience through communication they are not simply elucidating the latter, but are reintroducing the father's potential presence, not through any explicit reference to him, but through the mere introduction of a third element into the communicative duality.

When we employ the metaphor of the mirror, which Freud was the first to use, and which I admit can be a deforming mirror, we always forget that the formation of the couple of the image and the object depends on the presence of the third object, i.e. the mirror itself. Similarly when we speak of the dual relationship in analysis, we forget that third element represented by the setting, which is its homologue. It is said that the setting represents holding and maternal care. But the 'work of the mirror' itself, so obvious in the analysis of difficult cases, is neglected. One could say that the psychic counterpart of the physical activity of maternal care is alone able, metaphorically, to replace physical activity, which is reduced to silence by the setting. It is only thus that the situation can evolve towards symbolization. The psychic functioning of the analyst has been compared to the fantasy activity of the mother's reverie (Bion, 1962) which is undeniably an integral part of holding and maternal care. Faced with the diffuse discharge of the patient which spreads and invades the space, the analyst responds using his capacity for empathy, with a mechanism of elaboration which presupposes the inhibition of the aim of the drive in itself. The effect of lessening the inhibition of aim in the patient prevents that retention of experience which is necessary for the formation of mnemic traces, on which the activity of remembering depends. This is all the more so because the discharge is permeated with destructive elements which oppose the construction of links, and whose attacks are directed at the thought processes. Everything happens as if it were the analyst who was moving towards the registration of experience which could not have taken place. From this follows the idea that these patients find themselves more closely caught in current conflicts (Giovacchini, 1972c, 1973). The response by way of countertransference is that which should have taken place on the part of the object.

Drives seek satisfaction by means of the object, but where this is impossible, due to inhibition of aim imposed by the setting, there remains the avenue of elaboration and verbalization. What is it that causes the lack of elaboration in the patient, so that it has to be supplied by the analyst? In normal psychic functioning each of the components used by the psychic apparatus has a specific function and a direction (from drive to verbalization) which allow the formation of correspondent relationships between differing functions (e.g. between the identity of perception and the identity of thought). All psychic functioning is based on a series of connections which relate one element to another. The simplest example is the relationship between a dream and a daydream. More complicated connections can lead one to compare primary and secondary processes. These relationships are not only ones of opposition, but also of collaboration, since if it were otherwise we would never be able to move from one system to another and to translate e.g. manifest content into latent content. But we know that this is only possible through intensive work. The dream work reflects the work of the analysis of the dream. All this implies that these connections can be established on the basis of a functional distinction: that the dream be considered as a dream, that the thought be considered as a thought, etc. But at the same time a dream is something other than a simple dream, a thought something other than a simple thought, etc. We find again the dual nature of the connection-reunion and/or separation. This is what we call the internal connections of symbolization. They bind the different elements of the same formation (in dreams, fantasies, thoughts, etc.) and of the formations, simultaneously ensuring the continuity and discontinuity of psychic life. In the analytic work, this implies, on the part of the patient, that he take the analyst for what he is, and at the same time for what he is not, as himself and not himself, but being able at the same time to maintain the distinction. It also implies that, conversely, the analyst can have the same attitude towards the patient.

In the structures with which we are dealing it is very difficult to establish the internal connections of symbolization, because the different types are used as 'things' (Bion, 1962, 1963). Dreams, far from constituting an object of psychic reality linked to the body (Pontalis, 1974), and delimiting an internal personal space (Khan, 1972c), have an evacuative function. Fantasies can represent a compulsive activity destined to fill a void (Winnicott, 1971) or are considered as facts (Bion, 1963). Affects have a representative function (Green, 1973) and actions no longer have the power to transform reality. At best they serve to ensure a communicative function, but more often they relieve the psyche of an intolerable quantity of stimuli. In fact the whole of psychic functioning is impregnated by the model of action which is the consequence of the impossibility of reducing the massive quantity of affects, which have not been able to be influenced by the elaboration of thought, or have only been able to arrive at a caricature of it (Segal, 1972). Bion (1963) has made great advances in the study of internal mental functioning. The economic point of view is all the more important here, provided one does not restrict it to quantitative connections and includes the role of the object in its capacity for transformation. It is also the function of the setting to tolerate extreme tensions and to reduce them, through the mental apparatus of the analyst, in order to arrive eventually at those objects of thought capable of occupying the potential space.

Narcissism and object relations

We are now confronted by a third topographic model elaborated from the analytic space in terms of self and object. But while the object belongs to the oldest psychoanalytic tradition, the self, of recent origin, remains an imprecise concept used in very different senses (Hartmann, 1950; Jacobson, 1964; Winnicott, 1960a; Lichtenstein, 1965). The rebirth of interest in narcissism, after its eclipse by the study of object relations, shows how difficult it is to engage in deep study of this kind without feeling the need for a complementary point of view. From this came the concept of the self. However, any serious discussion of the question must tackle the problem of primary narcissism. Its complete refutation by Balint in favour of primary love has not, despite apparently convincing arguments, prevented other writers from defending its autonomy (Grunberger, 1971; Kohut, 1971; Lichtenstein, 1964). Rosenfeld (1971b) linked it to the death instinct, but subordinated it to object relations. The uncertainty of our opinions on the subject probably goes back to Freud who, having introduced narcissism into his theory, rapidly lost interest in it and turned towards the death instinct, which we know has provoked resistance among some analysts. The Kleinian school, which has adopted Freud's point of view, seems to me to have maintained the confusion, absorbing the death instinct into the aggression which was originally projected on to the object. Even when it is an internal object the aggression is directed centrifugally.

The return of narcissism is not limited to explicit references to it. An ever-widening tendency exists towards the desexualization of the analytic field, as if we were returning surreptitiously to a restricted conception of sexuality. On the other hand, we have seen the development of ideas which allude to a central non-libidinal ego (Fairbairn, 1952) or to a state of being in which all instinctual qualities are denied (Winnicott and his disciples). In my opinion it is only a question here of problems concerning primary narcissism, as Winnicott none the less saw (1971b), without being precise on this point. The fact is that primary narcissism is the subject of contradictory definitions in Freud's work. Sometimes he means that which allows the unification of auto-erotic drives, contributing to the feeling of individual unity, and sometimes he means an original cathexis of the undifferentiated ego, with no reference to unity. Writers rely sometimes on one definition, sometimes on the other. I will base myself on the second. Unlike Kohut, I think that it is indeed the orientation of cathexes which points to the primitive narcissistic nature, whereas the quality of the cathexes (the grandiose self, the mirror transference and the idealization of the object), which eventually encompasses the object in the form of 'self-object', is secondary in sequence. These aspects relate to 'unifying' narcissism and not to primary narcissism in its strict sense.

Lewin (1954) has reminded us that in the analytic situation the wish to sleep, i.e. to achieve as full a state of narcissistic regression as possible, dominates the scene, just as it is the ultimate wish in dreams. The narcissism of sleep and the narcissism of dreams are distinct. It is significant that the oral triad which Lewin describes consists of a double relationship (e.g. eat—be eaten) and a tendency towards zero (falling asleep). Winnicott, following his description of the false self (which one can equally see as a double since it deals with the formation on the periphery of the self of the creation of a self-image which conforms to what the mother wishes), comes to the conclusion, in a remarkable article, that the real self is silent and isolated in a state of permanent non-communication. Even the title of his paper is revealing: 'Communicating and non-communicating leading to the study of certain opposites' (1963a). Here again it seems that the construction of opposites is related to a state of non-communication. For Winnicott, this lack of communication is in no way pathological, since it strives to protect that which is most essential to the self, which must never be communicated and which the analyst must learn to respect. But it seems that towards the end of his work Winnicott went even further, beyond the protective space which shelters subjective objects (see his 1971 addendum to the article on transitional objects; Winnicott, 1974), by formulating these problems more radically: in a way which recognizes the role and importance of emptiness. For example, 'Emptiness is a prerequisite to gather in' and 'It can be said that only out of non-existence can existence start' (Winnicott, 1974). All this invites us to reconsider Freud's metapsychological hypothesis of *primary absolute narcissism* as a tendency to come as close as possible to the zero degree of excitation rather than as a reference to unity. Clinical practice too makes us more and more aware of this, and from a technical point of view a writer like Bion – who is nevertheless a Kleinian – recommends to the analyst to attain a state without memory or desire, a state of the unknowable but yet a starting point for all knowledge (1970). This concept of narcissism, although held by a minority of analysts, has been the object of fruitful thinking, but has been centred for most of the time on its positive aspect, which takes as its model the state of satiation that follows satisfaction and allows quietude to be re-established. Its negative counterpart has met much resistance as far as theoretical formulations are concerned. However, the majority of writers have recognized that most defensive manoeuvres of patients with borderline states and psychoses attempt to struggle, not only against the primitive persecutory fears and the associated threat of annihilation, but also against the confrontation with emptiness which is probably the most intolerable of states, feared by patients, and whose scars leave a state of eternal dissatisfaction.

In my experience relapses, outbreaks of aggression and periodic collapses after marked progress all point to a need to maintain a relation 'th a bad internal object at all costs. As soon as the bad object loses its power there seems to be no other solution than to make it reappear, to proceed to resurrect it in the form of another bad object, which resembles the first like a brother and with which the patient identifies. It is less a question of the indestructibility of the bad object or of the wish to be certain of controlling it in this way, than of the fear that its disappearance will leave the patient confronted by the horrors of emptiness, without any possibility of ever being able to provide a replacement in the shape of a good object, even though this latter would be available. The object is bad, but it is good that it exists even though it does not exist as a good object. The cycle of destruction and reappearance recalls the hydra with its multiple heads, and seems to repeat the model of a theory (in the sense in which the term was used earlier) of the construction of the object which Freud said was knowable in hatred. But this compulsive repetition is due to the fact that here emptiness can only be cathected negatively. The abandonment of the object does not lead to the cathexis of a personal space, but to a tantalizing aspiration towards nothingness which drags the patient to a bottomless pit and eventually to negative hallucinations of himself. This tendency towards nothingness is far more than the aggression which is only one of its consequences. It is the real significance of the death instinct. Maternal deficiency aids it, but does it create it? One may wonder why we need so much care to prevent its appearance. Since something has not been provided by the object, there is no choice other than this flight towards nothingness. It is as if it were a question of finding the state of peace and quietude which follows satisfaction by its opposite, the non-existence of all hope of satisfaction. It is there that we find the solution of despair, when the struggle has been abandoned. Even those writers who emphasize to a large degree the domain of aggression have been forced to recognize its existence (Stone, 1971). We find traces of it in the psychotic kernel (blank psychosis) just as in what has recently been called the 'blank self' (Giovacchini, 1972*b*).

Thus we must join together the two effects of primary narcissism, i.e. the positive effect which follows regression after satisfaction and the negative effect which constructs a death-like quietus out of emptiness and nothingness.

I have put forward elsewhere a theory of primary narcissism (Green, 1967*b*) as a structure and not simply as a state which, alongside the whole positive aspect of object relations (in the visible, audible sense), be they good or bad, gives way to the negative aspect (in the invisible, silent sense). This negative aspect is formed by the introjection which takes place at the same time as maternal care forms the object relation. This is the relation to the structural framework of that care through the negative hallucination of the mother during her absence. That is the obverse of that of which the hallucinatory realization of the wish is one side. The space which is thus delimited, side by side with that of object relations, is a neutral space capable of being fed in part by the space of object relations but distinct from it. It constitutes the basis of identification when relationships aid the continuity of the feeling of existence (forming the personal secret space). On the other hand, it may empty itself by means of the aspirations towards non-existence, through the expression of an ideal, a self-sufficiency which is progressively reduced in the direction of self-annihilation (Green, 1967*b*, 1969*a*). One must not formulate things simply in terms of space. Radical decathexis also affects time through a frantic capacity to suspend experience (far beyond repression) and to create 'dead times' where no symbolization can take place (see the 'foreclosure' of Lacan, 1966).

The clinical application of this theory can be seen during the course of analysis, and it is this which stimulates the analyst's imagination most of all, whereas an excess of projections often has shock-like effects. But even in the most classical analysis something of it remains. This leads us to reconsider the question of silence in treatment. It is not enough to say that side by side with his communications the patient preserves within him a silent zone. One must add that the analysis develops as though the patient had delegated this silent function to the silence of the analyst. Thus the analysis evolves between the doubles of communication and the zero of silence. However, silence, as we know, can be experienced in certain borderline situations (*situations limites*) as the silence of death. This confronts us with a difficult technical choice. At one extreme is the technique proposed by Balint, which tries to organize experience as little as possible so as to allow it to develop under the benevolent protection of the analyst and his attentive ear, in order to encourage the 'new beginning'. At the other extreme is the Kleinian technique, whose aim is, on the contrary, to organize the experience as much as possible through interpretative verbalization. But is there not a contradiction in maintaining that object relations in the psychotic part of the personality have undergone a premature formation, and in responding to it with interpretations that are in danger of reproducing this same prematurity? Is there not a danger of overfilling the psychic space, when one should be helping to form the positive cathexis of the empty space? What is it that is structured in this way? The skeleton of experience, or its flesh which the patient needs to live? With these reservations I must acknowledge the difficulty of the cases whose treatment the Kleinians undertake and which compel one's respect. Between the two extremes is Winnicott's technique, which gives the setting its appropriate place, and recommends the acceptance of these unformed states and the non-intrusive attitude. He supplements through verbalization the lack of maternal care in order to encourage the emergence of a relationship to the ego and to the object, until the moment is reached when the analyst can become a transitional object and the analytic space a potential area of play and field of illusion. If I feel in harmony with Winnicott's technique, and if I aspire to it without being able to master it, it is because, despite the risk of fostering dependence, it seems to me to be the only one which gives the notion of absence its rightful place. The dilemma which places in opposition the intrusive presence – which leads to delusion (*délire*) – and the emptiness of negative narcissism which leads to psychic death, is modified by transforming delusion into play, and death into absence, through the creation of the playground of potential space. This requires one to take into account the notion of distance (Bouvet, 1958). Absence is potential presence, a condition for the possibility not only of transitional objects but also of potential objects which are necessary to the formation of thought (see Bion's 'non-breast', 1963, 1970). These objects are neither present nor tangible objects, but objects of relationships. Perhaps analysis only aims at the patient's capacity to be alone (in the presence of the analyst), but in a solitude peopled by play (Winnicott, 1958). We are too rigid or too idealistic if we think that it is a question of transforming primary processes into secondary ones. It would be more accurate to say that it is a question of initiating play between primary and secondary processes by means of processes which I propose to call tertiary (Green, 1972) and which have no existence other than that of processes of relationship.

CONCLUDING REMARKS

To conclude does not mean to close the work, but to open the discussion and to leave the floor to others. The solution to the crisis in which psychoanalysis finds itself does not lie within analysis alone. But analysis holds some cards with which its destiny will be played. Its future will depend on the way it finds in which to preserve its Freudian heritage while integrating its later acquisitions. For Freud there was no previous knowledge. Undoubtedly it needed his creative genius to invent psychoanalysis. Freud's work has become the basis of our knowledge. But an analyst cannot practise psychoanalysis and keep it alive by applying knowledge. He must attempt to be creative to the limits of his ability. This is perhaps what has made some among us extend the limits of the analysable. It is remarkable that the attempt to analyse these states has resulted in such a flowering of imaginative theories – too many for some, i.e. too many theories and too much imagination. All these theories strive to construct pre-histories where there is not even any evidence of a history. Above all, this shows us that we cannot do without a mythical origin, just as a small child must construct theories, even romances, about his birth and infancy. Undoubtedly our role is not to imagine, but to explain and to transform. However, Freud had the courage to write, 'Without metapsychological speculation and theorizing – I had almost said "phantasying" – we shall not get another step forward' (1937c, p. 225).[1] We cannot accept that our theories are fantasies. The best solution would be to accept that they are not the expression of scientific truth but an approximation to it, its analogue. Then there is no harm in constructing a myth of origins, provided we know that it can only be a myth.

In the last twenty years psychoanalytic theory has seen the considerable development of the genetic point of view (see the discussion in Lebovici & Soulé, 1970). Without embarking on a critique of our psychoanalytic concepts of development, of which many seem to me to adopt a non-psychoanalytic notion of time, it seems to me that the time has come to pay more attention to problems of communication, without limiting it to verbal communication, but taking in its most inchoate forms. That is what has led me to stress the role of symbolization, that of the object, of the analytic setting and also that of non-communication. Perhaps this will also allow us to tackle the problem of communication between analysts. Outsiders are frequently amazed that people whose profession is listening to patients are so bad at listening to one another. My hope is that this chapter, which shows that we all have similar problems to face, will contribute towards our listening to one another.

SUMMARY

This chapter has been guided by a personal theme while taking into account the psychoanalytic contributions of others.

1. The emphasis placed on the changes within the analyst was designed to show that, as well as changes within the patient, one must also consider the double created by the changes within the analyst, due to his capacity for constructing, by complementarity, in his mental functioning, a figure homologous to that of the patient.

2. The problem of indications for analysis has been approached from the point of view of the gap between the analyst's understanding and the patient's material, and from that of the evaluation of the mobilizing

[1] Freud uses the term 'the Witch (*die Hexe*) Metapsychology' . . .

effect of the analyst's communication on the patient's mental functioning, i.e. on the possibility – which varies with each case and with each analyst – of forming an analytic object (a symbol) by the meeting of the two parties.

3. The description of the implicit model of a borderline state by putting splitting (a condition for the formation of a double) and decathexis (as a striving towards the zero state) in the dominant position shows us that borderline states raise the question of the limits of analysability in the dilemma between delusion and death.

4. The attention given to the analytic setting and to mental functioning attempted to structure the conditions necessary for the formation of the analytic object through symbolization, by taking into account the intervention of the third element, which is the setting, in the dual relationship.

5. The place of primary narcissism gives us a point of view which complements the preceding one. In other words, alongside the doubles of communication of object relations is an encapsulated personal space which is a narcissistic domain, positively cathected in the silent self of being, or negatively cathected in the aspiration towards non-being. The dimension of absence, essential to psychic development, finds its place in the potential space between the self and the object.

This chapter does not claim to solve the crisis facing psychoanalysis, but only to raise some of the contradictions inherent in a theoretical pluralism and a heterogeneous practice. We have, above all, attempted to formulate an image of psychoanalysis which reflects personal experience and gives it a conceptual form.

psychosis, particularly latent schizophrenias presenting an apparently neurotic set of symptoms'. They stress the vagueness of the field covered by such a definition, which includes psychotic, perverted, and delinquent personalites; they seem to prefer that the term be more closely linked to 'pseudoneurotic schizophrenia'. Implied here are two concepts: the borderline as a neurotic set of symptoms is a fallacy, and the borderline as a psychotic set of symptoms is schizophrenia.

Moore and Fine (1967) give the following definition in their glossary: 'A descriptive term referring to a group of conditions which manifest both neurotic and psychotic phenomena without fitting unequivocally into either diagnostic category' (p. 19). Apparently no different from the French definition. But in fact the American glossary implies a difference. Even though its authors' further comments stress the defensive nature of the borderline's neurotic symptoms, what I find important for my investigation is that, according to their definition of the borderline, neither kind of symptom, neurotic or psychotic, fits the traditional conception of neurosis or psychosis.

Rycroft (1968) is less equivocal. He observes that the borderline case defies any attempt at classification. Yet he considers the problem from the point of view of psychosis alone and observes that in the borderline personality structure the defence is of a psychotic type, though the person's behaviour is not. Parenthetically, Rycroft rejects the idea that neurosis and psychosis are mutually exclusive.

As consulting dictionaries has proved of little help, let me pause for a moment and ask: Who or what is borderline? The important thing about such a question is the distinction between to *have* something borderline and to *be* borderline. I can *be* a citizen or *heimatlos*, but to be borderline – that is difficult for me to conceive.

The professional dictionaries tell me this much: borders are located at different places by different experts. So let me turn to my own personal experience. What are my borders? The skin envelope or container comes immediately to mind. But as definite and important as it may appear to me, my skin container is discontinuous. The tissue of flesh is interrupted by other tissues, or it presents holes, which act as gates. We can call them custom houses or inspectors: eyes, ears, nose, mouth, anus, urethra, vagina. Mouth, anus, sex organs – the so-called erotogenic zones – are important because they function in two ways: in and out. I am thus presented with two problems. The first is the nature or structure of the border; the second is the circulation in and out of its gates. But what are the borders or frontiers of my psyche? What are the laws governing the circulation through the gates of my psychic borders? What is the relation of the psyche and its borders to these gates? Two types of laws come to mind, two laws working in tandem – the pleasure-unpleasure principle and the reality principle. The reality principle is of particular importance for my investigation as it pertains to the existence or non-existence of the object, hence to the self.

Several types of borders are encountered in nature: lines or surfaces, with or without circulation through the frontier, or an osmotic membrane, which affords communication with an adequate selection of what has to be taken in or kept out, or, if there is trouble, what has to be rejected, what is unwelcome inside; and finally, a blurred division in some state of intersection, a border resembling the meeting of two clouds. In case of danger, an osmotic border can open up to unburden the inside from the troublesome stimuli. But other measures are possible: for instance, the stultification of the line, a kind of mortification, or the blurring of the border, creating instead a fragile limit, a no-man's-land. To be a borderline implies that a border protects one's self from crossing over or from being crossed over, from being invaded, and thus becoming a *moving border* (not *having*, but *being* such a border). This in turn implies a loss of distinction between space *and* time.

It is rather obvious that even apparently ordinary definitions of the borderline contain nuances betraying different points of view. In my view, one should not try to understand the symptoms of the borderline patient in terms of psychosis. Neither should one try to identify the borderline's psychotic condition with schizophrenia. Finally, I would question the generally accepted notion that neurotic symptoms have a definite function. Before elaborating on my point of view, however, I propose that we examine some other models.

CONCEPTUAL FRAMEWORKS AND MODELS OF BORDERLINE STATES

My intention is not to review the extensive literature on the subject. I shall therefore restrict myself to the work and views of those who have dealt with borderline cases in the psychoanalytic situation. I propose to classify such contributions in terms of three lines of thought: Freudian, Kleinian, and Winnicottian.

There are very few indications in Freud's own work that help in understanding borderline cases. In 'Neurosis and psychosis' Freud states: '. . . it will be possible for the ego to avoid a rupture in any direction by deforming itself, by submitting to encroachments on its own unity and even perhaps by effecting a cleavage or division of itself. In this way the inconsistencies, eccentricities and follies of men would appear in a similar light to their sexual perversions, through the acceptance of which they spare themselves repressions.

'In conclusion, there remains to be considered the question of what the mechanism, analogous to repression can be by means of which the ego detaches itself from the external world. This cannot, I think, be answered without fresh investigations; but such a mechanism, it would seem, must, like repression, comprise a withdrawal of the cathexis sent out by the ego' (Freud 1924*b*, pp. 152–3).

Several points are relevant to our discussion: the ego's avoidance of rupture, presumably of its borders, 'in any direction'; the ego's submission to 'encroachments' (today we would probably use the term impingements); the defence mechanism of ego 'cleavage or division of itself' (which today we would call splitting); the assumption that we need to create a clinical model for the ego deformation analogous to the sexual perversions; and finally, the hypothesis that ego cleavage (splitting) must involve a withdrawal of cathexis, which would make it a psychotic mechanism.

Freud (1924*e*) follows up his reflections on the nature of psychosis. He states: 'neurosis does not disavow the reality, it only ignores it; psychosis disavows it and tries to replace it' (p. 185). It is obvious that the concept of disavowal is different from repression in that disavowal is a psychotic mechanism dealing with external reality, whereas neurosis and repression deal with internal reality. Freud elaborates on this point: 'In a psychosis, the transforming of reality is carried out upon the psychical precipitates of former relations to it – *that is, upon the memory-traces, ideas and judgements which have been previously derived from reality and by which reality was represented in the mind*' (*ibid.*, p. 185; italics mine). Freud indicates the crucial role that cognition and the ability to deal not only with drives but also with ideas and judgments play in psychosis. Freud's statement underscores the importance of Bion's (1962) concept of the K (knowledge) and his emphasis on thought processes in psychosis. The creation of a neo-reality in psychosis is analogous to the neurotic *world of fantasy*, 'a domain which became separated from the real external world at the time of the introduction of the reality principle' (Freud, 1924*e*, p. 187). The final lines of Freud's article stress the difference between psychosis and neurosis in the use of fantasy – anticipating Winnicott's work on 'playing', and that of Klein, Segal, Khan, and myself, among others, on 'symbolism' and borderline states: 'But whereas the new, imaginary external world of a psychosis attempts to put itself in the place of external reality, that of a neurosis, on the contrary, is apt, *like the play of children* [italics mine], to attach itself to a piece of reality – a different piece from the one against which it has to defend itself – and to lend that piece a special importance and a secret meaning which we (not always quite appropriately) call a *symbolic* one. Thus we see that both in neurosis and psychosis there comes into consideration the question not only of a *loss of reality* but also of a *substitute for reality*' (*ibid.*, p. 187).

Freud's search for an answer to the problem of psychosis led him to the dynamics of borderline thinking, described in his article 'Negation' (1925*h*). In my view, Freud's pair of opposites – Yes or No – coexist with neither-Yes-nor-No mental structure, which, with regard to reality, finds expression in the feeling that the object is and is not real, or the object is neither real nor unreal (fantasied).

We may schematize Freud's ideas in the following manner:

	(IR)	(ER)
Pr_2	P–UP	Pr_2
	Yes-No	Yes-No
Pr_1	UP–P	?
	Yes	

At first a vertical border separates 'good' psychic reality (IR) from 'bad' external reality (ER). This division coincides with the separation of 'Yes' (inside) from 'No' (outside), according to the pleasure-unpleasure principle. A second development is represented by the horizontal border, which separates the pleasurable and unpleasurable inside. But because of repression, what corresponds to the unpleasurable in the conscious-preconscious corresponds to the pleasurable in the repressed. The vertical and horizontal lines thus indicate the separation between psychic reality (IR) on the left and external reality on the right (ER). In psychic reality, we have the secondary process (Pr_2) on the conscious level, with pleasurable (P) and unpleasurable affects (UP) linked with a Yes-or-No system (Yes-No), corresponding to the secondary process (Pr_2) of the external world. Hence a similarity between the conscious and the real. On the other hand, in psychic reality we also have the repressed, i.e., the system of a reversed opposition of the pleasurable-unpleasurable affect (antagonistic to the corresponding conscious affects) and a system of judgment where 'No' is unthinkable. Hence a conflict between the conscious and the unconscious and, in turn, between the unconscious and the external world. But we can assume that the unconscious is in some sort of correspondence with the unknown (?) of the external world.

This set of propositions is echoed in 'Analysis terminable and interminable' (1937*c*), an inexhaustible source of ideas for psychoanalysts with regard to theory and practice. Here once again Freud reiterates his belief in the importance of early traumas or early ego distortions with fixations to primitive defence mechanisms. He embellishes this with formulations about constitutional factors and peculiarities of the libido (inertia, viscosity, extreme fluidity and mobility of the cathexes), factors he seems to take for granted, but which require in fact a thorough investigation of their meaning and origin. On the other hand, even if not all of us agree with Freud's conception of the death instincts, few would deny the crucial importance of aggression – even if variously understood and conceptualized – in the etiology of psychosis and borderline states.

I would place the work of Bergeret (1974a) along this theoretical developmental line. His extensive knowledge of the literature allows him to make a good synthesis. He describes two kinds of disorganizing traumas. An early infantile trauma, with severe frustrations and the threat of object loss, leads to a precocious pseudo latency. This kind of disorganizing trauma accounts for a common body of borderline states (*tronc commun des états-limites*) and a provisional ego organization. A second kind of disorganizing trauma may occur in late adolescence – adolescence itself becoming prolonged beyond its normal end. Such trauma, accompanied by disruptive anxiety states, results in the reorganization of the provisional ego toward three alternative pathological outcomes: neurosis, psychosis, or psychosomatic regression. Two other ways of negotiation are found by the beleaguered ego: perversion and character disorder.

Another developmental theory basically along Freudian lines is that of Kernberg (1975). His formulations are supported not only by his own clinical experience, but by his vast knowledge of the literature, which he is able to reinterpret and integrate in an original and imaginative way.

As Kernberg's writings on the borderline personality organization are well known, I shall limit myself to his general frame of reference. Kernberg uses a double-sided model: structural and genetic-dynamic. This structural point of view has reference to (a) a topographical model as developed by Freud, (b) Hartmann's ego psychology, and (c) the structural derivatives of object relations. Borderline states, according to Kernberg, are characterized by: (a) non-specific manifestations of ego weakness, (b) a shift toward primary-process thinking, and (c) specific defensive operations, which he views from the vantage point of internalized object relations.

Kernberg stresses the importance of splitting between 'good' and 'bad' internal objects and self-images. He believes that the major defect in the development of borderline pathology lies in the individual's incapacity to synthesize the positive and negative introjections and identifications. Note that Kernberg considers the borderline personality organization not as fluctuating or labile, but as a style type of structure.

From the genetic-dynamic point of view, Kernberg stresses the importance of oral fixations. His conceptualization in this respect is distinct from the Kleinian view, which he criticizes. But along with Klein, he believes that pregenital aggression induces premature development of oedipal striving.

In conclusion, I shall define Kernberg's theory as a *borderline* one – bordering between ego psychology and the Kleinian point of view.

We may now turn to the work of Melanie Klein and her followers. I refer to only one of Klein's papers, 'Notes on some schizoid mechanisms' (1946), which I find particularly relevant to the subject of borderline disorders. Most important is her assumption that object relations exist from the beginning of life. She also emphasizes the destructive potential of the infant mind and its primitive defences of splitting, idealization, and projective identification. Moreover, she recognizes the importance of the narcissistic nature of schizoid object relations and describes the connection between schizoid and manic-depressive phenomena. Segal and Rosenfeld, among other followers, have elaborated and developed Klein's views with reference to adult borderline patients.

Special mention should be made of Bion's work. Even though nearly all his contributions are focused on the problems of psychosis, his 1957 paper 'Differentiation of the psychotic from the non-psychotic personalities' is an important contribution to the literature of borderline disorders. The richness and originality of Bion's ideas defy summarization. His contributions are most significant in that they confront Freud's ideas about the psychic apparatus, especially as it concerns thought processes, and Klein's conceptualization of object relations, especially her view of projective identification as a basic defence mechanism. Bion points to the precocious mental development or 'precipitation' of psychotic individuals and argues that defence should be conceived not in terms of regression, but as rapid 'anticipation' – something that impairs the development of the psychic apparatus for secondary-process thinking. His recognition of depressive functions in language processes is also an original and relevant contribution. Instead of a maturational use of language resources, there is, according to Bion, a fixation to 'ideograms', which hinders the evolution of thought processes toward a mind structure dependent on verbal thought.

In his later work (1962), Bion assumes the existence of three factors: L (love) and H (hate), with K (knowledge) as a primary concept of equal importance to love and hate. He also postulates the relations $O \rightarrow K$, where O stands for the unknowable object and the state of the unknowable (godness, absolute truth, the infinite), leading to a state of knowledge that deals with what is acknowledgeable. Finally, his analysis of the relation between 'container' and 'content' offers valuable clues to the study of the psychic structures.

But it is Winnicott (1965, 1971a, 1971b, 1975) who is specifically, in my opinion, *the analyst of the borderline*. His inimitable style and original conceptualization do not lend themselves to easy summarization. Winnicott's apparent clarity is misleading, and frequently one reads authors inspired by his contributions who do not do justice to the subtle and rich complexity of his ideas. His emphasis on the 'facilitating environment', 'primary maternal concern', and 'holding' has led to a shift of attention from the overall internal object to the role of the external object. In fact, however, Winnicott is much more interested in the *interplay* of the external and the internal. What he directs our attention to is precisely the *area of the intermediate*, and the failure to create it. He gives us a joint model of clinical setting and psychic functioning. He describes the fate of symbolization and the impairment of the functional value of the transitional field, as well as transitional phenomena in borderline cases, by insisting on the fact that for these patients the setting and the analyst do not represent the mother – they *are* the mother. His conceptualization of the 'false self' refers to the effects of an overdemanding adaptation to the need-supplying object.

Much less attention has been given to Winnicott's late concepts of 'non-communication', 'void', and 'emptiness'. His theory of the 'gap' and the impossibility to create out of it another form of reunion with the object in the building of the 'potential space' opens new horizons of understanding, inducing the analyst to new ways of observing his own reaction as a tool for comprehending the paradoxes of borderline systems of thought. In what he calls 'the negative side of relationships', Winnicott (1971b) gives useful clues for the understanding of clinical features of the borderline individual, in whom a sense of lack and a feeling of nothingness predominate. Countertransference thus becomes the analyst's privileged instrument for work with such patients. The analyst must pay attention not only to what is present, but also to the missing links, which are not hidden but experienced as gaps, the only things that are real for the borderline patient. The essence of Winnicott's thought is contained in the last lines of *Playing and Reality* (1971b), which he names his 'tail piece'. Here he defines conceptualization (the psychic functioning that creates the subjective object) and perception (the objectively perceived object), pointing out an inherent paradox, 'one that we must accept and that is not for resolution'.

Winnicott's work has influenced Khan's (1974) and Milner's (1968) theoretical development. Khan has given us the concept of the 'cumulative trauma', describing infantile neurosis as a 'false-self organization' and pointing out the role of the interplay of the analyst's senses in the appraisal of transferential manifestations. The necessity to establish a contractual distance prevents the analyst from indulging in merging regressions or intruding into the secrecy of the patient's 'potential space'. Like Winnicott, Khan is aware of the importance of the aliveness of the analytic situation.

Milner has outstandingly illustrated the modifications required for analytic work with borderline patients. Her major contribution lies in the recognition of the need for tolerance of unorganized states in the analyst's mind, from which growth and creativity stem. Her contributions to the dynamics of symbolism and her criticism of the conceptualization of primary process as a lower form of psychic activity constitute the basis of a better understanding of primary-process thinking in borderline disorders. I would like to add here that in borderline thinking we have the result of a destructive perversion of primary-process thinking, rather than a genuine expression of what primary process is supposed to be in infancy.

I have made only one reference to the French literature, but as I have been strongly influenced by it, I feel that I should not close this section without mentioning some important, even though indirect, contributions to the borderline psychopathology by my fellow countrymen. Bouvet's (1967) description of pregenital structures and especially of depersonalization neurosis, as well as the work of his followers from the Paris school of psychosomatics (Marty, Fain, de M'Uzan, and David), have enriched our understanding of the borderline. Bouvet's concept of *rapprocher* and of psychic distance has been carefully applied to the handling of difficult cases. Lacan's (1966) ideas on psychosis, especially his attempt to clarify Freud's concept of 'deferred action', of 'foreclosure' (*Verwerfung*) and its role in his theory of the Name of the Father, are stimulating, even if other aspects of Lacan's writings may be highly questionable.

To conclude this partial review of the literature, I shall list the issues relevant to our topic: (1) the role of the *ego*, *the self*, and *narcissism*, with the early defence mechanisms of dissociation and splitting, and their consequences: decathexis and projective identification; (2) the function of *object relations*, with special attention to pregenital aggression and its influence on thought processes; (3) the presence of *psychotic anxiety* and its impact on the binding function of psychic processes, with consequences for verbal thought; (4) the failures in the creation of a *transitional space*, with the dual, coexisting function of the pleasure principle and the reality principle, and a double-bind pattern of relations; (5) the *condensation of pregenital and genital aims*, giving a double meaning to each of them, which automatically refers one to the other; (6) the role of a *complementary relation* in the analytic setting, the countertransference becoming a conveyor for the patient's communication more than an obstacle to his understanding; and (7) the notion of *psychic distance*, necessary to avoid both lack of communication and intrusion.

THE CONCEPT OF THE BORDERLINE

Most, if not all, of the preceding contributors base their theoretical assumptions mainly on the genetic point of view. Even those who take into account the topographic model and the concomitant structural point of view subsume it under an overall genetic rubric.

In *An Outline of Psycho-Analysis* Freud wrote: 'A child's first erotic object is the mother's breast that nourishes it; love has its origin in attachment to the satisfied need for nourishment. There is no doubt that, to begin with, the child does not distinguish between the breast and its own body; when the breast has to be separated from the body and shifted to the *"outside"* because the child so often finds it absent, it carries with it as an *"object"* a part of the original narcissistic libidinal cathexis. The first object is later completed into the person of the child's mother, who not only nourishes it but also looks after it and thus arouses in it a number of other physical sensations, pleasurable and unpleasurable' (1940a, p. 188).

In this instance Freud conceived the birth of the object as separate from the child's own body as a gradual process. But on other, earlier occasions, he spoke about a clear-cut separation from the outset (1925h). His concept of the original reality ego indicates that he saw the child as able to distinguish between internal and external sources of excitation from the beginning. Such ideas seem contradictory unless we assume that there is a distinction between inside and outside that antedates the distinction between the child's body and the mother's breast. Indeed, in his paper 'Negation' Freud made a clear-cut distinction between the pleasure principle and the reality principle, which arises with the development of reality testing. As he put it, '. . . it is evident that a precondition for the setting up of reality-testing is that objects shall have been lost which once brought real satisfaction' (1925h, p. 238). In

Freud's view, at least as I understand it, this development is not a progressive, slow change, since it requires the function of judgment to decide whether the object exists or not. The function of judgment is related to primary instinctual impulses and 'is not made possible until the creation of the symbol of negation has endowed thinking with a first measure of freedom from the consequences of repression and, with it, from the compulsion of the pleasure principle' (*ibid.*, p. 239).

Because of the sovereignty of the reality principle, the realm of fantasy is created as a private domain. This development allows for an important observation: *each time a separation occurs between a couple of mental opposites – two terms, two functions, two processes – at least one of the two split-off elements tends to re-include some part of the opposite, excluded element.*

On the other hand, if the psychic apparatus has the *illusion of a mutative transformation,* a retrospective view of its former functioning allows us to assume that, in fact, the transformation was *gradual,* involving the overlapping of different models of functioning, of two areas, and of the dual relation between the self and the object.

Let us now shift our attention to some other relevant metapsychological concepts formulated by Freud. Let us consider the nature of the topographic model. Freud states: 'In thinking of this division of the personality into an ego, a super-ego and an id, you will not, of course, have pictured sharp frontiers like the artificial ones drawn in political geography. We cannot do justice to the characteristics of the mind by linear outlines like those in a drawing or in primitive painting, but rather by areas of colour melting into one another as they are presented by modern artists. After making the separation we must allow what we have separated to merge together once more. You must not judge too harshly a first attempt at giving a pictorial representation of something so intangible as psychical processes. It is highly probable that the development of these divisions is subject to great variations in different individuals; it is possible that in the course of actual functioning they may change and go through a temporary phase of involution' (1933*a*, p. 79).

The function of judgment is established gradually. Conversely, the reconstruction in the psychic apparatus of the past experience of this gradual process as a mutation is important for the establishment of the judging process in reality testing. The major difficulty therefore lies in the coexistence of different ego states: tolerance of 'shadows, doubts and mysteries' and/or capacity to decide between the Yes and the No, the existent and the non-existent. Imagination and rationality are so necessary to each other that any imbalance in the one would be detrimental to the other, leading to a global impairment of mental functioning.

In *Civilization and Its Discontents*, Freud discusses the blurring of mental frontiers that occurs even in normal persons and relates it to the return of an undifferentiated infantile state of mind, characterized by an 'oceanic feeling'. He concludes: 'The fact remains that only in the mind is such a preservation of all the earlier stages alongside of the final form possible, and that we are not in a position to represent this phenomenon in pictorial terms' (1930a, p. 71).

Here again we find Freud wishing to use pictorial metaphors, even though he is aware of their inadequacy. The pictorial way of communicating, in theory or in mental functioning, has a transitional function between the two other main modes of human communication: affects, which in essence are not representable in pictorial form, and thought, which consists of relations independent of the terms it brings into relation. Splitting is therefore a normal process enabling one to achieve communication out of the verbally uncommunicable affects and thought processes. As such, splitting never disappears but undergoes transformations with the help of a holding, containing, *optimally distant, and time-delaying object*. Even though splitting can separate, it never succeeds in a complete way. This is also true in a clinical sense with the 'Splitting of the ego in the process of defence' (1940e), as Freud pointed out in his posthumously published paper, where the concept of disavowal is once more implicated.

In a companion paper Freud (1940a) brings forward the importance of splitting in the psychoses. Even in the severely disturbed patient suffering from hallucinatory confusion, the normal ego is not totally absorbed by the regressive condition – *a fortiori* in less severe cases. As Freud puts it: 'Two psychical attitudes have been formed instead of a single one – one the normal one, which takes account of reality, and another which under the influence of the instincts detaches the ego from reality. The two exist alongside of each other. The issue depends on their relative strength' (p. 202).

I would like to close this section by showing that not only are the frontiers between the ego and reality variable, but even the instinct, as Freud conceived it, undergoes analogous variations in its intrinsic functioning. According to Freud, 'an "instinct" appears to us as a *concept on the frontier* between the mental and the somatic, as the psychical representative of the stimuli originating from within the organism and reaching the mind, as a measure of the demand made upon the mind for work in consequence of its connection with the body' (1915c, pp. 121–2; italics mine).

This so frequently quoted, deceptively simple statement of Freud's can be a source of endless reflection. My understanding of it is as follows:

1. The instinct (*Trieb*) is a concept.
2. The concept is on the *frontier* between two domains.
3. Freud opposes one single word, the 'mind' (*Seele*), as the function of the 'mental' (*psychisch*), to two words expressing the same idea: the 'somatic' (*somatisch*), or the 'organism', and the 'body' (*Körper*). One may raise the question: Are these different synonyms used to avoid fastidious repetition, or do the words in fact refer to semantic distinctions?
4. The instinct is a *psychical representative* of stimuli. This psychical representative must not be confused with the *ideational representative*, which, along with a quota of affect, forms the instinctual representatives in the psyche.
5. The instinct is defined as a *process*, a progression involving pressure or energy, which can only be felt and understood as a measure of a demand upon the mind for work. In my opinion, it is clear that the measure of such a demand for work is of variable strength, and the frontiers between the organism and its mind are not sharply delineated. So within this concept of the frontier (*Grenzbegriff*) one can also think of borderline states between the somatic and the mental or psychic, between the body and the mind, on which a process of transformation is at work.

In conclusion, we can say that *nowhere* does there exist clear-cut splitting: within the instincts; between body and mind; within the ego and its interrelations to the id, the superego, and reality. Therefore we have to consider the borderline as a *moving and fluctuating* frontier, both in normality and in severe illness, and as the most basic concept in psychoanalysis, which cannot be understood in pictorial terms (representations) but has to be conceived in terms of processes of transformations of *energy* and *symbolization* (force and meaning).

On the other hand, one basic function of the psyche is to strive for *separation* in order to foster adaptation, individuation, and autonomy. But these aims will not be attained unless the *disjunctive* process is accompanied by a *conjunctive* one, where the aim is to re-establish communication with the split-off elements to the extent possible. This is the work of *symbolization*, which requires the splitting of two elements and their conjunction in order to create a third element, which is composed of the two split-off elements, each of them remaining the same and becoming in reunion a different one.

A HYPOTHESIS OR CONCEPTUAL FRAMEWORK
CONCERNING BORDERLINE PATIENTS

As I indicated earlier, the borderline case is less of a frontier than a no-man's-land, an entire field whose borders are vague. Its population has to be sorted out. Grinker's (1977) attempt is in this respect a classificatory one. Yet we are in need of catalogues not only of symptoms or of classificatory tables, but also of ordinal concepts. To this end I propose a conceptual framework such as outlined in the previous chapter, and extracted from the analytic situation. I would like to stress that the borderline cases closer to neurosis often afford us the greatest opportunity to grasp the nature of the problem, because they are amenable to the deep scrutiny of psychoanalytic investigation. Illustrative case material may give the reader the impression that the patient is neurotic, but the analyst knows that he is dealing with a borderline case. This knowledge is based on the affective quality of the patient's communication and the analyst's own inner response to it, which are difficult to convey in writing – unless one writes poetry. In this connection, I should mention the function of countertransference, which can serve as a very precise tool in the understanding of borderline patients.

To begin with, one must trace the hypothetical limits of the psychic field. There are two, of a different nature: *soma* and *acting*. In my analysis of Freud's definition of an instinct (*Trieb*), I pointed to the multiplicity of terms attributed to the somatic sphere and raised the question of synonymity or semantic difference. Here I shall draw a distinction between the somatic, which I relate to the organism (a biological entity), and the body, which I relate to libidinal cathexis. We assume that the aim of an instinct is achieved by what Freud calls 'specific action', which can transform a helpless situation into a satisfactory experience after the failure of hallucinatory wish-fulfiment. We know that 'acting out' is the opposite of a specific action (in Freud's sense). The main function of acting out – or reactive behaviour – is to pare or to parade. I have in mind the French word *parer*, meaning to cope with, to counteract, to protect oneself, to avoid, to ward off. The aim here is to precipitate the organism into action in order to bypass psychical reality. Thus, one might say that the psychical field is delineated by both aspects of the instinct: its source (somatic) and its aim (acting). It is difficult to assign one basic function to the psychic field, as it seems to have more than one. But in order to clarify my idea, and at the risk of oversimplifying things, I shall advance a hypothesis.

Freud assumed that the basic function of the psychic field was the *lowering of unpleasurable tension*. Hartmann's ego psychology assumes that the basic function is *adaptation*, an assertion not contradictory to Freud's, though implying a shift in emphasis. The British School considers that *growth* is this basic function. I suggest that this basic function is *representation*. This should be understood in a very broad sense, as including representation of both the external and the internal world. It also includes a pluralistic mode of representation, not only through an ideational content but also through acts, affects, bodily states, language, ideas, and thoughts. As Castoriadis-Aulagnier (1975) suggests, it is as if any activity of the psychic apparatus had the function of building the representation of whatever is to be represented, and also the representation of the functioning of the psychic apparatus itself. The psychical field is under a double influence: the *pressure* of the instinct pushing toward the realization of the specific action, and the impact of the need-satisfying object through representation.

Freud has endlessly stressed the importance of reality testing in distinguishing between representation, which obeys the pleasure principle, and perception, which is under the power of the reality principle. The aim of the instinct requires, especially at the beginning, a devoted person to act as a need-satisfying object, and at the same time as substitute for the child's embryonic ego. Both functions are fused and embodied in the mother's breast – i.e., the mother's care. The child's ego acts individually when separation between breast and child finally takes place. This gradual process is evidently accompanied by periodic phases of reunion with the object, when the former phase is re-established in fact; and of periodic phases when the child tries to re-establish, alone, the lost paradise of fusion with the maternal object or breast. But the inevitable frustrations and disappointments of the growing process compel him to tolerate, alongside the feeling of well-being, the discontent and anger which are fixated in archaic forms of representation, for which Bion (1957) has proposed the concept of the 'ideogram'. The attempt to separate the 'good' from the 'bad', the pleasurable from the unpleasurable, and the obligation to achieve separation instead of giving birth to the distinction between self and object (inside and outside, somatic and psychic, fantasy and reality, 'good' and 'bad') engender splitting in borderlines. In a set of complementary, opposite terms, each separated term admits the symmetrical complement; for example, the shadow of its light, its phantom more than its fantasy. But inevitably, it will be again re-united in some other area of the psychic space. In severely disturbed cases the result is a radical exclusion: splitting.

To some extent, splitting is necessary to the work of the psychic apparatus, which must not be overburdened and overwhelmed by tension and has, in order to survive, to refind the *quality* of well-being. On the other hand, radical splitting puts aside and away factors indispensable for the work of representation. Therefore splitting, instead of functioning as a useful limitation, causes amputation in the ego. For, with regard to the kind of splitting I am talking about here, not only destructive instinctual representations are split off, but also, in the same process, important parts of the ego itself (Bion, 1962, 1963).

The cause of splitting is understood differently, depending on one's conceptual framework. For Freud the splitting I am discussing is an expression of the death instinct, as opposed to the unifying action of Eros. For Melanie Klein it is also the result of the death-instinct operations, but as related to the fear of annihilation and directed toward the object. Freud's death instinct is a separating force, which operates primarily internally, even at the cellular level, without necessarily being felt as destructive; rather it is seen as disjunctive. In Klein's theory, it is the *affect* and not the idea of destruction that comes into play. For Winnicott splitting or dissociation is also related to destruction but with major differences. First, Winnicott assumes that early destructive experiences, because of the ego's immaturity, cannot be felt as such; lacking integration, they are more like unthinkable 'agonies'. Second, the attitude of the external environment is of utmost importance in containing these disintegrated states.

In my view, splitting is hardly conceivable without its complementary term: confusion. The child's splitting is a very basic reaction to the object's attitude, which can be twofold: (1) a lack of fusion on the part of the mother, to the effect that even in the actual experiences of encounter the child meets a *blank breast*; (2) an excess of fusion, the mother being unable to renounce for the sake of her child's growth the paradisiac bliss regained through the experience of pregnancy.

The child-breast separation is bound to a double consent, a two-party contract relating mother and child with reference to a potential third party – the father – who is present from the beginning in the mother's mind. The paradoxical result of splitting in this instance is that (a) something will be excluded, warded off, disavowed, and in fact become unworkable or unthinkable; and (b) the split-off terms will come back in a manner analogous to the return of the repressed, with the difference that they will have an intrusive, persecutory quality by way of projective identification. In other words, splitting in this instance results in the polarity 'loss-intrusion'.

It would be quite erroneous to think that splitting occurs only or mainly during the separation of the external from the internal. In fact, splitting also occurs, and perhaps even predominantly, between psyche and soma, and consequently between bodily sensations and affects. This dissociation may take subtle forms, as in the isolation process disjoining affect representation and thought. Needless to say, motor action itself may also be split off from the psychic world. What I want to stress here is that the two frontiers established by splitting are between the somatic and the libidinal body on the one side, and between psychical reality and external reality, involving the libidinal body and action, on the other.

As a consequence, we may assume that the split-off soma will intrude into the psychic sphere in the form of psychosomatic symptoms, hysteria, or hypochondriasis. The difference between psychosomatic symptoms and conversion hysteria is that whereas conversion symptoms are built in a symbolic fashion and are related to the libidinal body, psychosomatic symptoms are not of a symbolic nature. They are somatic manifestations loaded with refined, 'pure' aggression. Hypochondriacal symptoms, on the other hand, are painful representations of somatic organs filled with narcissistic, delibidinized and destructive libido.

Considering the second frontier, one may assume that there is the same lack of symbolization in 'acting out'. Insofar as it is a symptom, acting out may have a symbolic meaning for the analyst, but none from the patient's point of view. It is a mere discharge, the patient being blind to its possible meaning. It is not linked to anything other than its manifest, rationalized content. Here lies the difference between acting out and parapraxis, which is something devoid of meaning but which rapidly acquires a meaning by means of the associations that follow its narrative. In short, we may say that somatic (or psychosomatic) reactions and acting out have the same function: discharge to ward off psychic reality.

One can now understand the difference between splitting and repression. In repression, the psychic energy is bound. Links are intact and recombined with other representations or affects – id derivatives. The original terms in the associative link are replaced by others, but the linking function is only transformed, not altered. In splitting, the links are destroyed or so impaired that only by intensive effort can the analyst guess what they could have been. I therefore strongly object to the notion that borderline patients engage in primary-process thinking.

The implications of this differentiation between repression and splitting are of momentous importance. The return of the repressed gives rise to signal anxiety. The return of the split-off elements is accompanied by feelings of severe threat, of 'helplessness' (Freud's *Hilflosigkeit*), 'annihilation' (Klein, 1946), 'nameless dread' (Bion, 1970), 'disintegration' or 'agonies' (Winnicott, 1958). When the narcissistic cathexes are mainly threatened, the experience is characterized by 'blankness' (Green, 1969*b*).

Let us now consider the concepts that define the psychic sphere, for so far I have only examined those elements rejected from the psychic sphere. They are the same: *splitting* and *repression*. Just as repression is a mechanism directed inward, splitting here is active on its inner side. Let me clarify what I mean.

The idea of splitting in the psychic sphere poses problems. It is clear that splitting in borderline disorders is not the same as repression in neurosis or splitting in the psychoses. I have pointed out that repression in neurosis is accompanied by internal symbolization, which can be witnessed in the return of the repressed. With respect to psychosis, we may say that splitting acts as minute splitting, as Klein and her followers have observed. Nor is splitting in the borderline simply reduced to the kind of cleavage that takes place in depression, though depression and mental breakdown are constant threats in borderline disorders. In my opinion, the specificity of the borderline lies in the fact that splitting develops on two levels: splitting *between* the psychic and the non-psychic (soma and outside world) and splitting *within* the psychic sphere. The splitting between the inside and the outside is determined by the constitution of an ego container, and ego holder or ego envelope, whose limits are well delineated but do not function as a protective shield. In fact, ego boundaries are largely elastic. Nevertheless this flexibility is not conducive to adaptive behaviour; rather, it acts like a fluctuation of expansion, retraction, or both, in coping with *separation (loss) anxiety, intrusion (implosion) anxiety*, or both. This variability of ego boundaries is not felt as an enrichment of experience but as a loss of control, as the last defensive measure against implosion, disintegration, or loss. This ego envelope, this inefficient shield, protects the vulnerable ego, which is both rigid and lacking cohesiveness. The inner splitting reveals that the ego is composed of different, non-communicating nuclei. These ego nuclei can aptly be designated as *archipelagos*.

By means of this metaphor I shall try to describe some unique characteristics of these psychic structures. Instead of a myriad of islands surrounded by an ocean, one might think of isolated pieces of land delineated by void space. These islands remain without the possibility of connection with each other. There is a lack of cohesiveness, a lack of unity, and above all a lack of coherence and an impression of contradictory sets of relations – roughly speaking, the coexistence of contradictory thoughts, affects, fantasies, but moreover contradictory byproducts of the pleasure principle, the reality principle, or both. This failure in integration gives the observer a feeling of aloofness, an absence of vitality, as these separated islands of egos (self-object relations) do not succeed in forming one individual being. In my view, these islands of ego nuclei are less important than their surrounding space, which I have described as void. Futility, lack of awareness of presence, limited contact are all expressions of the same basic emptiness that characterizes the experience of the borderline person. Again, like Bion, I stress the importance of the linking function or, to remain in Freud's conceptual framework, of the binding function of Eros. The discourse of the borderline is not a chain of words, representations, or affects, but rather – like a pearl necklace without a string – words, representations, affects contiguous in space and time but not in meaning. It is up to the observer to establish the missing links with his own psychic apparatus.

I have suggested that the mechanism of splitting operates alongside a mechanism best identified as primary depression. In my view, all other mechanisms of psychic defence (projective and introjective identification, denial, omnipotence, etc.) are consequences of the basic mechanism of splitting, which is one of the two polar mechanisms of the psychic apparatus. The other polarity is depression. By depression I do not mean what is usually described by this term, but rather a *radical decathexis*, which engenders blank states of mind without any affective components, pain, or suffering. The clinical features associated with this mechanism are a series of phenomena about which borderline patients complain: difficulty of mental representations, impairment of concentration, impossibility of thinking – all of which have been described before as *blank psychosis* (Donnet and Green, 1973). It is the psychotic kernel. This primary depression may lead either to a random recathexis by instinctual energy (predominantly aggression) and a reinforcement of splitting, or to feelings of nonexistence and unreality of self- and object-images. When there is a chance for further maturation, the normal depressive position becomes a regressive pool for this primary depression. To ward off the threat of primary depression, precipitate and premature object relations occur, and adolescence is inordinately prolonged. Impossibility of mourning and of tolerating guilt feelings are striking features responsible for acting out psychopathic or as-if personality behaviour, polymorphous perversions, drug addiction, and alcoholism. These two basic mechanisms, splitting and primary depression, take place within the inner reality of the self. I have already commented on the elasticity of ego boundaries as a mode of reaction to loss, separation or intrusion anxiety, or both.

In my view, one needs to consider *two borderline areas* in the psychic apparatus. First, an intermediary area between the unconscious and the conscious-preconscious; its manifestation is the dream. Second, the area of play or illusion – Winnicott's 'potential space'. Borderline patients are characterized by a failure to create functional byproducts of the potential space; instead of manifesting transitional phenomena, they create symptoms to fulfil the function of transitional phenomena. By this I do not mean to say that borderline patients are unable to create transitional objects or phenomena. To say such a thing would be to ignore the fact that many artists are borderline personalities. In fact it can only be said that, from the point of view of the psychic apparatus of such individuals, transitional objects or phenomena have no functional value, as they do for others.

As many workers in the field have realized, dream analysis in the treatment of the borderline is, as a rule, unproductive. The reason seems to be that borderline patients' dreams do not express wish-fulfilment but rather serve a function of evacuation. As Bion (1962) has pointed out, the 'dream barrier' is an important function of the psychic apparatus. It seems that in borderline cases, even though the dream barrier is effective, the dream's purpose is not the working through of instinct derivatives, but rather the unburdening of the psychic apparatus from painful stimuli or, in Bion's terms, from 'accretion'. The dreams of borderline patients are not characterized by condensation but by concretization. One can also observe dream failures in these patients: wakening in order to prevent dreaming or to find themselves surrounded by a strange, disquieting atmosphere, which constitutes a transitional dream state akin to a nightmare. In more successful instances, dreams are actualizations of the self in the dream space, attempts to reformulate traumatic experiences (Khan, 1974). In such instances, the most significant thing in analyzing a dream is not the dream's latent content but *the dreamer's experience*.

Let us now turn to another aspect of the problem. The content of the unconscious is made up of object relations, involving either part objects or whole objects (persons). The history of object relations is made up of pregenital fixations and regressions in a more or less predictable sequence of pre-oedipal and oedipal phases of development. In describing 'blank psychosis', Donnet and I (1973) have proposed the concept of *bi-triangulation* or *tri-dyadic relationships*. In this type of Oedipus-like complex, there is a triangular relationship in which the two parental figures are experienced as affective polar opposites.

A normal person nurtures ambivalent feelings, both positive and negative, for each parent. In borderline persons, however, there is a split between the two parents along the notions of the 'bad' and the 'good', the 'persecutory' and the 'idealized'; one parent is felt as 'all bad' and the other as 'all good'. In this relationship the 'good' parental object is perceived as weak and ineffective and the overvaluation of the 'good' idealization is of no help against the omnipotent 'badness' of the other parent. The fear that abandonment by the 'bad' intruding parental object will lead nowhere but to a desert, and that the idealized 'good' object is unavailable, too distant and unreliable, brings the borderline patient to an insoluble dilemma. Shapiro and his co-workers (1975) have described how the borderline may be the receptacle of complementary disturbed parents, each projecting onto the child the denied part of his or her sick personality. However, the division of good and bad between two objects uncovers that of one two-sided object.

When Winnicott postulated the concept of the 'false self', he gave us a way of understanding the function of narcissistic features in borderline patients. As the 'false self' is built not on the patient's real experiences, but on the compliance to the mother's image of her child, the 'false self' organization serves the object's narcissism rather than that of the self – hence one paradox of the existence of narcissistic features and the feeling that they are of a different nature from the usual features of so-called narcissistic personalities. The answer to this contradictory assessment is that the 'false self' is supplied by a borrowed narcissism – the object's narcissism. Consequently, the mental functioning of the bewildered analyst appears as the double of the patient's mental functioning and object relations: symmetrical, complementary, or opposite.

It is quite remarkable that the dead-end issues facing the borderline patient are experienced by him not only in his mental functioning and object relations as reactivated in the transference, but also in his real life. They force him to move constantly from one place to another, to travel away in order to escape the 'bad' object and reach the 'good' one in some ideal holy land, only to be recaptured by some substitute figure of the 'bad' object, some silly agent of the 'bad' object sent to torment him and bring him back to his detested nest.

Concerning the borderline's mental functioning, one may observe a paradoxical mode of elaboration. I have already commented on the role of splitting. I can add that the different components of the psychic apparatus are all confused. There is no clear distinction between thoughts, representations, and affects. Rational thinking is difficult because the thought processes are loaded with massive quantities of affects, and they cannot be detached from the instincts except by way of an intensive splitting, sometimes accompanied by magical beliefs and narcissistically invested omnipotence. Also, in considering the border-line's mental representations, one can see that there is such a con-glomeration of affects and representations that affects act in fact as representations and representations act as affects. Moreover, one can say that acting (as opposed to specific action) is the true model of the mind here, whether directed inward, producing psychosomatic symp-toms, or outward, by way of acting out. Acting is not limited to actions; fantasies, dreams, words take the function of action. Acting fills space and does not tolerate the suspension of experience. The reason for such intolerance for the suspension of experience is the belief that no creation, no knowledge can emerge from it. Suspension is equated with inertia or, as Khan (1974) has described it, resourceless dependence. Basic trust is fundamental for the acceptance of passivity. Passivity is always felt as the supreme threat, open to all kinds of dangers in the hands of the omnipotent 'bad' object.

I shall now propose a final hypothesis with respect to the borderline's judgment and reality testing. According to the reality principle, the psychic apparatus has to decide whether the object is or is not there: *'Yes' or 'No'*. According to the pleasure principle, and as negation does not exist in the primary process of the unconscious, there is only 'Yes'. Winnicott has described the status of the transitional object, which combines the 'Yes' and the 'No', as the transitional is- and is-not-the-breast. One can find precursors of Winnicott's observations in Freud's description of the cotton-reel game (1920*g*) and in his description of the fetish (1927*e*). But I think that there is one more way of dealing with this crucial issue of deciding whether the object is or is not, and that is illustrated by the judgment of the borderline patient. There is a fourth possible answer: *neither 'Yes' nor 'No'*. This is an alternate choice to the refusal of choice. The transitional object is a *positive refusal*; it is either a 'Yes' or a 'No'. The symptoms of the borderline, standing for transitional objects, offer a *negative refusal of choice*: neither 'Yes' nor 'No'. One could express the same relation in experiential terms by asking the question: 'Is the object dead (lost) or alive (found)?' or 'Am I dead or alive?' – to which he may answer: *'Neither Yes nor No.'*

A related concept that may prove useful to our discussion is Lacan's (1966) 'absence'. As I understand it, the concept refers to neither loss nor death. Lacan's 'absence' has an intermediate status, being halfway between intrusion and loss. Excess of presence is intrusion; excess of absence is loss. The presence-absence pair cannot be dissociated. The two terms are interrelated, as are perception and representation. But a tremendous effort is necessary in order to be able to tolerate absence, to differentiate it from loss, and to give to the representational world its full role in one's imagination and thought. Only the absence of the object can be the stimulus for imagination and thinking, in other words, for psychic creativeness and aliveness. Winnicott's (1958) concept of the capacity to be alone *in the mother's presence* and Bion's (1970) *negative capability* come to mind.

To conclude, I would like to offer one more hypothesis. This concerns the notion of *tertiary process*, not materialized but made of conjunctive and disjunctive mechanisms in order to act as go-between of primary and secondary process. It is the most efficient mode of establishing a flexible mental equilibrium and the richest tool for creativity, safeguarding against the nuisance of splitting, whose excess leads to psychic death. Yet splitting is essential in providing a way out of confusion. Such is the fate of human bondage, that it has to serve two contrary masters – separation and reunion – one or the other, or both.

4

Projection

From Projective Identification to Project

The verb *to project*, the adjective *projective*, the nouns *projection* and *project* do not belong exclusively to the terminology of psychoanalysis. These terms are used in a number of other disciplines; ballistics, physics, geometry, architecture, and physiology all attribute their own specific meanings to projection. Even philosophy, thanks to Condillac, has a theory of projection, according to which 'sensations, felt originally as simple modifications of the mental state, are then "projected" outside of the self (that is to say, localized at points in space other than where the thinking subject imagines himself to be), and only then acquire the appearance of independent reality' (Lalande, 1951). This description brings us quickly to the heart of the problem: the relationship of projection to reality via the medium of appearance. Psychoanalytic theory, which is based on clinical experience, thanks to Freud, lays claim to the concept of projection by specifying it. It is regrettable, however, that Freud either abandoned the idea of clarifying this concept or destroyed the rough draft of the paper which was to have been included in the *Metapsychology*. Since Freud, there has been no shortage of contributions to the theory of projection. The concept of *projective identification* has dominated the metapsychology of Melanie Klein and her pupils, most notably Bion (1967). For some time the writings of psychoanalysts have featured a term long considered the preserve of Sartre and his disciples and, even more recently, of molecular biology: the *project*.

Where, how, and why projection in light of these two concepts?

SUMMARY OF BASIC FACTS AND FUNDAMENTAL PROBLEMS

A certain number of clinical and theoretical facts must be reviewed before Freud's work on projection can be examined (Laplanche & Pontalis, 1973).

This chapter was first published in *Object and Self: A Developmental Approach* (Essays in honor of E. Jacobson), edited by S. Tuttman, C. Kaye and M. Zimmerman (International Universities Press, New York, 1981). It is dedicated to Denise Braunschweig, and the translation is by Jacques Houis and J. Naiman.

1. Projection is linked to a primary defence mechanism fundamentally defined by the action of expelling, of casting out (to project = to spit, to vomit) something from within which is unpleasant, disagreeable, even intolerable, but which had previously been introjected.

2. Projection has the effect of placing outside (outside of the ego) something judged undesirable (or excessively desired), but which had arisen inside. The danger is thus externalized.

3. Projection by externalizing is a means of self-defence against the internal by means of a counter-excitation, which treats the instinctual drive (internal excitation) as if it were a perception (external excitation).

4. Projection, which is a universal and normal defence, can become pathological inasmuch as it entails a radical misreading of the instinctual drives found within the subject.

5. Via displacement of the subject's cathexes towards the exterior, projection leads to a knowledge of the object which, although greatly dependent on the subject's input and therefore a distorted perception of the object's reality, nevertheless allows for a real knowledge of the object's unconscious. Of course, this knowledge of the object's unconscious is acquired at a cost – a radical misreading of the subject's unconscious; but the detour via knowledge of the object does constitute, by way of reflection, an implicit yet concealed knowledge of the subject.

This basic summary brings up a number of fundamental problems:

1. Projection is solidly linked to introjection: the projected can only be what has already been introjected. Only that which has been swallowed can be vomited.

2. Projection raises the question of the distinction between inside and outside, that is to say, of the split which allows this distinction to be made. This split is twofold since it affects not only the division of the inner world from the outer world, but also the division of the inner world into conscious-preconscious on the one hand, and unconscious on the other.

3. Projection is inextricably linked to perception. A *passage à la limite* allows a dimension of the id (the projected material) to be transformed into a dimension of the ego (that which is perceived by projection).

4. Closely related to paranoia, projection raises the question of the relationship between, on the one hand, the shifting of an excess not tolerated by the psychic apparatus, which periodically expels what it cannot master, and, on the other hand, the subject's radical misreading which is expressed in delusions.

5. Projection forces us to examine the relationship between the subject and the other. The other, as we have seen, is both known and

unknown: unknown because he is visible only through the distorting mirror that is the subject's image of him; known because this image corresponds nevertheless to a certain reality. Freud (1937d) acknowledged this when he said that every delusion contains a kernel of truth.

This implies that:

1. There is a homologous or isomorphic relationship between the subject and the object since a kernel of truth links both of them through the delusion.

2. This knowledge/lack of knowledge (misreading) relationship is the product of a *construction*. This construction is not only *in* the other's space, but is also *of* that space as the externalization of the subject's inner space. This construction is a *theoretical construct*, a theory of the object which refers back to the theory of the subject, as the theory of what is foreclosed within his *own* space.

PROJECTION AND INSTINCTUAL DRIVE

Let us return to a more down-to-earth metapsychology. When we link, as Freud did, projection to instinctual drive, we return to the most basic concept in psychoanalysis; the primordial and definitive distinction that Freud drew between internal and external excitation is the basis of metapsychology. The instinctual drive or internal excitation is that constant tension which cannot be eliminated and from which we cannot flee. The complexity and obscurity of this concept of instinctual drive stem from the fact that it joins an internal somatic source to an external psychic object. Thus the instinctual drive and its '*Regung*' (and we know that certain experts on Freud's writings refuse to see any difference between the two) connect a source located in the depths of the body to an object outside of this body which alone is able to extinguish the fire located – if I may be forgiven this paradox – at its source. The instinctual drive is destined, therefore, to be projected – to the extent that it is only by becoming bound, in order to reach the object capable of satisfying its aim, that the instinctual drive *exits toward the object*, tracing the path that leads movement to the object, hence to its aim. This path is necessarily projective in that it is directed outward, where the object is located.[1] We know that this path is unavoidable because the subject lacks the object; it is not available to him. In an ideal situation, where the object becomes

---

[1] It must also be stressed that the movement by which the instinctual drive becomes bound, a forward movement, sets off its own reactive movement and engenders a reflection of the forward movement into its backward opposite. Alongside this movement, toward the outside, there is then, from the outset, a corresponding movement of return to the inside. The orientation is from the start both centrifugal and centripetal.

immediately available when it is needed, there is no projection because the subject is spared the path and only has to greet the object which anticipates his desires. I have called this an *ideal situation*. It is, in fact, the nucleus of what we call *idealization* of the object – an object which is never the cause of any frustration and, consequently, of any projection. There is nothing to project. The subject has no project (to use the word in its most ordinary sense), because the object has anticipated it.[1] There is also nothing to project, in the more restricted sense of the word, because there is no frustration; therefore there is no aggression, since aggression arises from the need to release tension, and without frustration there is no tension. We are well acquainted with the other side of this coin: the dependence on the feeding object, and the blockage of psychic activity that we encounter in transferences where the analyst is idealized. But this idealization is, as we know, a primitive defence, like projection,[2] because this ideal situation, like all ideal situations, cannot exist. Frustration is therefore inevitable and, as a consequence, so is projection.

This brings me to the most basic form of projection where, after projection is a mode of the instinctual drive, the projected material is the undesirable, that is to say, the unpleasant, the intolerable. A question arises which the theory of projection finds difficult to answer: does this type of projection imply that the distinction between inside and outside has already been acquired? Freud addressed this problem by postulating the existence of a reality ego which distinguishes, from the start, between the ego and the outer world by detecting the internal or external origins of excitation. What seems essential to me, in this case, is the attempt to cast off, through a centrifugal movement, that part of the body where the tension is felt. This is less a projection than an *excorporation*, of which the motor discharge is the behavioural manifestation – cries, tears, motor agitation. Here, a discussion of whether or not the outside as such exists, seems of little importance to me. The outside, then, is the 'out of' or the 'outside of' – Get out, demons! – Leave my body! This initial action performs excorporation, exorcism.[3] In my opinion, one can speak of projection only when an object can receive the excorporated. A *projective plane* is then constituted which receives the projected material.

---

[1] In his studies of the mother-child relationship, Winnicott (1978) clearly described the developmental phase dominated by this problem, but which, for me, extends well beyond this phase.

[2] In fact, this idealization is itself a projection of the ego's idealization onto the object – at least in the Kleinian conception where the good, like the bad, is projected after denial.

[3] I note in passing that for Tausk (1933), the first projection takes place inside the body and corresponds to finding the object for the first time. One could validly agree that this point in time necessarily precedes preliminary expulsion.

Before going any further, let me reiterate that only what has been incorporated can be excorporated. This can happen retroactively. In other words, the good object is not experienced as good when pleasure is obtained from it. Rather, this pleasure is perceived as such when it is lacking, cruelly lacking, and its place is taken by the unpleasure of the lack, which is the lack of the pleasurable object, the lack of pleasure. The search for pleasure is therefore, in essence, the attempt to recover a lost pleasure. The possibility of pleasure – which I do not intend to deny – is always shadowed by its negative double, the nostalgia for the rediscovery of lost pleasure. Add to this orientation toward the past the project for the future: 'Next time I'll keep it and I'll never lose it again.' Such is the fantasy-promise of the object's return. Fidelity is sworn to it. Nevertheless, when the joy of rediscovery has passed, the threat of loss reappears. And the cycle begins again – incorporation, loss, desire, frustration, aggression, excorporation.

But this view of things is far too simple. It accounts only for the centrifugal aspect of expulsive projection. If we generalize the hypothesis according to which any progressive movement is reflexive and creates its inverted double in the form of a retrogressive movement, we can see that the projective movement is accompanied by an introjective movement. In other words, the excorporation of something previously incorporated provokes a partial reincorporation of the excorporated. It is as if, whatever the effort to expel the bad, something were opposed to its loss, which in the final analysis remains a narcissistic amputation. The 'beyond' of *Beyond the Pleasure Principle* (Freud, 1920g) is at work here in the shape of a return to the previous state, be it unpleasant or even unbearable, where perhaps we find one of the earliest forms of primary masochism as well as one of the subject's first reflections.[1]

Later, when the object is cathected, when its existence (preceding its perception) is 'experienced', the aim inhibition, which prevents both a complete erotic fusion with the object and its total destruction by the death instinct, will provide a structure for this retroaction. This dual reversal (into its opposite and against itself) constitutes, along with splitting, one of the fundamental structuring activities of the instinctual drive. Projection, as Braunschweig (1971) and Fain (1966), as well as myself, have shown, manifests itself then as a negation, or rather, a *diversion*, of the dual reversal.

[1] It must be carefully stressed that this excorporation of the instinctual drive is the precondition of the ego's cathexis, this exclusion being the matrix for subsequent splitting and for the cathexis, in due time, of the object as a replica of the ego, but with the additional task of working through its loss.

PROJECTIVE IDENTIFICATION

Projection begins when the object provides a surface for projection. This suggests the metaphor of the mirror. But before dealing with this very special object, I would like to consider the case of objects which do not provide a reflecting surface. Other less narcissistically cathected objects crop up, beside the breast and the mirror. This is where the Kleinian concept of projective identification comes in. According to Hanna Segal (1973), 'Projective identification is the result of the projection of parts of the self into an object. It may result in the object being perceived as having acquired the characteristics of the projected part of the self but it can also result in the self becoming identified with the object of its projection' (p. 126).

Rosenfeld (1969) delineated the functions of projective identification in the transference. It can be used (1) to communicate pre-verbal experiences, (2) to deny psychic reality by expelling bad parts of the ego, and (3) to control the body of the transference object.

Projective identification is a defence primarily triggered by primitive aggression. Whether it is due to frustration or envy, it reflects an omnipotent narcissistic position. It implies a premature splitting. It often leads to the establishment of a parasitic relationship in which the analyst replaces the patient's ego. Projective identification contributes to creating in the subject an absolute split between the inner and outer world.

The features I have just reviewed indicate that projection arises simultaneously with splitting. External projection onto an object creates the distinction between an inside (the ego), and an outside (the object), which are divided by the metaphorical barrier of the space that separates them and helps to make them distinct. At the same time, however, this separation is accompanied by its denial. The accompanying fusion takes the shape of the subject's identification with the parts projected onto the object, through a kind of return to sender. In sum, we are faced with the two accepted meanings of the term *to identify*: one meaning in which an object is identified *by* the projection, leading to a second meaning, identification *with* the object, as if the vacuum created by the expulsion were immediately filled by the projection's return.

Bion (1967) gives a metaphorical description of the processes involved in projective identification.[1] Everything happens as if the parts expelled from the ego carry not only the bad objects but also the ego's bad parts.

---

[1] The original concept of projective identification is reworked and greatly changed in Bion's subsequent works.

Projected onto external objects, these parts rush into the objects and attempt to seize control of them. What follows is a struggle between the external objects perceived as real and those parasitized by the invasion, the former trying to both poison and master the latter. The world becomes a world of malevolent objects, of bizarre ghosts, hostile to the ego. Worse yet, the real objects, parasitized by the fantasized bad ones which now control them are attracted to their former habitat and try to force their way back into the cradle of the ego where they were born. There follows a struggle against their intrusion and a desire actively to resist them. Once more we can detect the reciprocating motion at work, which gives us the alternating images of progression-projection and regression-introjection. This motion belonged to the internal sequence of the instinctual drive movement at its formation. It now shifts over into the field of interaction between the ego and the object.

This image, which is not unlike science fiction – and what is science fiction if not a delusional dream – paints a picture of projection in schizophrenia. As such it would seem to be worthy of attention; on the other hand, it is less satisfactory in addressing paranoia than Freud's conception, which seems more heuristically fertile.

FORECLOSED PROJECTION

Projective identification is midway between excorporation and projection. Excorporation, a primitive expulsion, seeks only to project as far as possible in a centrifugal way.[1] Where? Everywhere and nowhere. What is projected is not localized in any precise place; it infiltrates the surrounding space, giving it that affective tone characteristic of the persecutory experience. Unlike projective identification, excorporation dwells not *within* things but *between* them. In projective identification, on the contrary, a receptacle is needed: the analyst's body or the mother's, which allows itself to be more or less passively penetrated by the projected parts. This effusion of objects and narcissism greatly drains the ego, making it anaemic. It results in a fragmentation affect which reflects the holes left behind by the projected and exiled parts of the ego. One might think that this loss in the ego would bring about a compensatory outpouring of the id's energies to fill the gap. But that would be tantamount to sending a new Trojan horse into the ego. The result is not an increase in energy capable of restoring the ego's narcissistic and object deficits. It is, rather, an excess of destructive energy, because of the instinctual defusion which would further increase the need to project

---

[1] Language forces me to use this imprecise word, since there is no centre here. The desire to avoid a neologism led me not to use the more exact term *locofugal*.

outside and lock the ego in a struggle against the return of the repressed. It is what Freud calls the *repression of reality* in psychosis. The ego's negative hallucination is periodically filled with the products of projection and reconstitutes itself indefinitely.

The foregoing shows the extent to which the meanings Freud gave to projection differ. In his work on Schreber's autobiography, Freud gives two definitions which would appear contradictory:

1. 'An internal perception is suppressed and, instead, its content, after undergoing a certain kind of distortion, enters consciousness in the form of an external perception' (1911c, p. 66). Let us note that this involves the effect of a repression followed by a distortion which allows access to consciousness, but only after a displacement which changes the internal perception into an external perception. It is then possible to say that *projection changes instinctual drive into perception*. This process is not limited to paranoia, however, since it also applies perfectly to phobia and to dream.

2. 'It was incorrect to say that the perception which was suppressed internally is projected outwards; the truth is rather, as we now see, that what was abolished internally returns from without' (*ibid.*, p. 71).

The change in definitions involves the difference between 'repression' and 'abolition' on the one hand, and, on the other, the distinction between projection from the inside toward the outside and the return of the abolished from the outside to the inside. It is a clear reversal in direction, centrifugal in the first case, centripetal in the second. Freud is specifying psychotic projection: the abolition that Lacan (1956) has called *foreclosure*, thereby eliminating the phase of centrifugal projection, and considering projection the return of projected material, no aspect of which allows us to think that the return was preceded by a departure. A synthetic definition would allow us to think of projection as an uninterrupted coming and going, the first phase of which is foreclosed in the paranoiac.

These considerations permit a breakdown of projective operations into their component parts:

Phase 0: Foreclosed – I (a man) love him (a man).
Phase 1: The verb turns into its opposite – I don't love him, I hate him.
Phase 2: The subject and object trade places – I hate him. He hates me.
Phase 3: Rationalization – I don't love him. I hate him because he's persecuting me.

Lacan's formulation prompts several comments:

1. Changing the verb into its opposite suggests that the coming and going, a bringing together (I love him), is turned into an estrangement (I hate him). *Aversion is the reversion of a desire perceived as a perversion* (i.e., homosexuality). In this connection, it should be noted that Freud's expression, 'I love him', may lack precision. It would be better to say, 'I want to be loved', which implies that the desire is initially a passive one, an active desire to be loved passively (and masochistically). The verb's reversal thus implies a switch from passivity to activity (I love him), and then into its opposite (I hate him), a double reversal.

2. The inversion of subject and object suggests an identification between the terms 'I' and 'he' which become interchangeable: 'I am him'; 'He is me.' Strictly speaking, there is no actual reversal onto the person himself. In relation to 'I hate him', 'He hates me' becomes a primarily passive construction: 'I am hated by him.' This formula has the advantage of preserving the 'I' of 'I hate him.' The shift to the 'he' effects a shift to the object: 'It is he who hates me.' There is an almost imperceptible nuance in the difference between 'I am hated by him' and 'He hates me.' This nuance, nevertheless, accounts for the change in the initiative inherent in the shift from the passive 'I' to the active 'he'. A structure of exchange between the two split entities then takes over. The split between the 'I' and the 'he' is retained; the two terms are not confused but exchanged. Three possibilities emerge:

1. No splitting. I = he = everything = nothing.

2. The presence of a split, but with the possibility of substituting the split terms: love/hate, I/he, and the exclusion of one of the two.

3. Splitting with coexistence of the two terms separated by the split, in spite of the contradiction. I love him and/or I hate him; I hate him and/or he hates me. Both are true. This is the path to splitting as it appears in fetishism.

THE OTHER

By introducing the 'he' we are brought to the issue of the other. The other is the non-ego and the non-I: non-ego insofar as it is what my ego refuses to be and casts out of itself; non-I insofar as it is distinct from my person and not to be confused with my identity. When Lacan says of the Other that it is the 'place of the truth', he is referring to this other which corresponds to the foreclosed part of the ego, and which, because of its object status, is able to arouse my wish and consequently reveal me to myself.

But these remarks remain limited in scope. They are complemented by Freud's work (1922*b*) which added considerably to the entire theory of projection. It is not true that projection restricts me to an absolute misreading of reality. Projection is a measure of knowledge and constitutes access to a certain truth. What is projected onto the other undeniably reveals something about him: something the object's ego mistakes but the projecting subject recognizes. Thus, Othello is not mistaken when he senses in Desdemona a certain attraction for Cassio. His own desire for Cassio is foreclosed. My conclusion is that projection can reveal something about the object, and that what is foreclosed is the projecting subject's wish. In the final analysis the other is none other than the subject's own unconscious. At this point, difficulties surface which had heretofore gone unnoticed.

If the 'projector' (the one who projects) can, while attributing to the object his own wishes, arrive at a real knowledge of said object, projection cannot be completely dismissed, as it becomes a mode of knowledge. This brings to mind Clérambault's remark to a patient afflicted with delusional jealousy: 'May it please God that it should be enough to be cuckolded in order not to be delusional!' To admit this is to offer the hypothesis of a certain homology or isomorphism[1] between the I and the other, since the I's projection – which is constructed according to the I's unconscious, but foreclosed – has its true counterpart in the unconscious of the other. On the other hand, it also means setting up the option of either (a) knowing the self and considering the other unknowable, or (b) knowing the other and considering the self unknowable. Here, I am touching, on the question of the construction of the other's space. This construct is 'theoretical' in much the same way as Freud's concept of sexual theory. The other exists; I cannot ignore his existence. But I can only know him through myself. At the same time I cannot know the space of the other within me. Nevertheless, if I can get to know the other – with a knowledge that is truthful even though projected, and even if by knowing him I mistake myself – it is in constituting his space that I construct my own at the same time.

It follows that the other's wish, which I adopt, becomes the basis for the division within myself. In other words, the unity acquired at great expense by the ego, through narcissistic cathexis, can be attained only by referring to the pairs persecuted/persecutor, ego/object, inside/outside, conscious/unconscious. The conjunction-disjunction – internal conscious ego/external other's unconscious – is reflected in the conjunction-disjunction – internal conscious ego/other's internal unconscious.

---

[1] The geometric sense of the term is applicable.

This process implies the functioning of a surface-to-surface relationship, since mirror reflection is at work here. This is a good time to recall that Freud defines the ego as the body's surface of projection; the other is its mirror.[1] The mirror established on the surface of the ego's projection is the meeting place for the body projected from within and the other's image from without. Both sides of this mirror would, in other words, reflect, creating an image the components of which belong as much to the inside as to the outside.

It is clear that this logic is contrary to the logic of psychoanalysis, which argues that knowledge of the other improves as the subject pushes back the limits of his own unconscious. My conclusion is that this factor of deception must be a characteristic of the logic of paranoia.

THE NARCISSISTIC HOMOEROTIC OBJECT AND
THE PROJECTIVE SCREEN

It may be that the solution to these theoretical difficulties is provided by Freud's (1911c) study of the mechanisms of paranoia: 'we can assert that the length of *the step back from sublimated homosexuality to narcissism* is a measure of the amount of *regression* characteristic of paranoia' (p. 72). The recognition of homosexuality in paranoia by post-Freudian authors has not always taken into account the relationship between *sublimated* homosexuality and narcissism. It is difficult to know precisely what Freud is trying to tell us here. It is not a question of perverse homosexuality but of a homosexuality which has been sublimated, that is to say, displaced, inhibited as to aim, and *desexualized*. The relationship between a sublimated homoerotic object and the subject's narcissism has not been worked out. It is their correspondence which allows the exchange between ego and other. The ego, especially in its ideal part, is formed by narcissistic cathexes which have effected the desexualization, the aim inhibition, and the displacement of sexual interests. It therefore corresponds exactly to the image of the other as a sublimated homoerotic object. It is understandable that the ego allows itself to be so easily fascinated by an object fashioned from the subject's own narcissistic desires.[2] Just as God made man in his own image, the paranoiac makes the object resemble himself. It was inevitable that we would turn to the

---

[1] Let us note, however, that this reflection is not the totality of the ego-other relationship, but its fascinating narcissistic component coexisting with an 'objective' knowledge of the other. Nevertheless, this knowledge is subjugated in the projection-foreclosure for reasons I am about to go into.

[2] This is the essential difference between phobic projection, in which there is a shift of libidinal cathexis, and paranoid projection, in which there is a shift of narcissistic projection.

idea of a mirror's surface – or even better and closer to Freud's theory – to a projector and screen. Narcissism allows the ego to be unified. In other words, the transition from ego instincts to narcissism occurs through the constitution of the ego's projective plane as a reflecting surface. The narcissistically cathected ego tries to become an object to the id by attempting a seduction. It takes on the characteristics of the ideal object. The narcissism gathers its energy from the desexualization of the instinctual drives which come from the id and which the ego appropriates. Since the purpose of this narcissistic seduction is for the ego to model itself after the ideal object, it seems logical that this reflected and reflecting (projected and projecting) narcissism will constitute a projective screen upon which a homologous image of the other will appear. The cathexis of the other will project onto him the image of the ego and, in turn, the other will project this image onto the ego, reinforcing its deception. In paranoia this cathexis bears the mark of homoeroticism, a unity of subject and object based on each having the same sexual appearance. We must add, however, that such a cathexis is sublimated and narcissistic. In other words, there is a relationship of narcissistic identification between the ego and the other through their mutual projections. This projective current is duplicated by an introjective current, the other absorbing the ego's projections and vice versa. To the projective screen on the surface of the ego corresponds another projective screen located outside of the ego in the mirror formed by the other. The situation is alienating in that neither the ego nor the other can locate each other because the image is constantly bouncing back and forth between the ego's internal mirror and the other's external mirror. When the paranoiac becomes aware of this, he no longer knows where he is, he is no longer sure of the efficacy of projection, the split loses its effectiveness, he depersonalizes.

In paranoia the other, the object of the wish, is the blank screen upon which the subject's interior film materializes. This 'movie', encountering a surface capable of receiving its signs, distributes those features capable of reflecting to the projecting subject the structures of his narcissism. Here, adding to the outside corresponds to subtracting from within; as if the more we see outside, the blanker the internal screen. The more the other shows its signs, the more blank the subject becomes. Absolved of his wishes, he becomes a virgin surface passively receiving the other's messages. Henceforth, fascinated by the other in reality, his eye is glued to the screen without being able to tear itself away from it – to the extent that he can no longer distinguish between the eye of the camera and the image on the screen. His eye is *in* the image on the screen and is an integral part of the projected feature. It is the screen and the projection, all in one. This position is the opposite of the neurotic's who, although succumbing to fascination, nevertheless retains the ability to see himself seeing. His eye witnesses the spectacle precisely insofar as he sees himself with the eye of another who is *absent* from the spectacle.

Thus, the key to the enigma is in this narcissistic relationship. This conforms to the clinical data, since we are dealing with paranoid psychosis. It could be that things are additionally complicated by the fact that I attributed to paranoid projection the maintenance of the split, with both parties switching places. The split is not constituted by the screen since the screen is not recognized as such, but by the distinction effected between love and hate, as between I and he. In fact, it is not the whole eye which is projected; it is the bad eye, the one you have to get rid of – forbidden, passive, homosexual love; a narcissistic homosexual love which, because of its cathectic requirements, endangers maintenance of the ego's narcissism.

Because of foreclosure, however, the split remains totally unconscious and the projected material – the bad eye – stays glued to the fabric of the screen. This eye, rather than looking, is destined to be looked at. The alienation created by this relationship of narcissistic fascination stems from the fact that it involves cathexes belonging to the subject's being rather than to his having. One could say that 'Someone is keeping an eye on him', provided that one supplements this expression with another which says, 'He's got someone under his skin.'

The narcissistic cathexis of the object must necessarily return to the ego, since it belongs to it. It is therefore not the ordinary return of repressed libidinal material, but is a reappropriation, as inevitable as it is undesirable – hence the intense struggle surrounding the projection's return from the outside. The narcissistic cathexis seeks to reenter its own home, while repression aims at closing the door. This is the essential difference between paranoid projection and phobia.

Finally, in this structure, paranoid projection specifies the role of homosexuality: it is foreclosed and narcissistic. Bak (1946) and Mallet (1966) have emphasized its link with masochism, which is not surprising when one considers the links between narcissism and masochism. Masochism itself undergoes an important transformation. By turning into its opposite, it shows itself in a clear sadism toward the object (I do not love him, I hate him.). What seems to me characteristic of paranoia, compared with the more regressive, schizo-paranoid forms, is that sadism cathects a unified object which has boundaries identified by the subject and with which the subject identifies. Indeed, narcissistic and homoerotic cathexis provides sadism with a framework. Instead of the diffuse sadism of projective identification, we are dealing with a sadism that is concentrated and applied to a single object. Identification has replaced scattering. A single split has replaced multiple splits (fragmentation). Sadism seems to be a product of the rejection of primary masochism, the more advanced forms of which are expressed by a rejection of passivity. Sadism contributes to the formation of the ego as a unified entity, through the dominance it asserts over the object of its attentions. On the other hand, the reintegration of this sadism turns back into masochism to the extent that the ego is a victim of the superego's supervision. The split becomes internal between a resexualized superego, allied to the id, which persecutes the ego and leads to an ever-increasing alienation. The ego's response is the foreclosed projection of this masochism, now transformed into the object's sadism toward the subject: 'He hates me,' allowing for self-defence.

The formation of delusion deserves its name of *neoreality* because foreclosure radically rejects the subject's wish. The struggle is shifted into the real or, more specifically, into the *social reality* of ego and other, a struggle that opposes neoreality to the real which is subject to repression – repression of reality.

TWO VERSIONS OF PRIMARY NARCISSISM

We know that Freud (1920g) gave contradictory versions of primary narcissism. Sometimes he refers to *absolute* primary narcissism as the reduction of tension to the zero level in accordance with the Nirvana principle; sometimes he refers to the result of the passage from autoerotism to the subject's unification. In a previous work (1967), I defended certain hypotheses regarding the relationship of primary narcissism to the death instinct and the wish for nothing, nothingness, emptiness. I put forth the idea that the negative hallucination of the mother could provide a framework, an empty frame to be filled by object cathexes and ego cathexes. What I am now presenting is the *form* – and I stress this word – taken by the subject's cathexes and the object's cathexes in a relationship of narcissistic complementarity. The object here is modeled on the subject's unified narcissism: the ego and the other are in a relationship of mutual doubling; the one is the other's double. The split is in place, but the terms complement each other and change places, as they always must. Any other outcome is denied them. *Othello* can end only in Desdemona's murder and Othello's suicide; there is no alternative. In the final analysis, the subject's unity is always a fallacy. He oscillates between nothing, zero and the pair he forms with his double: the narcissistic homoerotic object.

The role of the double (Green, 1970) becomes evident here. It is at once the same and the other, since it stretches resemblance to the point of identity, while preserving otherness through some minimal differences. Mallet (1966) has stressed the older brother's role in male paranoia. This role could be explained by the fact that such a brother is an intermediate imago between the subject and his father, favouring narcissistic identification and the homoerotic object choice. At the same time, the small difference separating the brothers is never eliminated, thus constantly frustrating the subject's wish to reach the narcissistically cathected double's enviable position. Such is the other, my fellowman, my brother. There must be a metapsychological status for such a position.

We can view it as one of the variants encompassed by Winnicott's concept of the transitional object, a transition between the subject and the object perceived in its difference, between inside and outside, love and hate, the narcissistic and the object-related. Winnicott (1975) defined the transitional object as the first non-ego possession, placing it more on the 'having' side (not-me possession). In my opinion, the double belongs in the 'being' category. It is the non-being of being, that which being cannot consent to being and cannot help but be. It seems evident that the double is essentially the first object with which the subject changes place. To move away from this compulsory and absolutely determined exchange to an exchange that takes difference into account, however, the double must be repressed (but acknowledged as such, therefore capable of being symbolized) and the field of exchange based on other objects which are not totally stamped with the seal of the subject's narcissism – though I do not think the subject ever frees himself from his narcissistic projection onto the object. This projection, however, no longer constitutes a screen because the eye has torn itself away and now considers its projections from the outside (enabling it to question their projective origin, whatever the value of projection as knowledge). In the transference, the analysand can, at the beginning, score a bull's eye by guessing the truth about his analyst. In the middle of analysis, the analysand is less interested in the projection's content than in its motivation, to the extent that this motivation refers him back to himself. At the end, the analysand arrives both at a real and at a truthful knowledge of the reality of his unconscious and of the being of his analyst. It is what will allow him to express his wish elsewhere, in the elaboration of his own project.

FROM PROJECTIVE IDENTIFICATION TO PROJECT

We have moved from projective identification to project, if we accept that the wish is always a project. The air of existentialism emanating from this word should not prevent us from using it.[1] What I wish to stress here is that each one of the phases has a corresponding phase belonging to a complementary series. To the *excorporation* of the beginning corresponds *incorporation*: the taking into the subject's body of the object which will be expelled. To Melanie Klein's *projective identification* corresponds *introjective identification*, defined by Segal (1964) as the result of the process by which 'the object is introjected into the ego which then identifies with some or all of its characteristics' (p. 105). To *projection* corresponds *introjection*. To the *project* (wish) corresponds *identification*. Without exception, Freudian thought works in pairs. Such is the whole history of the transference which, in those fortunate cases where it can be and is analyzed, ends in the freed play of the wish outside of the transference substitutes of analyst and in identification with the analyzing function.

These pairs involve specific cathexes of erogenous zones. In my opinion, the incorporation-excorporation pair calls forth a primarily oral relationship. The introjective identification-projective identification pair implies the participation of the anal zone (or perhaps better, both oral and anal). The introjection-projection pair, so strongly marked by narcissism, brings into play the matrix of the phallic-narcissistic relationships, in its search for a complete homoerotic unity and mutuality.

In the various phases I have outlined, the pairing of object libido and narcissistic libido must be taken into consideration. The cathexis of erogenous zones concentrates a great quantity of libidinal cathexis in these areas, making these sites of exchange between inside and outside veritable foci. Beyond these erogenous zones, however, the body's surface is narcissistically cathected. As the mouth and anus, being poles of entry and exit, are libidinally cathected, so is the rest of the body's surface negatively cathected when these orifices close. The closed mouth and the contracted anus allow for the filling of the body cavity and an increase in tension at the periphery. In the phallic narcissistic position of paranoia, sublimated, desexualized homosexuality corresponds to the intense narcissistic cathexis of the body's surface, including the penis's, as cathexis of the phallic 'shape'. In extreme cases, this penis can become foreclosed in the real as an influencing machine. One could add that when the ego's constitution is primarily narcissistic, the other represents its phallic complement; and when the other is narcissistically cathected,

[1] It was already used by Castoriadis-Aulagnier (1968, 1975).

the ego assumes the phallic function. Only the advent of castration and sexual differences introduces the dimension of both the oedipus complex and neurosis. In this regard, the real, which can be considered as existing from the beginning (see the reality ego of the beginning, in Freud), and which acquired definite structure during the anal phase, is formed in two stages: first, with the appearance of the Oedipus complex (the two differences, between the sexes and between the generations), and then with the acquisition of the knowledge of the vagina after puberty. Sexual reality is the matrix of a real acquisition of the real. Without wanting to sound pedantic, I stress that this knowledge of the vagina is the precondition of genuine procreation, the effect of which is to increase the possibilities of exchange through the triangulation of the parental couple and the creation of sibling relationships. This progression is also seen in the evolution of the transference in neurotic patients.

We know that the evolution of the transference is marked by the interplay of resistances and interpretations. The analyst's interpretation is related to the patient's projections. It is nevertheless received, in the very early stages of analysis, as if it were a delusional interpretation. In the eyes – or rather, to the ears – of the analysand, the analyst reacts to his speech like a paranoiac who believes that all the messages he receives concern him, whereas nothing, in the language confined by social conventions, would allow for such egocentrism. I should note, however, that the abuse of the power of interpretation which takes the form of 'interpreting everything' leads to the same result as projective defence in the patient: rationalization. The analyst rationalizes his inexact interpretations to salvage his power of interpretation.

The work of interpretation leads to displacement of the analyst's simulated and manifest paranoia as the analysand's silent and latent paranoia is recognized. Through *projective induction* and the analysis of projection, interpretation contributes to the gradual lifting of the split between conscious and unconscious, and to a better functioning of the relationship between internal and external reality. Moreover, the split must be maintained and preserved, failing which there would be confusion between subject and object, internal and external worlds. In other words, whereas interpretation extends the field of Eros, it leaves to Thanatos the task of delimiting the separations which are indispensable to maintaining the split. It should be made clear that this analysis of the split should lead, not to the simple intellectual acceptance of the repressed, but to the affective acknowledgment of its reality. The 'belief' which originally lulled the ego into illusions about its reality to the detriment of that of the unconscious now becomes belief in the two-sidedness of the subject and in the influence of the unconscious on the ego. But the completed analysis – even if it was imperfect – also leads to a belief, undoubtedly limited but unquestionably effective, in the ego's potential for change as it reacquires the strength it used to exhaust in countercathexes. The split is therefore maintained, while a recognition is affirmed of an external reality regulated by its own laws and an internal reality governed by the all-powerful wish. It might be helpful here to recall that for Freud the result of analysis was the lifting of the excessive sexualization of object relations and the shift of cathexes to the social sphere, in the shape of sublimated activities.

SOCIAL REALITY

One could then question the extent of the split between internal and external reality, and determine the boundaries of analysis. This question leads one to envisage the limits of interpretation in the non-therapeutic applications of psychoanalysis.

It may be necessary to refine our distinctions. The distinction between external and internal reality is basic yet vague. Internal reality is not just the reality of the wish, it is also the reality of the body as the place of need. External reality also is not so simple. I propose a distinction, within external reality, between social reality and physical reality. There would be two extremes: the reality of the body and that of the physical world, which would connect, even though one belongs to internal reality and the other to external reality; and two intermediate terms, the psychic reality of the wish and social reality, which are closely interrelated.

Social reality would be subject to the reality of the wish as well as to the specific order linking men in their struggle to master nature and to satisfy their needs. Thus the objects of social reality would be intrinsically double, to the extent that they are at once linked to the world of the wish and external to it. Here the most difficult part remains: to recognize what in social reality obeys the laws of the realm that corresponds to the physical world. The problem here may be that the function of such a realm is to create a mimetic equivalent of natural laws.

For psychoanalysts the fact that culture is based on wish does not require further proof. But culture is also something else; it implies a technological and political development somewhat independent of wish. This is one more ambiguity of the other. The other is the object of my wish, yet he exists as such, such as my wish will never be able to define him, to justify his existence. I cannot apprehend him, not only because he is the object of a never-fulfilled wish (which guarantees that the lack will have its inalienable space), but also because he exists out of my range. This distinction is the basis of the split between the object-related and the objective. It remains to be seen whether the objective can be an area of study for psychoanalysis when it goes beyond the objectivity of the wish. The extent to which Freud's position implies a difficult choice should be noted. A confirmed materialist, he believed profoundly in the world's objectivity. Yet he also believed in the unknowability of this object world because of the enormous impact of subjectivity on our judgments. Nothing in him, however, led to scepticism; rather, he was impelled to the tireless work of acquiring knowledge in order to attain the greatest possible objectivity in the knowledge of both the inner and the outer world. It should be noted that this position implies that nothing should be entirely subjective in our knowledge of reality or entirely objective either.

Since paranoia has occupied the centre of this study of projection, I can hypothetically determine its place in culture as belonging to the realm of social reality. I would maintain that any active culture is based on an implicit paranoia. This paranoia is found in the split which allows the identity of a culture to be affirmed through the difference and rejection of another culture, in so far as it is considered foreign, other. At the same time the foreign culture is loaded with all the evils against which the active culture defends itself, through the considerable narcissistic cathexis effected by casting the other culture into outer darkness. The evil it refuses to recognize in itself, it denounces mercilessly in the other. Any active culture, just as in paranoia, also supposes a reinforcing of sublimated homosexual links among its members. Even so, this sublimation is relative – cultural activity results in a considerable resexualization of social relations, just as in paranoia.

Finally, another aspect of group psychology, the members of an active culture have a tendency to substitute for their ego ideal the feared object on the model of the primitive horde's all-powerful father (Freud, 1921c).[1] Today, when the gods are dead, the Other as seat of the truth is represented by the deification of the leader. Social structures die and are reborn continually.

One wonders if the very condition of a culture's activity does not reside in its paranoia, otherwise referred to as ideology or group mysticism, according to Bion (1959). Messianism is part of the ideology of any culture; it is supported by the idealizing relationship it establishes with itself, justifying its demands with the claim that it is only seeking the

---

[1] In societies where this relationship is less important, mutual identification is dominant, which does not alter the validity of the above statement.

elimination of evil (a basic paranoid concern), after which the golden age of shared beatitude will reign, and paradise lost will be rediscovered. This does not mean that I reject all cultures indiscriminately, since I have in mind only those characteristics of social reality which belong to the realm of the wish; and I have maintained, on the contrary, that the world of the wish is not sufficient in and of itself to define a social reality which has its objective dimension. When Freud (1930a) ends *Civilization and Its Discontents* by referring to the possible destruction of the human race and the resulting anxiety, he is not referring to neurotic anxiety but to *Realangst*, fear in the face of real danger.

The task of psychoanalysts as a cultural group is to avoid this alienating situation through continual analysis of our conflicts with social reality, both with other psychoanalytic groups and within our own group – to avoid the various divisions which split us into subgroups. This 'permanent analysis' must pursue the dual task of going as far as possible within the limits of the analyzable, and acknowledging the existence of the extra-analytic, according to Donnet's (1973) formula, as the objective dimension of being. This is yet another impossible aspect of our profession, since it is the task of each one of us to draw the shifting boundaries that guide our steps.

The greatest contribution of Denise Braunschweig's profound 'Psychoanalysis and reality' (1971) may be that it shows us that reality is not the real. Reality is what happens *in* the real, what is shown by the painting on the white canvas, with its dramatic or dramatized images, its forces, its tensions, its history and structure. The real is something else; it is the empty frame, the white canvas or the projective screen, altogether different from what is happening *within* the frame and *on* the canvas. Where reality is dramatic, the real is neutral. Whether the planet rediscovers its mythical golden age or is blown up by its own destructiveness, the real could not care less. It will continue to exist in one form or another, whether or not there is anyone there to take cognizance of it, to laugh or cry about it.

5

Aggression, Femininity, Paranoia and Reality

According to Freud, aggression is the outward expression of the destructive instincts. Theoretically speaking, aggression makes no distinction between the sexes. Nevertheless, its nature and function lead us to question its specific expression in female sexuality. In contradistinction to the male, the integration of aggression in feminine identification seems less obvious.

In man, masculine identification calls for aggression, both in carrying out the sexual function and in the many activities involving aim-inhibited drives and displacements, especially social ones, such as professional competition, sports, games, as well as the tragic game of war. Of course, social changes are bringing increasingly larger numbers of women to share such activities with men, from infancy on. The opening to women of social activities that used to be reserved for men has led to an attenuation, in its social aspects, of the difference between the sexes. However, we wish to stress that such an attenuation is, to a large extent, superficial. Freud's opinion (1937c, p. 250) that what is repudiated in *both* sexes is femininity may be aptly recalled at this point.

From this viewpoint, what becomes of woman's aggressive drives? The question may be examined from two angles: (1) the antagonism between erotic and destructive drives, and (2) the antinomy of identifications reflecting sexual difference.

How can women integrate their aggressive drives when their libidinal development does not facilitate discharge and displacement? What happens in those cases where successful integration is blocked (Freud, 1933a, p. 116)? I am not considering the case of the virile, castrating or phallic woman, the subject of so many studies, but rather certain less recognized aspects of aggression in women. I wish to discuss these from two points of view: (1) narcissism (the role of secondary narcissism in

This paper was presented at the 27th International Psychoanalytical Congress, Vienna, in July 1971, and published in the *International Journal of Psycho-Analysis* (1972) 53. The translation is by Dr Alexander Lloyd.

identification is well known); (2) the pre-oedipal stages with their corresponding object-relations.

FEMININITY AND PARANOIA

After stating that hysteria in women is closely related to the pre-oedipal relationship with the mother, Freud adds, in his article on female sexuality: 'and further, in this dependence on the mother we have the germs of later paranoia in women' (1931*b*, p. 227). With regard to paranoia in men, fixation to the mother has also been stressed by many later writers. In my opinion, an important factor in masculine paranoia is that it constitutes a struggle on two fronts: one against femininity and the other against hostility (to the father). In this case, therefore, femininity and aggression are united in the same radical rejection.

Freud describes the mechanism of paranoia in the Schreber case in a striking statement: 'We can assert that the *length of the step back from sublimated homosexuality to narcissism* is a measure of the amount of *regression* characteristic of paranoia' (1911*c*, p. 72). In his letters to Fliess, Freud had already observed that paranoia undoes identifications. Psychoanalytic experience has taught us that the paranoiac is caught in the same dilemma as the hysteric: 'Who am I, man or woman?' However, whereas the hysteric asks the question in terms of secondary identification, it seems that the paranoiac does so in terms of primary identification. One could even say that the fact that the question is not acknowledged is specific to the paranoiac's basic rejection of femininity; the question reappears, but in the patient's delusions, or is diluted in a system of projective interpretations which deny its cardinal importance.

As in the hysteric, there is a narcissistic vacillation in the paranoiac which is expressed by depersonalization. The consequences are different: in hysteria, depersonalization only temporarily endangers the state of reality, whereas in paranoia reality is basically recast to form a new reality, that of the delusion. The splitting extends beyond the limits of the inner world and involves external reality. Splitting may affect only one significant person: the object of the delusion. In this case only those parts of reality related to the latter are cathected delusionally, the rest of reality being more or less preserved. It is interesting to note that the most striking examples of this mechanism are found in erotomania and delusive jealousy, both misfortunes of love.

Our experience has taught us that the paranoiac has resexualized social relations to an extremely high degree, as is borne out by the fact that paranoid traits are common in those individuals who hypercathect the social aspects of their life. The paranoiac aspires to eliminate evil completely; he wants to rid the world of destruction in all its forms; so he starts by effecting a rejection: disavowal or repudiation (*Verleugnung* or *Verwerfung*) of his own destructive aggression. He wants to be filled only with love. Having expelled evil, he now has to accept everything in the name of love and sovereign good. Then he meets the other or others, and finds them evil and violent. This is where his conflict begins: if he accepts their violence passively he will be destroyed, but if he is to struggle against their violence, he has to use violence himself. Thus one of my patients told me that if it were in his power he would have forced the Nazis to grow roses in concentration camps under the threat of machine guns. His aim in life was to make weakness his supreme strength, and so weaken his super-powerful enemy. Bak (1946) and Mallet (1966) have stressed the fact that in paranoiacs destructive drives are converted into masochism. The most far-reaching effects of masochism are combined here in the three forms described by Freud: feminine, moral and erotogenic (1924c, p. 160). Thus the paranoiac combines moral masochism (literally and figuratively) with feminine masochism in what might be called, as Mallet has suggested, a degradation of drives, a process different from regression and closer to dedifferentiation. Erotogenic masochism, however, is well concealed. Conversely, certain masochistic perverts show many paranoid character traits.

THE INTERNAL AND EXTERNAL ORIENTATION
OF AGGRESSIVE DRIVES

We shall now return to the psychosexual difference between boys and girls in the development of aggression. A parallel might be drawn here: the fact that aggression in the boy is turned outwards may correspond to the fact that his genital organs are external. In the female, the internal location of her genitals may be related to the internal orientation of aggression. Internal orientation of aggressive drives and the inhibitory retention that follows have many consequences; among others, it may represent a permanent danger to object-cathexes (the latter being continually threatened with destruction or damage) and a protective reinforcement of some narcissistic cathexes alike. Whether it is only protective is still questionable to my mind. At the juncture of these two types of cathexes, homosexual cathexes are to be found: their role is paramount in the construction of secondary identification.

In women, various strata can be demonstrated and interrelated: refusal of femininity and a masculinity complex, tenacious hostility towards the mother (a mixture of love and hate) referring to both the oedipal and the pre-oedipal levels of the conflict; its extreme form is envy of the mother's breast and of its creative power (Klein, 1957). This form of envy is expressed by refusal to identify with the mother other than by projective identification, resulting in an alienating identification. Envy of the creative ability of the mother's breast is of considerable importance in women because their sexual destiny is child-bearing.

This does not mean that this type of envy is not important in the boy; his wish to have a baby is also very strong. Displacement and desexualization of this wish lead to masculine creativeness if the wish is not paralysed by conflict. This does not mean that women are withdrawn from creativeness, but that the pathway is probably more complicated in their case. The wish to create is extremely strong in the paranoid (or the psychotic), notably so in transsexualism. Delusional hypochondria and delusions of being poisoned may be understood as disguised fulfilments of such wishes. However, we must emphasize the fact that sexual destiny inscribes into the very flesh of the girl and the woman the desire for child-bearing. It is well known that excessive counter-cathexis of aggression is dangerous in small children of both sexes: contained, internalized and defused aggression endangers object cathexes because defused, destructive cathexes may impede the development of erotic cathexes related to good experiences or to the experience of good objects. In addition to having to solve this conflict, girls are also faced with another difficulty: if aggressive drives are too freely expressed outwards, feminine identification is in danger of being dominated by its masculine counterpart (in the double identification of the Oedipus complex).

We have thus come to the idea that femininity corresponds to an extremely intense cathexis of the inner world due both to fixation and to defensive mechanisms. We would not be the first to remark that, among psychoanalysts, feminine insight is more developed than masculine insight. We now have to study relations between internal and external reality.

EXTERNAL REALITY AND INTERNAL REALITY

The ambiguousness of the notion of reality in psychoanalysis is largely due to the fact that the same word applied to both psychic reality and external reality. For the unconscious, only the first counts, i.e. the inner world of unconscious fantasies. However, in order to be preserved, internal reality must reckon with external reality. Dominance of the reality principle protects the pleasure principle (Freud, 1911b, p. 223), hence the importance of taking external reality into consideration, for both analyst and analysand. It is indeed a prerequisite of psychoanalytic treatment that the analytic field be limited by the boundaries of the inner world and that extra-analytic reality should not become the source of any major dangers (as in psychosis). In this connection, Freud refers to a *repression of reality* (1924e, p. 183). What does he mean by that? It is our opinion that the psychotic subject submits perception (or the various types of perception) to intensive counter-cathexis. Bion (1967) speaks of attacks on the linking functions of the data coming from reality, of hatred of reality, both external and internal, and of a struggle against awareness. Delusion is an attempt to create a new reality. The world of the paranoiac is no better than our world, but, as Freud said, at least he can live in it.

Delusion, the psychotic symptom, screens external reality just as the neurotic symptom covers up the internal reality of desire stemming from instinctual forces. Delusional neo-reality can, as we have said, be limited to one single object. Anything involving the object is then submitted to delusional elaboration, contrary to what occurs in schizophrenia, where regression is deeper and more massive, and affects a large part of relations with the outside world. The paranoiac's object is a homosexual object, an object with the same sex as the subject. In women, the mother or the sister is this object. Here we recall a fundamental difference between men and women. For the little girl the first object, the mother, is a future homosexual object, whereas for the boy the first object is the future heterosexual one. In the oedipal stage, the boy establishes the original heterosexual object as the object of his desire and, after puberty, he needs only effect a displacement to a final object by identification with his later homosexual object. In the little girl the Oedipus situation requires that she become detached from her *original* homosexual object before being in a position to cathect a heterosexual one (Freud, 1933a). In the oedipal phase, the strength of the earlier homosexual ties opposes the cathexis of the more recent heterosexual ones. After puberty, the same conflict recurs. All this would lead one to think that homosexuality, latent or sublimated, plays a more important part in women than in men. Male homosexuality might be more directly related to the problem of castration in that the homoerotic object-choice implies the presence of a penis in both partners, whereas in female homosexuals fixation to the original object would play the leading role. In the transference – we are referring here to transference resistance of the erotic type – the female patient who says she is in love with her male analyst is frequently making a maternal transference and one that is often fiercely denied and frequently has delusional undertones. This is well known.

Thus a parallel may be drawn between the delusional neo-reality of the paranoiac and, other things being equal, the paranoid relationship of a daughter to her mother. This relationship is obviously an inextricable mixture of love and hate. Each time love is expressed, hate is repressed and *vice versa*. The patient often accepts intellectually the analyst's interpretations of the maternal aspects of the transference, but immediately adds: 'If only you knew how *really* nasty my mother was to me.' The element of truth hidden behind oedipal rivalry corresponds to that of the delusional patient who *really* does provoke ill-will but is unconscious of his hostility. To overcome the corresponding situation in the mother-daughter relationship is particularly difficult because of the mutual impingement of the primary object-relationship and of the lineament of secondary narcissism, the latter being supplied by the feelings of 'sameness' in the representative processes of identity.

INCORPORATION OF THE OBJECT IN WOMEN

Psychoanalytical studies have amply demonstrated the widespread fear of penetration in women. During coitus the penis is admitted to a certain extent. When penetration is consciously accepted, it may still be rejected because of vaginismus or dyspareunia, contraction or pain which prevent intromission, or it may occur in a way that prevents deep penetration (Bonaparte, 1953). The penis is commonly symbolized as a knife. Refusal to incorporate the penis is related to a double fear: fear *for* the penis and fear *of* the penis; fear of damaging or castrating the penis, but also fear that the penis might injure and destroy the internal genitals and the inside of the abdomen. We believe that the anatomical location of the female genitals is such that the little girl imagines that there is an abdomino-vaginal communication (between the genitals and the inside of her body) by which the swollen penis might be 'swallowed'. Coitus during pregnancy is particularly feared, as though it might destroy the baby by perforation, etc., and even before pregnancy there is a fear that it may destroy the baby's future nest. These early fears, probably related to a recurrence of the fear of destroying the mother's breast, constitute a repetition of persecutory anxiety and fantasied attacks against the mother's abdomen. The object of the infant's attacks is the mother's centre of creativity or its products (milk, faeces, babies, etc.). The wish to have a baby may serve to reassure the woman of her internal capacity for reparation. To create a healthy child would then be a proof that destructive aggression has been neutralized by erotic libido. Anxiety over destruction is not only a fear of destroying, but also a wish to destroy and to enjoy doing so. Therefore the woman must face a combination of two types of fantasies: the fantasy of destroying the mother's body (all girls consider themselves potential mothers from a very early age), and the fantasy of being damaged by that most desirable and feared object, the father's penis. The wish to be deeply penetrated, admitted intellectually more than actually accepted, is often accompanied by an identification with the aggressor. Separating from the penis after coitus constitues an additional difficulty; loss of the penis and loss of the breast may be considered as identical in the unconscious.

Corresponding difficulties encountered by men derive mainly from feminine identification: psychotic, perverted, neurotic homosexuality, more or less complete impotence, ejaculatio praecox, phobic avoidance of women or misogyny and fear of deep sexual or emotional involvement with a feminine object, with particular features related to every occurrence mentioned.

Thus women have to find a compromise between the fear of object loss, which could lead to mourning of a depressive type (hysterical depression is indeed common in women) and dangerous incorporation which generates persecutory anxiety. On the whole, an intermediate position must be found between an object that is too exclusively internal (internalized through fusion or a devouring absorption) and an object that is overtly external (externalized by disavowal or rejection) and therefore subject to loss. Jones's (1927) concept of aphanisis needs more examination in this light and may have new possible extensions (Freud, 1933*a*).

HERCULES SPINNING AT THE FEET OF OMPHALE

The compromise in which a basic fantasy of feminine sexuality might be exemplified is that of Hercules spinning at the feet of Omphale. We find here a typically feminine wish to have constantly at her side the man of her desire in a double role – protecting and virile like the father, and at the same time being used as if he were the mother. Man is feminized here, not so much because the woman wants to castrate him but because she wants to be sure of his *loving, maternal, reassuring and undangerous role*. The object here is neither external nor internal, but at a point where the two meet. The ancient Greeks display once more their deep intuition of the meaning of myths; 'Omphale' is related to *omphalos*, which meant both 'navel' and 'umbilical cord' (Delcourt, 1955, pp. 144, 150).

In the transference of female patients of this type, the analyst is treated as though he were Hercules. They claim that he gives them an impression of strength, of power, yet they reproach him with *being too strong*. They are afraid of his strength, afraid of the projected power, and especially afraid of the reintrojection of this projected power. They may then feel overwhelmed by too much pleasure in fantasied orgasm, especially since pleasure and power are considered capable of destroying all the good objects that provide this pleasure. Here again there is a coalescence of the omnipotent, phallic mother and the father bearing an overpowerful phallus. The envied penis is the object that brings a feeling of fulfilment: vagina filled by a penis, uterus filled by a baby, abdomen full of food and head full of knowledge. But by idealizing the analyst with this power and this absolute weapon, one runs the risk of being unable to find any object outside the transference capable of replacing him. The fixation to the idealized parental objects (primary or secondary) prevents any form of displacement that could allow for real satisfaction in the outside world. The patient attempts to prove to the analyst that he is irreplaceable. This blockage can be overcome only by analysing the object aspect (the father fixation) and the narcissistic counterpart (the mother fixation). The same also applies to male patients with marked feminine tendencies. The dilemma that occurs in an inverted Oedipus complex is well known. One must either be the passive object of an omnipotent phallic mother or else be used by the father in coitus. If only one of the horns of the dilemma is analysed, an important part of the basic conflict will not be touched. This predisposes to relapse after the termination of analysis. In both sexes analysis of femininity and of aggression must be carried to its farthest limits to prevent this.

THE ROLE OF MOTHER-FIXATION IN FEMALE SEXUALITY

The preceding remarks may provide a hypothesis concerning the central controversy in feminine sexuality: the respective roles of clitoris and vagina in childhood. Should one continue to place clitoris and vagina in opposition (as one might schematically oppose Freud's theories to those of Melanie Klein) or would it be better to make a distinction between the external erotogenic zones and the internal erotogenic ones? The external erotogenic zones are the clitoris and the labia majora and minora, while the internal erotogenic zones comprise the deeper part of the vagina and the cervix. Sexual excitation is first produced by the arousal of the external erotogenic zones. Masturbation in the little girl is most probably external and superficial. But we know that what counts in masturbatory satisfaction is the collusion of organpleasure and pleasure derived from fantasy. The fantasies accompanying early clitoral and external vaginal masturbation reintroduce traces of oral experiences. Satisfaction can thus bring oral and phallic fantasies into play at the same time. On the other hand, internal arousal of the erotogenic zones requires deep penetration. Accounts of early sexual satisfaction related to stimulation of the internal vaginal zones are most uncommon in the course of psychoanalysis in spite of contrary opinion on this point (Sherfey, 1966; Barnett, 1966).[1] Internal vaginal satisfaction encounters fantasies related to the anal phase for the very reason that it involves the fantasy of a communication between vagina and abdomen. The anal passage is a preferential one for fantasies of pregnancy or childbirth. It is, of course, difficult to distinguish what is strictly anal in the destructive aggression described above, since oral fixations clearly play a considerable role.

In any case, it seems probable that Freud was right in saying (following Lou Andreas-Salomé) that the vagina is 'taken on lease from the anus' (1917c, p. 133) and that little girls' sexuality is phallocentric. But one may also add, in accordance with Melanie Klein, that early oral fixations infiltrate the infantile sexuality of the little girl. In the course of libidinal development, clitoral excitation is likely to become autonomous, and consequently penis envy is able to develop, along with the series of 'little ones' that become separated from one's body (Freud, 1918b, p. 84): faeces (money, presents), baby, penis. The moment the little girl becomes aware through visual perception that the boy has a penis and that the mother's body does not, she can 'enter the Oedipus situation', according to Freud's expression (1933a). That is to say, she has gradually to give up the mother in order to conquer the father. We have shown why the work of mourning implied is so difficult. It involves erotic cathexes related to the mother ('the first seducer') and aggressive cathexes alike. Actually, it is less a matter of mourning than of displacement, of *transference* of cathexes on to the father, the possessor of the penis; a displacement from the internal on to the external. We wish to state once more that the transference of aggressive cathexes is as vital as that of erotic ones (Luquet-Parat, 1964). This displacement on to the father is indispensable if the final post-pubertal displacements are to take place and thus permit cathexes of a non-parental, masculine figure. But the original fixations cause this chain to break at its weakest link. Since Freud, it has frequently been noted that after a stage during which the husband or male partner plays the role of a father-substitute, he again becomes, following a period of cohabitation, a mother-substitute, particularly in hysterics (Freud, 1931b, pp. 230–1). The relationship to the man is marked by extreme ambivalence: a demand for absolute love, constant presence and continual emotional demands, coupled with

[1] Sherfey's (1966) assertions, based on the research of Masters & Johnson, need thorough examination and criticism; see Gillespie's valuable remarks (1969). The non-participation of the motionless upper two-thirds of the vagina in 'recordable' orgasm does not necessarily mean that it does not interfere with some sort of pleasure though some signs of activity are demonstrated in the descent, swelling and contractions of the cervix towards it, which are strongest in pregnancy and masturbation.

permanent dissatisfaction and open aggressiveness verging on *envy*. This envy becomes attached to every aspect of his life from which the woman feels excluded (professional life, friendships, leisure, etc.). When aggressive factors prevail over erotic cathexes, the relationship either ends in separation or leads to the establishment of a sado-masochistic relation which psychoanalysis frequently can neither change nor dissolve. Of course, the complicity of the male partner (due to his homosexual components) is conducive to the maintenance of such a relationship. One may speak in these cases of a 'psychotic' or 'delusional' relationship to the mother of homosexual origin.

These remarks may lead to the reconsideration of the existence or absence of specific feminine guilt mechanisms in women. Educational features will, of course, interfere with these mechanisms, but it will be worth exploring whether a specific structure may be found owing to the peculiarities of the development and transformations of aggressive drives in women and their narcissistic links.

FANTASY AND ANATOMY: SEXUAL DESTINY

We have placed some importance on *anatomical* considerations in this study. These are rarely taken into account in psychoanalysis. It has even been asserted that differences in anatomy do not prevent identical fantasies (Viderman, 1967). It is true that fantasy ignores anatomy in the same way as psychic reality ignores external reality. To reduce the difference of the sexes to differences in anatomy would certainly not be fruitful. The unconscious does appear to take no account of anatomical reality, for children of either sex assume that there is only *one sex*: boys think that all humans have penises and girls think everyone is built like themselves. This lasts until boys discover that the penis may be absent and girls discover that it exists. This leads to a re-evaluation of their anatomical conception of the difference between the sexes. But this manner of basing anatomical difference on the presence or absence of the penis does not, of course, correspond to anatomical reality. And we would like to complete this phallocentric manner of representing the difference of the sexes by the notion of *sexual destiny*. In dealing with the dissolution of the Oedipus complex, Freud, paraphrasing Napoleon, recalls that *anatomy is destiny* (1924*d*, p. 178). We now find with sexual destiny a *sexual reality* alongside internal and external reality. However far fantasy and denial may be pushed (and transsexualism is an example of the lengths to which this may go), it remains true that even if surgical miracles may change a person's sex, it is impossible to change his sexual destiny. As a matter of fact, paraphrasing Marjorie Brierley, we would say that sexual destiny is cathected before it is perceived. Perceptual discoveries blur these cathexes and sexual destiny is attained by the hazards which counteract its achievement: bisexuality. Beyond anatomy, a deeper truth is found joining the positive and negative aspects. A man cannot bear children; a woman cannot inseminate. Thus anatomy would enhance the core of reality around which fantasy is constructed towards the deeper truth. Under these conditions, anatomy would decide what *direction* the cathexes should take: towards external discharge in the boy, towards internal capture in the girl. The issue here, of course, can be only partially situated at the level of the pleasure principle. The idea of *sexual destiny* is one that almost transcends the personal level: we have no option with regard to it. But it does not prevent us from creating the fantasy that one may choose one's sexual destiny.

6
Moral Narcissism

Virtue is not merely like the combatant whose sole
concern in the fight is to keep his sword polished;
but it has even started the fight simply to preserve
its weapons. And not merely is it unable to use its
own weapons, but it must also preserve intact those
of its enemy, and protect them against its own
attack, seeing they are all noble parts of the good,
on hehalf of which it entered the field of battle.

HEGEL *The Phenomenology of Mind*

Because you have no inkling of these ills;
The happiest life consists in ignorance. . . .

SOPHOCLES *Ajax*

OEDIPUS AND AJAX

The legendary heroes of antiquity provide the psychoanalyst with an
inexhaustible source of material of which he does not hesitate to avail
himself fully, Usually he calls upon these lofty figures in order to
embellish a thesis. I will work from an opposition that allows each of us to
refer from a memory, to a common example that might then recall one or
another of our patients. Dodds, in his book *The Greeks and the Irrational*
(1951), opposes the civilizations of shame to the civilizations of guilt. It is
not irrelevant to recall here that according to Dodds the idea of guilt is
connected to an interiorization, we would say an internalization, of the
notion of fault or sin: it is the result of divine transgression. Shame,
however, is the lot of fatality, a mark of the wrath of the gods, of an Ate, a
merciless punishment barely related to an objective fault, unless it be
that of immoderation. Shame falls upon its victims inexorably: without
doubt one must inpute it less to a god than to a demon – infernal power.
Dodds ties the civilization of shame to a sociotribal mode in which the
father is omnipotent and knows no authority above his own, whereas the
civilization of guilt, moving toward a relative monotheism, implies a law

This paper appeared originally in French in *Revue française de Psychanalyse*, vol. 33, 1969. It
was first published in English in the *International Journal of Psychoanalytic Psychotherapy*, edited
by Robert Langs, vol. VIII, 1980–81. The translation is by Nancy Osthues.

above the father's. In each of the two cases even the reparation of the fault is different. The passage from shame to guilt is a road leading from the idea of impurity and pollution to consciousness of a moral wrong. In short, shame is a fact where human responsibility barely plays a part: it is a lot of the gods, striking the man liable to pride or *hubris*, whereas guilt is the consequence of a fault; it carries the sense of a transgression. The first corresponds to the talion ethic, the second to the ethics of a more understanding justice.

Without generalizing to any great extent, it seems that one might oppose these two problematical questions, shame and guilt, by comparing the cases of Ajax and Oedipus. Ajax, you may remember, was next to Achilles the bravest of the Greeks. When Achilles died, Ajax hoped to be given his weapons, but instead they were offered to Ulysses. The details of how this came about vary, depending on which version of the myth you refer to. According to the earliest, the choice was made by the Trojans, who, defeated by the Greeks, named the enemy they most feared. They named Ulysses who, though perhaps not the bravest, was nonetheless the most dangerous because the most cunning. According to later versions – and Sophocles sided with this tradition – it was the Greeks themselves who chose Ulysses.

Ajax thought this choice unjust and insulting. He decided to take violent revenge: execute the Atridae – Agamemnon and Menelaus – take prisoner the Argives, and capture Ulysses that he might whip him to death. However, Athena, offended by Ajax for having refused her aid during the battle with the Trojans, drove him insane. Instead of carrying out his exploit by fighting with those he wanted to punish, he destroyed the Greek's flocks in a bloody slaughter while in a state of madness. The perpetrator of this hecatomb recovered his sanity only once the wrong had been done. Sane again, he understood his madness. Twice mad, with grief and with shame because he was unable to triumph either by right or by force, his pride wounded, he killed himself by falling upon – some say and it is probable – by impaling himself upon Hector's sword, which he had received as a trophy.

Reading Sophocles, one realizes that shame is the key word of his tragedy. 'The loud voiced rumour, mother of my shame,' says the chorus upon learning of the massacre. Madness itself is an excuse for nothing – it is the worst shame of all – since it is a sign of the reprobation of a god. Here madness carries dishonour, because it is responsible for a murderous act devoid of glory. It ridicules a hero who aspires to the highest degree of bravery by forcing him to savagely destroy harmless animals. It burdens him with 'grievous conceits of his infatuate glee'. As soon as sanity returns, it is evident that death is the only possible solution. Ajax, having lost his honour, can no longer live in the light of day. No tie can resist the temptation of nothingness. Parents, wife, children, all of whom will be practically reduced to slavery by his death, do not suffice to hold him back. He aspires to hell, praying for the night of death: 'O darkness, now my light.' He leaves his remains behind him like an impurity and lets those who held him in contempt decide what course to take: exposure to the vultures or reparative burial. The ethic of moderation is stated by the messenger: ' "For lives presumptuous and unprofitable fail beneath sore misfortunes wrought by heaven," the seer declared, "whenever seed of man ceases to think as fits humanity!" '

It seems to me fitting to compare the example of Ajax with that of Oedipus. Oedipus's crime was no less great. His excuse was disregard, deception on the part of the gods. The punishment which he inflicted upon himself obliged him to accept the loss of his eyes, which desired to see too much; to banish himself, with the help of his daughter Antigone; to live among men with his impurity and consume it. Before his death, he even allowed himself to become a subject of litigation and contestation between his sons (whom he later cursed), his brother-in-law, and Theseus (under whose protection he had placed himself). In the woods of Colonus, on the outskirts of Athens, Oedipus waited for a sign from the gods. After the revelation of his faults, his life was entirely devoid of pleasure, but it was the life given by the gods and the gods took it back when they saw fit. Above all, Oedipus then clung to his objects. They were his very life as they helped him remain alive. He could not abandon them, even at the cost of becoming a sinister stake in the games of his children. Oedipus hated some of his children (his sons, naturally) but paternally loved his daughters, even though they were the fruit of incest.

You can see that we have opposed two problematical questions corresponding to two types of object choice and object cathexis: in the case of Oedipus, objectal object cathexis, generated through the transgression of guilt; in the case of Ajax, narcissistic object cathexis, generated through the disappointment of shame.

CLINICAL ASPECTS OF NARCISSISM: MORAL NARCISSISM

The apologue of Ajax, which served as an introduction, leads us directly to a question: Does it not seem evident that this form of narcissism is in some way related to masochism? Is not self-punishment in the foreground here? Before we settle the question and decide whether masochism is, after all, what best qualifies the theme of Ajax – who does not seek punishment but rather inflicts it upon himself in order to save his honour, another key word of narcissism – let us stop here for a moment and take a look at the relationship between masochism and narcissism.

While discussing tension-unpleasure and relaxation-pleasure in 'The economic problem of masochism' (1924c), Freud was led to dissect masochism, as an expression of the death instinct, into three substructures: erotogenic masochism, feminine masochism, and moral masochism. I would like to propose a similar dismemberment based not upon the effects of the death instinct – a theory to which I adhere completely – but rather upon those of narcissism. It appears to me from clinical observation that one can distinguish several varieties or substructures of narcissism:

Bodily narcissism concerns either the perception (affect) of the body or display of the body. It is the body as object of the Other's gaze insofar as the one is extrinsic to the other, just as narcissism or the feeling of the body (the body as experienced from within) is a narcissism of the scrutiny of the Other insofar as the one is intrinsic to the other. Consciousness of the body and perception of the body are its elementary bases (Green 1967a).

Intellectual narcissism becomes evident when intelligence takes over self-control with superabundant self-confidence despite contradiction by the facts. There is stubborn and untiring repetition that 'that doesn't keep it from being so'. This form, which I will discuss no further, recalls the illusion of domination by intellectualization. This is a secondary form of omnipotence of thought, an omnipotence of thought brought about by secondary processes.

Moral narcissism will be described in a later section.

In *The Ego and the Id*, Freud (1923b) attributed to each instance a specific material. What the instinct is to the id, the perception is to the ego, and the ideal to the superego. This ideal is the result of instinctual renunciation; it opens the indefinitely rejected horizon of illusion. It therefore appears that moral narcissism – insofar as the relationship between morality and superego is clearly established – must be included in a close relationship of ego/superego or, more precisely, since it is a matter of the function of the ideal, of the ego ideal/superego. What follows will show that the id is in no way an outsider to the situation. If we suppose that the id is dominated by the antagonism between *life instincts* and *death instincts*, that the ego undergoes a perpetual exchange of cathexes between the *ego* and the *object*, and that the superego is torn between the *renunciation of satisfaction* and the *mirages of illusion*, we suppose that the ego, in its state of double dependence on the id and the superego, serves not two masters but rather four, since each of the latter is split in two. This is what usually happens to everybody; no one is free of moral narcissism. Therefore, the pleasure in our relationships is due to the general economy of these relationships, provided that the life instinct prevails over the death instinct and that the consolations of illusion prevail over pride in instinctual renunciation. But this is not always the case. The pathological structure of narcissism we should like to describe is characterized by an economy that heavily burdens the ego by the double consequence of the victory of the death instinct and of instinctual renunciation, which confers upon the Nirvana principle (the lowering of tensions to a zero level) a relative preeminence over the pleasure principle. This follows from what has just been posited – the predominance of pride over the satisfactions of illusion. Hence an overcathexis of the ego to the detriment of the object.

Does not the dominating effect of the death instinct and of instinctual renunciation take us back to the severity of the masochistic superego? Approximately yes. Precisely no.

MASOCHISTIC FANTASIES AND NARCISSISTIC FANTASIES

'The true masochist,' writes Freud (1924c), 'always turns his cheek whenever he has a chance of receiving a blow.' This is not the case with the moral narcissist. Paraphrasing Freud, we would say, 'The true moral narcissist always volunteers himself whenever he sees a chance of renouncing a satisfaction.' Let us, in effect compare masochistic fantasies, so revealing, with narcissistic fantasies. Concerning masochism, it is a matter of being beaten, humiliated, befouled, reduced to passivity (but a passivity that demands the presence of the Other). Lacan (1966) feels, in regard to the masochist's requirement of the Other, that it arouses anxiety in the latter to a point where the sadist can no longer sustain his desire for fear of destroying the object of his pleasure.

None of this holds for the narcissist. For him it is a matter of being pure and therefore alone, and of renouncing the world – its pleasures as well as its displeasures – since we know that one can always get some pleasure out of displeasure. Subversion of the subject by the inversion of pleasure is within the grasp of many. What is more difficult and more tempting is to be beyond pleasure-seeking displeasure without seeking pain by vowing endurance. This is done through poverty, destitution, solitude, even hermitage – all states that bring one closer to God. Is God hungry or thirsty, is God dependent upon the love, the hatred of men? Some of the latter may believe so but they do not know who the true God is: the Unnameable. This profound asceticism, described by Anna Freud (1936) as a defence mechanism common to adolescence in the normal development of the individual, and to which Pierre Mâle (1956) has often returned in his studies on the adolescent, can take pathological forms. Suffering will not be sought, but neither will it be avoided, no matter how much energy is employed by the subject to do so. Freud (1924c) has said of the masochist that in fact he desires to be treated like a child. The moral narcissist's plan is just the opposite. Like the child he is, he desires to resemble the parents who, for one part of him, have no problem dominating their instincts. In other words, he wants to be a grown-up. The consequences will be different in the two cases. Through his masochism, the masochist masks an unpunished fault, the result of a transgression in the face of which he feels guilty. The moral narcissist has committed no fault other than that of remaining tied to his infantile megalomania and is always in debt to his ego-ideal. The consequence of this is that he does not feel guilty but rather *is ashamed of being nothing more than what he is or of pretending to be more than what he is.* Perhaps one can say that masochism operates on the level of a relationship concerning possession of what is improperly obtained – 'Ill-gotten gains seldom prosper' – whereas narcissism is situated on the level of a relationship concerning being: 'One is as one is.' In the case of moral masochism the subject is punished not so much for the fault but for his masochism, Freud reminds us. Libidinal coexcitement uses the road of unpleasure as one of the most secret passages leading to a pleasure of which the subject is unaware. This is seen in the 'Rat Man', who told Freud about the torture which aroused his horror and reprobation yet felt a pleasure of which he was unaware. In moral narcissism, whose aims fail (as do those of masochism), punishment or shame is brought about by the insatiable redoubling of pride. Honour is never in a position of safety. All is lost because nothing can clean the impurity of soiled honour unless it be new renunciations which will impoverish the relationships with the object, leaving all the glory for narcissism.

The dominant trait of the opposition is revealed here: through the negation of pleasure and the search for unpleasure, the masochist maintains a rich tie to the object which the narcissist tries to abandon. Use of the adjective *rich* may be criticized because we are accustomed to giving the word normative qualities. Otherwise we might say a *substantial* relationship with the objects, insofar as, in their turn, the latter nourish the fantasied objects which, finally, the subject will feed upon.

To resolve this conflict the narcissist will attempt increasingly to impoverish his object relationships in order to reduce the ego to its vital object minimum, thus emerging triumphant. This attempt is constantly frustrated by the instincts, which require that the satisfaction pass through an object. The only solution is a narcissistic cathexis of the subject, and we know that when the object withdraws itself, is lost, or disappoints, the result is depression (Pasche, 1969).

This remark leads us to understand the particularities of these patients' cures. Whereas masochistic patients present problems, anticipated by Freud, of a negative therapeutic reaction that perpetually underlines the need for self-punishment, moral narcissists, faithful and irreproachable patients, lead us, through a progressive rarefaction of their cathexes, to a dependent behaviour where the need for love and, more precisely, the esteem of the analyst is the oxygen without which the patient can no longer breathe. More precisely, it is a question of a need for a special kind of love, as it is aiming for the recognition of the sacrifice of pleasure.

But, as Freud (1924c) wrote, 'even the subject's destruction of himself cannot take place without libidinal satisfaction'. What satisfaction does the moral narcissist find in his impoverishment? The feeling of being better because of renunciation, is the foundation of human pride. This recalls the relationship between this clinical form of narcissism and the primary narcissism of the child and its tie to autoerotism.

If it was Freud who said that masochism resexualizes morality, we would like to add: *narcissism turns morality into an autoerotic pleasure in which the pleasure itself will be suppressed.*

PARTIAL ASPECTS AND DERIVATIVES OF MORAL NARCISSISM

The opposition between masochistic and narcissistic fantasies has allowed us to come to the heart of the principal aspect of this structure. We shall now briefly consider some of its partial or derived aspects before outlining its metapsychology.

We have already mentioned *asceticism*, when it lasts beyond adolescence and becomes a life style. This asceticism is quite different from that which subtends a religious conviction or a rule, again in the religious sense of the term. It is, in fact, unconscious. It uses as a pretext limitations of a material nature in order to force the ego to consent to a progressive shrinking of its cathexes so as to tighten the ties between desire and need, bringing the order of the former to the level of the order of the latter. One drinks, one eats only for survival, not for pleasure. One eliminates dependence in regard to the object and to desire (insofar as it is different) through meagre autoerotism, devoid of fantasies, whose aim is relief through hygienic evacuation. Or else one operates a massive displacement onto work and immediately puts into action a pseudosublimation which is more of a reaction formation than a destiny of instinct through inhibition, aim displacement, and secondary desexualization. This pseudo-sublimation will have a delusional character because of its megalomanic undertones amalgamated with an overall idealization which implies denial of its instinctual roots.

These last remarks lead us to consider a second aspect of moral narcissism. We discover it behind the features of a syndrome rarely mentioned but nonetheless very frequent: *affective immaturity.* Affective immaturity, which we have learned to recognize little by little, is not a benign form of conflict solution; far from it. On the one hand, the term *immaturity* is well deserved because this is indeed a case of retardation whose consequences are as serious for the affective cathexes of the subject as intellectual retardation is for the cognitive investments. On the other hand, affective immaturity is based upon a substratum of denial of desire and its instinctual base. This denial justifies the fact that early authors such as Codet and Laforgue (1925) classified it as *schizonia*, a psychotic form. One is often astonished by the quasi-paranoid form of behaviour. Affective immaturity is the appanage of young girls but is found also in young men – with, however, a more serious prognosis. We know its banal aspects: sentimentality, not sensitivity; a horror of human appetites, oral or sexual, a failure in sublimation which would imply their acceptance; the fear of sex, especially of the penis, which conceals a desire (present in both sexes) of an absolute and incommensurable nature; and the attachment to daydreams that are childish, affected, and willingly messianic. One recognizes these people in everyday life because they often put themselves in the position of a scapegoat; this does not bother them, so sure are they of their superiority over common people.

Perhaps these cursory elements are not sufficient to enable us to distinguish between hysteria and affective immaturity. The essential difference seems to me to reside in the exorbitant amount of tribute paid to the ego-ideal in affective retardation. Here we must recall Melanie Klein's remarks on idealization (1946). She saw idealization as one of the most primitive and most fundamental of defence mechanisms; idealization centred on the object or the self. It is this distinction of an economic order that enables us to establish more clearly the separation between hysteria and affective retardation, as though the latter were the product of a highly exaggerated narcissism in the face of a growing decathexis of the object.

One might fall into the trap of seeing behind all of this behaviour nothing more than a defensive position against instinctual cathexis. What characterizes these choices is, above all, immense pride – behind the misleading forms of intense humility – having nothing in common with the ordinary possibilities of narcissism. While there is, it is true, a defensive meaning to this sheltering of the instinct and its objects from vicissitudes, one may imagine that this arrangement would protect the subject. This cannot be denied, and one sometimes has the impression that the patient feels intense anxiety because cathexis appears to carry with it the considerable risk of disorganization of the ego. Just as the stimulus barrier protects the ego by refusing external stimuli which exceed a certain amount and which, because of their intensity, would put the fragile organization of the ego in danger, so in this case the refusal of the instinct is aiming for a similar protection. It is more exact to say that these patients feel extremely fragile and have the idea that admission of the instinct into their consciousness would imply for them the danger of perverse or psychotic behaviour. One patient told me that if she did not watch herself constantly, if she let herself become passive, it would not be long before she would become a bum. Now, everybody is a bit of a bum – on Sunday, during a vacation – and more or less accepts this; the moral narcissist cannot. This is why it seems necessary to insist upon the narcissistic cathexis of pride.

Messianism is accompanied in women by an identification with the Virgin Mary, who 'conceived without sin', a phrase whose consequences have been so serious for female sexuality; it is a much more dangerous notion than 'to sin without conceiving', to which women also aspire. In men, the equivalent is identification with the Paschal Lamb. This is not simply a matter of being crucified or of having one's throat cut; it implies being innocent as a lamb when the holocaust arrives. However, we know that the innocent have often been accused by history of crimes they allowed in order to remain pure.

This idealized behaviour, always destined to failure because of the conflict with reality, carries with itself, as we have already stated, shame rather than guilt, dependence rather than independence. The idealization includes certain particularities within the analytic cure:

1. The *analytic object* is difficult of access, for the material is buried beneath the narcissistic cloak of what Winnicott would here call a *false self*.

2. The *narcissistic wound* is felt to be an infraction, an inevitable condition of the coming to light of the objectal material. Here mystification is directed not only toward desire but also toward the subject's narcissism, toward the guardian of his narcissistic unity, an essential condition of the desire for life.

3. The cure is anchored in *actively passive resistance* in order to satisfy the subject's desire for dependence, a dependence having the power to make

him stay with the analyst eternally and to bind the analyst to his chair, like a butterfly caught in the net of the analytic situation.

4. The desire for *unconditional love* is the sole desire of these subjects. This desire takes the form of a desire for esteem, of a narcissistic valorization whose express condition is the burial or putting aside of drive conflict and of access to pleasure tied to the use of the erotogenic zones.

·5. *Projection* is a corollary of this desire and is put into play with the tactical aim of provoking the analyst's reassuring denial. 'Assure me that you do not see in me a fallen angel, depraved, banished, who has lost the right to be held in esteem.'

THE METAPSYCHOLOGY OF MORAL NARCISSISM

What we have just outlined in descriptive terms must now receive its metapsychological credentials. (I use the term *metapsychology* in its general meaning.) Thus we must examine the relation of moral narcissism to (a) the varieties of countercathexes; to (b) other aspects of narcissism; to (c) the development of the libido – erotogenic zones and object relations; (d) id, ego, and superego; and (e) bisexuality and the death instinct.

The varieties of countercathexis

The concept of the defence mechanism has been considerably extended since Freud. However, the multiplicity of defensive forms (the catalogue of which is to be found in the work of Anna Freud [1936]) does not enable us to account for the structural particularities of the major forms of the nosography which one tries vainly to ignore. Our only hope lies in a reflection concerning countercathexis – repression seen as a defence, *not the first* but nonetheless the most important in the individual's psychic future. (I am thinking here of the distinction in Latin between *prima* and *summa*.) In effect, Freud described a series of forms which we must now recapitulate and whose function is to regulate – to encircle – all of the other defences.

1. *Rejection* or *Verwerfung*, which some, along with Lacan (1966), translate as *forclusion* (English *foreclosure*). One can argue about the word but not about the thing itself, which implies radical refusal of the instinct or the instinct presentation and which, directly or in disguise, expels the instincts, which nonetheless return through reality, by way of projection.

2. *Denial* or *disavowal*, depending on the translation, or *Verleugnung*, repression of perception.

3. *Repression* itself or *Verdrängung*, which is specifically directed toward the affect and the instinct representative (Freud, 1927*e*).

4. Finally, *negation, Verneinung*, which is directed toward the faculty of judgment. This is an admission into the conscience in a negative form. 'It is not' is equal to 'It is.'

In its clearest and most characteristic aspects, moral narcissism seems to correspond to an intermediate situation somewhere between rejection and disavowal – between *Verwerfung* and *Verleugnung*. Here we shall point out the seriousness of its structure, which brings it close to psychosis.

Several arguments support this opinion. First, the idea that it is a question of a form of 'narcissistic' neurosis, something which clinical studies have accustomed us to consider with uneasiness. Next there is the dynamic itself of the conflicts, which implies a refusal of instincts associated with a refusal of reality. There is a refusal to see the world as it is, that is, as a battlefield upon which human appetites indulge in an endless combat. Finally, there is the considerable megalomania of moral narcissism, which implies a refusal of object cathexis by the ego. Nonetheless, it is not a matter of a repression of reality as in psychosis but more so of a denial, a disavowal of the order of the world and of the personal participation of the subject's desire. In this regard, if we recall that Freud describes disavowal in connection with the fetish tied to the sight of castration, we can see that the moral narcissist engages in a function of similar filling up by stopping with an omnipotent divine image the holes through which the absence of protection reveals itself, while offering himself in an effort to obstruct this unbearable deficiency. 'If God does not exist, then anything is permitted,' says the hero of Dostoyevsky's *The Devils*. 'If God does not exist, then it is permitted for me to replace him and to be the example which will cause belief in God. I will therefore be God by proxy.' One understands that the failure of this undertaking brings about depression (in accord with the mode of all-or-nothing) without mediation.

Other aspects of narcissism

The three aspects of narcissism we have particularized – moral, intellectual, and bodily narcissism – present themselves as variants of the cathexis which, for defensive reasons or for reasons of identification, are preferred according to the individual conflict configuration. But, just as the narcissistic relationship is inseparable from the object relationship, the diverse aspects of narcissism are interdependent.

In particular, moral narcissism has a very close relationship with intellectual narcissism. We recall that we understand intellectual narcissism to be that form of self-sufficiency and solitary valorization which makes up for the lack of human desires with intellectual mastery or intellectual seduction. It is not rare for moral narcissism to ally itself with intellectual narcissism and to find in this kind of displacement an addition to pseudo-sublimation. A hypertrophy of desexualized cathexes, which ordinarily occasions the displacement of partial pre-genital instincts (scoptophilia-exhibitionism and sado-masochism), supports moral narcissism. We know of the affinity certain religious orders have for intellectual erudition. The aim of this intellectual research of a moral or philosophic character is to find through philosophy, or God, *reasons* for an ethic which opposes an instinctual life, which views it as something that must at any price be not just repressed or surpassed, but *extinguished*. The shame felt for having an instinctual life like every other human being gives the impression of hypocrisy concerning the unavowed aim of the work. This shame is displaced into intellectual activity which becomes highly guilt-ridden. A term is lacking here: one would have to say that it becomes *shame-ridden*, as though the vigilant superego were to become an extra-lucid persecutor who remembers and reads behind the intellectual justification the desire for absolution for the remnants of instinctual life which continue to torment the ego. Also punished is the fantasy of grandeur included in this kind of search, which aims, rationally and intellectually, to increase the moral superiority of the subject.

In other cases intellectual activity, a synonym for the paternal phallus, undergoes an evolution so that childhood efforts made in school become objects of blocking during adolescence.

Here one ought to go more deeply into an analysis of sublimation and of regression from action to thought. As this would enlarge our field beyond the limits we have set, a brief discussion must suffice:

Intellectual activity, accompanied by fantasy or not, is highly eroticized and guilt-ridden, but is above all *felt to be shameful*. It is accompanied by cephalalgia, insomnia, difficulty in concentration or in reading, and inability to put knowledge to use. It is considered shameful because the subject, while engaging in this activity, relates it to sexuality: 'I read works of a high human or moral value, but I do so in order to fool those around me and to pass myself off as what I am not – since my mind is not pure and since I have sexual desires.' It is not rare in this case to find that the mother has accused the child of pretension or of unhealthy curiosity.

Intellectual activity can also represent an escape hatch for *aggressive instincts*. To read is to incorporate power of a destructive nature; to read is to feed upon the corpses of the parents, whom one kills through reading, through the possession of knowledge.

In the case of moral narcissism, intellectual activity and the exercise of thought are supported by a *reconstruction of the world* – the establishment of a morality, a truly paranoid activity which constantly remakes and remodels reality according to a pattern in which everything instinctual will be omitted or resolved without conflict.

To sum up, the percept-consciousness system, insofar as it is narcissistically cathected, is in a state of 'surveillance', tightly controlled and thwarted by the superego, just as in the delusion of observation; it has, however, a different type of economic equilibrium.

But it is above all with bodily narcissism, as one might suspect, that moral narcissism has the closest relationship. The body as an appearance and source of pleasure, of seduction and conquest of others, is banished. In the case of the moral narcissist, hell is not other people – narcissism has eliminated them – but rather, the body. The body is the Other, resurrected in spite of attempts to wipe out its traces. The body is a limitation, a servitude, a termination. This is why the uneasiness experienced is primordially a *bodily uneasiness* which expresses itself in the fact that these subjects are so ill-at-ease with themselves. For them the session of analysis which allows the body to speak (intestinal sounds, vasomotor reactions, sweating, sensations of cold or heat) is a torment because, though they can silence or control their fantasies, they are helpless as to their bodies. The body is their absolute master – their shame. (This intolerance of bodily reactions suggests a reprisal against the body and its drives related to an early relationship with the mother – she herself being reluctant to admit her own libidinal trends, which are reactivated through the baby's reactions.) This is why, on the analyst's couch, these subjects are petrified, immobile. They lie down in a stereotyped manner, allowing themselves neither change of position nor any kind of movement. It is understandable that visceral motor activity bursts out in the face of this driving silence of the relational life. This is, of course, nothing but the displacement of the sexual body, of that which does not dare name itself. During a session of analysis, a fit of vasomotor reaction will cause the subject to blush, and the emotion will bring on the tears which are the expression of the humiliation of desire. So, contrary to the pleas of the body, its appearance will become repulsive, harsh, discouraging – even to an analyst undemanding of the criteria of attraction.

We are pointing out those aspects which appear to be defensive, but here again we must not neglect the hidden and prideful pleasure to be found behind this humility. 'I am neither man nor woman, I am neuter,' one such patient said to me. It is, however, important to note that this uneasiness, painful though it may be, is a sign of life. When after the analysand has succeeded in controlling the anxiety in all its forms, including the visceral – and this is not so impossible as one might think – the moment of silence arrives and then he experiences an impression of frightful blankness. The lead helmet of psychic suffering has been replaced by the lid of the coffin, and what is now experienced is a feeling of inexistence, of non-being, of an interior emptiness far more intolerable than what the subject was to be protected from. Before, at least, something was happening, whereas control of the body prefigures a definitive sleep, a premonition of death.

Psychic development: erotogenic zones and the relation to the object

This dependence upon the body that we find in the narcissist, and particularly in the moral narcissist, is rooted in the relationship with the mother. We know that love is the key to human development. In the latter part of his work, Freud never ceased comparing the imprescriptible demands of the instinct with the no less imprescriptible demands of civilization requiring renunciation of the instinct. All development is marked by this antinomy. In *Moses and Monotheism* Freud gives us the following: 'When the ego has brought the super-ego the sacrifice of an instinctual renunciation, it expects to be rewarded by receiving more love from it. The consciousness of deserving love is felt by it as pride. At the time when the authority had not yet been internalized as a super-ego, there could be the same relation between the threat of loss of love and the claims of instinct; there was a feeling of security and satisfaction when one had achieved an instinctual renunciation out of love for one's parents. But this happy feeling could only assume the particular narcissistic character of pride after the authority had itself become a portion of the ego' (1939a, p. 117).

This passage shows that it is necessary to look at the notion of development from at least two angles: on one hand, the development of the object-libido from orality to the phallic and then genital phases; on the other, the narcissistic libido from absolute dependence to genital interdependence. Now, the security which must be gained can only be acquired – so as not to suffer the loss of a parent's love – through instinctual renunciation, which permits the acquisition of self-esteem. The supremacy of the pleasure principle, as well as evolution, is possible only if from the start the mother guarantees the satisfaction of needs, so that the field of desire can open as the order of the significant. This is so also in the sphere of narcissism, which can establish itself only insofar as the security of the ego is assured by the mother. However, this security and the order of need can suffer from a precocious conflictualization brought on by the mother. Then one witnesses the crushing of desire and its being dealt with as need. Also, the narcissistic wound, because of the *impossibility of experiencing omnipotence* and therefore of surmounting it, brings with itself excessive dependence upon the maternal object that assures security. The mother becomes the pillar of an omnipotence attributed to her, accompanied by an idealization whose psychosis-inducing character is well known, particularly since it must be accompanied by the crushing of libidinal desire. This omnipotence is even more easily created because it corresponds to the mother's desire to bear a child without the contribution of the father's penis. In short, it is as though the child, because of his conception with the help of this penis, were a debased, damaged product.

D. W. Winnicott has worked on this problem of dependence. He has shown how the splitting of the remaining part of the psyche from what has been refused leads to the construction and adoption of what he calls a '*false self*' (Winnicott, 1975).

The fact that this problematical narcissism is contemporaneous with an orality in which dependence upon the breast is very real, increases this reinforcement of dependence even more. During the anal phase – when, as we know, cultural constraints are important – the demands of renunciation become imperatives and reaction formations predominate; at best one will end up with an obsessive and rigid character, at worst with a camouflaged psychopathic paranoid form bearing fantasies of incorporation of a dangerous and restrictive object animated by an antilibidinal omnipotence. All of these pregenital relics will heavily mark the phallic phase and will confer upon the boy's castration anxiety a fundamentally devalorizing character, and upon the girl's penis envy an avidity of which she will be ashamed and from which she will hide as best she can.

Id, ego, superego

Let us examine narcissism in relation to the id. Here we can speak only of primary narcissism. In a recent work I demonstrated the necessity of distinguishing between that which pertains to the id, which is usually described by the term *elation* or *narcissistic expansion*, and that which is the exclusive domain of primary narcissism, which I characterize as the lowering of tensions to zero level. We have just seen that the level of moral narcissism is to use morality as a crutch in order to free itself from the vicissitudes involved in the tie to the object and therefore, by this roundabout method, to obtain liberation from the servitudes attached to the object relation, in order to give the id and the ego the means to be loved by a demanding superego and a tyrannical ego-ideal. However, their effort at mystification fails: first of all because the superego is not so easily fooled; second because the demands of the id continue to be voiced in spite of the ascetic manoeuvres of the ego.

If what I have said is so – that is, if moral narcissism turns morality into an autoerotic pleasure – then one understands better how the ego can be interested in these operations, using all the means at the disposition of secondary narcissim, robbing the cathexes destined to objects. Here is the travesty which permits it to say to the id, according to Freud's phrase, 'Look, I am so like the object, you can as well love me.' One might add, 'And at least I am pure, pure of any suspicion, pure of any impurity.'

However, it is definitely between the superego and the ego-ideal that the relationship is the closest. We have often insisted upon what Freud described in 1923 (and to which he never ceased to return since that date) as the order of the phenomena proper to the superego: the function of the ideal, which is to the superego what the instinct is to the id and what perception is to the ego (Freud, 1923b). Briefly recapitulating: if, at the start, everything is id, everything is instinct and, more precisely, antagonism of the instincts (Eros and destructive instincts), the differentiation as to the external world leads to the existence of a corticalization of the ego that differentiates perception and, correlatively, the instinct presentation. The division into ego and superego, plus the fact that the latter plunges its roots into the id, brings along with repression the need to represent the world as one desires it and also as it is – that is, in such a way that a system of connotations permits control of it. Secondarily or in compensation this leads to the setting up of the function of the ideal desire's revenge upon reality. This function – a function of illusion – makes possible the spheres of fantasy, art, religion.

For the moral narcissist, the ideal, which is capable of evolution while renouncing none of its original demands, retains its original force. Finding its first application in the aggrandizement of the parents, that is, in the idealization of their image, the ego ideal preserves all the characteristics of the relationship with the parents, the mother in particular. In the case of these subjects, the love of their ego-ideal is as indispensable as the love they expect from their mothers, as indispensable as the nourishment given by the mother whose love was the first illusion. 'I am nourished, therefore I am loved,' says the moral narcissist.

'Anyone who is not ready to nourish me cannot really love me.' During therapy, the moral narcissist will demand and try to obtain the same unconditional nourishment, or love, by means of privation and reduction of cathexes (the very opposite of the aims pursued by the therapy). This is an attempt to assure the domination over and the servitude by the Other. Here again we find the tie of love and security of which we spoke. To be sheltered – sheltered from a world which favours excitation – by the analyst's narcissistic love as guarantee of survival, of security, of love: that is the desire of the moral narcissist.

And the superego? We now discover one of moral narcissism's most fitting traits. In fact, the moral narcissist lives in a state of constant tension between the ego-ideal and the superego. The idealizing function of the ego-ideal is seen for what it is: its function of decoy, of diverted occult satisfaction, of troubled innocence. The superego reveals the trap of this travesty and refuses to be taken in. In turn the ego-ideal tries, through its sacrifices and holocausts, to ridicule the superego, which then pierces the 'sin of pride' of megalomania and severely punishes the ego for its masquerade.

The ego-ideal of the moral narcissist builds itself upon the vestiges of the ideal ego: that is, upon a force of omnipotent idealizing satisfaction which is ignorant of the limitations of castration and which therefore has less to do with the Oedipus complex of the oedipal phase than with the preceding phases.

Here we would like to bring to your attention a remark concerning the religious superego. Every superego carries in itself a germ of religion because it is created through an identification not with the parents but rather with the parents' superego: that is, an identification with the dead father, the ancestor. However, not every superego merits the qualifying term *religious*. A specific feature of any religion is that it takes the superego as foundation and forms it into a system – the dogma – a necessary mediator of paternal prohibition. It is certainly this feature that Freud was referring to when he called religion the obsessional neurosis of humanity. Conversely, since there is reciprocity, he also maintained that obsessional neurosis is the tragicomic travesty of a private religion. Moral narcissists have numerous similarities to obsessives, especially in regard to the intense desexualization they try to instill in their relationships with the object and also in the profound aggression which they camouflage. We have already mentioned the relation to paranoia. Grouping these observations, one can say that the more the ties to the object are maintained, the more the relationships will be obsessional. The more these ties are detached, the more the relationship will be paranoid. Any failure, in the first case as well as the second, any deception inflicted upon the ego-ideal by the object, brings on depression.

Let us say more concerning the relationship between shame and guilt, and about Dodds' speculation that Greek mythology finds its echo in individual pathological structures. Shame, as we have said, is of a narcissistic order, whereas guilt is of an objectal order. This is not all. One may also think that these feelings, the bases of the first reaction formations long before the Oedipus complex, are constitutive of the precursors of the superego. This occurs before the interiorization of the superego, heir to the Oedipus complex. Therefore, linking shame to the pregenital phases of development explains not only its narcissistic prevalence but also its cruel and intransigent character that allows no possibility of reparation.

Certainly this is a matter of schematic opposition. Both shame and guilt always coexist. However, in the analysis a distinction must be made. Guilt in relation to masturbation is tied to the fear of castration; shame has an irrational, primary and absolute character. Shame is not a question of the fear of castration but rather of the prohibition of any contact with the castrated person, insofar as he is the proof, the mark of an indelible impurity that can be acquired on contact. It must be stated that only a defusion of narcissism and the object-tie enables shame to have such a great importance. As any defusion favours the liberation of the death instinct, suicide because of shame can be better understood.

Let us go back to the ego. A point concerning sublimation was left suspended and deserves our further attention. I have mentioned pseudo-sublimation, a sublimation others might call a defensive sublimation. To my way of thinking, this conception is not apt; it puts a true sublimation, an expression of what is most noble in man, in opposition to a defensive sublimation, nothing more than a failed sublimation. Undeniably, there do exist sublimations which are the offspring of certain pathological forms. These can be viewed as emergency exits from conflict, without necessarily being reaction formations. And insofar as any sublimation is governed by the threat of castration, this leads to the need to end the Oedipus complex, at the risk of running even more serious risks for the libidinal economy. Thus sublimation has the destiny of an instinct. It is therefore a defence, one favoured by the existence of instincts whose aims are inhibited.

What there is to say about moral narcissism in this respect is instructive. One can observe not only these escape sublimations, for which the subject will later pay dearly, but also a process of inhibition, indeed a halting of the sublimation by secondary guilt (we must not forget that shame is always first) in the partial impulses, scoptophilia in particular. When the subject tends toward pseudo-sublimation, this mechanism is only on rare occasions a pleasure: of a lesser value than sexual pleasure, and at a higher price, but a pleasure nonetheless. The essential part of this observation of the ego is the completion of the constitution of what Winnicott calls a *false* self. This takes over the idealizing and depriving behaviour at the cost of what is called authenticity, the difference being that the process *is totally unconscious*.

In the face of this *false self* it is important not to disregard its economic function. I have already mentioned that which in the midst of moral narcissism acts as a defensive process, as well as that which acts as a substitute satisfaction (pride). But one must not neglect the essential economic consideration that makes moral narcissism and the *false self* that *subtends it* the backbone of these subjects' egos. It is therefore dangerous to attack it, at the risk of seeing the entire structure crumble. Life, with its potential of disappointments, very often does just this and then comes depression or, succeeding this, suicide.

Bisexuality and the death instinct

The last aim of narcissism is the obliteration of the trace of the Other in one's desire, therefore the abolition of the primary difference, the difference between One and the Other. But what is the meaning of the abolition of this primary difference in regard to the return to the maternal breast? The aim of moral narcissism in this abolition of tension to zero level is either death or immortality, which is the same thing. This explains why, confronted by these patients, we have the feeling that their life is a protracted suicide, even when they appear to have given up the idea of a violent death. However, this suicidal form reveals the fact that object inanition, consumption are sacrifices for the love of a terrible god: self-idealization. With the suppression of the primary difference, one simultaneously brings about the abolition of all the other differences and, it goes without saying of the *sexual difference*. It is basically the same thing to say that desire must be reduced to zero level and to say that one must do without the object which is the *object of lack* – the object becoming a sign that one is limited, unachieved, and incomplete. Freud, in *Beyond the Pleasure Principle* (1920a), refers to the Platonic myth of the androgyne, a figure evoking the fantasy of a primitive completion prior to sexual differentiation. For the moral narcissist the inconveniences of sexual differentiation must be supressed by self-sufficiency. Narcissistic wholeness is not a sign of health but rather a mirage of death.

Moral narcissism is a narcissism which is positive and negative at the same time. It is positive in its concentration of energy upon a fragile and threatened ego; negative because it is a valorization, not of satisfaction, not of frustration (this would be so in the case of masochism), but of *privation*. Autoprivation becomes the best bulwark against castration.

Here appears the need for a differential analysis, according to the nature of the deficiency, that is to say, according to sex. One cannot repeat this often enough: the fear of castration concerns both sexes. Penis envy concerns both sexes but with different particularities from the start. The man fears castration of what he has, the woman of what she could have. The woman desires a penis insofar as it is her destiny, through coition or procreation, for example. The man desires a penis insofar as his, like the female clirotis, is never sufficiently valorizing. We must remember the indestructibility of these desires.

Moral narcissism enlightens us in this respect. In the case of a man, it leads, through the behaviour of deprivation, to the following defence: 'I cannot be castrated because I have nothing left, I am stripped of everything and have put all my belongings at the disposition of whoever wants to take them.' In the case of a woman the reasoning would be: 'I have nothing but I want nothing more than the nothing I have.' This monastic vocation in man or woman is an attempt to deny the lack or, on the contrary, to love it. 'I lack nothing. I have therefore nothing to lose and even if I did lack something I would love this lack as though it were myself.' Castration continues to lead this chase, because this deficiency will be displaced in the direction of the moral perfection to which the moral narcissist aspires and which will constantly leave him far from his self-imposed demands. There, shame will expose its face, which will have to be covered with a shroud.

One does not wipe out the trace of the Other, not even in the desire of the One, because the Other will have taken on the face of the One and will repeat to it unceasingly: 'You must love only me. No one but me deserves to be loved.' But who is hiding behind the mask? The double, the image in the mirror? The doubles come to live in the frame of the *negative hallucination of the mother*.

We cannot return to this concept, which I have recently elaborated (1967). Here we will extend this hypothesis by demonstrating that if negative hallucination is the base upon which moral narcissism stands in its relationship with primary narcissism, then the father is involved. The negation of the absence of maternal environment joins with the father as primordial absence, as an absence of the principle of kinship, whose ulterior ties with the Law will be perceived. In the case of moral narcissism it cannot be denied that this detour is aiming only for the possession of a phallus – a paternal phallus – as a principle of universal domination. The negation of this desire in the form of a celebration of renunciation does not in the least change its ultimate aim. Also, it is not by chance that in both sexes it is a matter of a negation of castration. God is asexual but God is the father. For the moral narcissist his phallus is disincarnate, void of his substance, an abstract and hollow mould.

Before finishing with the relation between moral narcissism and the death instinct, we must return to the subject of idealization. It is greatly to the merit of Melanie Klein (1946) to have given idealization the place it deserves. For her, idealization is the result of the primordial splitting between the good and the bad object and, correspondingly, between the good and the bad ego. This dichotomy overlaps the one that exists between the idealized object (or ego) and the persecuting object (or ego) in the paranoid-schizoid phase. Consequently, the excessive idealization of the object or of the ego appears as the result of the splitting. Through this, there is an attempt to maintain in exclusion (in the ego as in the object) all persecutory parts. This point is confirmed in clinical work. The idealization of the ego is always the corollary of an extremely threatening feeling, for the object as well as for the ego. This joins our observations on the importance of destructive aggression in moral narcissists. Idealization joins forces with omnipotence in order to abolish, neutralize, or destroy the destructive instincts that threaten the object and, through retaliation, the ego.

Here one can perceive more clearly the relations with masochism which pose many questions in the interpretation of moral narcissism. I consider masochism to represent the failure of the neutralization of the destructive instincts oriented toward the ego: hence the failure of moral narcissism and of its work of idealization. Moral narcissism must therefore be understood to be, at the same time, the success of the defence and, consequently, success in the search for megalomaniacal pleasure beyond masochism, the megalomania being due to the liberation from conflict tensions. It must be clear that moral narcissism is not the only way out in the face of a masochism that might attain the ego; rather, it is only one of several methods used to keep this threat in the background.

Should we conclude that moral narcissism is a protection from masochism? I do not think so, for the reason that it is the dichotomy between idealization and persecution that is primary. The splitting shows the two positions at the same time. It is necessary to emphasize the fact that idealization is no less mutilating than persecution, in that it removes the subject from the circuit of object relations. In order to be

understood more clearly, I would say that persecution underlies paranoid delusion, whereas idealization underlies schizophrenia in its most
hebephrenic forms. In its milder forms, this problem is obviously less
evident. Melanie Klein would say that in these cases the depressive stage
has been reached. This explains why the breakdown of the moral
narcissist takes on the face of depression and not that of delusion or
schizophrenia. In all of these cases, one can see that it is the intensity of
the destructive instincts, uncontrolled by the splitting, and the accentua-
tion of idealization that are responsible for the regression. Thus, the two
positions, idealization and persecution, go hand in hand. Beyond this
there is a chaotic state which does not recognize the primary symbolizing
division, that of good and bad.

TECHNICAL IMPLICATIONS IN THE TREATMENT
OF MORAL NARCISSISTS

The cure of moral narcissists poses delicate problems. I have already
pointed out some of the more serious obstacles to the treatment's
evolution. They involve difficulty of access to material tied to the object
relation beyond the reconstitution of narcissistic dependence upon the
mother (and therefore upon the analyst). In my experience it appears
that the key to these cures involves, as always, a desire for the analyst,
and a provocation of the analyst's countertransference. For eventually
the analyst, knowing that he must continue such a relationship, finally
feels that he is his patient's prisoner. He becomes the other pole of
dependence, as in those cases when one does not quite know what
distinguishes the jailer from the man he is guarding. The analyst is then
tempted to modify this analytic situation in order to make it advance.
Since the least guilt-inducing variant is kindness, the analyst offers his
love, without realizing that he is pouring the first jet into the Danaides'
barrel. But the fact is that the desire for this love is always insatiable and
that one must also expect to see the reserves of love used up: they are
limited and therefore exhaustible. It seems to me that in that case the
analyst commits a technical error because he is responding to a desire of
the patient, a move we know to be always perilous. Since it is a matter of
moral narcissism, the analyst then becomes a substitute moralist, indeed
a priest. The result is that the analysis loses its specific feature, the spring
of its efficacy. It is exactly as if one were to choose to respond to a
delusional symptomatology by placing oneself on the level of its manifest
expression. To do so is to create an impasse.

The second possibility is that of the transference interpretation. As
long as it remains expressed objectively through the words of the analyst,

there is only a slight echo in this material covered by the narcissistic carapace. One might as well try to awaken the sexual desire of someone dressed in armour. Resignation remains. It is certainly the least dangerous of all these attitudes. Let it be, let it happen. Since the privations required by therapy have no effect other than that of reinforcing the moral narcissism, the analyst then risks engaging himself in an interminable analysis, the patient's need for dependence thus being largely satisfied.

So it seems that no solution appears. There is, however, one that I would not dare mention here without apprehension, if in certain cases it had not allowed me to make perceptible advances. It is a matter of (and the undertaking is perilous) analyzing narcissism. Analyzing narcissism is a project which, in more than one way, could appear impossible. However, after a sufficient passage of time when the transference is after all established and the repetition behaviour has been analyzed, the analyst can resolve to pronounce the key words: shame, pride, honour, dishonour, micromania, and megalomania. And he can thereby free the subject of a part of his burden, since the worst frustration a patient can feel during an analysis is not to be understood. As tough as the interpretation may be, as cruel as it can be to hear the truth, it is less cruel than the iron yoke in which the patient feels imprisoned. Often the analyst cannot bring himself to use this method, because he has the feeling he is traumatizing his patient. He therefore puts up a good front while within he is ill at ease. If we believe in the unconscious we ought to suppose that these attitudes, camouflaged by the civility of analytical relations, are perceptible to the patient, through the most subtle indications.

The analyst must be an artisan of the separation from the patient, with the condition, however, that the patient does not feel that this separation is a way of getting rid of him. Moreover, let us add that often those who treat these patients, when face to face with the realization of their subjects' inaccessibility, get rid of them in most affable ways, at least superficially. In short, we defend here nothing other than a technique of truth, certainly not an orthopaedic technique.

This interpretive attitude can at times permit access to the idealization persecution problem, and can thereby uncover what is lurking in the persecution implicit beneath the façade of idealization. Protection from persecution (on the part of the object and suffered by the ego; on the part of the ego and suffered by the object) is, at the same time, an escape from persecution in a camouflaged form. Through this, the object-tie to the mother can be reconstituted. Then the ego's reproaches concerning the object and the object's reproaches concerning the ego will be evident. Recourse to narcissistic sufficiency can be accounted for only by the deficiency of the object, whether this deficiency is real or the result of inability to satisfy the unquenchable needs of the child.

HEROIC FIGURES OF MORAL NARCISSISM

Everything I have elaborated here, except for my apologue of Oedipus and Ajax, is drawn from observation of patients. Their implied narcissistic regression makes them caricatures of the normal portraits that anyone may discover among those around him. While not quite caricatures, certain heroic figures – other than Ajax, who is an extreme case – may be contemplated.

Think of Brutus, for example, as portrayed in Shakespeare's *Julius Caesar*. Brutus assassinated Caesar not because of desire or ambition but because of patriotism, because he was a republican and saw in his adoptive father a threat to the virtue of Rome. When one assassinates for virtue, afterwards one is never virtuous enough to justify the assassination: therefore this refusal to tie oneself by oath to the other conspirators, as each has to answer only to his own conscience.

> . . . No, not an oath . . .
> And what other oath
> Than honesty to honesty engaged
> That this shall be or we will fall for it?
>   (Act II, sc. 1)

Above all, honour! Brutus has already warned us: 'I love the name of honour more than I fear death' (Act I, sc. ii).

And so, in consequence of this principle, this act of insanity by this least of political debutants (Cassius is aware of this and warns Brutus that he doesn't know what he's doing, an act permitting the most feared of his rivals, Marc Antony, to make the funeral oration). And so also, before the battle he must fight, the violent reproaches to the courageous Cassius, his ally, whom he accuses of being what we would call today a war profiteer. And so, finally, his suicide, offered as supplementary evidence of his incorruptible virtue. His heroic cause, however, is not necessarily that of the Republic, of the state, or of power.

Love also has its heroes of moral narcissism. The most beautiful of them all is the analyst's patron saint, Don Quixote, particularly cherished by Freud. Recall the episode in which Quixote goes to the Sierra

Morena and wants to live there as a hermit. He strips himself of his few possessions and begins to tear his clothing, to batter his body, and to leap around madly, all of which astonishes Sancho Panza. When the latter demands an explanation, the illusioned hildago explains to this common man that he is only conforming to the rules of the code of love as stipulated in the novels of chivalry. Quixote is looking for the feat capable of perpetuating his name in the name of love, a love which must not only be pure, with no sign of carnal desire, but which must also totally dispossess him of his fortune. He must come to this destitution of himself and of his individualty, by imitation of Amadis or Roland, to the point of madness – or at least an imitation of it. 'But I have now to rend my garments, scatter my arms about, and dash my head against these rocks; with other things of the like sort which will strike you with admiration.' This he says to Sancho Panza, who tries in vain to reason with him. 'Mad I am and mad I must be,' adds Quixote whose madness here is a sign of virtue. And of Quixote's description of Dulcinea as the 'ever honoured lady,' Sancho sees only that 'she will pitch the bar with the lustiest swain in the parish; straight and vigorous, and I warrant can make her part good with any knight-errant that shall have her for his lady. Oh, what a pair of lungs and a voice she has . . . and the very best of her is, that she is not at all coy, but as bold as a court-lady. . . .' Certainly this is not the way Quixote sees Dulcinea. One can say that here it cannot be a matter of narcissism but rather of objectal love; it is for the love object that Quixote inflicts upon himself privations and cruelty. But no, it is only a matter of the narcissistic projection of an idealized image and it is not the least of the strokes of genius of Cervantes that he ends his book with Quixote's repudiation: 'No more of that, I beseech you,' replied Don Quixote, 'all the use I shall make of these follies at present is to heighten my repentance."'

Doubtless Quixote and Sancho Panza exist only on paper. But they live in us if not in themselves. In the same way, is not Falstaff the absolutely and completely amoral narcissist, whose monologue on honour merits both our reprobation for its coarseness and our admiration for its truth? We are caught between an indispensable illusion and a no less indispensable truth.

All of these figures have been described by a philosopher. Have you not recognized, again and again in these pages, Hegel and his beautiful soul? Concerned about the order of the world, wanting to change it but anxious for his virtue, he would like to knead the dough with which man is made, while at the same time keeping his hands clean. But beware of doing as Hegel, who, having immortalized this beautiful soul with his pen, could only conclude *The Phenomenology of Mind* with a triumph that could well have been that of the beautiful soul.

That beautiful soul of moral conscience, do we not feel how close it can come to the delusion of presumption, to this law of the heart whose reference is paranoia? In any case, its narcissistic character has not escaped Hegel: 'Contemplation of itself is its *objective* existence, and this objective element is the utterance of its knowledge and will as a *universal*.' There is even its tie to the most primary narcissism: 'We see then here, self-consciousness withdrawn into the inmost retreats of its being, with all externality, as such, gone and vanished from it – returned into the intuition of the ego as altogether identical with the ego, and intuition where this ego is all that is essential, and all that exists.' The consequence of this is 'absolute untruth, which collapses within itself'.

Would we appear to be engaging in the denunciation of virtue and the defence of vice? To do so would be to give in to a fashion which today sees Sade as our saviour. We will content ourselves with the recalling of this truth, pointed out by Freud, who indissolubly tied sexuality and morality, the diversion of one automatically bringing about the diversion of the other. Georges Bataille (1957), to whom tribute must be paid, has profoundly understood this consubstantiality of erotism and the sacred. 'I must earn your love,' a patient said. To which I answered: 'Yes, but what kind of love are you talking about?' She was obliged to recognize, in spite of her vain and hopeless efforts, that Eros, that black angel, for her had turned white.

CONCLUSION

Several points have been left in suspense. First of all, it is necessary to point out that the structure of moral narcissism here is rigidly final. It characterizes certain patients by the predominance of its features. No one is totally free of moral narcissism. One can also call attention to this structural particularity as a phase in the analysis of certain patients. Also, concerning some of the cases I have described, though they may well have the outlines of this structure, they are not definitively tied to it. They can evolve – experience has taught us this – and can attain other positions. It is with satisfaction that we can observe favourable evolutions in cases where they were no longer hoped for.

Let us also take another look at the ties between moral narcissism and moral masochism. It is useful to distinguish them. Is not one a camouflage for the other? Rather than consider their relationship in terms of the covering of one by the other, I think that, if their relationship is dialectical, it is nonetheless a matter of a different series. If, however, one must admit their oneness, I would say that the true masochism is moral narcissism, insofar as there exists in the latter an attempt to reduce the tensions to zero level – the final aim of masochism insofar as its destiny is tied to the death instinct and the Nirvana principle. To repeat: the connection with suffering implies the relationship with the object – narcissism reduces the subject to itself, toward the zero which is the subject.

Desexualization is directed toward the libidinal and aggressive instincts, toward the object and toward the ego. The open range given to the death instinct is aiming for the annihilation of the subject considered as the last fantasy. Here death and immortality converge.

Truthfully, extreme solutions are never encountered; all that one establishes in the clinic, and particularly in the selectivity of the *psychoanalytic* clinic, are orientations toward curves, moving to their asymptotic limits. In this regard, the relations between shame and guilt are much more complex than we have said. However, the destructive character of shame is major: *guilt can be shared, shame can not be*. Nonetheless, ties form between shame and guilt: one can be ashamed of one's guilt, one can feel guilty about one's shame. But the analyst clearly distinguishes the splitting planes when, faced by his patient, he feels the extent to which guilt can be tied to its unconscious sources and how it can be partially surpassed when analyzed. Shame by contrast takes on an irreparable character. The transformation of pleasure into unpleasure is a solution for guilt; for shame, the only thing possible is the path of negative narcissism. A neutralization of affects is at work, a deadly enterprise where a labour of Sisyphus is carried out. I love no one. I love only myself. I love myself. I do not love. I do not. I. O. The progression is the same for hate: I hate no one. I hate only myself. I hate myself. I do not hate. I do not. I. O. This progression of propositions illustrates the evolution toward the affirmation of the megalomaniacal 'I' in the last stage before its disappearance.

7
The Dead Mother

If one had to choose a single characteristic to differentiate between present-day analyses and analyses as one imagines them to have been in the past, it would surely be found among the problems of mourning. This is what the title of this essay, the dead mother, is intended to suggest. However, to avoid all misunderstanding, I wish to make it clear that I shall not be discussing here the psychical consequences of the real death of the mother, but rather that of an imago which has been constituted in the child's mind, following maternal depression, brutally transforming a living object, which was a source of vitality for the child, into a distant figure, toneless, practically inanimate, deeply impregnating the cathexes of certain patients whom we have in analysis, and weighing on the destiny of their object-libidinal and narcissistic future. Thus, the dead mother, contrary to what one might think, is a mother who remains alive but who is, so to speak, psychically dead in the eyes of the young child in her care.

The consequence of the real death of the mother – especially when this is due to suicide – is extremely harmful to the child whom she leaves behind. One can immediately attach to this event the symptomatology to which it gives rise, even if the analysis reveals later that the catastrophe was only irreparable because of the mother-child relationship which existed prior to her death. In fact, in this case, one should even be able to describe modes of relationship which come close to those that I wish to expound here. But the reality of the loss, its final and irrevocable nature, will have changed the former relationship in a decisive way. So I shall not be referring to conflicts that relate to such a situation. Nor shall I take into account the analyses of patients who have sought help for a recognized depressive symptomatology.

Effectively, the reasons which motivated the analysands of whom I am going to speak to undertake an analysis barely touch on the characteristic aspects of depression, in the preliminary interviews. On the other hand, the analyst immediately perceives the narcissistic nature of the conflicts that are invoked, connected as they are with character neurosis

This chapter, written in 1980 and dedicated to Catherine Parat, is translated by Katherine Aubertin. It was published in French in *Narcissisme de vie. Narcissisme de mort* (Green, 1983).

and its consequences on the patient's love-life and professional activity.

Before examining the clinical framework that I have just defined, by exclusion, I must briefly mention a few references which have been the second source of my ideas – my patients having been the first. The reflections which follow owe much to authors who have laid the foundations of what we know about the problems of mourning: Freud, Karl Abraham and Melanie Klein. But in particular the more recent studies of Winnicott (1971b), Kohut (1971), N. Abraham (1978), Torok (1978) and Rosolato (1975) have set me on this path.

Here then is the statement on which I shall be concentrating:

The most widely shared psychoanalytic theory entertains two ideas. The first is that of *object-loss* as a fundamental moment in the structuring of the human psyche, at which time a new relation to reality is introduced. Henceforward the psyche is governed by the reality principle, which takes precedence over the pleasure principle which it also protects. This first idea is a theoretical concept and not the result of observation, for this shows that a gradual evolution, rather than a mutative leap, has taken place. The second generally accepted idea is that of a *depressive position*, but this is interpreted variously by different authors. This second idea combines observed fact and theoretical concept for both Melanie Klein and Winnicott. Both ideas, it should be noted, are linked to a general situation referring to an unavoidable event in the process of development. If previous disturbances in the mother-child relationship make its passage or its resolution more difficult, the absence of such disturbances and the good quality of maternal care cannot help the child to avoid living through this period, which plays a formative role in the organization of his psyche.

Besides, these are patients, whatever their presenting structure may be, who seem to suffer from more or less intermittent and more or less invalidating depressive traits, which seem to go beyond the normal depressive reaction that periodically affects everyone. For we know that a subject who never experiences any depression is probably more disturbed than someone who is occasionally depressed.

So the question I ask myself is this: 'What is the relation that one can establish between object-loss and the depressive position, as general given facts, and the singularity of the characteristics of this depressive configuration, which is central, but often submerged among other symptoms which more or less camouflage it? What are the processes that develop around this centre? What constitutes this centre in psychic reality?

THE DEAD FATHER AND THE DEAD MOTHER

Psychoanalytic theory, which is founded on the interpretation of Freudian thought, allots a major role to the concept of the dead father, whose fundamental function is the genesis of the superego, as outlined in *Totem and Taboo* (Freud, 1912–13). When one considers the Oedipus complex as a structure, and not merely as a phase of libidinal development, this is a coherent point of view. Other concepts derive from this: the superego in classical theory, the Law and the Symbolic in Lacanian thought. This group of concepts is linked by the reference to castration and to sublimation as the fate of the instincts.

On the other hand, we never hear of the dead mother from a structural point of view. There may be allusions to this in certain individual cases, as in the case of Marie Bonaparte's analysis of Edgar Poe, but that concerns a particular event: the loss of the mother at a very early age. There is a limitation imposed here by a purely realistic point of view. It is not possible to explain this exclusion by invoking the Oedipus complex, because one could refer to it in connection with the girl's Oedipus complex, or again with the boy's inverted Oedipus complex. In fact the answer lies elsewhere. Matricide does not involve the dead mother as a concept, on the contrary; and the concept which is underlined by the dead father, that is to say the reference to the ancestor, to filiation, to genealogy, refers back to the primitive crime and the guilt which is its consequence.

So it is surprising that the general model of mourning that underlies this concept makes no mention of the bereavement of the mother, nor the loss of the breast. I am alluding to this not because these are supposed to be prior to it, but because one is forced to notice that there is no articulation between these two concepts.

In *Inhibitions, Symptoms and Anxiety* Freud (1926d) categorized castration anxiety by including it in a series which also comprises anxiety about the loss of a loved object, or a loss of its love, anxiety of the superego, and anxiety at the threat of the loss of the protecting superego. We know, besides, that he was careful to make the distinction between anxiety, pain and mourning.

I do not intend to discuss in detail Freud's thinking on this point, because this would lead me away from my subject, but I should like to make one remark: with castration it is the same as with repression. First, Freud well knew that, concerning both, there exist as many other forms of anxiety as other varieties of repression and even other defence mechanisms. In both cases he considers the possibility of the existence of chronologically earlier forms, from which the one and the other derive.

However, in both cases he specifically fixes castration anxiety and repression as a centre, in relation to which he places the other types of anxiety and different varieties of repression, whether they come before or after, which is proof of the structural and genetic character of Freudian thought. This is clearly stated when he makes a primal fantasy of the Oedipus myth, which is relatively independent of the vicissitudes of the conjuncture which gives it its specificity for any given patient. Thus, even in the cases where he notes the presence of an inverted Oedipus complex, as in the 'Wolf Man', he asserts that the father, object of the patient's erotic wishes, remains nonetheless the castrator.

This structural function implies a constitutive conception of the psychical order – that constitutes a symbolical organization – which is programmed by the primal fantasies. This path has not always been followed by Freud's successors. But globally it seems that French psychoanalytic thought, in spite of its divergences, has followed Freud on this point. On the one hand, reference to castration as a model has obliged authors to 'castratize', if I may express myself thus, all other forms of anxiety; one speaks of anal or narcissistic castration, for example. On the other hand, by giving an anthropological interpretation of Freudian theory, one relates all the varieties of anxiety to the concept of lack in Lacanian theory. Now, I believe that, in both cases, one is doing violence as much to experience as to theory to save the unity and generalization of a concept.

It may be surprising that on this point I seem to dissociate myself from a structural point of view that I have always defended. Thus, what I would propose, instead of conforming to the opinion of those who divide anxiety into different types according to the age at which it appears in the life of the subject, would be rather a structural conception which would be organized not around one centre or one paradigm, but around at least two, in accordance with a distinctive characteristic, different from those which have been proposed to date.

Castration anxiety can be legitimately described as subsuming the group of anxieties linked by the ' "little one" detachable part of the body', whether it be penis, faeces or baby. What gives this class unity is that castration is always evoked in the context of a bodily wound associated with a bloody act. I attach more importance to the idea of 'red' anxiety than to its relation to a part-object.

On the contrary, whether referring to the concept of the loss of the breast, or of object-loss, and even of threats relative to the loss of the superego or its protection, and in a general manner, to all threats of abandonment, the context is never bloody. To be sure, all forms of anxiety are accompanied by destructiveness; castration too, because the wound is, of course, the result of a destruction. But this destructiveness has nothing to do with a bloody mutilation. It bears the colours of mourning: black or white.[1] Black as in severe depression, or blank as in states of emptiness to which one now pays justified attention.

I defend the hypothesis that the sinister black of depression, which we can legitimately relate to the hatred we observe in the psychoanalysis of depressed subjects, is only a secondary product, a consequence rather than a cause, of a 'blank' anxiety which expresses a loss that has been experienced on a narcissistic level.

Having already described negative hallucination and blank psychosis, I shall not return to what I have said on the subject, but I shall attach blank anxiety or blank mourning to this series.

The category of 'blankness' – negative hallucination, blank psychosis, blank mourning, all connected to what one might call the problem of emptiness, or of the negative, in our clinical practice – is the result of one of the components of primary repression: massive decathexis, both radical and temporary, which leaves traces in the unconscious in the form of 'psychical holes'. These will be filled in by recathexes, which are the expression of destructiveness which has thus been freed by the weakening of libidinal erotic cathexis. Manifestations of hatred and the following process of reparation are manifestations which are secondary to this central decathexis of the maternal primary object. One can understand that this view modifies even analytic technique, because to limit oneself to interpreting hatred in structures which take on depressive characteristics amounts to never approaching the primary core of this constellation.

The Oedipus complex should be maintained as the essential symbolic matrix to which it is always important to refer, even in cases of so-called pre-genital or pre-oedipal regression, which implies the reference to an axiomatic triangulation. However advanced the analysis of the decathexis of the primary object, may be, the fate of the human psyche is to have always *two* objects and never one alone, however far one goes back to try to understand the earliest psychical structure. This does not mean to say that one must adhere to a conception of a primitive Oedipus complex – phylogenetic – where the father as such would be present, in the form of his penis (I am thinking of Melanie Klein's conception of the early Oedipus complex: the father's penis in the mother's womb). The father

---

[1] '*Noir ou blanc*' – in French *blanc* can mean either 'white' or 'blank'. In this chapter it has the latter meaning, 'empty', throughout. [Translator's note.]

is there, both in the mother and the child, from the beginning. More exactly, *between* the mother and child. From the mother's side this is expressed in her desire for the father, of which the child is the realisation. On the side of the child, everything which introduces the anticipation of a third person, each time that the mother is not wholly present and her devotion to the child is neither total nor absolute (at least in the illusion he maintains in this regard, before it is pertinent to speak of object-loss), will be, retrospectively, attributable to the father.

It is thus that one must account for the solidarity which links the metaphoric loss of the breast, the symbolic mutation of the relation between pleasure and reality – established retrospectively as principles – the prohibition of incest, and the double figuration of the images of mother and father, potentially reunited in the fantasy of a hypothetical primal scene which takes place outside the subject. It is from this scene that the subject *excludes himself* and constitutes himself in the absence of affective representation, which gives birth to fantasy, which is a production of the subject's 'madness'.

Why is this metaphorical? The recourse to metaphor, which holds good for every essential element of psychoanalytic theory, is particularly necessary here. In chapter 3, I pointed out that there are two Freudian versions of the loss of the breast. The first, which is theoretical and conceptual, is that to which Freud refers in his article 'Negation' (1925*h*). Freud talks about it as though it implies a unique, instantaneous, basic event – decisive, it goes without saying, because its repercussion on the function of judgement is fundamental. In the second version, in *An Outline of Psychoanalysis* (1940*a*) in particular, he adopts a position which is less theoretical than descriptive, as though he were applying himself to infant-observation, so much in vogue today. He accounts for the phenomenon, not theoretically, but in a 'narrative' form, if I may so describe it, where one understands that this loss is a process of progressive evolution which advances step by step. Now, I believe that the theoretical and descriptive approaches are mutually exclusive, rather as perception and memory exclude each other in theory. The recourse to this comparison is not only analogical. In the 'theory' that the subject elaborates about himself, the mutative interpretation is always retrospective. It is in the aftermath that this theory of the lost object is formed, and acquires its unique, instantaneous, decisive, irrevocable and basic characteristic.

The recourse to metaphor is not only justified from a diachronic point of view, but also from a synchronic point of view. The fiercest partisans of the reference to the loss of the breast in contemporary psychoanalytic theory, the Kleinians, now admit, humbly watering down their wine, that the breast is just a word to designate the mother, this, to the satisfaction of non-Kleinian theoreticians who often psychologize psychoanalysis. One must retain the metaphor of the breast, for the breast, like the penis, can only be symbolic. However intense the pleasure of sucking linked to the nipple, or the teat, might be, erogenous pleasure has the power to concentrate within itself everything of the mother that is not the breast: her smell, her skin, her look and the thousand other components that 'make up' the mother. The metonymical object has become metaphor to the object.

One may note in passing that we have no difficulty in reasoning in the same manner when we speak of loving sexual intercourse, in reducing the whole of a relationship, which is far more complex, to the pairing 'penis-vagina', and in relating its mishaps to castration anxiety.

From this one may understand that, by going more deeply into the problems relating to the dead mother, I refer to them as to a metaphor, independent of the bereavement of a real object.

THE DEAD MOTHER COMPLEX

The dead mother complex is a revelation of the transference. When the subject presents himself to the analyst for the first time, the symptoms of which he complains are not essentially of a depressive kind. Most of the time these symptoms indicate more or less acute conflicts with objects who are close. It is not infrequent that a patient spontaneously recounts a personal history where the analyst thinks to himself that here, at a given moment, a childhood depression should or could have been located, of which the subject makes no mention. This depression, which has sometimes appeared sporadically in the clinical history, only breaks into the open in the transference. As for the classic neurotic symptoms, they are present but of secondary value or, even if they are important, the analyst has the feeling that the analysis of their genesis will not furnish the key to the conflict. On the contrary, the problems pertaining to narcissism are in the foreground where the demands of the ego ideal are considerable, in synergy with or in opposition to the superego. The feeling of impotence is evident. Impotence to withdraw from a conflictual situation, impotence to love, to make the most of one's talents, to multiply one's assets, or, when this does take place, a profound dissatisfaction with the results.

When the analysis is underway, the transference will reveal, sometimes quite rapidly but more often after long years of analysis, a singular depression. The analyst has the feeling of a discordance between the *transference depression* – an expression that I am coining on this occasion to oppose it to transference neurosis – and the behaviour outside the analysis where depression does not blow up, because nothing indicates that the entourage perceives it clearly, which nevertheless does not prevent the people close to him from suffering from the object-relationship that the analysand establishes with them.

What this transference depression indicates is the repetition of an infantile depression, the characteristics of which may usefully be specified.

It does not concern the loss of a real object; the problem of a real separation with the object who would have abandoned the subject is not what is in question here. The fact may exist, but it is not this that constitutes the dead mother complex.

The essential characteristic of this depression is that it takes place in the presence of the object, which is itself absorbed by a bereavement. The mother, for one reason or another, is depressed. Here the variety of precipitating factors is very large. Of course, among the principal causes of this kind of maternal depression, one finds the loss of a person dear to her: child, parent, close friend, or any other object strongly cathected by the mother. But it may also be a depression triggered off by a deception which inflicts a narcissistic wound: a change of fortune in the nuclear family or the family of origin, a liaison of the father who neglects the mother, humiliation, etc. In any event the mother's sorrow and lessening of interest in her infant are in the foreground.

It should be noted that the most serious instance is the death of a child at an early age, as all authors have understood. In particular there is a cause which remains totally hidden, because the manifest signs by which the child could recognize it, and thus gain retrospective knowledge of it, is never possible because it rests on a secret: a miscarriage of the mother, which must be reconstructed by the analysis from minute indications; a hypothetical construction, of course, which renders a coherence to what is expressed in the clinical material, which can be attached to earlier periods of the subject's history.

What comes about then is a brutal change of the maternal imago, which is truly mutative. Until then there is an authentic vitality present in the subject, which comes to a sudden halt, remaining seized from then on in the same place, which testifies to a rich and happy relationship with the mother. The infant felt loved, notwithstanding the risks that the most ideal of relationships presupposes. Photos of the young baby in the family album show him to be gay, lively, interested, carrying much potentiality, whereas later snapshots show the loss of this initial happiness. All seems to have ended, as with the disappearance of ancient civilizations, the cause of which is sought in vain by historians, who make the hypothesis of an earthquake to explain the death and the destruction of palace, temple, edifices and dwellings, of which nothing is left but ruins. Here the disaster is limited to a *cold core*, which will eventually be overcome, but which leaves an indelible mark on the erotic cathexes of the subjects in question.

The transformation in the psychical life, at the moment of the mother's sudden bereavement when she has become abruptly detached from her infant, is experienced by the child as a catastrophe; because, without any warning signal, love has been lost at one blow. One does not need to give a lengthy description of the narcissistic traumatism that this change represents. One must however point out that it constitutes a premature disillusionment and that it carries in its wake, besides the loss of love, the loss of *meaning*, for the baby disposes of no explication to account for what has happened. Of course, being at the centre of the maternal universe, it is clear that he interprets this deception as the consequence of his drives towards the object. This will be especially serious if the complex of the dead mother occurs at the moment when the child discovers the existence of the third person, the father, and that the new attachment should be interpreted by him as the reason for the mother's detachment. In any case, here there is a premature and unstable triangulation. For either, as I have just said, the withdrawal of the mother's love is attributed to the mother's attachment to the father, or this withdrawal will provoke an early and particularly intense attachment to the father, felt to be the saviour from the conflict taking place between mother and infant. Now, in reality, the father more often than not does not respond to the child's distress. The subject is thus caught between a dead mother and an inaccessible father, either because the latter is principally preoccupied by the state of the mother, without bringing help to the infant, or because he leaves the mother-child couple to cope with this situation alone.

After the child has attempted in vain to repair the mother who is absorbed by her bereavement, which has made him feel the measure of his impotence, after having experienced the loss of his mother's love and the threat of the loss of the mother herself, and after he has fought against anxiety by various active methods, amongst which agitation, insomnia and nocturnal terrors are indications, the ego will deploy a series of defences of a different kind.

The first and most important is a unique movement with two aspects: *the decathexis of the maternal object and the unconscious identification with the dead*

mother. The decathexis, which is principally affective, but also representative, constitutes a psychical murder of the object, accomplished
without hatred. One will understand that the mother's affliction excludes the emergence of any contingency of hatred susceptible of damaging her image even more.

No instinctual destructiveness is to be inferred from this operation of
decathexis of the maternal image. Its result is the constitution of a hole in
the texture of object-relations with the mother, which does not prevent
the surrounding cathexes from being maintained, just as the mother's
bereavement modifies her fundamental attitude with regard to the child,
whom she feels incapable of loving, but whom she continues to love just
as she continues to take care of him. However, as one says, 'her heart is
not in it'.

The other aspect of the decathexis is the primary mode of identification with the object. This mirror-identification is almost obligatory, after
reactions of complementarity (artificial gaiety, agitation, etc.) have
failed. This reactive symmetry is the only means by which to establish a
reunion with the mother – perhaps by way of sympathy. In fact there is
no real reparation, but a mimicry, with the aim of continuing to possess
the object (who one can no longer have) by becoming, not like it but, the
object itself. This identification, which is the condition of the renounce-
ment to the object and at the same time its conservation in a cannibalistic
manner, is unconscious from the start. Here there is a difference from the
decathexis, which becomes unconscious later on, because in this second
case the withdrawal is retaliatory; it endeavours to get rid of the object,
whereas the identification comes about unawares to the ego of the
subject and against his will. Here is where its alienating characteristic
lies.

The ulterior object-relations, the subject, who is prey to the repetition-
compulsion, will actively employ the decathexis of an object who is about
to bring disappointment, repeating the old defence, but, he will remain
totally unconscious of his identification with the dead mother, with
whom he reunites henceforth in recathecting the traces of the trauma.

The second fact is, as I have pointed out, *the loss of meaning*. The
'construction' of the breast, of which pleasure is the cause, the aim and
the guarantor, has collapsed all at once, without reason. Even if one were
to imagine the reversal of the situation by the subject, who in a negative
megalomania, would attribute the responsibility for the mutation to
himself, there is a totally disproportional gap between the fault he could
reproach himself for having committed and the intensity of the maternal
reaction. At the most, he might imagine this fault to be linked with his

manner of being rather than with some forbidden wish; in fact, it becomes forbidden for him to be.

This position, which could induce the child to let himself die, because of the impossibility of diverting destructive aggressivity to the outside, because of the vulnerability of the maternal image, obliges him to find someone responsible for the mother's black mood, though he be a scapegoat. It is the father who is designated to this effect. There is in any case, I repeat, an early triangular situation, because child, mother and the unknown object of the mother's bereavement are present at the same time. The unknown object of the bereavement and the father are then condensed for the infant, creating a precocious Oedipus complex.

This whole situation, arising from the loss of meaning, leads to a second front of defence:

the releasing of secondary hatred, which is neither primary nor fundamental, brings into play regressive wishes of incorporation, but also anal features which are coloured with manic sadism where it is a matter of dominating, soiling, taking vengeance upon the object, etc.

auto-erotic excitation establishes itself in the search for pure sensual pleasure, organ pleasure at the limit, without tenderness, ruthless, which is not necessarily accompanied by sadistic fantasy, but which remains stamped with a reticence to love the object. This is the foundation for hysterical identifications to come. There is a precocious dissociation between the body and the psyche, as between sensuality and tenderness, and a blocking of love. The object is sought after for its capacity to release isolated enjoyment of an erogenous zone (or more than one) without the confluence of a shared enjoyment of two objects, more or less totalized.

Finally, and more particularly, *the quest for lost meaning structures the early development of the fantasmatic and the intellectual capacities of the ego.* The development of a frantic need for play which does not come about as in the freedom for playing, but under the *compulsion to imagine*, just as intellectual development is inscribed in a *compulsion to think*. Performance and auto-reparation go hand in hand to coincide with the same goal: the preservation of a capacity to surmount the dismay over the loss of the breast, by the creation of a patched breast, a piece of cognitive fabric which is destined to mask the hole left by the decathexis, while secondary hatred and erotic excitation teem on the edge of an abyss of emptiness.

The overcathected intellectual capacity necessarily comprises a considerable part of projection. Contrary to widespread opinion, projection is not always false reasoning. This may be the case but not necessarily. What defines projection is not the true or false character of what is projected, but the operation which consists in transferring to the outside scene – the scene of the object – the investigation, even the guessing, of what has had to be rejected and abolished from within. The infant has made the cruel experience of his dependence on the variations of the mother's moods. Henceforth he devotes his efforts to guessing or anticipating.

The compromised unity of the ego which has a hole in it from now on, realizes itself either on the level of fantasy, which gives open expression to artistic creation, or on the level of knowledge, which is at the origin of highly productive intellectualization. It is evident that one is witnessing an attempt to master the traumatic situation. But this attempt is doomed to fail. Not that it fails where it has displaced the theatre of operations. These precocious idealized sublimations are the outcome of premature and probably precipitated psychical formations, but I see no reason, apart from bending to a normative ideology, to contest their authenticity. Their failure lies elsewhere. The sublimations reveal their incapacity to play a stabilizing role in the psychical economy, because the subject remains vulnerable on a particular point, which is his love life. In this area, a wound will awaken a psychical pain and one will witness a resurrection of the dead mother, who, for the entire critical period when she remains in the foreground, dissolves all the subject's sublimatory acquisitions, which are not lost, but which remain momentarily blocked. Sometimes it is love which sets the development of the sublimated acquisitions in motion again, and sometimes it is the latter which attempt to liberate love. Both may combine their efforts for a time, but soon the destructiveness overwhelms the possibilities of the subject who does not dispose of the necessary cathexes to establish a lasting object-relation and to commit himself progressively to a deeper personal involvement which implies concern for the other. Thus, inevitably, it is either the disappointment in the object or that in the ego which puts an end to the experience, with the reappearance of the feeling of failure and incapacity. The patient has the feeling that a malediction weighs upon him, that there is no end to the dead mother's dying, and that it holds him prisoner. Pain, a narcissistic feeling, surfaces again. It is a hurt which is situated on the edge of the wound, colouring all the cathexes, filling in the effects of hatred, of erotic excitement, the loss of the breast. In a state of psychical pain, it is as impossible to hate as to love, impossible to find enjoyment, albeit masochistic, impossible to think; only a feeling of a captivity which dispossesses the ego of itself and alienates it to an unrepresentable figure.

The subject's trajectory evokes a hunt in quest of an unintrojectable object, without the possibility of renouncing it or of losing it, and indeed, the possibility of accepting its introjection into the ego, which is cathected by the dead mother. In all, the subject's objects remain constantly at the limit of the ego, not wholly within, and not quite without. And with good reason, for the place is occupied, in its centre, by the dead mother.

For a long period, the analysis of these subjects will proceed with the examination of the classic conflicts: Oedipus complex, pregenital fix-ations, anal and oral. Repression reposing on infantile sexuality, on aggressivity, will have been interpreted without cease. Probably some progress has become manifest. But it hardly convinces the analyst, even if the analysand himself seeks comfort by underlining the points on which there would be cause for satisfaction.

In fact, all this psychoanalytic work remains subject to spectacular collapses, where everything again seems to be as on the first day, to the point where the analysand realizes that he can no longer continue to bluff himself and he finds himself forced to admit to the insufficiency of the transferential object: the analyst, in spite of the relational manoeuvres with the supporting objects of lateral transference which had helped him, the patient, to avoid approaching the central core of the conflict.

In these cures, I finally understood that I had remained deaf to a certain discourse that my analysands had left me to guess. Behind the eternal complaints about the mother's unkindness, or her lack of under-standing or her rigidity, I guessed the defensive value of these comments, against intense homosexuality. Feminine homosexuality in both sexes, for in the boy it is the feminine part of the psychical personality which expresses itself thus, very often in the search for paternal compensation. But I continued to ask myself why this situation prolonged itself. *My deafness related to the fact that, behind the complaints concerning the mother's doings, her actions, the shadow of her absence was profiled.* In fact the enquiry against X concerned a mother who was absorbed, either with herself or with something else, unreachable without echo, but always sad. A silent mother, even if talkative. When she was present, she remained indiffe-rent, even when she was plying the child with her reproaches. Thus, I was able to represent this situation for myself quite differently.

The dead mother had taken away with her, in the decathexis of which she had been the object, the major portion of the love with which she had been cathected before her bereavement: her look, the tone of her voice, her smell, the memory of her caress. The loss of physical contact carried with it the repression of the memory traces of her touch. She had been buried alive, but her tomb itself had disappeared. The hole that gaped in its place made solitude dreadful, as though the subject ran the risk of being sunk in it, body and possessions. In this connection I now think that the concept of *holding*, of which Winnicott spoke, does not explain the feeling of vertiginous falling that some of our patients experience. This seems to me to be far more in relation to an experience of psychical collapse, which would be to the psyche what fainting is to the physical body. The object has been encapsulated and its trace has been lost through decathexis; primary identification with the dead mother took place, transforming positive identification into negative identification, i.e. identification with the hole left by the decathexis (and not identification with the object), and to this emptiness, which is filled in and suddenly manifests itself through an affective hallucination of the dead mother, as soon as a new object is periodically chosen to occupy this space.

All that can be observed around this nucleus organizes itself with a triple objective:

– to keep the ego alive: through hatred for the object, through the search for exciting pleasure, through the quest for meaning;

– to reanimate the dead mother, to interest her, to distract her, to give her a renewed taste for life, to make her smile and laugh;

– to rivalize with the object of her bereavement in the early triangulation.

This type of patient presents us with serious technical problems which I shall not go into here. On this point, I refer the reader to my paper on the analyst's silence (Green, 1979*a*). I greatly fear that the rule of silence, in these cases, only perpetuates the transference of blank mourning for the mother. I will add that I do not believe that the Kleinian technique of the systematic interpretation of destructiveness is of much help here. On the other hand, Winnicott's position, as it is expressed in his article 'The use of an object and relating through identification' (Winnicott, 1971*b*), seems appropriate to me. But I fear that Winnicott somewhat underestimated the sexual fantasies, especially the primal scene, which I will take up later on.

FROZEN LOVE AND ITS VICISSITUDES: THE BREAST, THE OEDIPUS COMPLEX, THE PRIMAL SCENE

Ambivalence is a fundamental trait of the cathexes of depressives. What is the case in the dead mother complex? When I described above the affective and representative decathexis of which hatred is the consequence, this description was incomplete. What one must understand, in the structure that I have expounded, is that the inability to love only derives from ambivalence, and hence from an overload of hatred, in the measure that what comes first is *love frozen* by the decathexis. The object is in hibernation, as it were, conserved by the cold. This operation comes about unknown to the subject, in the following way. Decathexis is withdrawal of cathexis which takes place (pre)consciously. Repressed hatred is the result of instinctual defusion, all unbinding and thus weakening the erotic-libidinal cathexis, which, as a consequence, frees the destructive cathexes. By withdrawing his cathexes, the subject believes he has brought them back within his ego, for want of being able to displace them onto another object, a substitute object, but he ignores that he has left behind, has alienated, his love for the object, which has fallen into the *oubliettes* of primary repression. Consciously, he believes his reserve of love to be intact, available for another love when the occasion arises. He declares himself ready to become attached to another object, if he appears to be friendly and he feels loved by him. He thinks the primary object no longer counts for him. In truth, he will encounter the inability to love, not only because of ambivalence, but because his love is still mortgaged to the dead mother. The subject is rich but he can give nothing in spite of his generosity, for he does not reap enjoyment from it.

In the course of the transference, the defensive sexualization which took place up to now, always involving intense pregenital satisfactions and remarkable sexual performance, comes to a sudden halt, and the analysand finds his sexual life diminishing or fading away almost to nothing. According to him, it is a matter neither of inhibition nor of the loss of sexual appetite: it is simply that no one is desirable, or, if perchance someone is, it is he or she who is not attracted in return. A profuse, dispersed, multiple, fleeting sexual life no longer brings any satisfaction.

Arrested in their capacity to love, subjects who are under the empire of the dead mother can only aspire to autonomy. Sharing remains forbidden to them. Thus, solitude, which was a situation creating anxiety and to be avoided, changes sign. From negative it becomes positive. Having previously been shunned, it is now sought after. The subject nestles into it. He becomes his own mother, but remains prisoner to her economy of survival. He thinks he has got rid of his dead mother. In fact, she only leaves him in peace in the measure that she herself is left in peace. As long as there is no candidate to the succession, she can well let her child survive, certain to be the only one to possess this inaccessible love.

This cold core burns like ice, and numbs like it as well, but as long as it is felt to be cold, love remains unavailable. These are barely metaphors. These analysands complain of being cold even in the heat. They are cold below the surface of the skin, in their bones; they feel chilled by a funereal shiver, wrapped in their shroud. Everything happens as though the core of love frozen by the dead mother does not prevent the ulterior evolution towards the Oedipus complex, in the same way that the fixation will be ultimately overcome in the life of the individual. These subjects may outwardly have a more or less satisfactory professional life; they marry and have children. For a while all seems well. But soon the repetition of conflicts contributes to turning the two essential sectors of life, love and work, into failure: professional life, even when profoundly absorbing, becomes disappointing, and marital relations lead to profound disturbances in love, sexuality and affective communication. It is in any case this last which is most lacking. As for sexuality, it depends on the later or earlier appearance of the dead mother complex. It may be relatively preserved but only up to a certain point. Love, finally, is never completely satisfied. Thus, at one extreme, it is completely impossible, or, at best, it is somewhat mutilated or inhibited. There must not be too much: too much love, too much pleasure, too much enjoyment, whereas on the contrary the parental function is hyperinvested. However, this function is more often than not infiltrated by narcissism: children are loved on condition that they fulfil the narcissistic objectives which the parents have not succeeded in accomplishing themselves.

Thus, if the Oedipus complex is reached and even bypassed, the dead mother complex will give it a particularly dramatic aspect. Fixation to the mother will prevent the girl from ever being able to cathect the imago of the father, without the fear of losing the mother's love; or else if love for the father is deeply repressed, without her being able to avoid transferring onto the father's imago a large part of the characteristics that have been projected onto the mother. Not the dead mother, but her opposite, the phallic mother whose structure I have attempted to describe (Green, 1968). The boy projects a similar imago onto the mother, while the father is the object of a homosexuality which is not very structuring but makes him into an inaccessible being and, as in the familiar descriptions, insignificant or tired, depressed and overwhelmed by this phallic mother. In all cases there is a regression to anality. In anality the subject not only regresses from the Oedipus complex backwards, in every sense of the term, but also protects himself by the anal buttress against the tendency towards oral regression to which one is always thrown back by the dead mother, because the dead mother complex and the metaphoric loss of the breast reverberate each other. One also always finds the use of reality as a defence, as though the subject feels the need to cling to the presence of what is perceived as real and untouched by any projection, because he is far from sure of the distinction between fantasy and reality, which he does his utmost to keep apart. Fantasy must be only fantasy, which means that one witnesses, at the limit, the negation of psychical reality. When reality and fantasy are telescoped together, intense anxiety appears. Subjective and objective are confused, which gives the subject the impression of a threat of psychosis. Order must be maintained at any price, by a structuring anal reference which allows splitting to continue to function, and above all keeps the subject away from what he has learned of his unconscious. This is to say that psychoanalysis allows him to understand others better than to see clearly within himself. Whence the inevitable disappointment with the results of the analysis, though it is strongly cathected, albeit more often narcissistically.

The dead mother refuses to die a second death. Very often, the analyst says to himself: 'This time it's done, the old woman is really dead, he (or she) will finally be able to live and I shall be able to breathe a little.' Then a small traumatism appears in the transference or in life which gives the maternal imago renewed vitality, if I may put it this way. It is because she is a thousand-headed hydra whom one believes one has beheaded with each blow; whereas in fact only one of its heads has been struck off. Where then is the beast's neck?

A habitual preconception expects one to delve to the deepest level: to the primordial breast. This is a mistake: that is not where the fundamental fantasy lies. For, in the same way that it is the relation with the second object in the Oedipus situation that retroactively reveals the complex which affects the primary object, the mother, likewise, it is not by attacking the oral relation face on that one can extirpate the core of the complex. The solution is to be found in the prototype of the Oedipus complex, in the symbolic matrix which allows for its construction. Then the dead mother complex delivers its secret: it is the fantasy of the primal scene.

Contemporary psychoanalysis has understood, many indications attest to it – belatedly, it is true – that if the Oedipus complex remains the indispensable structural reference, the determining conditions for it are not to be sought in its oral, anal or phallic forerunners, seen from the angle of realistic references – for orality, anality or phallicisity depend on partly real object relations – nor either in a generalized fantasizing of their structure, 'à la Klein', but in the isomorphic fantasy of the Oedipus complex: that of the primal scene. I emphasize this fantasy of the primal scene to stress the difference here from the Freudian position as it is expounded in the 'Wolf Man' (Freud, 1918*b*), where in the controversy with Jung, Freud searches for proof of its reality. Now, what counts in the primal scene is not that one has witnessed it but precisely the contrary, namely that it has taken place in the absence of the subject.

In the case with which we are concerned, the fantasy of the primal scene is of capital importance. For it is on the occasion of an encounter between a conjuncture and a structure, which brings *two* objects into play, that the subject will be confronted with memory traces in relation to the dead mother. These memory traces have been forcibly repressed by decathexis. They remain, so to speak, in abeyance within the subject, who has only kept a very incomplete memory of the period relative to the complex. Sometimes a screen memory, of an anodyne nature, is all that is left of it. The fantasy of the primal scene will not only recathect these vestiges, but will confer to them, through a new cathexis, new effects which constitute a real *conflagration*, that sets fire to the structure which gives the complex of the dead mother retrospective significance.

Every resurgence of this fantasy constitutes a *projective actualization*, the projection aiming to assuage the narcissistic wound. By actualized projection I designate a process through which the projection not only rids the subject of his inner tensions by projecting them onto the object, but constitutes a *revivifying* and not a *reminiscence*, an *actual* traumatic and dramatic repetition. What happens to the fantasy of the primal scene in the case that concerns us? On one hand the subject takes account of the insuperable distance that separates him from the mother. This distance makes him realize his impotent rage at being unable to establish contact with the object, in the strictest sense of the term. On the other hand the subject feels himself incapable of awakening this dead mother, of animating her, or rendering life to her. But, on this occasion, instead of his rival being the object who had captivated the dead mother in her experience of bereavement, on the contrary, he becomes the third party who shows himself apt, against all expectation, to return her to life and to give her the pleasure of orgasm.

This is where the revolting aspect of the situation lies, which reactivates the loss of narcissistic omnipotence and awakens the feeling of an incommensurable libidinal infirmity. Of course, in reaction to this situation there will be a series of consequences which may come singly or in groups:

1. The persecution by this fantasy and hatred for the two objects which form a couple to the detriment of the subject.

2. The classic interpretation of the primal scene as a sadistic scene, but where the essential feature is that the mother either has no orgasm and suffers, or else has orgasm in spite of herself, forced to it by the father's violence.

3. A variation of the last situation; when the mother experiences orgasm, she becomes cruel, hypocritical, playing it up, a sort of lewd monster, that makes her the Sphinx of the Oedipus myth, rather than' Oedipus' mother.

4. The alternating identification with the two imagos: with the dead mother, whether she remains in her unaltered state or gives herself up to a sado-masochistic type of erotic excitation; with the father, the dead mother's aggressor (necrophilic fantasy), or he who repairs her, through sexual union. More often, depending on the moment, the subject passes from the one to the other of these identifications.

5. Erotic and aggressive delibidinalization of the primal scene to the advantage of intense intellectual activity, which restores narcissism in the face of this confusing situation, where the quest for meaning (which was lost anew) results in the formation of a sexual theory and stimulates an extensive 'intellectual' activity, which re-establishes the wounded narcissistic omnipotence by sacrificing libidinal satisfaction. Another solution: artistic creation, which is the support for a fantasy of auto-satisfaction.

6. The negation, 'en bloc', of the whole fantasy. Ignorance of everything pertaining to sexual relations is highly cathected, making the emptiness of the dead mother and the obliteration of the primal scene coincide for the subject. The fantasy of the primal scene becomes the central axis of the subject's life which overshadows the dead mother complex. This is developed in two directions: forwards and backwards.

Forwards, there is the anticipation of the Oedipus complex, which will then be experienced according to the schema of defences against the anxiety of the primal scene. The three anti-erotic factors, namely hatred, homosexuality and narcissism, will conjugate their effects so that the Oedipus complex is adversely structured.

Backwards, the relation to the breast is the object of a radical reinterpretation. This becomes significant retrospectively. The blank mourning for the dead mother reflects back to the breast which, superficially, is laden with destructive projections. In fact it is less a question of a bad breast, which is ungiving, than a breast which, even when it does give, is an absent breast (and not lost), absorbed with nostalgia for a relation that is grieved for; a breast which can neither be full nor filling. The consequence of this is that the recathexis of the happy relation to the breast that existed prior to the occurrence of the dead mother complex, is this time affected with the fleeting signal of a catastrophic threat, and, if I dare say so, it is a *false breast*, carried within a *false self*, nourishing a *false baby*. This happiness was only a decoy. 'I have never been loved' becomes a new outcry which the subject will cling to and which he strives to confirm in his subsequent love-life. It is evident that one is faced with a situation of mourning which is impossible, and that the metaphoric loss of the breast cannot be worked through for this reason. It is necessary to add a precision concerning oral cannibalistic fantasies. Contrary to what happens in melancholia, here there is no regression to this phase. What one witnesses above all is an identification with the dead mother on the level of the oral relation and with the defences which arise from it, the subject's fearing to the utmost either the ultimate loss of the object or the invasion of emptiness.

The analysis of the transference by means of these three positions will lead to the rediscovery of the early happiness that existed prior to the appearance of the dead mother complex. This takes a great deal of time, and one has to work it over more than once before marking a victory, namely before blank mourning and its resonance with castration anxiety allow one to reach a transferential repetition of a happy relationship with a mother who is alive at last and desirous of the father. This result supposes one has passed through the analysis of the narcissistic wound, which consumed the child in the mother's bereavement.

THE CHARACTERISTICS OF THE TRANSFERENCE

I cannot dwell on the technical implications which arise in those cases where one may identify the dead mother complex in the transference. This transference presents remarkable features. The patient is strongly attached to the analysis – the analysis more than the analyst. Not that the analyst escapes from it, but the cathexis of the transferential object, though it seems to present the whole scale of the libidinal spectrum, takes deep root in a tonality of a narcissistic nature. Beyond acknowledged expressions which give rise to affects, which are very often dramatized, this can be explained by secret disaffection. This is justified by a rationalization of the type 'I know the transference is but a lure, and everything is quite impossible to carry out with you, in the name of reality: so what is the use?'. This position is accompanied by the idealization of the analyst's image, whether it is a question of maintaining it as it is, or of being seductive, to attract his interest and his admiration.

Seduction takes place in the area of the intellectual quest, the search for lost meaning, which reassures intellectual narcissism and which constitutes as many precious gifts for the analyst; all the more so to the extent that this activity is accompanied by a richness of representation and a gift for auto-interpretation which is quite remarkable, that contrasts with its meagre effect on the patient's life, which is only slightly modified, especially in the affective sphere.

The analysand's language often adopts rhetoric here, which I described in an article concerning narcissism (Green, 1976): narrative style. Its role is to move the analyst, to implicate him, to call him to witness in the recital of conflicts which are encountered outside; like a child telling his mother of his day at school and the thousand small dramas which he has experienced, to attract her interest and make her participate in what he has been through during her absence.

One may guess that narrative style is hardly associative. When associations are produced, they coincide with a movement of discrete withdrawal, which makes one feel that all is said as though it were the analysis of someone else, who is not present at the session. The subject disconnects, becomes detached, so as not to be overcome by revivifying emotion, rather than reminiscence. When he gives way to it, naked despair shows itself.

In fact there are two notable traits in the transference. The first is the non-domestication of the instincts: the subject cannot renounce incestuous desire, nor, as a consequence, consent to mourning for the mother. The second, and more remarkable trait, is that the analysis induces emptiness. This is to say that, when the analyst succeeds in touching an important element of the nuclear complex of the dead mother, for a brief instant, the subject feels himself to be empty, blank, as though he were deprived of a stop-gap object, and a guard against madness. Effectively, behind the dead mother complex, behind the blank mourning for the mother, one catches a glimpse of the mad passion of which she is, and remains, the object, that renders mourning for her an impossible experience. The subject's entire structure aims at a fundamental fantasy: to nourish the dead mother, to maintain her perpetually embalmed. This is what the analysand does to the analyst: he feeds him with the analysis, not to help himself to live outside the analysis, but to prolong it into an interminable process. For the subject wants to be the mother's polar star, the ideal child, who takes the place of an ideal dead object, who is necessarily invincible, because not living, which is to be imperfect, limited, finite.

The transference is the geometric space of condensations and displacements reverberating between the fantasy of the primal scene, the Oedipus complex and the oral relation which are constituted by a double inscription: peripheral, luring and central, veracious, around the blank mourning for the dead mother. What is essentially lost here is contact with the mother, who is secretly maintained in the depths of the psyche, and concerning whom all attempts of replacement by substitute objects are destined to fail.

The dead mother complex gives the analyst the choice between two technical attitudes. The first is the classic solution. It carries the danger of repeating the relation to the dead mother by an attitude of silence. But I fear that, if this complex is not noticed, the analysis may sink into funereal boredom, or into the illusion of a libidinal life, finally rediscovered. In any event, the time for despair cannot be avoided and disillusionment will be harsh. The second, which I prefer, is that which, by using the setting as a transitional space, makes an ever-living object of the analyst, who is interested, awakened by his analysand, giving proof of his vitality by the associative links he communicates to him, without ever leaving his neutrality. For the capacity to support disillusion will depend on the way the analysand feels himself to be narcissistically invested by the analyst. It is thus essential that the latter remains constantly awake to what the patient is saying, without falling into intrusive interpretation. To establish links which are proffered by the preconscious, which supports the tertiary processes, without short-circuiting it by going directly to the unconscious fantasy, is never intrusive. And, if the patient does express this feeling, it is quite possible to show him, without being excessively traumatizing, the defensive role of this feeling against a pleasure which provokes anxiety.

For one will have understood that it is passivity that is at the heart of the conflict, here: passivity or passivation as primary feminity, feminity common to the mother and the infant. The blank mourning for the dead mother will be the common body of their deceased loves.

When analysis has succeeded in rendering life, at least partially, to the aspect of the child which is identified with the dead mother, a strange reversal will take place. Restored vitality remains the prey of a captive identification. What then happens is not easily interpretable. The former dependency of the child upon the mother, at a time when the infant still needs the adult, becomes inverted. From now on, the relation between the child and the dead mother is turned inside-out like the fingers of a glove. The healed child owes his health to the incomplete reparation of the mother who remains ill. This is translated by the fact that it is then the mother who depends on the child. This seems to me to be a different movement from that which is usually described as reparation. It has less to do with positive acts, which are the expression of remorse, than simply a sacrifice of this vitality on the altar of the mother, by renouncing the use of these new potentialities of the ego, to obtain possible pleasures. The interpretation to give the analysand then is that everything is happening as though his activity were aimed at furnishing the analysis with an occasion to interpret, less for himself than for the analyst, as though it were the analyst who needed the analysand, contrary to what had been the case previously.

How is one to explain this change? Behind the manifest situation there is an inverted vampiric fantasy. The patient spends his life nourishing his dead, as though he alone has charge of it. Keeper of the tomb, sole possessor of the key of the vault, he fulfils his function of foster-parent in secret. He keeps the dead mother prisoner, and she remains his personal property. The mother has become the infant of the child. It is for him to repair her narcissistic wound.

A paradox arises here: if the mother is in mourning, dead, she is lost to the subject, but at least, however afflicted she may be, she is there. Dead and present, but present nonetheless. The subject can take care of her, attempt to awaken her, to cure her. But in return, if cured, she awakens and is animate and lives, the subject loses her again, for she abandons him to go about her own affairs, and to become attached to other objects – with the result that the subject is caught between two losses: presence in death, or absence in life. Hence the extreme ambivalence concerning the desire to bring the dead mother back to life.

METAPSYCHOLOGICAL HYPOTHESES: THE EFFACEMENT OF THE PRIMARY OBJECT AND THE FRAMING STRUCTURE[1]

Contemporary clinical psychoanalysis has been engaged in defining more precisely the characteristics of the most primitive maternal imago. In this respect Melanie Klein's work accomplished a mutation in theory even though she was mainly concerned with the internal object, as she was able to represent it, as much through the analysis of children as through the analysis of adults of psychotic structure, and without taking account of the part played by the mother in the constitution of her imago. Winnicott's work was born of this neglect. But Klein's disciples, without sharing Winnicott's views, recognized the necessity of readjusting her ideas on this subject, starting with Bion. In fact, Melanie Klein went to the limit of what could be attributable to a group of innate dispositions concerning the respective strength of the death and life instincts present in the baby, the maternal variable hardly entering into the question. In this she was following Freud's lead.

Above all, Kleinian contributions concentrated on projections relative

---

[1] 'La structure encadrante'. This notion combines in the word 'cadre' the meaning of 'frame', but is also used in the French sense of the 'setting', 'le cadre analytique' (of technical importance in this paper). [Translator's note.]

to the bad object. Up to a point this was justified in the face of Freud's denial of their authenticity. Frequently one has noted the way he overshadowed the 'bad mother' with his immovable faith in the quasi-paradisical bond uniting the mother to her infant. So it fell to Melanie Klein to touch up this *partiel* and partial picture of the mother-infant relationship, and this all the more easily as the cases she analysed – whether children or adults –, being mainly of a maniaco-depressive or psychotic structure, revealed the evidence of such projections. Thus an abundant literature describes to the full this omnipresent internal breast which threatens the infant with annihilation, with fragmentation and infernal cruelty of all kinds, that a mirror-relation links with the baby, who defends himself, as well he may, by projection. When the schizo-paranoid phase starts to give way to the depressive position, the latter, which coincides with the unification that links the object and the ego, has as a fundamental characteristic the progressive cessation of the projec-tive activity, and the fact that the infant becomes able to assume his own aggressive drives – he becomes 'responsible' with regard to them, in a way –, which in turn encourages him to take care of the maternal object, to worry about her, to fear losing her, by reflecting his aggressivity onto himself by way of archaic guilt and with the aim of reparation. This is why, more than ever, there is no question here of incriminating the mother.

In the configuration that I have described, where vestiges of the bad object may persist, as a source of hatred, I suspect that hostile character-istics are secondary to a primary imago of the mother, where she happened to be devitalized by a mirror reaction of the child who was affected by her bereavement. This leads us to develop the hypothesis that has already been proposed. When conditions are favourable to the inevitable separation between the mother and the child, a decisive mutation arises in the depths of the ego. The maternal object in the form of the primary object of fusion fades away, to leave the place to the ego's own cathexes which will found his personal narcissism. Henceforth the ego will be able to cathect its own objects, distinct from the primitive object. But this effacement of the mother does not make the primitive object disappear completely. The primary object becomes a 'framing-structure' for the ego, sheltering the negative hallucination of the mother. Most certainly, the representations of the mother continue to exist and are projected inside this framing structure onto the backdrop of the negative hallucination of the primary object. But they are no longer *frame-representations* or, to make myself clearer, representations that fuse what comes from the mother with what comes from the child. One may as well say that they are no longer representations whose corresponding affects express a vital character, which is indispensable for the baby's existence. These primitive representations hardly deserve the name of representations. They are the compounds of barely outlined representations, probably of a hallucinatory nature rather than representative, and of loaded affects which one could almost call affective hallucinations. This is just as true in the hopeful anticipation of satisfaction as in states of want. When these are prolonged, they give rise to the emotions of anger, rage and then catastrophic despair. Now the effacement of the maternal object that has been transformed into a framing structure comes about when love for the object is sufficiently sure to play this role of a container of representative space. This latter is no longer threatened with cracking; it can face waiting and even temporary depression, the child feeling supported by the maternal object even when it is not there. The framework, when all is said and done, offers the guarantee of the maternal presence in her absence, and can be filled with fantasy of all kinds, to the point of, and including, aggressive violent fantasies which will not imperil the container. The space which is thus framed constitutes the receptacle of the ego; it surrounds an empty field, so to speak, which will be occupied by erotic and aggressive cathexes, in the form of object representations. This emptiness is never perceived by the subject, because the libido has cathected the psychical space. Thus it plays the role of primordial matrix of the cathexes to come.

However, if a traumatism such as blank mourning occurs before the infant has been able to establish this framework solidly enough, there is no psychical space available within the ego. The ego is limited by this framing structure, but in the circumstances this frame surrounds a conflictual space which strives to hold the mother's image captive, struggling against its disappearance, and alternately noting the revival of the memory traces of lost love, with nostalgia, which is expressed by the impression of painful vacuity. These alternations reproduce the ancient conflict of unsuccessful primary repression, in the measure that the effacement of the primordial object will not have been an acceptable experience, nor mutually accepted, by the two parties of the former mother-infant symbiosis.

Arguments on the theme of the antagonism between primary narcissism and primary object-love are perhaps . . . without object. All depends on the point of view adopted. That primary object-love can be observed straightaway by a third party, an onlooker, can hardly be disputed. On the other hand, that this love should be narcissistic from the child's point of view could hardly be otherwise. Doubtless, the debate has been obscured by differing uses of the term of primary narcissism. If by such a term one wishes to designate a primitive form of relation where all cathexes come from the child to start with – which is probably distinct from auto-erotism which has already elected certain erogenous zones on the baby's body – then, there is certainly a characteristic primary narcissistic structure of inaugural forms of cathexis. But if one means by primary narcissism the accomplishment of a feeling of unity which is established only after a phase dominated by fragmentation, then one must conceive of primary narcissism and object-love as two modes of cathexis centred around opposite and distinct polarities. For my part, I see here two successive moments of our mythical construction of the psychical apparatus. I am inclined to believe that the earliest primary narcissism encompasses *all* cathexes in a confused way, including primary object-love, and even what we might symmetrically call primary object-hatred, because it is this early subject-object indistinction which characterizes the type and quality of the cathexes. Thus it is that, when separation is accomplished, one may with justification oppose later primary narcissism, in the sense of designating the sole cathexes of the ego, as distinct from object cathexes.

To complete this description, I propose to distinguish a *positive* primary narcissism (attachable to Eros), tending towards unity and identity, from a *negative* primary narcissism (attachable to the destructive instincts), which is not manifested by hatred towards the object – this is perfectly compatible with the withdrawal of positive primary narcissism – but by the tendency of the ego to undo its unity and to proceed towards nought. This is clinically manifest by the feeling of emptiness.

What we have described under the name of the dead mother complex helps us to understand the failures of favourable evolution. We watch the failure of the experience of individuating separation (Mahler) where the juvenile ego, instead of constituting the receptacle for cathexes to come, after separation, relentlessly endeavours to retain the primary object and relive, repetitively, its loss, which on the level of the primary ego (which is melded with the object) gives rise to the feeling of narcissistic depletion, expressed phenomenologically by the sentiment of emptiness, so characteristic of depression, which is always the result of a narcissistic wound experienced on the level of the ego.

The object is 'dead' (in the sense of not alive, even though no real death has come about); hence it draws the ego towards a deathly, deserted universe. The mother's blank mourning induces blank mourning in the infant, burying a part of his ego in the maternal necropolis. To nourish the dead mother amounts, then, to maintaining the earliest love for the primordial object under the seal of secrecy enshrouded by the primary repression of an ill-accomplished separation, of the two partners of primitive fusion.[1]

It seems to me that psychoanalysts should have little difficulty in recognizing a familiar clinical configuration in the description of the dead mother complex, which may however differ in one or another aspect from my own account of it. Psychoanalytic theory is elaborated from a limited number of observations, and it may well be that what I have described covers at the same time sufficiently general characteristics to coincide with the experiences of others, and more singular characteristics which would be particular to the patients I have had in analysis.

Although I may perhaps have schematized the structure of this dead mother complex, it is quite possible that it may be found in more rudimentary forms. In this case one might imagine that the traumatic experience to which I have alluded has been either more discrete or more tardy, taking place at a time when the child was better able to support its consequences, and thus having only to resort to *partiel* depression, more moderate, and easier to overcome.

It may seem surprising that I should attribute such an important role to a maternal traumatism, at a period in psychoanalysis when one tends to insist a great deal more on the vicissitudes of intra-psychical organization and when one is more prudent about the role played by conjuncture. As I indicated at the outset of this work, the depressive position is a fact that is now recognized by all authors, whatever explanations they may give. On the other hand, the depressing effects of early separations between mother and infant have been described for years, without however, any general accord being established between the importance of the trauma and the observed depressive manifestations. In the dead mother complex, the situation cannot be reduced to the level of the

---

[1] What I have just described cannot fail to evoke the very interesting ideas of N. Abraham and M. Torok. However, even if, on numerous points, our conceptions converge, they differ elsewhere on a theme to which I attach great importance, namely the clinical and metapsychological significance of states of emptiness. The manner in which I attempt to account for them is taken up in a continuous thread of thought, where, after having tried to define the heuristic value of the concept of negative hallucination and proposing the concept of 'blank psychosis' with J. L. Donnet, I have in this work been engaged on the elucidation of what I call blank mourning. One might summarize these differences by stating that narcissism constitutes the axis of my theoretical reflection, whereas N. Abraham and M. Torok are essentially concerned with the relation between incorporation and introjection, with the crypt-like effect to which they give rise.

common depressive position, nor assimilated with the serious traumat-
isms of real separations. In the case that I describe, there has been no
effective break in the continuity of the mother-infant relationship.
However, independently of the spontaneous evolution towards the
depressive position, there has been an important maternal contribution
which intervenes, disturbing the positive outcome of the depressive
phase and complicating the conflict, because of the reality of maternal
decathexis which is sufficiently perceptible, by the infant, to wound his
narcissism. This configuration seems to me to conform to Freud's views
on the aetiology of the neuroses – in the wide sense –, where the child's
psychical make-up is formed by the combination of his personal inheri-
ted dispositions and the events of his earliest infancy.

FREUD AND THE DEAD MOTHER

The starting-point of this work is contemporary clinical experience
which is the outcome of Freud's writings. I have not adopted the usual
course, namely to begin by seeking out the new approaches that Freud's
work opens up, but have preferred on the contrary to leave this until the
end of the chapter. In fact it is only at a late stage, almost at the end of
proceedings, that repression in me has lifted, and that I have remembered retrospectively something in Freud that can be related to my
subject. It is not in 'Mourning and melancholia' (1917e) that I found
Freud's support, but in *The Interpretation of Dreams* (1900a).

In the last chapter of the *Traumdeutung*, and already in the first edition,
Freud tells a final personal dream concerning the arousal by dreams
(*ibid.*, p. 583). It is the dream of the 'beloved mother', and the only
childhood dream he recounted, either in this work or in his published
correspondence. In this matter, Fliess' psychical deafness made one of
Freud's dead mothers of him, after having been his eldest brother. With
the help of previous interpretations by Eva Rosenfeld and Alexander
Grinstein, Didier Anzieu (1986) gives a remarkable analysis of it. Here I
cannot go into all the details of this dream or the multiple commentaries
to which it gives rise. I shall limit myself to the reminder that its manifest
content shows 'my beloved mother, with a peculiarly peaceful, sleeping
expression on her features, being carried into the room by two (or three)
people with birds' beaks and laid upon the bed'. The dreamer awakes in
tears and screaming, interrupts his parents' sleep. It is an anxiety dream
which is interrupted on waking. The commentators who analyze this
dream, beginning with Freud himself, do not pay sufficient attention to
the fact that it is a dream that could not be dreamed, a dream that may
have been a dream, if ever it had been dreamed through, one would

almost have to construct the end. Which, the two or the three – an essential hesitation –, will join the mother in her sleep? In his uncertainty, the dreamer can stand no more; he interrupts, killing two birds with one stone – the dream and the parents' sleep. Detailed analysis of the dream, both by Freud and his commentators, ends up with the conjunction of two themes: that of the dead mother and that of sexual intercourse. In other words, we find confirmation of my hypothesis concerning the relation between the dead mother, the primal scene and the Oedipus complex; here, besides the object of desire, two (or three) people with birds' beaks are brought into play.

The associations shed light on the origin of these people derived from the Philippson Bible. Grinstein's enquiry (1972) allows one to attach this representation to figure 15 of this Bible, which was a gift of Freud's father, an illustration which becomes the object of a condensation. In effect, in this illustration, it is not a question of gods with falcons' heads, which was Freud's first association, but of two pharaonic personages of Lower Egypt – I emphasize Lower – while the birds surmount the columns of the bed. I think this is an important condensation, for it displaces the birds from the mother's bed to the head of the personages, who are two here, and not three. Thus the mother is perhaps attributed with a bird-penis.[1] The corresponding text illustrates the verse 'King David follows the litter (of Abner)', which, as Anzieu remarks, abounds with themes of incest, parricide and, I stress this, fratricide.

Anzieu interprets the two personages correctly, I believe, as the representations of Jacob Freud, grandfatherly image, and Philipp, the younger half-brother of Freud, paternal image. This because, as everyone knows, Philipp, who was born in 1836, was himself only one year younger than Freud's mother, and Freud had Philipp's eldest son Emanuel as a playmate. In the dream the dead mother has the expression of the maternal grandfather on his deathbed, on October 3, 1865, when Sigmund was nine and a half. Thus this is a bereavement which must have resonated upon the relationship between Amalie Freud and her son. The commentators have noted the erroneous dating in this dream, which was not rectified by Freud. He says he dreamed it when he was seven or eight years old, i.e., a year and a half or two years prior to the time of the grandfather's death, which is impossible. Whereas others have simply noted the error and corrected it, it seems to me a revealing lapsus, and it leads me to conclude that it is not the bereavement of the maternal grandfather that is in question, but a former bereavement. The

[1] Bird = *oiseau*, also a familiar term for penis. [Translator's note.]

significant period in the error – a gap of one and a half to two years – reminds me of another bereavement of the mother: that of Freud's younger brother, Julius, who was born when Sigmund was seventeen months old (almost a year and a half) and who died when he was twenty-three months old (nearly two). Hence the double explication: *two (or three)* people, namely Jacob, Philipp or Jabob, Philipp and *Philippson*: Philipp's son, Julius; because in 1859, when Freud was three, he dreads that his mother might be pregnant again, like the Nanny, and that Philipp might have shut her in the cupboard, have her 'boxed up'.

This, I shall note in passing, is why the young initiator, the *concierge*'s son who reveals the information on sexual intercourse, is supposedly called Philipp. It is Philipp who copulates with Amalie, and it is Philippson (Julius) who allows Sigmund to understand the relation between copulating, giving birth and dying . . . Julius' name will be forgotten, that of the painter Julius Mosen, who Freud writes about in his letter to Fliess, on August 26, 1898 (Masson, 1985). Mosen-Moses, we know what follows and also Freud's insistence on making an Egyptian of Moses, namely, to make the point clearly, the son, not of Amalie and Jacob, but of the concierge, or if need be, of Amalie and Philipp. This also sheds light on Freud's conquest of Rome, if one remembers that he quotes Livy (Freud 1900a, p. 398n) in connection with the incestuous dreams of Julius Caesar.

I understand better the importance of this age, eighteen months, in Freud's works. It is the age of his grandson playing with the wooden reel (mother dead–mother resurrected), who died when he was about two, and which will be an occasion for intense mourning, though it is minimized. This is also the age at which the Wolf Man supposedly witnessed the primal scene.

Anzieu makes two remarks which link with my own deductions. He shows, concerning the preconscious elaboration of Freud, the *rapprochement* that there is between Freud and Bion, who, besides love and hatred, gave a specific place to knowledge as a primordial reference within the psychical apparatus: the quest for meaning. Finally, he concludes that one should hold suspect Freud's insistence on reducing the specific anxiety of the dream, anxiety over the mother's death, to something else.

There is only one other hypothesis pending, that of the oral relationship. Another dream which is in keeping with that of the 'beloved mother' refers to this, where the mother appears to be alive: the dream of the 'Three Fates' (1900a, pp. 204–5). In this dream Freud's mother is making *Knödel*, and while little Sigmund is waiting to eat them she intimates that he should wait until she is ready ('these were not definite spoken words', Freud adds). One knows that his associations with this passage concern death. But further on, when he has put the analysis of the dream aside, he comes back to it, to write: 'My dream of the three Fates was clearly a hunger dream. But it shifted the craving for nourishment back to a child's longing for his mother's breast, and it made use of an innocent desire as a screen for a more serious one which could not be so openly displayed' (*ibid.*, p. 233). Probably, and how can one deny it when the context is so pertinent, but here again it would be as well to remain suspicious. One should especially question this triple image of woman in Freud's thinking, which is examined again in the 'Theme of the Three Caskets': the mother, the wife (or beloved), and death. The censure of the beloved has been much discussed in recent years (e.g. Fain and Braunschweig, 1971). I in my turn wish to point out the censure of the dead mother: the mother of silence as heavy as lead.

Now our trilogy is complete. Here we are again referred to the metaphoric loss of the breast, interrelating with the Oedipus complex, or the primal scene fantasy, and that of the dead mother. The lesson of the dead mother is that she too must die one day so that another may be loved. But this death must be slow and gentle so that the memory of her love does not perish, but may nourish the love that she will generously offer to her who takes her place.

Thus we have come full circle. It is again significant retrospectively. I have known of these dreams for many years, as well as the commentaries to which they have given rise. One and the other were printed in my mind as significant memory traces of something that seemed to me to be obscurely important, without my knowing exactly how or why. These traces have been recathected by the discourse of certain analysands whom, at a given moment, I was able to hear, though not before. Is it this discourse that permitted me to rediscover Freud's written word, or is it the cryptomnesia of this reading that made me permeable to my analysands' words? In a rectilinear conception of time, this hypothesis is the correct one. In the light of Freud's concept of deferred action, it is the other that is true. Be it what it may, in the concept of deferred action, nothing is more mysterious than this preliminary statute of a registered meaning which remains in abeyance in the psyche while awaiting its revelation. For it is a question of 'meaning', otherwise it would not have been able to be recorded in the psyche. But this meaning-in-waiting is only truly significant when it is reawakened by a recathexis which takes place in an absolutely different context. What meaning is this? A lost meaning, refound? It would give too much credit to this presignificative structure, and its rediscovery is much more of the order of a discovery. Perhaps potential meaning which only lacks the analytic – or poetic? – experience to become a veridical experience.

8

Conceptions of Affect

It is no exaggeration to say that, in psychoanalysis as it is practised today, work on the affects commands a large part of our efforts. There is no favourable outcome which does not involve an affective change. We would like to have at our disposal a satisfactory theory of affects, but that is not the case. Unable to have such a theory at our disposal, we would prefer it if we did not have to encumber ourselves with previous theoretical conceptions, in order to have an entirely new look at the question. That is hardly possible. These difficulties have two sources. The first stems from the very nature of affects. It is difficult to speak of something which is, in essence, only partially communicable, as affects often are, at any rate more so than any other phenomena observed in analysis. The second difficulty lies in our preconceptions and in the very manner in which the problems were posed from the' beginning of Freudian theory. If the first difficulty constitutes an obstacle which is not easily overcome, the second can lead to an enlightening thought. It is easier to talk about what has been said about affect, and the way in which affect has been conceived, than about affect itself. Affect constitutes a challenge to thought.

AFFECT ACCORDING TO FREUD

Freud struggled with the problem of affect all his life, especially in the period from *Studies on Hysteria* (1893–95) to *Inhibitions, Symptoms and Anxiety* (1926). I shall select four 'moments' in time from his work: *The Interpretation of Dreams* (1900); 'Papers on Metapsychology' (Freud, 1915c, d, e, 1917d, e; all written in 1915); *The Ego and the Id* (1923); and finally *Inhibitions, Symptoms and Anxiety* (1926). On these four occasions Freud fashions or refashions a global formulation of his overall concep-

This paper was written for circulation before the 30th International Psychoanalytical Congress held in Jerusalem in August 1977, and was published in *The International Journal of Psycho-Analysis* (1977) 58, in a translation by Trevor Hartnup. The main theme of the Congress was 'Affects and the Psychoanalytic Situation', and my purpose was to elucidate the theory of affect and to provide the historical background to the concept. For a fuller account I refer the reader to my book *Le discours vivant* (Green, 1973), which begins with a detailed critical analysis of Freud's notion of affect and then turns to other studies and my personal contribution, which, for lack of space, could not all be mentioned here.

tion of psychic activity, and each formulation involves taking a position on affect, clear evidence that the theoretical status of the notion cannot be examined in isolation.

From the origins of psychoanalysis to The Interpretation of Dreams

Even before *Studies on Hysteria*, in his work on 'Organic and hysterical motor paralyses' (1893c, written in 1888), Freud had introduced the notion of a quota of affect (*Affektbetrag*) which provides every impression and every psychical event with a measurable quantity, *de jure*, if not *de facto*, of which the ego seeks to divest itself either by means of a motor reaction or by associative psychical activity. It can be said that from this moment the Freudian conception of affect implicitly reveals its presuppositions.

1. Affect is a quantity (of energy) which accompanies the events of psychic life. It is a charge more or less comparable to the electric charge of a nervous impulse.

2. The ego represents the part of the psychic apparatus which serves as the homeostatic 'binding agent' and has a constant cathexis. Its role is to moderate excessive variations in psychic life, by the quota of affect when it appears to threaten its organization, which is secured by an optimal mobility of the cathexes.

3. Two paths are offered to the ego to fulfil its function: motility, that is to say the spending of the quantity by discharge (specific action) and making links by associative work. Associative psychic activity is a means of binding the quota.of affect, dividing it up, distributing it whilst fragmenting it and translating it into small quantities attached to an assembly of interconnected representations. However, the work of fragmentation has its failures: a trifling impression of no pathogenic value can afterwards become traumatic.

What will weigh heavily on the future of the conception of affect is the subordination of the subjective quality of affect to its objective expression: the quantity whose measurement escapes our knowledge.

The 'studies on hysteria' (Freud & Breuer, 1895d) are centred on the theory of blocked affect. Freud imagines a permanent dialogue between affect and representation, one mobilizing the other and vice versa, according to the circumstances. The solution offered by psychotherapy, 'talking cure', is that language can function as a substitute for action, which offers affect an alternative solution to abreaction. It is in the article 'The neuro-psychoses of defence' that Freud (1894a) gives the clearest formulation, distinguishing in a decisive fashion the *quota of affect or sum of excitation*, an expression fundamentally quantitative in nature, and the representational *memory-traces*. In his letter to Fliess of May 21, 1894 (Masson, 1985), Freud already describes three vicissitudes of affect which are different from those of representations: conversion, displacement and transposition into anxiety.

The work of the psychic apparatus in relation to affects is parallel to and different from that of representations.

The origin of affects is distinct from that of representations. Referring to Darwin, Freud conceives affect as the posthumous representative of what were, in the dim and distant prehistoric past, adaptive and highly motivated actions. We see that for Freud the organic substratum of affective life is much more pronounced than for the representations. Affect is a mnemic trace of actions which belong to the phylogenetic past of the species. On this point Freud remains faithful to tradition, which has not entirely disappeared, which sets the origin of affect back in biology and the animal basis of Man. The traces of this conception are preserved in the imagery of language.

Draft G (*ibid.*) and then the 'Project' (Freud, 1895), both written in 1895, go a long way into the research of this physiological basis of affect. It is true that when Freud was laying down the main lines of his theory, he worked from clinical experience, but the fundamental fact is that, however new the use he made of the conceptual instruments of the period, their inescapable limitations obliged him to define the new continent, whose structure he discovered, in terms of a duality which raised great difficulties. Seen in relation to consciousness or, rather, to the theories of consciousness current at his time, the Unconscious presents a double picture: on the one hand, a semantic system revealing another meaning or another way in which meaning functions and, on the other hand, a system of connotations of the meaning which is more dependent on biology and transforms the emotional quality attached to the conscious meaning not only into another quality (pleasure into unpleasure) but, in the end, into 'pure' quantity. Thus, *in the theory*, the unconscious will suffer the consequences of the difference in treatment imposed on information coming from outside or inside, giving the latter another meaning (latent, disguised or repressed) and transforming it into pure quantity without quality.

These conclusions are not surprising since, for Freud, the role of the psychic apparatus is to divest itself of excessive excitations which interfere with its functioning. However, there is a contradiction, or at least an apparent contradiction, in postulating that the psychic apparatus is disposed to seek pleasure and at the same time to avoid tension. The theoretical solution consists in a greater insistence on the avoidance of unpleasure and envisaging pleasure as a lessening of tension. This solution was to impose itself on Freud till 1924, that is for nearly thirty years. It follows from this that, having put the qualitative dimension of affect second to its quantitative variations, Freud conceives of affect above all as a disorganizing factor in the psychic apparatus. It is not negligible to recall that the initial example mentioned by Freud in the 'Project' is that of the experience of pleasure against which he sets the experience of pain (and not unpleasure). It then becomes understandable that Freud's theoretical system turns towards the search for solutions to the disorganization induced by the affect of pain, and that quantity appears as the concept most adequate to account for this. Whilst already recognizing the importance of the experience of pleasure, Freud essentially takes his position from the point of view of the detrimental consequences of affect on the functioning of thinking. This point of view enables us to attach the beginnings of Freudian theory to the dawning of a tradition which raises the exercise of scientific thought to the human ideal. One could say that the goal of the psychic apparatus is less to derive the maximum from the wealth of affective experience than to be able to master such an experience by thought and confront it with the known facts of the external and internal worlds. The whole of the third part of the 'Project' makes this clear.

Freud's thinking in the 'Project' is intricate and complex. But it is essential to arrive at an understanding of it, for the initial hypotheses determined what followed, whatever changes he brought to them later. I regret that the limits of this study constrain me to extreme condensation. This condensation is inevitable, for each notion links up with the mass of other notions and I must limit myself here solely to the examination of affect. The first time that the term 'affect' appears in the 'Project', that is, in this first attempt at theoretical systemization, it is indicated as the *reproduction* of an experience (Freud, 1895, p. 320). That is to say that affect is conceived as of one of the modalities of the organism's memory. Freud is obliged to call it into play when dealing with the 'reproduction' of *secretory* neurones which, when they are excited cause '*the generation in the interior of the body of something which operates as a stimulus* upon the endogenous paths of conduction to ψ (*ibid.*; my italics). Let us hold on to this expression, for it will surface again almost thirty years later. What Freud means is that, on the one hand, the affect is not the emotional state of the primitive experience, but its reproduction, and that the purely mnemic aspect (a recathexis of the perceptive trace), on the other hand, is not sufficient to explain the rise in the observable level which follows the recathexis of the hostile mnemic image in the experience of pain. The connection which he establishes with the secretory neurones brings in the givens of the interior of the body. It is not a question of the physical body, but of the body in its relation to the system ψ. The text does not say so very clearly, but there are good reasons for making this deduction as follows. Freud specifies firstly that these secretory neurones, in contrast to the motor neurones, do not conduct the excitation into the muscles in order to divest the psychic apparatus of it. Their stimulus on the endogenous paths of conduction to ψ does not destroy the quantity (i.e. the concept of quantity, cf. Strachey in Freud *SE* 1, pp. 289 and 392), but increases it in roundabout ways. Returning to these neurones, Freud gives them the name of 'key neurones'.[1]

Thus, the affect is the liberated product of the friction between the hostile mnemic image and the stimulus occasioned by the products of the secretory neurones, on 'the endogenous paths of conduction leading to ψ'. If we wished to go further into the implications of this theoretical draft on the theory of affect, we must go back in the text. At the end of Section 9 ('The functioning of the apparatus') Freud (*ibid.*) states that the ψ system also received excitation from the interior of the body. He therefore divides the ψ neurones into neurones of the *pallium* which are cathected from φ and the *nuclear* neurones which are cathected from the endogenous paths of conduction (p. 315). At the end of the following section (10), which precisely deals with the 'endogenous paths of conduction', Freud comes to the conclusion that these paths, which in the ψ system transport the excitation arising from the interior of the body, can receive a supplementary investment of quantity $Q\dot\eta$ and that this new contribution entails a structural modification. He writes: 'Here ψ is at the mercy of Q, and it is thus that in the interior of the system there arises the impulsion which sustains all psychical activity. We know this power as the *will* – the derivative of the *instincts*' (p. 317). It is Freud's first formulation of the drive.

We are now in a position to understand that in Freud's thinking affect corresponds to the liberating phenomenon accomplished through the medium of the groups of neurones known as secretory, or key neurones, belonging to the nuclear neurones which are excited by the evocation of the hostile mnemic image. It is essential to be clear that *it is not the mnemic*

---

[1] But which neurones? In the manuscript Freud wrote: 'the motor neurones' and the editors, Strachey as well as his predecessors, adopt the hypothesis that it is a mistake and Freud meant to write 'the secretory neurones'. That is possible. If, however, we were to respect what Freud had written, we might reach the conclusion that Freud wished to give this subcategory of motor neurones the name of key neurones which is to say that the secretory neurones, about which there is no doubt, have a key command role for motility in relation to the system ψ.

image itself (the representational basis) which induces this excitation, but its facilitation, that is to say its cathexis (cf. ibid., p. 321 *and* p. 319) *and that it is this cathexis which is at the root of drive functioning.* To be sure, Freud expresses himself here in confused terms, seeking an intermediary language between the neuronic apparatus and the psychic apparatus and no doubt he presents in but a confused way what he wants to express by the notion of cathexis, but he knows that he must not confuse the image and the cathexis. The affect therefore appears as a result of a previously established trace maintained by facilitations, and liable to be actualized upon the repetition of an experience which threatens to evoke the previous experience, whether of pleasure or of unpleasure. It corresponds to what happens on the level of the wishful states, which result in 'hallucination'. However, what must be remembered is that affect is not a direct emotional expression, but a *trace*, a *residue*, awoken by a repetition. Its difference from the desire (or the wish) lies in its manifestation by a sudden liberation, whereas the latter is the product of summation. If more attention is paid to the phenomenon of pain, it is because it is the source of the primary defence (repression). The heuristic interest in this distinction is that as far as the destiny of the wish is concerned (what will later be called hallucinatory wish-fulfilment) the psychic apparatus can allow itself to be deceived by the creation of a representation which satisfies the wish, whereas affect which gives information about the internal state of the body cannot have recourse to this expedient and finds itself obliged to maintain the primary defence. The matter is even more important because the excitation of the ϕ system can be confused with internal excitations (*ibid.*, p. 334).

The pairing of wish and defence indicated to Freud that if he wished to further the elaboration of his *theory* of the psychic apparatus – for clearly, in my opinion, he was much further forward in relation to the workings of its functioning as manifested in the clinical situation – he would have to deal the cards again. That is to say that he would have to set the affects of the moving quantity within clearly established limits in order to come to a better understanding of the transformations to which they give rise. Defence has multiple functions: biological – to avoid the disorganizing effects of pain, social – so as not to contravene moral prohibitions. In waking life these two functions are so tightly interwoven that it is difficult not only to distinguish them, but also to extricate the function which is intrinsically psychic. Thus Freud's theoretical strategy would be modified in the following way: on the one hand, by using the space of sleep as a natural limit and considering the role played in it by the wish *which has already been fulfilled*; and by regarding the dream as a product of hallucinatory wish-fulfilment and evaluating the defence in it, not only in its limiting function, but in its instigation *of transformation*: the dream work. Freud understood only afterwards what it was that he had done (see his letter to Fliess of January 3/4, 1899, in Masson, 1985). However, there would be not only advantages in this solution which pushed the theory of the psychic apparatus definitely into its proper domain.

The Interpretation of Dreams (Freud, 1900a) bounded psychic space between its two poles: the pole of perception, curbed by the abolition of information from the outside world, and the pole of motility, reduced to its most simple expression by the relative paralysis of sleep. Freud had reached his objective: his theory of the psychic apparatus, but it was at the price of a fascination with representations, to the detriment of affects. Although Freud dedicated a section to the examination of affects, in the chapter on dream work, their role is at a secondary level. The dream experience is less important than the meaning of the dream from which the interpretation springs. The expressions of uninhibited affect considered by Freud have little effect in dreams which provoke an orgasm in the dreamer, and much more in anxiety dreams. It seems that, for Freud, affects in their raw state are failures of the dream work. This dream work as applied to affects led Freud to describe diverse mechanisms which, here again, continue to distinguish carefully between the work on representations and the work on affects. A very important differentiation appears here opposing: the *repression* of the content, and the *suppression* (inhibition) of affects; although the non-suppression of affects provokes repression, which makes the differentiation relative. Furthermore, we must note that the principal mechanisms of the dream work: condensation and displacement, influence simultaneously the representations and the affective charges. Why does Freud favour the representations to this extent, linking them to repression whose action would render psychic activity 'more unconscious' than suppression? My hypothesis is that Freud, at this stage of his work, was subject to preoccupations about demonstrability – as if, in centring the problem on affect and its subjective quality, he had run the risk of finding himself reproached for a subjectivity incompatible with the demonstration of the proof. In displacing the accent on to the representations, and showing the transforming mechanisms which they are subject to, he thinks that he will be better able to demonstrate in a convincing and scientific fashion the existence of the unconscious. In this way he offers the account of an objective method, verifiable by everyone, without the analyst being accused of taking his stand on the basis of affective intuitions which are subject to caution. We know that this aim has not been achieved. On the contrary, by exposing, even partially, the resources of subjectivity, he attracted to himself men whose vocation was to respond to psychic human suffering, having understood that the determinisms at work in their own psyches could not, in the name of science, be separated from their therapeutic vocation and their thirst for truth and knowledge. One can say that, from this moment on, affects will not cease to hold an ever uncomfortable position, to the extent that, in contrast to representations, it is impossible to refer to them theoretically outside the relationship to the object, already recognized by Freud in the 'Project', precisely in connection with the experience of satisfaction. However, the section on 'Affects in dreams' (Freud, 1900a) gives us very valuable indications of the trans-formations themselves on the affective level, which we cannot enter into in detail here. Let us take note however, that Freud already makes the hypothesis that the suppression of affects in the dream might result from the confrontation at the very heart of the dream between contradictory thoughts (*ibid.*, p. 468). Thus whatever revolution it may have accom-plished in relation to the 'Project' which is so impregnated with Freud's years in the laboratory, *The Interpretation of Dreams* is still more dependent on the ideal of a pure science than is usually said.

Metapsychology

The papers on metapsychology, written in 1915, appear to us as Freud's effort to grasp the totality of his fundamental concepts, just at the moment when he is pressing on with the theoretical change which he is not slow to accomplish by 1919.

It is remarkable that in the paper which opens the collection, namely 'Instincts and their vicissitudes' (Freud, 1915c), it is never a question of representations and even less of affect. As if at the drive level that crossroads between the body and the psyche, it was not possible to proceed with this separation, since the drive is an expression of a link between psychic activity and the body. But psychic activity can only be evaluated in the opposite circumstances, namely the separation between them, and can be estimated by the extent of a demand for work.

The article 'Repression' allowed Freud to clarify his conceptions and doubtless help his disciples towards a more precise idea of his theories. There he writes: 'In our discussions so far we have dealt with the repression of an instinctual representative, and by the latter we have understood an idea or group of ideas which is cathected with a definite quota of psychical energy (libido or interest) coming from an instinct. Clinical observation now obliges us to divide up what we have hitherto regarded as a single entity; for it shows us that despite the idea, some

other element representing the instinct has to be taken into account, and
that this other element undergoes vicissitudes of repression which may
be quite different from those undergone by the idea. For this other
element of the psychical representative, the term of *quota of affect* has been
generally adopted. It corresponds to the instinct so far as the latter has
become detached from the idea and finds expressions, proportionate to
its quantity, in processes which are sensed as affects (Freud, 1915*d*,
p. 152).

I propose to understand this quotation by making the distinction –
which is not always clearly made in Freud – between the *Triebrepräsentanz*
and the *Vorstellungsrepräsentanz* or *représentant – représentation* (Laplanche &
Pontalis, 1967; the 'ideational representative' in Anglo-Saxon terminology, cf. Laplanche & Pontalis, 1973). It was therefore the *Triebrepräsentanz* which could be divided into the *Vorstellungsrepräsentanz* and
affect which, logically speaking, ought to have been given the name of
Affektsrepräsentanz. What prevented Freud from coining this word is an
internal contradiction which it appears to contain in the conceptual
framework of his time. It seems to me that today there is nothing
unacceptable in this contradiction. It is in any case less unacceptable
than the contradiction which made Freud conceive of the unconscious
state of affect only in the form of a simple quota. Why does Freud give
affects a representative status, unless the word links back to a representation or group of representations – a vicissitude of perceptions. The
representatives, according to his thinking, are mnemic traces whereas
affects are discharge processes. Indeed, seen in close-up, if every psychic
operation mobilizes energy, the ideational representatives (*Vorstellungsrepräsentanz*) have, like language, a discharge function too; less than
affects, to be sure, but nonetheless inevitable. In fact, what must be
understood is that the economy of representations is on a different scale,
or is of a different order from the economy of affect, hence the corollary
that the respective destinies of representations and affects are different.
Freud describes three possible vicissitudes of quantity which bear
witness to the evolution of his early thinking. These are: (1) the
suppression of the instinct so that no trace of it is found; (2) the
appearance of an affect which is in some way or another qualitatively
coloured; and (3) the transformation into anxiety, of the psychical
energy of instincts.

The more his ideas developed, the more explicitly Freud placed
anxiety in the context of a theory of affect. This explains the following
opinion, which in the end gives pre-eminence to affect: 'We recall the fact
that the motive and purpose of repression was nothing else than the

avoidance of unpleasure. It follows that the vicissitude of the quota of affect belonging to the representative is far more important than the vicissitude of the idea, and this fact is decisive for our assessment of the process of repression. If a repression does not succeed in preventing feelings of unpleasure or anxiety from arising, we may say that it has failed, even though it may have achieved its purpose as far as the ideational portion is concerned' (Freud, 1915d, p. 153).

If repression in 1900 had, compared with inhibition, the function of rendering the content more 'unconscious', that is to say, of keeping it further away from consciousness, with fifteen years more clinical experience the role of repression was rather to neutralize the affect of unpleasure in a more radical fashion. Let us note that Freud does not take into consideration the problem of total affective neutralization whose effect would be to impoverish the ego, which could not control the effects of repression selectively in relation to unpleasure alone.

In 'The unconscious' Freud (1915e) asks questions about the existence of unconscious feelings. He shows himself faithful to his conception of the inhibition of affects, and emphasizes the contrast between content and affect. The content can appear in disguises which make it unrecognizable in consciousness, or is subject to the incessant play of permutations in the unconscious. The unconscious processes as a whole are deprived of quality and affect is above all a question of quantity, which, in contrast to the fate of the content, can essentially be diminished (even to extinction) or admitted to consciousness, where it assumes a defined quality. Up to this point, we understand the action of repression as quantitative. But where the problem becomes more complicated is in the theory of anxiety which implies a *transformation*. It is here, in my opinion, that we must enlarge Freud's economic point of view and understand that it is not only a question of quantitative variations but *qualitative transformations* – pleasure transformed into its opposite: anxiety, a form of unpleasure. At the time the influence of the idea of internal, secretory, vasomotor discharge dominated Freud's thinking. Thus he maintained the idea that to speak of *repressed* or *unconscious* affects is an abuse of language.

The theoretical problem of affect is conceived from the angle of mastery of the potential excess. If anxiety is the result of an accumulation of repressed libido, we have no way of explaining this transformation, since clinical practice presents us with diverse forms of anxiety and different types of unpleasurable affects which are distinct from anxiety. Hysterical conversion could dispense with an explanation, since the conflict was conducted towards a non-psychic sphere. The anxiety neurosis had also been divorced from the psychic conflict. Phobia, as an evolution and expression of anxiety hysteria, seemed to show the limited capacity of representations to circumvent anxiety. But already obsessional neurosis confronted Freud with the unavoidable problem of transformation, since it gives rise to the infiltration of the conflict into the sphere of action (rituals), of thought (doubt, and the distortion of causal relationships) and moral conscience (remorse), indicating a constant struggle against the instincts.

Many theoretical difficulties could have been removed if Freud had allowed that there were several modes of being in the unconscious, for representations and for affects. The latter might either be linked with representations or remain in a floating state, but they could undergo internal transformations – or what Freud called 'affective constructions' without granting them the right to complexity.

We could sum up the question by saying that, from the economic point of view, it is affect which has to be made unconscious by inhibition and that, from the topographical point of view, it is the representations which must be kept unconscious by repression. The economic hypothesis and the topographical hypothesis which Freud constantly sets in opposition to each other both fall under the sway of the dynamic point of view. It is impossible not to see that these contradictions are not pure speculations but have their origin in the fact that psychoanalysis is born out of hypnosis and catharsis, where pre-eminence is openly accorded to affect, which had either to be repressed, by the imposition of another representation in hypnosis, or to be got rid of by cathartic discharge. Freud's concern to keep the originality of psychoanalysis safe from all contamination from the origins from which it had separated is doubtless responsible for this subordination of affect to representation in the beginnings of the discipline which he founded. The fact that today we are present at a renaissance of comparable inspirational methods (bioenergy, gestalt, primal scream) shows that the problem remains ever present. The 'talking cure' founded on the recounting of words could have led Freud to make language play a crucial role in the theory of the Unconscious, since it would be logical, within the conceptual horizons of the day, to attach language to the vicissitudes of the representations. He resisted this temptation just as he was vigilant not to let himself become involved with affect, on the paths which he had abandoned. This is the reason for which, at the end of 'The unconscious', Freud (1915e) made clear that the unconscious is formed only of the representations of things, whereas it is for the Preconscious to link up the representation of things and the representation of words.

It does not seem like chance to us that the two essays at the end of the collection deal in the first instance (Freud, 1917*d*) with dreams, dominated by considerations of representability, and in the second place (Freud, 1917*e*) with mourning in its relationship to melancholia: a narcissistic neurosis, but an affective psychosis *par excellence*. Nor is it by chance that this paper was the starting point for the work of Abraham and of Melanie Klein.

I maintain that Freud had grasped the totality of his conception at the moment when he was preparing to change it. Indeed, no later than 1919, 'The uncanny' returns to the problem of affect and introduces for the first time repetition-compulsion which announces the final theory of the drives.

The Ego and the Id (1923)

After the rearrangement of the second topographical model, Freud returned in 1923 to the irritating problem of unconscious affect. If the fact appears uncontestable to him as far as unconscious feelings of guilt are concerned, the general problem remains. We appreciate the evolution of this thinking but also the constancy of his views from the following passage in *The Ego and the Id* (Freud, 1923*b*): 'Internal perceptions yield sensations of processes arising in the most diverse and certainly also in the deepest strata of the mental apparatus. Very little is known about the sensations and feelings; those belonging to the pleasure-unpleasure series may still be regarded as the best examples of them. They are more primordial, more elementary, than perceptions arising externally and they can come about even when consciousness is clouded. I have elsewhere [Freud, 1920*g*, p. 29] expressed my views about their greater economic significance and the metapsychological reasons for this. These sensations are multilocular, like external perceptions; they may come from different places simultaneously and may thus have different or even opposite qualities. . . . Let us call what becomes conscious as pleasure and unpleasure a quantitative and qualitative "something" in the course of mental events; the question then is whether this "something" can become conscious in the place where it is, or whether it must first be transmitted to the system *Pcpt.*' (pp. 21–22).

From reading this, it seems that external perceptions and internal perceptions are now brought together rather than contrasted. What Freud underlines in this new formulation is the more primitive, more elementary character of this type of sensation, and hence their deep bodily location. In fact, it is clear that in the course of Freud's theoretical development, he is led towards more and more similar formulations with which to talk about affects and instinctual impulses, whereas previously it was rather the ideational representative (*Vorstellungsrepräsentanz*) which most often served to denote the representative of the drive (*Triebrepräsentanz*). There is therefore a slide towards affect. It is equally possible to observe this in the definition which Freud gave of the id in Lecture 32 (Freud, 1933*a*) where all reference to representations is left out of the description. He even goes as far as to maintain that nothing corresponding to an idea or a content exists in the id. Nothing but instinctual impulses seeking discharge. We may wonder what role the introduction of the death instinct into this theory may have played in this re-evaluation of the relationship between the unconscious of the first topographical frame of reference and the id of the second one, if, as I believe, these two theoretical arguments indicate concepts which are much more distinct than is usually stressed.

The question of unconscious affect is still not resolved. Returning to the text that we have just quoted and to the mysterious 'something' which Freud mentions, what happens on the pathway which affect seeks towards consciousness. 'If the way forward is barred, they [sensations and feelings] do not come into being as sensations, although the "something" that corresponds to them in the course of excitation is the same as if they did. We then come to speak, in a condensed and not entirely correct manner, of "unconscious feelings", keeping up an analogy with unconscious ideas which is not altogether justifiable. Actually the difference is that, whereas with the *Ucs. ideas* connecting links must be created before they can be brought into the *Cs.*, with *feelings* which are themselves transmitted directly, this does not occur. In other words: the distinction between *Cs.* and *Pcs.* has no meaning where feelings are concerned; the *Pcs.* here drops out – and feelings are either conscious or unconscious. Even when they are attached to word-presentations, their becoming conscious is not due to that circumstance, but they become so directly' (Freud, 1923*b*, pp. 22–23).

In my opinion, it is difficult not to think of the spirit which inspires this text as akin to the spirit of section 1 of the 'Project' on 'The experience of pain'.

This passage indicates that Freud's reservations are terminological, and that there are several modes of existence in the unconscious, which enables us to speak of an unconscious modality for affect. In the end the essential difference between affect and representation is the impossibility of affects being in direct conjunction with the verbal mnemic traces. Thus we come back to the observation which I made at the beginning about the limitations of language in giving an account of affect. Verbalization induces the affect and most often by indirect paths. Affect is an original subjective modality. For all that, its expressive dimension does not exclude it from semantic material. This supposes the transmission of a communication from affect to affect, or a consensus on the spoken messages which refer to it, whilst the information retains an allusive status.

Was the way already open towards recognizing the importance of the *quality* of affect? In any case Freud submitted to this recognition in 'The economic problem of masochism' (1924*c*) in which he admits the existence of pleasurable tensions and unpleasurable *détentes*. 'Negation' (Freud, 1925*h*) brings great precision to bear on the question: language can, via denial, ease the drain of energy due to repression and surreptitiously allow the repressed into consciousness by a simple change of sign. The intellectual admission of the repressed represents the most unattackable of the defensive manoeuvres.

Finally, in his article 'Fetishism', Freud (1927*e*) comes to the point where, still mindful of the vicissitudes of the representation and that of the affect, he completely reverses his former views. Inhibition no longer comes into it: 'If we wanted to differentiate more sharply between the vicissitudes of the *idea* as distinct from that of the *affect* and reserve the word "*Verdrängung*" ("repression") for the affect, then the correct German word for the vicissitude of the idea would be "*Verleugnung*" ("disavowal")' (p. 153).

In the end it is indeed the affect which is repressed, a term which he formerly reserved for the representation. It is evidently no coincidence that this same period saw the emergence of Freud's two principal works on psychosis (Freud, 1924*b*, 1924*e*). He discreetly gives us to understand that he has perhaps neglected the relationship between perversion and psychosis too much up to now, but the splitting, in fetishism, opens a new way towards understanding this relationship. What is only sketched out in 1927 will be made more clearly explicit in *An Outline of Psycho-Analysis* (Freud, 1940*a*) by a comparison of splitting and fragmentation.

Inhibitions, Symptoms and Anxiety (1926)

Unavoidably, the second topographic model led Freud to propose a new theory of anxiety. This theory covers a wider clinical field than previously. It had to endeavour to take account of the limited forms of anxiety in the transference psychoneuroses, as well as the less circumscribed and more incapacitating forms, the acute repetitive forms (traumatic anxiety), the forms with somatic accompaniment (actual neuroses and anxiety neuroses) and the forms where the anxiety seems to have disappeared (neutralization). It had also to recognize the diverse psychogeneses of anxiety: anxiety aroused by the threat of object loss, anxiety aroused by the loss of the object's love, and anxiety aroused by the superego. And that is limiting ourselves to the aspects met in psychoanalytic experience without getting lost in speculative discussions on the anxiety aroused by the birth trauma, or on the difference between anxiety aroused by real danger and neurotic anxiety. Qualitative considerations henceforth took precedence over quantitative ones, although the latter could be neglected and the relationship between quantity and quality still remained obscure. Witness Freud's distinctions between anxiety and mourning. I must repeat that the first topographical model of the psychic apparatus was totally insufficient to give an account of these qualitative differences. So as not to overload this exposition I have set a limit on the questions raised in the previous theoretical discussions by the production of an excess of affect. If such a thing arises it is, according to Freud in 1926, because the operation of repression withdraws the cathexis from the representation and the affect is thus set free. We may therefore take the view that the process by which repression succeeds in keeping the drive representative out of consciousness implies that the counter-cathexis (the expenditure of energy for protective purposes) is concomitant with decathexis which consists precisely in 'disaffection' from the drive representation. Freud appears to have hesitated between two ideas. The first is that this disaffection was a consequence of the decathexis of the representation and in this situation the liberation of affect by discharge was secondary in every sense of the word. The second, attested by numerous passages, is that the first and definitive aim of decathexis should bear in the first place upon the affect. The creation of the second topographical model did not abolish the ambiguities. It is remarkable to note that Freud had the same hesitations – almost the same formulae when he raised the problem of the possibility of id anxiety, i.e. anxiety which is seated in the id, as when he attempted to reply to the question of unconscious affect in 1915 and 1923. 'Addendum A' (Freud, 1926d) leaves the question open. Freud's solution to the problem, making the distinction between signal anxiety and traumatic anxiety, and attributing to the ego a role in the unleashing of anxiety, has far-reaching theoretical implications. After the division between the somatic anxiety of actual neuroses and the psychic or psychosexual anxiety of the transference neuroses, and then the conception of anxiety as an effect of the accumulation of repressed libido, the new division contrasts a notifying function in signal anxiety and an energy function in traumatic anxiety which forces the limits of the stimulus barrier and repression. Two systems are visible here: the one which complies with the meaning, and the one which complies with the force. In a way, with the signal function of affect, the theory gave affective life the possibility of functioning in a way analogous to thought. The possibility of discharge in small quantities in signal anxiety is the equivalent of the method by which the psychic apparatus tests the outside world by means of small quantities of energy (cf. Freud, 1933a, p. 89). The gulf between affect and thought is reduced, and affect is no longer solely that disturber of thought. But the view is still that excess of affect, the eruption of massive quantities of affect, has a comparable effect to that of an external trauma, when the psychic apparatus is not prepared for it. The final theory of anxiety permits us to reopen the question of the relationship of trauma or fantasy. Without considering that the theoretical readjustments correspond entirely to this, from now on it is important to understand the interest in a conception of internal trauma created by the inevitable, but *quantitatively and qualitatively variable* failure of the object to provide mothering. The *Hilflosigkeit* leaves the baby powerless in the face of the demands of his primitive drive impulses, with no possibility of moderating the imperious nature of their demands for satisfaction, which create serious disorder in which all the sense-giving structures collapse and give way to a disorganization of the ego, which is as yet incapable of putting defences to work which might avert the intolerable anxiety. One may wonder if certain serious semantic distortions of communication might not have a comparable effect.

The importance of *Inhibitions, Symptoms and Anxiety* (Freud, 1926d) arises from the fact that Freud displaced the accent from the Oedipus complex, and its corollary of castration anxiety, on to separation anxiety. A parallel movement takes us from the role of the father – does Freud not call the Oedipus complex the '*Vaterkomplex*' – to the role of the mother who is at the centre of the child's anxieties which follow the catastrophe of the threat of her loss or the despair about her prolonged absence, which is manifested in traumatic anxiety. On the other hand, she also plays the opposing role of organizer of the means of re-establishing the continuity of the psychic experience. This she performs by the double role of repairing the less disastrous effects and repairing defences which can be put to work in future situations, which may, for a long time to come, give rise to the threat of danger. Faced with the regressive tendency which follows the internal trauma due to the combined effects and joint action of the disorganization and the defence against it, the mother, in her exchanges with the baby, offers the possibility of bringing anticipation into play via the cathexis of *representative and affective* mnemic traces which will permit the development of the symbolic function. However, one may be surprised that in this general re-evaluation Freud did not take sufficiently into consideration the relationship between the narcissistic investment and investment in the object and the implications of the role of the destructive instincts in affective development.

Conclusion

The initial division between representation and affect bears witness to Freud's care in distinguishing two subsystems in the unconscious, different both in their nature and in their vicissitudes. If the representation has pride of place in the beginning, it is perhaps because of the possibilities of illustration and above all demonstration which it offers. Furthermore, it is true that representations, being more closely allied to language than affect, which eludes it much more, appear to play a greater role in talking cure. That would explain why Freud discovered the transference relatively late, and early on considered it an obstacle. The representation appears to constitute the psychic material which is most favourable to psychotherapy.

The links between affect and the body drew it more to the biological side. Freud's equation of affect = quantity = economy had the disadvantage of neglecting the part played by the mechanisms in the production of quality and at the same time failing above all to recognize the role of the transformations implied in the concept of economy. Thanks to the evolution brought about by analytic experience, affect seems to have acquired more and more importance in Freudian theory. Its proximity to the drive impulse made it a better pointer to drive activity. Modifying the relationship between the unconscious and the id, the second topographical model puts the emphasis on the drive impulses and consequently on the affects. Furthermore, affect is granted unconscious status. It can be conscious or unconscious, whilst only the representations have, in addition, the preconscious status which links them to language. But analytic treatment using the transference, gives affect an increasingly large part to play. What has been neglected by the critical analysis of Freudian epistemology is the relationship between the undeniable shift of emphasis towards the affect–drive impulse complex and the final drive theory. Freud makes it clear that the energy at the source of production of anxiety is neutral and the fact that elsewhere he has also envisaged neutralization as a result of the work of the death instinct has theoretical consequences which have not been noticed. Anxiety, the prototype affect of analytic theory, now situated in the ego, works on two fronts: signal anxiety which brings the functioning of affective life more in line with that of thought, and traumatic anxiety which remains the expression of psychic disorganization which is unspeakable, in the strict sense of the word. This final theory of anxiety leads on to consideration of the maternal object as a source of semantic stimuli and at the same time as a solicitor of economic transformations. The meaning and the force combine their effects to help the child create a varied system of qualitatively differentiated affects rich in nuances whose value in communication is inestimable. There remains the displacement of emphasis from the *Vaterkomplex* on to the mother's role, which necessitates a link between a complex, from which Freud withdraws none of its organizing value in structuralization, and the relationship to the primary object, a link which one cannot reconcile with a strict genetic point of view. Nevertheless it remains that affect keeps its place as the *primary system* in Freudian theory, regulated by the pleasure-unpleasure principle, whose possibilities of transformation and evolution offer less room for man-oeuvre than the representations, whose evolution leads to the function of language and its relationship to thought. But, on the other hand, because the aim of psychoanalysis is to gain access to the most fundamental systems of psychic life, those which regulate the basic functioning of the psychic apparatus, the place taken by affect in the evolution of the theory is completely justified. As Freud gives us to understand in 'Negation' (1925*h*), there remain to be established the foundations of affective logic so as not to cut off the logic of the unconscious representations from that of affective life.

AFFECTS SINCE FREUD

Even in Freud's lifetime affect gained more and more ground in the clinical, theoretical and technical elaborations of his disciples. This is implicit in the work of Abraham, in some of Jones's work (e.g. Jones, 1929) and above all in the last period of Ferenczi's work (from 1929 to 1933). This orientation accompanied the growing difficulties encountered in the treatment of certain patients, with the result that less importance was given to the search for a solution to an enigma in the infantile conflict – as in the case of the 'Wolf Man' (Freud, 1918*b*) – and there was pressure to learn more about the early stages of development in the child, especially because analysts were having more and more to do with patients presenting more marked regressions. With the benefit of experience, they were in a better position to discover the foundations of regressions of a neurotic type. But what is most characteristic of the development of post-Freudian writing is that the homogeneity of his theoretical construction gives way to a diversified development in directions determined by the theoretical preferences of the dominant figures of the post-Freudian era of psychoanalysis. Hence a certain confusion for the present-day reader who would like to find unity in this diversity. From now on I shall abandon the historical point of view and cite the principal contributions, regrouping them according to the perspective which they take.

Hartmann's perspective, the genetic, structural and adaptive points of view

If Hartmann wrote little about affect, his theoretical views have influenced a number of authors, especially Anglo-Saxon ones. The best known is Rapaport (1953). His conception is psycho-biological, endeavouring to reconcile the hereditary predispositions, the function of discharge and the socio-communicative function. What creates a problem in such a task is the interpretation of concepts which are turned in a psychological direction. Ego psychology rather than psychoanalysis of the ego. The fact that this conception seeks to root its hypotheses in biology takes nothing away from its psychological style of thought, which is equally true of the sociological aspects which are occasionally incorporated. One can wonder if the addition of the genetic, structural and adaptive points of view to the three metapsychological points of view has not increased the movement either by the work of Hartmann himself, or by the fact that the psychologists (like Rapaport) found psychoanalytic theory more acceptable. In wanting to clarify the theory, they have suppressed contradictions which would have been better respected until psychoanalytic experience allowed a better formulation of what they concealed. A fruitful obscurity is worth more than a premature clarification. Perhaps it is paradoxical that we accord such a role to psychologists in a psychoanalytic movement which endeavours, on the other hand, to preserve itself from such an influence. But that is not the question, which is, rather, to ask whether in a psychoanalytical group dominated by medical training, psychology does not appear of necessity as the only compatible discipline to which one would delegate the task of resolving problems to which medical training offers no rigorous approach. It is remarkable that in Rapaport, more faithful to Freud in letter than in spirit, the relationship of the affect to the signal never leads to a reflection on the *sign* and in particular on language, in its relation to affects. If the economic point of view is maintained, it is not the object of a reflection on the processes of psychic transformations. The work as a whole comes under the criterion of a hierarchical development of 'motivations'.

Sometimes, however, the genetic orientation enables us to gather some valuable reflections based on observed facts, as in Engel's (1962) work which divides reactions to trauma into two types, active and passive, and describes depression withdrawal, as the ultimate reaction to catastrophe in immobility, and narcissistic withdrawal to a pre-object stage of undifferentiation. The necessity of speaking of a biological basis is reinforced in the work of Moore (1968). The adaptive function is similarly defended by Schur (1968), who is not afraid to advance the view that certain autonomous apparatuses serve the development of the id as well as that of the ego. It is in this spirit that a cognitive function may be recognized in affect, with signal anxiety as an expression of this. We must also credit Hartmann with the introduction of the concept of the *self*, understood in a different way by the English school. The exchanges between self and object pose the problem of the respective cathexis of each of them, the cathexis of the self-presentations and the self-images. The drop in this category of the cathexis is at the root of an id impulse responsible for affective storms. Affects in relation to the narcissistic wound (shame and humiliation) bear witness to the failure in the mastery of the self, an opinion already defended by Fenichel. The role of the maternal object, as an external object, takes a position of importance here and the subsequent internalization is partially explained, but on the other hand, the fantasy experience seems to be underestimated. According to this line of thinking, the ego becomes more and more a *central agent* of modulation and affective regulation, serving aims of adaptation to reality. If one can maintain that this orientation is only the development of late Freudian views on the ego, one cannot fail sometimes to have the feeling that the psychic apparatus is reduced to mechanisms whose functioning is simplified to too great a degree. It all happened as if the fundamental structure of affect had returned to the domain of biology outside psychoanalysis, and as if ever since Freud placed the seat of anxiety in the ego, it is this instance which has been almost the exclusive object of interest for psychoanalytic contributions of this sort, in which the ego is seen in relation to control of affects rather than in relation to the rich, varied and contradictory subjective experience of affects. This explains, in particular, the scepticism of American writers about the metapsychological conceptions of the English school, when they take primary affects back to the primitive object relationship instead of abandoning them to biology, and postulate the existence of a fantasy world to which the psychoanalysts from the other side of the Atlantic give but limited credibility, if any at all. The nub of the question is that there is no convergence of views about what is meant by an object in the diverse theoretical orientations.

On the other hand, the reference to the mechanics of the psychic apparatus would attract the opposite criticism. It is not reprehensible in itself *if one intends to place oneself on the highest level of theoretical generality*. But most frequently the question is approached only at an intermediary level which attempts to make the psychic apparatus as far as possible like a neuro-psychological apparatus, *at the level of model construction*. So, it is not by chance that Freud always mistrusted this orientation and it is certainly not because he accorded less influence to biology. If we had opted for such an orientation, we would doubtless have had to go much further, as G. Klein (1967) understood. Unfortunately, the stamp of psychological inspiration marks this path too. Other studies, however, whilst based on Hartmann's thinking, give the feeling, at least as far as I am concerned, of bearing clinical truth. The earliest of them is that of Edith Jacobson (1953) and is justly renowned. If her classification of affects is based on Hartmannian notions (I should rather say those of Hartmann, Kris and Loewenstein) of intra- and intersystemic tensions and if she, too, places the adaptation and mastery frame of reference at the centre of her work, her contribution, born out of remarkable clinical experience of affective psychoses, calls into question once more Freud's idea of discharge, by the substitution of a dynamic view in which the process is more important. In fact, affect must be taken in its evolutionary curve. It is born of tension and develops to discharge. Tensions and discharges coexist simultaneously in diverse parts of the psychic apparatus. The pleasure principle regulates the variations about an axis of average tension, starting with the extreme swings of the pendulum to pleasurable and unpleasurable affects. Jacobson gives equal interest to pleasurable and unpleasurable affects. Her perspective gives precedence above all to a homeostatic view of affective regulation, without confining herself to a purely phenomenological view.

Similarly, it is a homeostatic standpoint which defines the point of view of Joffe & Sandler (1968) and of Sandler (1972) who nevertheless insist above all on the constitution of emotional states of safety, whose genesis is envisaged according to their psycho-physiological base. The progressive differentiation of these states is concomitant with the child's representational world which crystallizes out of his automatic beginnings. These states of safety are learned through the experience of live feeling-states and are enriched by a gamut of nuances which distinguish them from the gratifications of primitive drive impulses, especially after their eruption, and by means of the capacity to differentiate need-satisfaction. The disorganizing role of anxiety lowers the feeling of safety and favours the return of maladaptive reactions. We might say that

Sandler has in mind above all the narcissistic roots of affect. Adaptation is necessary for the preservation of a basic state. The function of signal anxiety ensures the individual's safety by adapting its reaction to the circumstances of the danger. A scanning of information from internal or external sources is already constantly active to prevent the appearance of the conscious affective experience. The affective function is in a permanent state of change, one might add a permanent state of alert, evaluating moment by moment the respective images of self and object and striving for ideal states of the ego (the ego ideal). Any excessive departure from this state of grace is rejected, giving rise to a painful experience which for a long time can only be denied. The contradictions can multiply between a body state in disequilibrium and an ego finding its equilibrium in an adaptive solution of a defensive nature, which would take account for certain psychosomatic symptoms.

We can relate the preceding work to that of Peto (1967) which is dedicated to the study of affect control. The central idea advanced is also heir to the conceptions of Hartmann and Nunberg on the synthetic function of the ego. But the interest of Peto's work, whose clinical inspiration is tangible, lies in the picture he gives us of the affective processes of the mastery–submission dyad. A dialectic view of the analytic situation allows us to form an idea of the observable variations between the affect, which remains integrated with the other elements of the analytic process on the one hand, and on the other hand archaic and tempestuous affective states which exceed on all sides the means of containment in the psychic apparatus. One can throw down a bridge here between Peto's conceptions and those of Bouvet (1960). Valenstein (1962) produced an original conception of what he calls 'affectualization'. This can be observed when one is present at an agitated dramatization of the affective experience which blocks all insight, turning the analytic situation back into a cathartic experience and preventing any durcharbeiten ('working through').

A sure link unites resistance as a mode of defence to Bouvet's (1956) 'trop éprouver' ('excess of feeling') and also to Lewin's (1964) concept of screen affects, the affective homologue of the blank dream screens he described. Lewin successfully demonstrated the work of affective decondensation to which we devote ourselves in relation to affective constructions in order to distinguish the functional and structural differences between affect and intellect.

Valenstein, however, thinks that once a certain number of affective crises have been passed through, some real analytic work is possible. The theoretical inferences to be drawn from this about the idea–affect complex in the unconscious – and here we find views which are closer to Freud than to Hartmann – lead us to take into consideration the type of cognition appropriate to affect. He recommends to our attention the concept of *conation*, the expression of a wish-force tending towards action.

The study which seems farthest from the Hartmannian point of view is that of Schafer (1964). This critical article is too phenomenological in inspiration perhaps, but its merit lies in the description of affect from a non-genetic perspective. He underlines the importance of the complexity of affects, the ambiguity with its implications for their expressive value (whose existence is no more proof of authenticity than the absence of affects is necessarily a sign of dissimulation) and the necessity of considering them as part of a configuration. He calls in question the virtues of mastery of affect as a criterion of maturity. This purpose, according to Schafer, is served rather by their complex, contradictory and ambiguous nature. Finally, their communicating function is not only in relation to other people. On this point Modell (1971) tried to correct our negligence of the role of affects in collective psychology. But apart from this intercommunicating function, affects are at work in communication with oneself. Rangell (1967) was amazed that affects had too often been absent as a theme in analytic literature. If that is true, it is perhaps because the advancement of our thinking about affect can no longer proceed in isolation, but requires us to pay attention to those difficult cases where the affective dimension of the problem is in the foreground, but is itself subordinate to a perspective which implicitly encompasses it. It is the way followed, for example, by many psychoanalysts of the British Society.

I will now conclude my comments on this orientation of thinking, which I have regrouped somewhat arbitrarily under the heading of Hartmannian influence, because that seems to me to indicate the dominating tendency, and make more general remarks which spring from my reading of the most recent contributions (Pulver, 1971; Brenner, 1974; and Castelnuovo-Tedesco's 1974*b* report, of a panel of the American Psychoanalytic Association). One may wonder whether the absence of an accepted theory of affects is not due to the limitations of the analytic field. – What could be said about affects in the realm of classical analytical knowledge has reached a point where if it is not impossible to exceed it, it is at least unexceeded. Whatever may be the more or less useful clarifications (Pulver, 1971; Castelnuovo-Tedesco, 1974*a*) it all takes place as if respect of clinical facts could not involve more than a phenomenological description, paraphrased in metapsychological terms which add nothing to it. On the contrary, the use which is made of metapsychology in this context does not clarify the problem any more, it restricts it. What transpires from these debates is most frequently the need for unification at any cost. Similarly, when Brenner (1974) proposes a unified theory of affects, he can only do it from a position which supposes the problem is resolved, since he includes in the structure of affect the combination of feelings *and ideas*, when the whole question is to know how the 'idea' which forms an integral part of the nature of affect differs from what is conventionally called an idea, the content. If Freud came up against the enigma, it is just because he was fully aware of its implications on the level of mental functioning, that is to say of its repercussions on the unity of psychic processes. Faced with this difficulty, some American writers tend to seek support in paths of research capable of completing knowledge acquired in analytic practice. Quite naturally they go to developmental studies in search of complementary information, when these studies can teach us only about the baby's or child's *behaviour* and research conditions impose limitations on the researcher's empathy. It follows, among other things, that the implicit conception of the ego is more and more turned towards action, whereas the analytic situation draws the best of its learning from the very fact that the subject is constrained by the analytic relationship to put action in parentheses. When the need is felt to reach a more general degree of conceptualization, three directions present themselves:

(*a*) the *psychoneurological* direction (Moore, 1974) which attaches affect to cerebral or psycho-physiological structures (the relation of affect to automatic motor reactions or reflexes);

(*b*) the *information* direction (Rangell, 1974) which seems not to take account of the fact that the theory of information is built on the exclusion of affect; and

(*c*) the *psychological* direction which endeavours to put together the viewpoints of a linear conception of development and phenomenological introspection, which it joins by a disguised behaviourism.

The sum of these directions converge around the central concept of adaptation, even though affect, of all the components of the human psyche, is the one whose value to adaptation is the most fragile if one keeps to a strict view of the concept. One remains struck by the reticence of the American authors to call on the role of the analyst's feelings in the analytic relationship, not in the limited perspective of the 'tools' of treatment, but in a context where practice and theory could come together to understand the joint work of affect and verbalization and the implications which might be drawn from it as to the domain of communication and intrapsychic and intersubjective semantics. In this respect it must be noted that this absence of reference to the analyst's psychic functioning goes along with a very restrictive conception of the concept of object.

The object relations perspective and the influence of Melanie Klein

The way followed by the psychoanalysts of the British Society has been to endeavour to deepen the nature of the affective experience by taking less distance or fewer theoretical precautions in order to restore the quality such as the analyst experiences it through his patient. The piece of work by Jones (1929) which I have already referred to, developed above all the notion of the covering up of diverse types of affects by one another. What we retain is especially the notion he discovered of *aphanisis* which already presaged the clinical configurations which have been in question during recent years: the crushing of affect, massive inhibition including a drastic prohibition against experiencing the slightest libidinal gratification, petrification, etc. Although what Jones described does not entirely coincide with the matters in question today, I think it is legitimate to consider that Ferenczi's work of the same period already saw the precursory signs of what we recognize in the affective weaknesses of our most disturbed patients. But it was above all the affect-discharge relationship which was called in question by Glover (1939) and Brierley (1937). Glover pursued his research towards what Freud, as early as 1915, had called 'affective constructions' but which he would later prefer to define in terms of fusion of affects. The affects Glover took an interest in, probably under the influence of Melanie Klein: bursting, explosive affects of disintegration – are familiar to us today. His description should, in my opinion, be understood in his general conception of the nuclei of the ego.

It is with Brierley (1937) that affect will find its best advocate. She was one of the first to understand that one speaks of *object cathexes rather than of affective charge of ideas* and to underline the inadequacy of the quantitative standpoint. This article reflects remarkably the tendency of the English school to tie primary affective development to object relations. The cathexis precedes differentiation and cognitive discrimination. We see that, for writers of the English school, it is not a question of pushing affect back towards biology but, rather, of setting it in a framework of a primitive sensibility the vestiges of which must be sought by the analyst in the analytic situation through the transference and countertransference. Paula Heimann (1950) demonstrated its role as an affective instrument, which implies that the analyst does not retreat in the face of his own involvement in the relationship and that he undertakes to investigate his own affects as empathic echoes of those of the analysand, and that he lives them in a sort of identification with the self of the analysand or identification with the effect that the self wishes to have on the object. In this sense Brierley's article really opens a new era in the understanding of affect. According to her, the construction of primary affects is linked to their carriers. We are reminded of Winnicott's concept of 'holding'. The recognized role of the primitive mechanisms of introjection and projection as well as the correlations which result from the ego's relations with the good and bad objects are clearly described here. Rather than defend an idea of psychic maturity which might smack of normative morality, she remarks, on the contrary, that no one completes ego integration. There is no doubt about the existence of unconscious affects, or of 'pre-affects', as she puts it. In any case affective language is older than speech. This observation, already made by Freud, is retained in our idea of an affective *language*. Rycroft (1968a) had already pointed out that one of the peculiarites of affects was that they were felt by others and that they induced in other people identical or opposing reactions. And one can subscribe unreservedly to Brierley's formula when she designates the qualities necessary to analytic practice as those of a '*combination of intelligent insight and affective comprehension*'.

If only a few indications of Melanie Klein's influence are to be found in Brierley's article, one must acknowledge that her thinking has a great influence on her colleagues in the British Society. She has written little about affect but she has stated that the imagery which she uses to describe the functioning of the psychic apparatus relates to what she calls, for want of a better term: 'memories in feelings' (M. Klein, 1957). One might think that Melanie Klein has substituted for the classical Freudian opposition of representation and affect, *the elementary unity of fantasied affect* underlying what the patient says. Melanie Klein's work is undoubtedly important because of what it contains in itself, but it is even more so because of the impetus she has given to others. Bion, at the heart of the Kleinian group, placed affects in a state of connexion with thought. In the patient's mouth 'I feel that' substitutes for 'I think that' (Bion, 1963). Bion demonstrates in depth how massive amounts of affect, expelled by projective identification, return to the psychic apparatus, which is incapable of mastering these excessive quantities of accretions, which forbid thinking of the no-breast and alter the development of thought. Fairbairn (1952), taking his distance from the Kleinian system, seems above all to challenge the unconscious fantasying which Melanie Klein uses to picture the infantile psyche. So the paradox is that, in putting more accent on schizoid factors in the personality, that is to say on the defences against expression of affect, he penetrates more deeply into the affective universe by making a radical break with Freud's biologically inclined thinking. In this respect his studies of hysteria have value as a paradigm. The question of orthodoxy or heterodoxy in Fairbairn seems to me secondary to the progress which he enables psychoanalysts to accomplish, who, like Winnicott, saw their work more as an extension of that of Freud. Winnicott (1945), without having strictly speaking elaborated a conception of affect, only talks in fact about primary affective development. The importance that Winnicott accords in treatment to affects in the two partners in the analytic situation, led him to write his lucid article on 'Hate in the counter-transference' (1949). His approach leads to the thought that, no more than the analytic process can ignore the analyst's affects, the conception of development – in the first place affective development – cannot exclude the mother's affects and her capacity to tolerate, sustain and relay the affective messages to the baby, in a form which can be integrated by his self. Henceforth any conception of affect leaves its individual isolation and enters into the setting of affective communications whose specificity remains to be defined. With Winnicott it is not only the way of conceiving affect which changes, but there is also a new inspirational thought which replaces the specialized terminology of the category of affects, by reference to the living experience of the analytic climate, at those moments when regression draws the two partners into a world where it is no longer pertinent to talk of affect as an isolated fact. No more, according to him, than it seems adequate to use in analytic communication Kleinian fantasy structures, which, when communicated to the patient, impose on his living experience a restriction which is potentially damaging to the development of the process in the analytic setting. In the first place this is because these interpretations only permit the patient to make sense of what he lives at the expense of a depersonalization of the relationship, and imprisonment within the interpretative matrices which translate the unknown into the already known, and are revealed as inappropriate to a mode of relating in which the analyst, by his tolerance of the regressive needs of the patient, might facilitate evolution by declining to fix the experience in a mould which limits his freedom of movement in his psychic functioning. For the patients, who are dependent on affective communication, seem to need a sharing of their experience, which does not mean collusion with it, in a non-intrusive exchange which gives them a feeling of existence, in which sufficient space can be formed, albeit manufactured space, for their silent self, and where the defensive meaning of their state can be acquired without there being a compression of their inner world. It is quite possible that the functioning of the psychic apparatus described by Kleinian authors is largely correct. But this correctness is the product of a certain point of view which hides the only question which interests us: namely, how to modify this functioning. This implies that specific powers of communication with the patient should be found which are not unacceptable to him and which require a modification of the means of perception by which we apprehend the patient and simultaneously an interpretative technique which does not speak to him from the outside, even if it seeks to communicate what is most intimate to him. What can be admitted by the patient must conform, at least in part, to the way in which he received in himself the gifts of his internal world, as well as those of the external world. That is what springs from the contributions emerging from the way opened by Winnicott with Milner (1968) and Khan (1969, 1971).

Affect and language in the theoretical debates in France

If it is true that the problem of affect has been tackled above all in France in the context of the controversies around the work of Lacan, two points of view outside this debate must nevertheless be mentioned. Mallet (1969) remains faithful to the classical Freudian conception. The interest of his work rests on two points: on the one hand, the division between appetitive affects (*affects appetitifs*) and inhibitory affects, of which anxiety is the prototype, which give rise to the division between affects accepted by the ego and affects refused by the ego, and on the other hand, the distinction between appetitive affects and reactive affects (*affects réactionnels*). The complexity connected with affects comes from the fact that it is affect which enables the ego to experience itself by means of its feeling-states and in its relationship to the body. It is, therefore, information for the ego, but information which puts it under an obligation to take up a position. On the other hand, it gets out of the control of the ego which can inhibit action but is constrained to let itself be 'inflamed' by the affect. Whilst the ego can defend itself against the drive by modifications of aim and substitutions of object, defences against affect do not offer the same possibilities of a disguise which also allows indirect satisfactions. It is also by escaping control that affect assumes value for other people as a communication, which necessitates new defensive measures insofar as it carries inopportune and untimely messages. It is understood that the circuit of affective exchanges between their source (the id) and their domain (the ego), and at the very heart of the ego in relation to the object, gives rise to conflictual tensions more ungovernable than in the case of representations.

Whilst Mallet describes affective functioning at the most general level, Bouvet (1956) endeavours to define the distinctive characteristics of the pregenital structures, where the massive, stormy nature of affects is in the foreground. They express absolute demands, unencumbered by nuances and permeated with excessive projections. Like Valenstein, he notes the defensive character of emotional discharge in which affect is dissipated by the discharge so as to avoid elaboration, and the intense revival is accompanied by no work in depth but seeks immediate relief by exteriorization. In fact it is affective lability rather than the intensity of the discharge which is responsible for this kind of resistance.

The interest of Lacan's (1966) study lies partly in its stimulation of studies of affect. In spite of more and more numerous translations of Lacan's work and the interest aroused by them, this author's thinking remains, on the whole, not very well known. It is not my intention to examine it in detail in this paper, but only to pinpoint his position as regards affect. From this point of view we must remember that Lacan's fundamental thesis, 'The unconscious is structured like a language', shows links with changing ideas about structuralism in recent years, which has almost nothing in common with the meaning of the structural point of view in contemporary psychoanalysis. Lacan explicitly and clearly maintained that it was fruitless to try to give conceptual status to affect as an expression of undifferentiated psychic functioning (Lacan, 1966, p. 799). The originality of Lacan's position in modern structuralizing comes from his conception of the signifier (le signifiant). This term, which F. de Saussure uses to designate one of the two parts which together compose the sign (the other being what is signified, le signifié) refers to the unity of phonic matter and becomes, in the Lacanian system, the atomic element of the modality of meaning itself in the Unconscious, whose functioning enables us to hypothesize retroactively about the subject. Subject and structure are thus in a dialectic relationship. There is no sense in placing the subject outside the functioning of the structure. According to him, it is important to distinguish significance, attached to the performance of consciousness, from the action of the signifier (signifiant). Another of his formulae which has attained fame is: 'the signifier (signifiant) is that which represents a subject for another signifier'. Schematically, there are two 'atomic unities' (unités atomiques) of meaning between which an agent intervenes. The agent is considered in the perspective of the unconscious but supposes a relationship as in every intelligible connection and is represented by the very fact that *there* is a relationship. Finally, Lacan takes up again, in his system, the fundamental theoretical fact of psychoanalysis which Freud calls *binding* (when he talks of energy) or *association* (when he talks of analytic material) whilst seeking to give it a conceptual base. Basically, this procedure appears perfectly correct – but it is faulty insofar as Lacan seems obliged to lean on the structure of language to make his theoretical system work. If he is obliged to do it, it is certainly because, for modern linguistics, the classification of signifiers, in the Saussurian sense, is nothing other than the structuring of the system. The question is to know whether the dependence on words of the essential elements in analytic communication is sufficient to justify the creation of a psychoanalytic model whose paradigm is language, even if Lacan's model departs from the type of model which the paradigm relates to in linguistics. For example, one cannot rule out that the future of linguistic research – I am thinking of Chomsky's (1968) concept of the underlying structure – may come to consider the connection of the matrices of language in their relationship to matrices foreign to the language, which might require a revision of the theory of information starting from the concept of a plurality of codes. A psychoanalyst might at this point interpose, alongside the problem of the interaction and the intermingling of the diverse codes amongst each other, the essential hypothesis of conflict. This is a tendency which seems to be indicated in recent interdisciplinary confrontations from which psychoanalysts have unfortunately been missing (the Centre Royaumont Conference, see Morin & Piatelli-Palmarini, 1974). Analysts who have not accepted the postulates of this psychoanalytic approach have sought to show its inadequacy of inaccuracy by taking up what it leaves out. They have defended a different conception of the connexions between the drive and the unconscious (de M'Uzan, 1967*a*, *b*), or have re-established the right of affect to better consideration in relation to clinical experience. Thus, David (1966, 1967*a*, *b*) even described a new clinical phenomenon which he called 'affective perversion' (David, 1972) where the process of auto-affectation and the pleasure drawn from the bottling-up of affective consummation is preferred to the realization of instinctual impulses. Viderman (1970) reminded us of the indissociable activity of force and meaning in analytic experience and indicated precisely that the place of language in psychoanalysis could not be conceptualized within the framework of linguistics.

My own position (Green, 1962, 1966, 1970*a*, 1973) differs from those who have gone before in that I attempt a critique of the Lacanian system on the basis of its own hypotheses, some of which are accepted by myself.

For it is not sufficient to defend affects as if the situation were the product of some neglect on the part of the Lacanian system. On the contrary, this system must be approached as a sign of the necessity to re-evaluate certain of its principal positions. It stresses that taking language as a frame of reference for the Unconscious obliges us to take account of the situation in which words are faced with communicating about an experience which by definition is impossible to translate into words. I underline that if the analysand makes himself known by his words, it is completely impossible to give the words equal weight because of the different states of mind in which they are spoken. So in any case, reference to language implies a homogenous body of phonemes to sentences and a unified structure which is that of language itself. However, the unconscious is constituted of heterogeneous elements: representations of things and affects constitute its core. But this core relates to the body, to action and to language. Hence the existence of chains of representations of things and words, affects, body-states and actions. As Freud (1913*j*, p. 177) says: 'the unconscious speaks more than one dialect'. If one considers all the material not as signals but as meanings, one sees that, on the one hand, this borrowed term implies such an extension that it cannot belong to the vocabulary of linguistics, and that the 'chain of signifiers' (Lacan: *chaine signifiante*) implies the *heterogeneity of the signifiers*. I draw from this the theoretical consequence that since a semantic (rather than cognitive) function is accorded to affect, affect should take the place of meaning, if we cannot find another replacement term to designate the sense element, the word 'sense' being employed here, of course, in the setting of a structural psychoanalytic semantic. The participation of affective forms of communication in analytic material need not lead to language communication and non-verbal communication being set in opposition by cutting them off from each other but, on the contrary, should lead to a search for their common foundations from which diverse modes of intelligibility assume different modalities. All this implies the study of different types of liaison or concatenation and conflictual interaction which results from it, and which is itself subordinate to the fundamental conflicts of the psychic apparatus, which our conceptual tools translate unskilfully into theory, obliging us to make more or less appropriate theoretical choices. Take as examples the ego and adaptation in Hartmann, unconscious fantasy and object relations in M. Klein, the being and the experience in Winnicott. Reference to language, if it has the merit of putting the accent on the structure – which is indeed of decisive importance insofar as it relates to the structure of unconscious intelligibility – avoids the essential questions posed by structuration: What can be structured, by what, by whom? to arrive at what type(s) (in the singular or the plural) of structuring? Is it necessary to finish up with a more general structure, a place to accommodate the diverse structurings – or should one, on the other hand, accept the juxtaposition of structures which do not communicate with each other except by intermittent links? What is the meaning of pragmatic, if not theoretical, reference to the notion of integration in psychoanalysis? Is it only a question of a meeting between the subject and his structure, or is some new functioning installed?

All these questions lead back to the process of meaning in relation to the Other. But, then, the process of meaning is linked to the existence of the 'chains' of affect, a reformulation of Freud's concept of '*binding*' whether this applies to energy or to representations. However, this chain is not as in linear language: it is at the same time polygraphic (by virtue of the heterogeneity of the material in the communication) and polyphonic, putting diverse types of code into communication with each other: affective, representative and linguistic. This structure implies that affect is understood, like language, as a product of *psychic work*. Indeed, the economic point of view cannot, in these circumstances, be understood only as the expression of quantity but, rather, as the principle of *transformation of quantities and of quantities and qualities between each other*. Language without affect is a dead language: and affect without language is uncommunicable. Language is situated between the cry and the silence. Silence often makes heard the cry of psychic pain and behind the cry the call of silence is like comfort.

Clinical structures demonstrate convincingly that affect does not play there the role that Freud restrictively assigned to it, and that one must distinguish the different types of danger to which the defence mechanisms have found more or less precarious solutions. There are no doubt connections between castration anxiety and unthinkable anxieties, fear of annihilation, and of nameless dread, but it is the differences which are important to us. The same observation can be made of positive affect, the theoretical elaboration of which has not been pursued to the same extent, because it apparently poses less of a problem to the analyst. But it is significant that the field of perversion attracts our attention today in a very different way (Stoller, 1975). Lacan's concept of the symbolic as the key to the unconscious system would be much more acceptable if it could be related to a paradigm other than that of language, but one which makes language possible. This seems to have been best understood by Winnicott (1971*b*). In fact it is certainly because this concept is indispensable to any authentic renewal of theory that criticism of the exclusion of affect becomes a serious one.

In the end I distinguish two types of affect:

(1) Affect which is integrated as solid material into the other significant material in the unconscious (and preconscious) chain – in this case affect is subordinated to the organization of the chain and its meaning lies in the sequence which it belongs to. Here affect takes on the function of signifier (*signifiant*) like the representation or any other material coming into unconscious formations.

(2) By its intensity and its meaning (*signification*) affect overflows from the unconscious chain, like a river which leaves its bed and disorganizes communications, destroying the sense-making structures. In this second case, we are dealing not with a signal affect in the ego, but perhaps with real instinctual impulses from the id which have broken the ego's barriers and are advancing in force towards the heart of the ego in the manner of a *Blitzkrieg*. The disorganization of the chain is responsible for the traumatic affect which may paralyse or have a tendency towards compulsive action, if they do not bring in their wake a reaction of stupefied immobility. Thus in the preceding case, affect remains in the framework of a relationship susceptible to transformation by the work of elaboration in analytic association. In the second case, however, the possibilities of analysis – at least classical analysis – are overrun, driving the patient into defences which disable his psychic life.

If it is easy to agree with Lacan (1973) when he seems to imply that the problem of affect is linked to a body 'whose natural habitat is language', the question remains untouched insofar as there exists no consensus on the relationship between psychic reality and the body – de M'Uzan (1970) presented a psychoanalytical conception of this relationship in a dynamic perspective, surely guided by his competence in psychosomatics, when he differentiated between affect as a psychic phenomenon and psychosomatic economy (cf. also McDougall, 1974). The reader will doubtless not fail to be struck by the fact that I make as little reference as possible to the hypotheses of child development for the comprehension of affective phenomena, which seems strange and, to say the least, paradoxical. I abstain from it on purpose, in order not to add to the confusion which appears to me to reign in this domain. This confusion consists in mixing a model of understanding analytic communication with the implicit hypothesis of its relation to the earliest history of development. Discussions about the necessity for distinguishing between repetition of the past and later restructuring of this past add nothing to our understanding, but simply reveal our temptation continually to bring our difficulties in conceptualizing what goes on in the actualization of communication back to a temporal conception of unconscious psychic mechanisms which is only a little bit psychoanlytical in nature. The here and now is not the alternative solution, for it rests on the same implications: only the technique is different.

PERSONAL COMMENTS

If I can be allowed to end this contribution by some pointers towards the orientation of future research, I would like to stress the following points:

Because Freud has characterized affects as discharge processes, there has often been a tendency to understand them as physiological phenomena accompanied by their corresponding psychical expression as a whole. In fact, a simplification has taken place, replacing a more subtle conception present in Freud's work, even though his explanatory hypotheses remain doubtful. In his *Introductory Lectures* we find the most precise definition: 'And what is affect in the dynamic sense? It is in any case something highly composite. An affect includes in the first place particular motor innervations or discharges and secondly certain feelings; the latter are of two kinds – perceptions of the motor actions that have occurred and the direct feelings of pleasure and unpleasure which, as we say, give the affect its keynote' (Freud, 1916–17, p. 395).

This distinction between the sensation of the internal movement and the quality of affect seems, at first sight, of little importance. It may be significant in those patients whose analysis shows difficulties related to a fear of being invaded by their affective experience. The character of strange indetermination of their affects appears to them dreadful, threatening their relationships with their objects. In this case, it may be less the quality of the affect, frequently felt as inexpressible or unutterable, what is the source of their discomfort, than the feeling of the internal movement and of its tendency towards diffusion. The appearance of a more specified affect of unpleasure of the destructive type, whether projected or not, seems to be an attempt to stop the diffusion more than the fullest expression of the original affective quality. The above quoted descriptive statement is not enough. This was also Freud's own impression about his definition: 'But I do not think that with this enumeration we have arrived at the essence of an affect. We seem to see deeper in the case of some affects and to recognize that the core which holds the combination we have described together is the repetition of some particular significant experience. This experience could only be a very early impression of a very general nature, placed in the prehistory not of the individual but of the species' (Freud, 1917e, pp. 395–6).

He then alludes to the well-known analogy between the construction of affect and that of hysterical attacks, of which he reminds us here as he will repeat it later on. But what we have to retain from it, is their function of reminiscence. Therefore one can only be surprised when in 'Constructions in analysis' (Freud, 1937d) he gives to affects, to affective impulses and emotional connections, a great significance in the material and does not evoke this very function when he comes to the question of the different types of remembering. The reason for this seems to lie in the fact that Freud, at that point, identifies the affect with the 'upward drive' partly expressed in the compulsive belief in the delusions. In this instance one could understand that the fear of the perception of the internal movement is linked with affective diffusion – and not only because of its quality, but more on account of the delusional potentiality of the diffusion. The hypothesis of the phylogenic nature of affect, though open to doubt, underlines the fact that if the ego is the seat of affects, what it may be forced to admit within itself is of the most alien nature as compared with its structure. On the other hand, the idea of an affective status belonging to a model comparable to hysterical attacks enables us to think that the more primitive affects do not derogate them from the claim to a complex form of organization.

The whole question seems to me to lie in the wasteland between the two types of affects, already sensed by Freud, and in respect of which I have put forward a theoretical reformulation: affect with a semantic function as an element in the chain of signifiers (*chaine signifiante*), and affect overflowing the concatenation and spreading as it breaks the links in the chain. The analytic situation offers the opportunity for a meeting with an object, resulting in the birth of a projective transference, which finds its meaning *in situ*, and which the analyst enables the patient to reintegrate into his communication by making it retroactively acceptable in the analytic setting.

On the other hand, in difficult cases, the analyst's interpretation has the effect of unleashing an auto-traumatic process of internal defence, a reactive defence against an internal void in which intense affect, usually painful, is the only proof of his own existence that the analysand can give himself, and where affect, rather than serve to carry the meaning, takes care of the function of externalizing the self, within the limits of internal space, to all the parts of the psychic apparatus in which the object threatens to intervene inopportunely. It is here that the major conflictualization of affect is revealed. The effects of two distinct phenomena are superimposed upon one another. On the one hand, affects penetrate into the ego, which fears not only their violence or their crudity, but also their contradictory nature like opposite pairs of instinctual impulses. The ego feels endangered by the introduction of these tensions which threaten to compromise the homogeneity which it seeks to establish in its midst. On the other hand, it creates confusion in itself between affect and object cathexis, as if the affect threatened the ego's narcissism necessary for the establishment of the ego's self-observation. This function cannot be suspended in cases where affect leaves a choice only between separation-anxiety, leading to the death of affect, and anxiety about intrusion, which is experienced as a need to abandon self-observation and let the object take possession, and bring it face to face with projected drive impulses to which it must submit. The special quality of the analyst as object, and the inevitability of the relationship established with him through the ever-insufficient medium of the movement of words, can only reactivate, in a snowball effect, the impossibility of transforming affect into action without shattering the analytic setting, that fragile container of potentially dispersed relatedness. The limits of speech and the formal conventions of language then act only like additional internal excitations which increase internal tension. The solution then appears to be the evasion or, to be more accurate, the *extravasation* of affect, by a series of repetitive internal reactions which modify the functioning of thought. It is not a question of primary process functioning, for if such were the case the analyst involved in deciphering them would not share the patient's tension. The invasion, the impotence, the distress, all give rise to an internal panic which drives the subject to exceed the limits of psychic space by various mechanisms: confusion – which is in fact a dissemination and dilution of conflictual tensions; cathartic action operating like a massive affective storm; somatization; perverse excitation; or the overcathexis of external perception which monopolizes all psychic attention. All these manoeuvres arise from an attempt at dissociation and splitting, which can function in an isolated state resulting in the installation of a dead space in the heart of the subject. I am aware that I am not going beyond the level of a descriptive metaphor in this attempt at clarification.

It is tempting to think that all these defensive operations correspond to unconscious fantasies and to attribute an important role to projective identification. To that, I would reply that our theory of projection still masks many obscurities that I refuse to raise by schematizations, which often lead analysts to mirror, in their scientific contributions, the psychic activity of the patients who put us in difficulties, by recourse to stereotypes which become a kind of acting out in the theory. It seems

important to underline that unconscious fantasies are psychic elaborations which require work to have been accomplished by the psychic
apparatus. Patients' functioning as it appears through their material,
makes one think that, if the crudest unconscious fantasies described by
Kleinian writers were at the disposal of the psychic apparatus, these
patients would not need to present the transference reactions which they
show us. I think that there are serious disadvantages in the hypothesis
that the translation of communications to the analyst into interpretations couched in terms of unconscious fantasies, has precisely the aim of
promoting work which the patients appear unable to accomplish themselves. Instead of giving rein to the relationship, and creating a feeling of
freedom in the patient, the relief from the invasion of affect seems bound
to be paid for by precipitate understanding, which enters upon a straight
but narrow way. Interpretations in Kleinian technique come down in
the end to saying that such and such an element in the material
'represents' the mother, or the object, and to supplying verbal support
intended to induce this representation – which is not the same as
suggesting it. The remarkable understanding of archaic structures by
the followers of M. Klein is not in question, nor are their therapeutic
intentions. The real problem is to recognize that the representation,
which is in effect indispensable material for mental elaboration, must be
formed by psychic work in which there can be no short-cuts, and which
cannot be accomplished by the analyst's communicating 'ready-made'
representations (i.e. the verbalization of unconscious fantasies). This
elaboration of the representation remains at the centre of our analytic
work and we should recognize this from the fact that, more than
three-quarters of a century after the invention of psychoanalysis, we still
consider that the dream (nightmares included), whatever approach we
have to it, remains a personal creation of psychic activity, whose value as
a pointer to the capacity of the psychic apparatus for work, remains
irreplaceable. For the problem is not to inject representations already
elaborated by someone else, but to favour the processes which will
enable these representations to be put at the disposition of the analysand. One of the paradoxes in these complex affective structures is that,
whilst they are themselves under the influence of the most massive
primitive and archaic reactions, they remain extremely sensitive to the
nuances of the most subtle and differentiated qualities of affect in other
people. That is to say these qualities can be intuitively recognized in
someone else without the subject being able to take the risk of adopting
them for himself.

The problem is therefore to help the patient to distinguish in his internal psychic reality, a representation of the other person, so that co-existence with him can become an experience that will not cease to be conflictual, but which will be conflictual in a tolerable and mutually desirable way. This is only possible through an awakening of the self to psychic reality and by the establishment of live intrapsychic communication.

What seems to separate our point of view from Freud's, as far as affect is concerned, is not, in my opinion, what has been called his hydraulic model of the psychic apparatus, nor his references to biology or the economic point of view. On these questions, his formulations impede us more than his ideas. By contrast, it seems that where we differ from him considerably is over his postulation that 'all presentations originate from perceptions and are repetitions of them' (Freud, 1925*h*, p. 237). Today I think that we would accord a much larger role to affects in the transformation of mnemic traces, if not in their creation. We implicitly question ourselves on the mnemic traces of affective experiences. It is possible that the problem lies in the fact that *the psychic apparatus registers the traces of affective experiences before it is ready to establish mnemic traces of perceptions and that the whole aim of the work is to separate out the representations from the contradictory affective infiltrations, whose general tendency is towards diffusion, whilst the representations seek articulation.* Supplying content to what is experienced only in unrepresentable form, is a fundamental task of the psychic apparatus. If content is connected to sense, we must nevertheless remember that nonsense has two different meanings: *chaos* and *nothingness*. The confusion of these two is at the root of many of our misunderstandings.

For sense to emerge from the dilemma requires us to abandon our theoretical preconceptions, which have now demonstrated their heuristic limitations. For my part, I see no way out of our difficulties except by research into what I call *primary symbolization*, where the matrices of experience, unaware of the distinction between affect and representation, are formed on the basis of a primary logic, the expression of a minimal unconscious semantic, where we would find the figures of psychoanalytic rhetoric: repetition-compulsion, reversal (turning into the opposite and turning against the self), anticipation, mirroring, inclusion, exclusion, formation of the complement, mediation between inside and outside, the emergence of the category of intermediary, the situation between the same and the other, the constitution of movable limits, temporary splitting, the creation of substitutes, the setting up of screens and *finally* projective identification. The reader will notice that I can only indicate the direction of current research. These are the prerequisites for connections between symbolization and absence, as indicated in chapter 2 above.

In order to comprehend the reason of the irrational, we must rid ourselves of the psychoanalytic realism which infiltrates all our theories, even those which we judge the most unreal. And if we are in agreement in saying that for our patients it is a question of transforming a mode of survival into a living experience, we will not achieve this result by our good intentions alone, nor by our intuitive abilities. We shall only achieve it by doing justice to that complexity of the human mind, which Freud taught us how to reach, by breaking with the routines of traditional thought. I recall, in conclusion, that sentence from the 'Project' which was to guide our thoughts: 'Thus quantity in ϕ is expressed by the *complication* in ψ' (Freud, p. 515). It is for us to draw out the implications of that statement from contemporary clinical experience.

SUMMARY

By way of summary, it can be said that Freud's study of affect started from a point of view founded on coherent symptomatic groupings of neurotic symptoms, as a criterion for a discriminating study of the different vicissitudes of representations and affect, in the realms of the conscious and unconscious. As his work unfolded and his clinical experience grew, he progressively came to reverse the balance, in his final drive theory and the second topographical model, in favour of affects in relation to representations, as well as extending the role of anxiety and differentiating aspects of it. Above all, he began to think of the drive as more and more independent of the idea of content. If it is true that he came to recognize the value of the notion of quality (in pleasurable and unpleasurable states) late in the day; the economic point of view, on the other hand, was to be constantly recalled, so that its importance should not be neglected. Finally, his last period of work was to be marked by an insistence on the primitive distress of the young child, on the general psychological immaturity of the ego at birth and on a shift of emphasis towards the primary object, which, in the first part of his work, was conceived primarily as an object of pleasure (and a force for repression) and subsequently became an object of survival, for building the ego up against the disorganizing power of the drives when it failed against them. Nevertheless, Freud remains faithful to the end to the opposition of representation and affect.

In the second period, a new way of seeing the problems developed. The development of categories of syndromes no longer constituted the pertinent boundaries for evaluating psychic functioning. If allusion is still made to them, it is in order to stress the differences between the classical neuroses and clinical aspects of modern practice, where differentiated groups of syndromes carry less interest than types of functioning which are no longer distinguished in nosographical terms but according to general types of structure (character neuroses, borderline states, depression, psychotic or psychosomatic structures, etc.). Whilst reference continues to be made to the substance of the second topographical model, clinical formulations are more often made in terms of object relations and defence mechanisms. The distinction between affect and representations gave way to another distinction, implicitly considered to be more in accord with the analytic situation – that between cathexis and unconscious fantasy, whilst one theme emerged predominant: the study of the prehistory of the mother–child relationship, examined from different angles and in different ways, but with affective factors to the fore.

Finally, the concept of the self emerged from various directions, having been, so to speak, suppressed by the object-relations approach. Similarly, without denying its specificity, the function of fantasy is connoted by that of experience. Both are found again in the setting of communication between analyst and patient and inside each of them, which obliges us to consider the value, function, effects and specific modes of the affective exchanges at the core of mental functioning, and of the changes which appear desirable in the context of transformations expected in analyses. But then the question arises about the different sorts of meaning carried in the material, the different means of transmitting them, and the type of response which they induce or call for in the analyst. All of which comes down to three questions: What is the most appropriate form of response to the patient's affective communication, in order to secure better intrapsychic communication in him? What sort of logic is implied by this type of exchange on both sides? What is the connection between affect in this relationship and what might be called affective logic?

9

Passions and their Vicissitudes

On the Relation between Madness and Psychosis

> Everything in the sphere of this first attachment to
> the mother seemed to me difficult to grasp in analy-
> sis, so grey with age and shadowy and almost
> impossible to revivify, that it was as if it had
> succumbed to an especially inexorable repression.
> But perhaps I gained this impression because the
> women who were in analysis with me were able to
> cling to the very attachment to the father in which
> they had taken refuge from the early phase that was
> in question.
>
> Childhood love is boundless, it demands exclu-
> sive possession, it is not content with less than all.
>
> 'Female sexuality' (FREUD, 1931b)

MADNESS AND PASSION

Not so long ago, before it was considered fashionable by certain radicals
to call themselves *mad*, 'madness' was exiled from our vocabulary. In
the language of that time, one was not 'mad', one 'suffered from nerves'.
Nervous disorders covered a variety of states, from '*le mal du siècle*' to
mental alienation. Madness was also banished from professional jargon.
No one was mad; psychiatric science sorted and differentiated. It firmly
traced boundaries between normality, neurosis, perversion and psychosis. Freud himself did not escape from taxonomy to which he even richly
contributed.[1] Madness thus disappeared from the classification of disorders as a shameful reference, witness to the era when psychiatry was

Published originally in *Nouvelle Revue de Psychanalyse* (1980) 21. The translation is by
Katherine Aubertin.
[1] We should remember that Freud created a number of nosographic labels, as much to
differentiate the classes – *actual* neuroses, *psycho*-neuroses, *transference* neuroses, *narcissistic*
neuroses – as types within these classes (anxiety neurosis, anxiety hysteria, obsessional
neurosis), this entire terminology being of his own invention. In an unpublished work
presented to the Société Psychanalytique de Paris in 1962, I demonstrated that a coherent
psychoanalytic classification – that is to say, one founded on metapsychological differences
– is easy to pick out in Freud's writings.

stumbling through its infancy. Was not to speak of madness perhaps to refer to a terminology with as little scientific bearing as that of the vocabulary pertaining to possession? Or, was it not a way of consecrating the symptom together with all those who were afflicted with it, and at the same time forbidding oneself the possibility of an enlightened gaze – an exorcist's gaze – at that which called rather for a zoologist's or, better still, a botanist's observation? Long did psychiatry bear witness to the efforts of its greatest minds to conform to the ideal, not of medical science, which was still largely empiric, but to that of the natural sciences. Psychiatry still needed naturalists to bring the disorders of the mind within the boundaries of the disorders that nature imposes on the victims of its whim.

The scientific spirit, which dates back approximately to the eighteenth century, took hold of psychiatry. At the time the old term 'madness' was retained, but it was slowly broken down. It is true that classification came into being long before this, but, as Michel Foucault (1965) has shown, madness had changed its status. During the Middle Ages and the Renaissance, before the seventeenth century, madness was embellished with an aura that made a mystery of it, in the religious sense of this term; not only because its nature remained profoundly hidden, but also because something of the order of the divine, or the demoniac, showed through it. It was in league with passion – sometimes in the strictest sense: think of Sir Percival, who was possessed with his quest for the Grail, or even Tristan, whose love for Isolde was impeded by his obligations to his lord – not Mark alone but Christ himself. Love-passion, love-sufferance. For the passion of loving is that of 'endurance' and of 'submission': submitting to trials sent by God, as Christ, God and Son of God, himself had to suffer in his soul and his flesh. Here already is an indication of the idea that there could be no happy passion except in the acceptance of the Way of the Cross, or the imitation of it. Female saints understood this better perhaps than their male counterparts. And Lacan (1975) finds no difficulty in reading on the features of Bernini's Theresa the signs or symptoms of ecstasy.[1] She suffers, thus she is loved, for Christ gives her to live what he himself has lived through, a privilege accorded only to his heart's chosen. Psychiatrists of the nineteenth and twentieth centuries faced an awkward situation with the mystics. As with churchmen, their predicament was to separate the wheat from the tares; in other words, to distinguish divine from malignant manifesta-

[1] The French word *jouissance* has no exact English equivalent. The closest translation is enjoyment, which has lost the sexual 'orgasmic' connotation that it retains in French. Here translated as enjoyment, ecstasy, joy or pleasure. The verb: *jouir*. [Translator's note.]

tions. No doubt for many of them – but not for all – the problem was situated in distinguishing hysteria from delusional states, or, more precisely, erotomania.

Later, in the Renaissance, we again find love: *Don Quixote* – another erotomanic misadventure – which is warmly recommended by Freud to his fiancée. Here is something which says much about the passionate love he bore her; as though he sought to make her read between the lines of the voluminous correspondence he sent her: 'My Dulcinea, I love you, but I know my love is pure madness'.

To speak of Shakespeare's many references to madness is as common-place as to point out its link with passion. This reminder, however, is necessary. Polonius is not so mad (in a different sense) as to say, in the same breath, that this noble son is mad and that the cause is his love for Ophelia. He errs but little – repression compels: it is Gertrude whom he should have named.

The jealous love of Othello is obviously of a passionate nature; only, here again, it is a question of mistaken identity.[1] Besides these exotic passions, narcissistic passions produce the same effects of alienation: Richard III, Julius Caesar and Macbeth all die because of their un-quenchable ambition.

But each of these cases should be treated with caution: the diagnosis is open to dispute. The madness of Lear, however, is undeniable. If, in the previous examples, passion was as certain as madness was doubtful, here we have the opposite. There is no doubt about the madness; it is the passion that is less certain. Is Lear the victim of a passion? Freud, in 'The theme of the three caskets' (1913*f*), admitted that he had only tackled this question from one angle, and that psychoanalysis would have more to say about it. He was more interested with death than with love. Is not the disappointment inflicted by Lear's incestuous love-object, Cordelia, the indirect and distant cause of his insanity? For is it not rather the ingratitude of his two other more 'unnatural' daughters that precipitates him into madness (cf. Green, 1971)?

The link between madness and passion is endorsed by literature. The ideal of the Renaissance recognizes this conjunction, which simul-taneously inspires fascination, respect and fear. This recognition of the obscure powers of man made possible the revival of the classic tradition of tragedy, which inspired horror and pity. Madness and passion: two tributaries of the same river, the source of which is 'hubris'.

According to Foucault (1965), the triumph of reason resulted not only

---

[1] Cf. Green (1979), where I pointed out Othello's latent unconscious homosexual love for Cassius.

in the repression of madness but in that of passion as well. This was still allowed, within limits, in the theatre – if one thinks of the discussions on the relationship of Phaedra to God's grace:[1] rationalism chases passion from philosophy.

Descartes had great difficulty with his *Traité des passions*, which is his weakest work. Spinoza, who recognized far better the essence of desire, nevertheless had trouble with it. Pascal found no other way of defending his religious passion than to stake it on a demonstration that was supported by logic. On one side, there was the anxiety of emptiness; on the other, mathematics. And what between the two?

By the beginning of the eighteenth century, the concept of Nature had already begun its task of undermining God and religious passion. Psychiatry was born of this mutation. Not that it stopped being, sometimes unknowingly, profoundly religious: see Morel's theory of degenerescence (Morel, 1952). But the perspective now changes. The eye wishes to be objective, that is to say, without passion. It tries to assess fairly the physical and moral causes of madness, and, amongst these, passions play a major part.

Following Cartesian thought, literature focusses on the idea that passions are to be situated (in classification but probably also anatomically) at the point where mind and body meet. This is not surprising. That the mind should be affected is evident: derangement can be observed by anyone who is sound of mind. But the body is also manifestly shaken: witness the signs of exaltation or, in contrast, extreme prostration. Recent psychiatric science, we should note, differs little with Descartes in determining where the seat of passion is located. Twentieth-century physiology replaces the pineal gland with the hypothalamus, closely related to the pituitary, 'conductor of the endocrine concert', as the saying goes, which was still in usage when I was studying medicine. The inference here is that, between the nervous system regulating relational life and the internal medium submitted to humoral or hormonal variations, there is a bridging link between the mind and body.

No one searched as ardently for this organic substratum of passion as Clérambault, who in the great herbarium of psychiatric classification isolated it in what he called the '*Psychoses Passionnelles*', namely: '*Erotoma-*

---

[1] In tragedy and in comedy too, for Molière is no less a painter of passions than Racine. Here are depicted the passions of the middle classes, which are more easily encountered in everyday life. Since Lacan, Alceste's paranoïa is an accepted fact. But there is not only this. Arnolphe's jealousy, Don Juan's sexual collectionism, Oronte's bigotry, Monsieur Jourdain's social quest, Harpagon's avarice, Arganta's hypochondria, are passions measurable with those that inhabit the world of tragedy. They are no less tragic. They show that passion is not solely the prerogative of legendary figures.

nie', '*Délire de Jalousie*' and '*Délire de Revendication*' – requiring the use of capital letters (Clérambault, 1942). His theory is both organicist and intellectualist. Passion, or the affective phenomenon, plays but a small part in this. Clérambault's student, Jacques Borel, postulates, with others, that the 'basal' role of the affective disorders is linked to hypothalamo-pituitary malfunctioning.

Today there is little discussion of passion in psychiatry, and practically none in psychoanalysis.[1] This is not surprising, so far as the class of '*psychoses passionnelles*' is concerned. Clérambault's work, contemporary with that of Freud, has not touched psychoanalytic thought, except in the case of Lacan, for reasons that are too lengthy to go into here, but probably because both were sustained by a common adherence to a quasi-mathematical combination system. Whether it was a question of a combination of neurones for Clérambault or of signifiers for Lacan, there was less divergence between them, I believe, than between Clérambault and Freud. If psychoanalytic thought did not deem it necessary to attach particular interest to the '*psychoses passionnelles*', the reason was probably because for psychoanalysis it is implicit that all delusions – and not only the three forms canonized by Clérambault – are the fruit of repressed passion. However, this would be to dispose of the problem too swiftly, for it is true that Freud remained blind to madness, and this on two scores.

First, his work was born of neurosis (principally hysteria), and it evolved from this point of reference, taking psychosis (madness in the traditional sense) into account from this angle only, and even then, much less thoroughly; with reason, for Freud maintained that the narcissistic neuroses (which are the psychoses of traditional psychiatry) are unanalyzable. Thus there is little that can be said about them with any precision. Or else he was overlooking the psychotic as a person, as the case of Schreber's *Memoirs* proves: which is the analysis of a written work, and not that of a patient undergoing analysis. But the work not only passes over the psychotic as a person, it also passes over the wall of the asylum where Schreber was interned; as much as to say that Freud passes over Schreber's madness, though it concerns but a mad document.

Secondly, Freud approached neurosis in such a way as to purge it simultaneously of the passion and the madness that it continued nevertheless to transmit. That psychoanalytic theory has itself carried the mark of this repression, or suppression, is of no small consequence. This is what we will now examine.

---

[1] With the exception of Daniel Lagache, whose work on amorous jealousy (1947) has remained a classic.

PSYCHOSIS OR MADNESS?

When an analyst today finds himself in the analytic setting, two situations may arise. In the first of these eventualities, the organization of the symptoms, the associative style, the nature of the conflicts, the type of defence mechanisms, the development of the transference, all give him the impression that he is on familiar ground. What he has learned from reading Freud plus his classical training permits him to find his bearings in the analysis, and he has the feeling, with time, that the interpretation of the conflicts in the framework of the transference, and the resolution of the same, will permit a favourable termination of the analysis. One can no longer say that today these cases represent the majority, but they comfort the analyst with the feeling of a correlation between theory and practice, and they give him the impression of exercising a coherent activity. In the second eventuality, everything is different. The analyst has the feeling that nothing he has learned, especially about the clinical psychopathology of the neuroses, holds true here. He finds but few traces of what he has been taught; he is confused by the zigzagging course of the cure; he no longer recognizes the classic defence mechanisms; he is confronted with resistances of which he has never read a description; and the analysis unfolds in unfamiliar territory. If he tries to apply what he has learned concerning the clinical aspect of the neuroses, he has the feeling that it is a mere veneer, that he can only make sense of things by forcing his interpretations to fit the material. Thus it frequently happens in these cases (which may even be the majority) that the existence of a psychotic core is inferred, or a latent psychotic structure declared. This is a false solution to a real problem.

Psychoanalysis today, I suggest, is paying the price for an error which goes back to Freud. As I see it, in correcting that error it has fallen into other errors. The first of these is related to the conjuncture prevailing in Freud's time, which induced him to favour the field of neurosis and to base on it the whole construction of psychoanalytic metapsychology. The second error is to extend the field of psychosis symmetrically, misusing the term to the point of applying the same word to refer both to interned psychiatric patients and to the patients whom we have on our couches.

When we return to the source of psychoanalysis, that is to say to Freud's *Studies on Hysteria* (1895*d*), the reading of the case material raises questions which we have trouble answering. Do these hysterical patients, who manifest disquieting symptoms, with disorganized speech, twilight states, disturbed consciousness, and hallucinatory phenomena, merit the name of neurotics? One would tend rather to call them psychotic, yet that seems just as doubtful. The problem is that we appear only to have the choice of these two alternatives. To call these patients borderline merely leaves the question unresolved.

Freud, in order to see clearly in the chaotic and proteiform universe of hysteria, and to throw light upon it without which we would still be wandering in the dark, 'neurotified' hysteria according to the clinical categories of his time. His interest in fantasy, which he conceived of as a production of the unconscious rather than as the consequence of hypnoid states – which was Breuer's belief –, brought him to the theory of the Unconscious as a territory separate from consciousness, a segregated psychical nucleus obeying a causality peculiar to itself. Breuer already said of Anna O: '. . . indulging in a systematic day-dreaming, which she described as her private theatre' (Freud 1895d, p. 22). Freud qualified the unconscious in a similar manner in *The Interpretation of Dreams* (1900a): an 'other scene'. Without doubt, this conception allowed for a better understanding of the unconscious system of representations underlying symptoms. But by interesting himself exclusively with this theatrical fantasying in hysteria, Freud abandoned at the same time the pole of passion – which one called hysterical madness (*'folie hystérique'*) which left its trace in the 'attack'. In fact, these hysterics were no more neurotic than psychotic. They were 'mad'.

The hysterical attack had always been thought of as a theatrical manifestation or at worst as an expression of simulation, an act. Freud, who took the matter seriously, put an end to the moral condemnation of which hysterics were the victims, but he only displaced this theatricality to the internal world of psychic reality. The hypothesis of the unconscious unburdened these patients of the suspicion that weighed upon them. But by calling hysterics the victims of their private theatre, or of the indirect effects of this 'other scene', he only transposed the space of the theatre; he did not do away with it. One needs only to have witnessed a hysterical attack to be astonished by the way in which the ego's capacities are overwhelmed, and to be sensitive, through the agitation which seizes the subject, to the degree of madness which is openly expressed, by the energy which is unleashed on this occasion and by the feeling that at this moment the subject is literally 'out of his mind', inhabited by a violence which no one, not even himself, knew existed.

Nowadays hysteria is more discrete. It has not disappeared but it is hidden.[1] On the other hand, hysterical characters and phobic states of all kinds are still regularly found in analytic practice. Although a hysterical

---

[1] Asylum is found in neurology wards.

character no longer has attacks, he continues to make scenes, sometimes in the consulting room, but more often in the private space of the bedroom. Such scenes show the same sudden transformation of the individual, the same excitation, the sudden stiffening, the flow of words carried in an unknown tone of voice, accusing, sometimes murderous, followed by a 'fit (attack) of nerves', and collapse, where the subject loses possession of himself. What remains of this in the session? A story that purges the event of its momentary madness. The analyst does not witness the phobic attack either. Here again, more often than not, he only hears the story. Heedful of the patient's recital and his associations, he loses sight – a lack of imagination? – of what the patient's experience implies: a counterphobic attempt that has been thwarted, external pressure forcing him to face a phobogenic situation releasing keen anxiety and agitation, fits of crying, entreaties, all showing, behind these apparently limited manifestations, the persistence of this pole of passionate madness, expressed here in its negative aspects. The agoraphobic who needs to be accompanied to be able to venture into the street, to protect himself from the urge to seduce someone sexually or to exhibit himself, or the wish to be subjected to a sexual aggression, allows us to recognize these wishes behind his symptom. What he reveals when this protection is lacking, through the anxiety which masks these wishes, is not only his forbidden unconscious representations, but rather something that evokes the idea of demoniac possession, which is lost to our memory and which the hysterical attack recalls.

That Freud discovered the unconscious, with hysteria as his starting point, is no accident – hysteria which will always be associated with the question of Eros. The vast continent of sexuality was opened. But for all that, should one have linked sexuality with neuroses? To say that neuroses are the negative of perversion, to maintain that perversion originates in the child's polymorphous perversity, was to make a courageous discovery. But one can say the same thing about hysteria alone, in relation to perversion. When Freud approaches this in *Three Essays on the Theory of Sexuality* (1905d), one can well appreciate that the audaciousness of tackling a field dominated by the stigma of morality, with a view to understanding its genesis and mechanisms, obliged him at the same time to adopt a cool, lucid and objective attitude, and to consider the subjects under his scrutiny with the eye of the entomologist. When we compare these descriptions with what we learn in the analysis of a pervert, we recognize the mechanisms described, but something is missing from the description. In vain we search for the element of passionate frenzy, linked to an instinctual upsurge which pushes him to acts which can compromise his entire life, to senseless behaviour where he submits to the rule of blind compulsive force. We explain these acts as being caused by guilt or the need for self-punishment, which does not explain everything.

Think of the homosexual who, in every situation where he is faced with anxiety, be it castration anxiety or the fear of destruction, experiences a dominating, urgent need to do away with it by provoking the reassuring verification of the persistence of the penis, of any penis, on the body of another human being, and this is a frantic search which must end in the carrying out of an immediate act, in conditions very often damaging to the whole of the rest of his personality and for the accomplishments of his ego. Here again one is struck by the sudden encroachment of what seems to be a 'derangement of the senses, or of sense'.

Here one must remember what Freud says about the sudden aware-ness of female – more specifically maternal – castration in the small boy. A comparable event, he declares, with the threat to Throne and Altar. This is a matter of *anxiety*, but, even more, of the loss of an essential point of reference.

When throne and altar topple, suicide may follow in the wake. The fall of the symbol demonstrates the fact that the symbolic order is attached to the subject's very existence, which is not only his reason for living, but his passion to be. In other words, the presence of emblems is the price of life; or, to put it another way, the entire love of life is consubstantial with them.

Castration anxiety and the anxiety of object-loss not only exist in the relation of part to whole, or of contained to container; they are mutually reflected in Eros, which holds them together. But already the one and the other are taking form in relation to the Mother.

This erotic madness has a comical, ridiculous aspect, for those who are not prey to it; as, for example, in their reactions to the torments of the jealous lover, to his over-estimation of his sexual object, or to his sliding, unaware, towards delusion; which is fortunately usually temporary, when this jealousy is not paranoid.

When Freud, at the end of his work, gives increasing importance to the role played by splitting in fetishism and in psychosis, one is tempted to situate perversion closer to psychosis. This proximity is hardly justified if one examines the essence of real perversion. On the one hand, the erotic madness which is at work in perversion, as it is in hysteria, must be taken into account, though differently.

Freud started by discovering the role played by sexuality in the neuroses and in the structuring of the human psyche. Subsequently, he almost came to think of sexuality and love as opposites, especially in 'Instincts and their vicissitudes' (1915c). Later he proposed a unified theory of love, bringing together the forms which had remained distinct until then, that is, the amorous relationship of two adults, filial or parental love, friendship, the love of one's country or even of humanity. But it is only with his final theory of the instincts that sexuality and love are included in Eros, or the life instinct; as though to say that Eros is life itself.

When he thinks of the state of being in love[1] or of amorous passion, Freud follows the general consensus and repeats after so many others: 'Love is a short madness'. One must reason further: if Eros, the life instinct, includes sexuality and love to the point of identifying them with life itself, and if one recognizes that love necessarily entails this mad dimension, then all the vicissitudes of Eros are tainted with a potential madness which is at the core of what they manifest, and in every aspect arising from them, even in the most normal sexuality, even to its infantile roots.

So what has become of madness? Rather than characterize it as a disorder of reason, one should on the contrary stress the affective, passionate element which modifies the subject's relation to reality, electing a part or whole object, becoming more or less exclusively attached to it, reorganizing his perception of the world around it, and giving it a unique or irreplaceable aura by which the ego is captivated and alienated. An obsessive, over-estimated internal representation is formed around the object which justifies the subject's inner state. This seems to me to be true in all the forms of love that Freud united under that heading.

At all times men have known that they were mad. Philosophers have said so in different ways, but philosophy failed in its quest for wisdom and truth because it could not recognize the roots at the origin of this madness. Freud fully recognized, first in sexuality and then in the Eros of the final theory of the instincts, the fundamental role played by them in structuring the normal and the pathological human psyche. But besides

---

[1] On everything concerning the state of being in love, I recommend the excellent book of Christian David (1971). He has had the singular merit of questioning the economic interpretation of Freud, who saw the relation between object-love and self-love according to the model of communicating vessels. He rightly observes that object-love exalts narcissism and throws light on the connection between love and mourning. His work describing affective perversion and on bisexuality seems to me to fit into the same framework. As for erotic madness, nowhere does it appear to me to be better illustrated than in his fine analysis of Kleist's Penthesilea.

this, he minimized their intrinsically mad essence, which subsists in the normal individual as well as in the neurotic and the pervert.

It is still this same madness that suddenly appears in the anti-erotic structures: obsessions, depressions, narcissism. Obsessional isolation is only so powerful because its absence would give free rein to acts of hateful frenzy. Object-loss for the depressed individual can lead to behaviour which is not so different from that of the pervert, where the wish to find a substitute-object at any price can lead to compulsive addiction, and thence to accidental suicide. As for the narcissistic subject threatened by requests from others that upset his need for self-sufficiency and autonomy, he can be seized by murderous impulses which he feels are mad, to protect himself against the feeling of a violating encroachment on his internal space, similar to an impairing anal penetration.

For an experienced ear, even in the most ordinary of neurotic structures, with the most common symptoms, there comes a time when the feeling arises in the analyst's countertransference, that he is at grips with mad mental functioning; it is a passing moment, but it is crucial. Neurosis deceives us because the ego has conserved its relation to reality, because rational thought remains intact, because fantasy is contained within a limited territory. But one may ask oneself if the classic defence mechanisms, above all repression, but also all sorts of inhibition, the causes of which are ill-understood (inasmuch as they only concern the normal exercise of a function – sexuality, nourishment, work etc.), are exclusively deployed in the face of a risk of conflict with the superego, and if the disapproval of an internal parental authority is sufficient to explain the drastic nature of these prohibitions. Should one not rather think that it is the risk of the appearance of this potential madness in the execution of these functions that makes it so dangerous to carry them out, and so implicitly disorganizing for the ego?

Finally, if one evokes what Freud considers the most evoluated outcome of the instincts, that is to say sublimation, this is far from bringing us wisdom and serenity: the lives of artists show them to be prey to the same madness. I am not only referring to their private lives, but to their relation to their work. Despite what Freud says, scientists are no better off: the history of science abounds with examples where the official body of knowledge has been purged of all the aberrations that bind scientists to their science. Thus, alongside sublimated accomplishment of instinctual development, there remains a pole of blind passion which scientific virtue passes over in silence.

FREUD'S CASE HISTORIES:[1] NEUROSIS, PSYCHOSIS, BORDERLINE CASES

My hypothesis, that passion and madness were banished from neurosis at the same time, is borne out in Freud's writings from several different angles. It is demonstrated, theoretically and technically, in his case studies.

The 'Dora' case carries on from *The Interpretation of Dreams*. One knows that Freud both fails and admits his failure. But why? Doubtless because he fails to recognize Dora's homosexuality; but is it not also because his whole interest is focussed on his patient's dreams – in other words, on her unconscious representations – while minimizing her affects? For *two hours* (this is emphasized by Freud himself), Dora remains wrapped in silent admiration before the Sistine Madonna. Freud associates this event with a dream, for which he cannot be criticized. However, if, as he wrote, affects are suppressed in dreams, how in the analysis of the dream is one able to account for Dora's state of contemplation in the Dresden Gallery, where she preferred to go on her own, refusing the company of a cousin? Similarly, when Freud interprets Dora's supposed appendicitis as a fantasy of childbirth, he recognizes this meaning but forgets the fever which accompanied the symptom. The Dora analysis is also the first psychoanalytic elaboration of the transference(s), if one considers that the cases reported in *Studies on Hysteria* (1895*d*) belong to the pre-history of psychoanalysis. One may recall that at that period Freud felt impeded by the appearance of this undesirable factor. 'Practical experience, at all events, shows conclusively that there is no means of avoiding it, and that this latest creation of the disease must be combated like all earlier ones' (Freud, 1905*e*, p. 116). Analysts are familiar with this history of the transference, which began by considering this phenomenon as an arte-fact and a nuisance ('our cross') before it came to be the motor of the cure. What is less well known is that this initial standpoint of Freud proceeds straight from his theoretical options. By favouring unconscious representations over affects, and by centring the cure predominantly on the analysis of representations (i.e. dreams), Freud was obliged to keep the transference outside the analysis, because with it the primacy of affects over representations reappeared. And as at the beginning trans-ference is recognized as transference love – and this since *Studies on Hysteria* –, Freud is caught in a ceaseless struggle to undo the transfer-ence: there is a '*mésalliance*', a 'false connection' ('I am not he who you

---

[1] Freud's case studies of 'Dora' (1905*e*), 'Little Hans' (1909*b*), the 'Rat Man' (1909*d*), 'Schreber' (1911*c*), and the 'Wolf Man' (1918*b*). [Translator's note.]

take me to be') because amorous *passion* reappears with the transference. Freud was more at ease with the analysis of infantile sexuality, which belonged to a repressed past, and with the daydreams connected to it, than with the reality of love in the psychoanalytic situation. Dora really is 'mad'; she is capable of anything because her feelings of love push her not only to transfer them but to 'act them out'. Acts of vengeance, as we know. More than one hysteric has compromised her doctors in the same manner. So one must become master of the transference, which means to cool it down. Freud cannot have forgotten, even in the presence of a *'petite hysterie'*, the pandemonium created at the Salpêtrière, where Charcot's prestigious silhouette looked on at hysterical passion from his lofty standpoint. Of course, though Freud is not yet aware of it, the danger of transference is countertransference. Mr K pays the price for his passion for Dora, with a traffic accident – probably because he was all eyes for the young woman, to the point of being blind to the danger of the vehicles driving in the street. Freud adds in a footnote (1905e, p. 121, n. 7): 'We have here an interesting contribution to the problem of indirect attempts at suicide, which I have discussed in my *Psychopathology of Everyday Life*' (1901b, chapter 8). This is what passion can lead to! To master the transference is to safeguard against the storms of passion and their consequent avalanches. To approach unconscious meaning by means of dreams is to introduce a mediating distance, not only because dreams are the royal road leading to the unconscious, but also because this road is well guarded against dangerous false connections. We have the proof, thanks to Felix Deutsch, that Dora did not resemble this somewhat sympathetic young woman. That Freud lets none of this transpire comes no doubt from his own countertransference, which drove him to give a watered-down version of passion.

The four others analyses doubtless show the same inclination within Freud. 'Little Hans' ' violent affects, his love for his mother and jealousy towards his father make him 'mad'; in the sense that a lover calls himself 'madly in love' with his object. In this case, what do fantasies do? They disguise, displace, transform. Above all, they create a second theatre of operations, to which whatever is transmittable from an activated libido can be diverted; fantasy binds libido to representations. To concern oneself in preference to these representations is to analyse, but perhaps it is only to half-analyse, if the suffering caused by this impossible love is not taken into account. It is to fix ones attention to the 'sexual theories' of children while failing to recognize that the solution they present is only partial compared with the quantity of libido which they do not manage to bind by this means, and which remains a burden for the child.

Doubtless one needs to have had experience with psychotic or pre-psychotic children to be sufficiently moved by this. Anxiety-horses are not enough. An adult lacks empathy. When he sees a horse, he is already on the way to imagining himself as a rider, mastering his mount. He does not see it with the eyes of the *small* child, crushed by this mass susceptible of becoming animated, bolting, stamping, biting. No doubt these are the child's projections, but what are projected here are emotions, movements, forces. Instincts.

Dora is a woman, and Hans a little child, and one knows that women and children are more easily prey to their emotions. Does the picture change when Freud has to deal with a man of university education suffering from 'intellectual obsessions': the 'Rat Man', an 'intelligent man with a clear mind'? It is even worse! Because the transference of symptoms to an intellectual level shows up *the horror of a pleasure unknown to himself* which is provoked by the fantasy of rats *penetrating* – all emphasized by Freud himself, who adds: 'in the rectum' – indicating a wish to sodomise the lady of his fancy. What could be responsible for this intense repression and the multiple defences that reinforce it: the fantasy or the ecstasy? If one replies: fantasy, it is because it produces ecstasy. Thus, in the last analysis, it is ecstasy that one encounters in relation to the love-object. Here it is not love for the lady of his fancy that drives him mad, it is the defences of which desire becomes the object, transferring the perversion which connotes it to the revealing symptom of perverted thought. One can say the hysteric is 'mad about her body'. The obsessional becomes mad about his mind – which is logical, as regression from acting to thinking sexualizes the latter.

If psychoanalysis well deserves to be called the analysis of passions, it is because it also situates them at the intersection of mind and body, and by setting itself at this focal point it can see that – between hysteria and obsessional neurosis – each of these two extremes draws libido towards itself, when the libido cannot exercise a specific action which would release tension through an experience of satisfaction. The hysteric converts somatically, the obsessional into thought, and between the two the phobic is anxious. Libido is everywhere, but above all it is *'between'*.

That thought succumbs here under the weight of the libidinal burden, that it becomes the caricature of itself – for Freud sees a form of the *compulsion to understand* in obsessional doubt –, shows at the same time that here is the source of the epistemophilic instinct, and most likely the sexual theories. It is a question of binding an unquenchable libidinal tension, through meaning. The constraints of interpretation are born of the constraints of the libido.

Thought can go so far in this work of transformation that it can border on delusion, which is rationalized secondarily. Here it is pertinent to quote the 'Rat Man' himself when he *knows* the pleasure of sexual intercourse for the first time. 'This is glorious! One might murder one's father for this!' (1909*d*, p. 201). What is evidently not said, is *this*: 'With my mother'. But who is speaking here? It is the child in love. The adult would be besieged, obsessed, faced with this lifting of repression.

For once, Freud recognizes the inadequacy of the nosography; he who gave obsessions the name of obsessional *neurosis*. Talking of his patient's morbid thought processes, he writes: 'I think such structures as these deserve to be given the name of *deliria*' (*ibid.*, p. 222).[1] However, it is remarkable that it is in this work that Freud, having to evaluate the relation between ideational content and affect, justifies affect and says that the deformation is on the side of the idea. Thus, if the affect is true, madness is displaced onto the idea.

The following case, 'Schreber', might on the face of it have demonstrated madness. But this is not so. If, according to the criteria of traditional psychiatry, Schreber is mad, he is not so in the sense that I wish to give to the term in this chapter. Schreber is psychotic, which is very different. Certainly it is his homosexual passion for his father, *via* Flechsig, which lies behind his delusion, but Freud points to something else as well: not the reference to narcissism alone, the touchstone of psychosis, but the delusional idea of the end of the world, which implies the destruction of reality – whence the construction of a delusional neo-reality, necessary for survival. 'The universe is destroyed, I alone survive', as Freud says – but at what price? The price of ecstasy, would be Lacan's answer. Elsewhere we have shown that this was to hold Schreber's *screams* very cheaply, or his cry which echoed beyond the construction of his delusion. For the deluded person's '*belle construction*' – in the sense in which one speaks of '*belle indifférence*' of the hysteric – is the supportive system which is necessary to hold together his ego, which can only survive by attaching its life to the defence of his delusion. This alienation is literally what cuts Schreber off from the life of men. Ecstasy is without doubt an important benefit. It is primarily of a masochistic nature. Secondarily it is narcissistic. Psychosis is not madness. Today one is misled to think so, when 'elegies to madness' flourish everywhere, which have nothing to do with psychosis. Today's madness is our hysteria (cf. the last chapter in Donnet and Green, 1973).

The field of psychopathology seems to have been quite extensively

---

[1] Strachey notes that delirium used in French and German psychiatry often corresponds to the English 'delusion' (*ibid.*, p. 164). [Translator's note.]

covered: on one hand, hysteria, phobia, obsessional neurosis, analyzable transference psychoneurosis; on the other, paranoia and unanalyzable narcissistic neurosis, apart from the meditation on a written text. And this, when the most enigmatic case of psychoanalysis appears: the 'Wolf Man'. In his account of this case, Freud himself admits that it is distorted because 'only the infantile neurosis will be the object of this work'. It is distorted again by the controversy between Freud and Jung. But, as frequently happens, what one does is not quite what one thinks one is doing, and it is this text that permits Lacan to recognize the importance of foreclosure[1] as a mode of repression in psychotic structures. Here Freud proceeds, unknowingly, with a description of the fundamental mechanisms found in those to whom we refer today as borderline cases. For where should one situate the 'Wolf Man'? He is between madness and psychosis. On re-reading the text, one finds splitting clearly indicated. But it is also with this case that Freud encounters the cruel experience of transference. Once more a bias is introduced by Freud's interest, which overstresses the patient's *infantile* neurosis to the detriment of the transference neurosis. Split transference in all respects, masking the patient's psychotic structure: the analyst's countertransference is again in question. In the end, the only case in the five analyses where Freud's transference was not unduly taxed is the 'Rat Man'. For Hans and Schreber, there was no cause to question it: in neither case was Freud the analyst. And one cannot say that the analysis of either Dora or the 'Wolf Man' was conducted without hindrances.

Where then does the 'Wolf Man's' madness lie? Uncontestably in his bisexuality, which Freud noticed. But what he glimpsed at, rather than noticing, is the repercussion of this conflict on the patient's thought processes.

What strikes Freud is 'the patient's power of maintaining simultaneously the most various and contradictory libidinal cathexes, all of them capable of functioning side by side. His constant wavering between these (a characteristic which for a long time seemed to block the way to recovery and progress in the treatment) dominated the clinical picture during his adult illness, which I have scarcely been able to touch upon in these pages. This was undoubtedly a trait belonging to the general character of the unconscious, which in his case has persisted into processes that had become conscious. *But it showed itself only in the products of affective impulses* (it is I who underline); in the region of pure logic, he

---

[1] Cf. pp. 69, 91 above. *'Foreclusion'* – term introduced by J. Lacan (1966), denoting a specific defence mechanism; the primordial expulsion of a fundamental signifier from the subject's symbolic world. The German term is *Verwerfung*. [Translator's note.]

betrayed, on the contrary, a peculiar skill in unearthing contradictions and inconsistencies' (Freud 1918*b*, pp. 118–19). These lines are taken from the final pages of this study, and they impose certain questions concerning the relation between madness and psychosis. The 'Wolf Man's' madness, attached to his bisexual conflict, is connected to his fixation to the primal scene and his rage at being excluded from his parents' pleasure. This is well known. But what lies behind it? It is the impossibility of deciding between the wish to experience orgasm like his mother (via the anus) or like his father (via the penis). One knows that castration cannot be avoided in either of these two cases: it is the blind alley of the inverted Oedipus complex. But this erotic madness is doubled by mad jealousy. The 'Wolf Man' no longer knows whom he wishes to destroy with vengeance, his mother or his father, which explains his affective 'wavering' on both the erotic and aggressive levels. The 'Wolf Man's' psychosis lies elsewhere. It resides in his foreclosure, his wish to 'know nothing', as Lacan pointed out, but even more so it is in his double mode of functioning – one could almost call it an affective and intellectual 'double bind': a wavering contradiction of the emotions – an impeccable logic of thought. In fact it is a question of double logic. The one is affective, allowing opposites to coexist, it does not make a choice; the other functioning on the principle of the excluded middle.[1] Thus we may conclude that madness is compatible with the logic of the included middle coexisting with a latent psychosis where castration is repudiated; it obeys the excluded middle. In conclusion, the secondary type of 'pure logic' can isolate castration anxiety by displacing it elsewhere, repressing it, but not by foreclosure or repudiation into normality.

This comes down to stating that madness is a sort of antidote to insanity, in the measure that a repression exists which functions elsewhere, which recognizes castration anxiety; but it also means that in borderline cases the existence of a double mode of functioning is anti-psychotic, which prevents thought processes from toppling totally into delusion. For the 'Wolf Man' is not Schreber. Here the world is not destroyed and there is no neo-reality: only an external reality coexisting with his psychic reality.

For us, the five case histories are not only an inestimable record of Freud's practice of psychoanalysis and of his interpretative genius. Neither are they just the means by which we may assess the link between practice and theory in Freudian psychoanalysis. They are the most

[1] In French, '*le principe du tiers exclu*'; the word 'tiers' (third, third party or third person) takes on here the double significance of the middle referred to in Logic and the third person in the Oedipal triangulation. [Translator's note.]

striking reflection of the distance Freud covered between 1901 and 1915, on a path strewn with obstacles and surprises. It is less important to note in passing his limits when faced with the resistance of neurosis to recovery – not without a twinge of relief on our part ('Ah ha! He too met with failure!') – than to see with blinding clarity how the resolution of one problem gives rise to a dozen others; how the unmasking of neurosis comes up against something that resembles it and differs from it: borderline cases.

After 1915 the 'Wolf Man' haunts theory, ceaselessly. He reappears in certain papers without being named; in the article 'The unconscious' (1915e), about the patient who squeezes his blackheads and seems to think that 'a hole is a hole'; in *Inhibitions, Symptoms and Anxiety* (1926d), where Freud wonders about his phobia compared with that of 'Little Hans'; in 'Fetishism' (1927e), where the theory of the coexistence of two modes of logic appears through splitting; and surely too in 'Analysis terminable and interminable' (1937c), where the question arises concerning negative therapeutic reaction, its relation to the death instinct and to bisexuality. This was a turning point both in theory and in clinical practice. Was 'An infantile neurosis' (1918b) really an infantile *neurosis*? In all events, it does not appear to be an adult transference psychoneurosis. What then? A narcissistic neurosis, psychosis? It would be an abuse of language to use the same term for 'the Russian' and Schreber. Still, Freud postpones for a few more years the introduction of the destructive instincts, exactly as he postpones separating the narcissistic neuroses from the psychoses.

PASSION-INSTINCT

The five case histories all precede the 'Papers on Metapsychology' (1915c, d, e, 1917d, e).[1] The papers which constitute this latter work have a definite function. They represent Freud's return to and re-evaluation of the theory that he expounded at the beginning of his work, which was supported chronologically by the pillars consisting of *The Interpretation of Dreams* (1900a), *The Psychopathology of Everyday Life* (1901b), *Jokes and their Relation to the Unconscious* (1905c), *Three Essays on the Theory of Sexuality* (1905d) and the analysis of Dora (1905e). Between the '*grande hysterie*' of the *Studies* (1896d) and the '*petite hysterie*' of Dora, passion and madness had been expurgated. This had been necessary so that psychoanalysis could come into being by expelling catharsis and the method that had

---

[1] The 'Wolf Man' case study was published in 1918, but Freud explains that it was drafted in the winter of 1914–15.

resulted from it. The 'Metapsychology' reveals the contradictions born of this exclusion.

Most authors agree on 'localizing' passion where body and soul unite, whether they are Cartesian or not. Freud does not belong to this filiation, but the one from which he is the offspring does not escape this tradition. He learned psychiatry from Griesinger, whose preoccupations were centred around this problem, as has been shown in the work of Paul Guiraud (1950), principal defendant, in the preceding generation of the French school, of a 'sub-cortical mind', that is hypothalmic. Before Griesinger, the German romantic school carped a great deal over the relation between body and mind. Freud broke with both the physicalist school supported by his teacher Brücke and the psychiatry of his day. It is easy, however, to show that even with his most audacious innovations, these influences left their mark. One catches their echo even in his most personal contributions, that is, in those concepts of which he was the unquestionable creator.

If we return to the definition which is of central concern to psychoanalysis – not the unconscious but the instincts –, 'our mythology', I shall quote the definition that Freud (1915c) gives them, adding my own commentary (in parentheses).

'If (*hypothesis*) we now apply ourselves to considering mental life (*the life of the mind*) from a *biological* point of view, (*by adopting the 'vertex' of the science of life, which is the point of view of the somatic body*) an 'instinct' appears to us as a concept (*the concept, and not the phenomenon, of instinct, is between inverted commas*) on the frontier (*concept at the limit of what one can conceptualize*), between the mental and the somatic (*frontier concept,[1] at the limit, the point where the psychical and the somatic meet*), as the psychical representative of the stimuli originating from within the organism and reaching the mind, (*the concept of instinct echoes the notion of psychical representations; semantic displacement: which is between the psychical and the somatic, the psychical representative of stimuli originating in the interior of the body – in other words, instinct, although localized between mind and body, acquires the status of psychical representative, and tips the balance to this side whenever it reaches the neighbourhood of the psychical, although it arises within the body*), as a measure of the demand made upon the mind to work (*measure, thus quantity, to work, which means to transform*) in consequence of its connection with the body' (*the psychical submits to the quantity that comes from the body to which it is bound – in other words,*

---

[1] The French '*concept limite*' and '*cas limites*' refer to the above 'frontier concept' and 'borderline cases' respectively, which renders better account of the limitative aspects or notion of extremity contained in the German '*Grenzfall*'. See chapter 3 above, 'The Borderline Concept'.

what is psychical is the slave of the corporal; the body which does not work itself, imposes this labour on the psyche, like a slave-driver).

Are we so far from passion? Passion is opposed to action as suffering is the opposite of acting. The ego submits to the instincts as the psychical (in the sense of instinct) submits to the corporal. The subject suffers his passion. He is no longer the agent but the patient. Passion dominates him and subverts his reason – his entire mind in fact. It alienates him from his object. It commands his actions. He no longer acts but is acted upon; he puts on an act.

Freud was obliged to attach passion – the most common state is being in love – to a corporal substratum, with a somatic infrastructure: sexuality. Although originally he clearly distinguished between love and sexuality. What is more, he had the lucidity to make the distinction within the instinctual components, between source and drive, of an organic nature and goal and object of a psychical nature.[1] The difference between the former pair, rooted in the body, and the latter two, less dependent on the soma, is that these are *substitutable*. The body is fixed, riveted, unchangeable; the psyche is mobile, thus modifiable. The entire theory of sublimation is outlined in these hypotheses. A reversal takes place in passion; it is the object which becomes unique and irreplaceable. But the object of passion is nonetheless a displaced object, a metaphor.

Unique and irreplaceable: these two adjectives are quite naturally couched by the pen that writes about the love-object or the object of passion. Freud uses them each time he endeavours to describe the first relationship between an infant and his mother: 'the trait of overvaluing the loved one and regarding her as unique and irreplaceable can be seen to fall just as naturally into the context of the child's experience, for no one possesses more than one mother, and the relation to her is based on an event that is not open to doubt and cannot be repeated' (1910*h*, p. 169). This statement is repeated in *An Outline of Psychoanalysis* (1940*a*), and we shall return to it. But why the mother? After all, we also have but one father.

As for doubt, the family romance demonstrates that it may just as easily concern either parent. Later – as though by chance, one should note – the answer appears as the solution to the problem of seduction, whether it relates to psychical or material reality. The prototype of the theory of anaclitic object cathexis is maternal care. In providing for the natural and cultural needs of her infant, the mother is the source of all the child's first experiences of pleasure. She is doubly unique and

---

[1] Which results in the notion of *psycho*sexuality.

irreplaceable: for the child's life, and for the pleasure that she alone is apt to provide. Through passion this anaclitic situation becomes a metaphor, which means that, by having become the necessary and sufficient condition for the infant's existence, the object no longer has to ensure any function of satisfying his vital needs. It remains true, nevertheless, that in passion, object-loss can bring about the inhibition of important biological functions, as depression shows quite well. If mourning for a loved object can cause an authentic depression, we are tempted to reverse the proposition and ask whether melancholia, for instance, would not imply a passionate 'devouring', an oral-cannibalistic relationship to the object.

The key word of this definition of the instincts is *representative* (psychical). It tells us that instincts are *already* psychical; an instinct is a delegation, a mandate or an embassy from the body. It does not concern the somatic body, but only the *libidinal* body. Libido is already animate, which means not so much 'animal' as 'belonging to the soul', which is in an alienated relationship to its object, because dependent on it for peace of mind – satisfaction.

This formulation, which emphasizes the representative *quality* of the instinct, is counterbalanced by the notion of measurement, that is, quantity. Measurement of an exigency: the strength to transform so that tension does not remain bound up within this conflict, but may lead to appeasing satisfaction: crying will become language, and wishing demanding.

Here we are on familiar ground. Behind an abstract definition – for what else is a borderline concept? – we find again the fundamental cogs of theory: the representative, the quota of affect. The symbolic, the economic – meaning, force.

In *Le discours vivant* (Green, 1973) I examined the arguments that raged in France over the respective functions of representations and affects in Freud's work, and the consequence of these divergences of interpretation. The debate is not over. The school which adheres strictly to Lacanian theory excludes affect altogether – showering sarcasm on all who refer to it, in other words the whole psychoanalytic community –, and they take the statute of representation, which they have stripped down to the (bare) essentials, to the extreme – I was going to say disincarnate – to the ultimate concept of the *mathème*.[1] The unconscious is no longer structured like a verbal language but like a mathematical

---

[1] Term used by Lacan in his attempt to formalize the minimal element of the signifier, which can be mathematizable.

language. We are faced with mathematical idealities – the code has become cipher.

What is certain is that in the 'Metapsychology', and until the second topic was established, Freud not only gave precedence to representations over affects, but in certain places he uses instinctual representative synonymously with its ideational representative. With the exception of one detail which he brings up at the end of his article on the unconscious: '. . . the unconscious presentation is the presentation of the thing alone. The system Ucs contains the thing-cathexes of the objects, the first and true object-cathexes' (Freud 1915e, p. 201). Objects of what? The answer is clear: of instincts; and, I would add, of passion.

For, whether we are concerned with the representation or the affect, in both cases it is the psyche that suffers. That suffers the passion of a missing object. It is here that the representation of psychoanalytic theory differs from the traditional (philosophic) conception of representation. In the latter instance, though the representation remains linked to the absence of perception, the subject hardly suffers from this lack; it is not desire that is lacking, nor is it the quest for a renewed experience of satisfaction, nor the avoidance of painful experience.

In the 'Metapsychology', Freud seems to subject affects to a treatment[1] which he later regrets. Not only does chapter 2 of *The Ego and the Id* re-establish their rights in no uncertain terms, but one will hear Freud repeatedly complain, in the last part of his work, that one – that he – had too long neglected the quantitative factor. One generally takes this affirmation literally and merely expounds the role played by the quantitative factor. However, if Freud always linked quantity to affect, one must understand that the importance of the *affective* factor went unrecognized for too long, as well as the transformations to which it did or did not give rise. What, ultimately, is the strength of the instincts, or the nature of their fixation? Nothing less than the intensity of passion and its attachment to its object. And if all this takes root in infantile sexuality, the objects of passion are to be sought in part-objects – taken from the mother's body or from that of the infant – or whole objects: the parental imagos. So what are the 'archaic' anxieties, then, referred to by contemporary authors? They are the effect of narcissistic passions, precisely where no differentiation between ego and object is possible, where love

[1] A treatment all the more ambiguous because at one moment he only allows representations the status of repression, as opposed to affects which are only suppressed, and at the next moment he maintains that the destiny of affects is the most important determining factor in repression. I refer the reader to *Le discours vivant* (Green, 1973) for a discussion of these two points. See also chapter 8 of this book.

and destructivity *affect* the ego and the object at one blow. They are passions in the strict sense of the term, that is, loves which are painful, to the point of having to defend ourself from them with an alienating sacrifice.

Lacan (1966, 'On psychical causality') writes: 'At the beginning of this development we have the primordial ego, which is essentially alienated together with primitive sacrifice, which is essentially suicidal: which is the fundamental structure of Madness.' But this was before the unconscious was said to be structured like a language, in a text where passion is present on every page. Later the *discourse* on passion will be confounded with passion itself. Passion will have been transferred to the fountain-pen.

TRANSFERENCE MADNESS—TRANSFERENCE PSYCHOSIS

When one re-reads the literature on passion, one is struck by the analogy with Aesop's language: the best or the worst of things. One is bound to admit that it is more often the worst than the best.

In psychiatry, as in psychoanalysis, it is natural that authors insist more on what is worst, rather than what is best, because, by definition, the finest fruit does not grow in their orchards. Psychiatrists and psychoanalysts only harvest what is blighted or poisoned. They both know: passionate structures develop delusional transferences, the only instances where psychiatrist and analyst risk dying on the field of honour, with the greater likelihood of falling in so far as they fail to recognize its true nature, or deny that paranoia infiltrates the transferred affects. Paranoia – *'psychose passionnelle'* – is the analyst's *'bête noire'*. The psychiatrist can still find protection behind a certificate of internment. But the analyst? There is surely no analyst who has not had his eroto-manic patient. He is none too proud of the fact because, unless there has been a technical error, he cannot fail to ask himself what, in the counter-transference, could have given rise to this delusional effervescence.

Freud, who was aware of what happened to his older colleague Breuer, was no doubt more careful. Confronted with the instability of the transference, he made a point of taming all that could favour this form of resistance by the transference. But one wonders if he did not throw out the baby with the bath-water. For it is important here to make a distinction: between madness and psychosis. Madness is present in *all* transference. When it is not experienced with the transference, it shows up clearly, outside the analysis, in the analysand who acts out. Transfer-ence psychosis is different. Psychotic transference is characterized by the parasitic nature it takes on, as though its sole objective were to destroy the analytic setting, everything being destructively cathected (auto- or hetero-destructive), whether emanating from the analysand's communication or the analyst's interpretative reply. Paranoia only represents the radical aspect of this, in the feeling which the subject experiences that everything belonging to him, in the exchange, is rejected. All is the Other's fault. And with cause, for were it not so, the subject would either be threatened with schizophrenic fragmentation or, even worse, with melancholic suicide. This does sometimes happen.

Thus, while a whole section of the psychoanalytic movement advises prudence when latent psychosis is suspected, which is to say that it holds back or takes care to 'respect the subject's defence mechanisms', in other words, decides to leave things as they are – as Flechsig did with Schreber –, another section takes the risk of confronting the subject's madness, and even his psychosis. I am referring here to the Kleinians, to Winnicott, to Searles. Moreover, it is only when a subject's madness, and in certain cases his psychosis, enters into the transference situation that analysis is really taking place. Everything new that has been said in psychoanalysis, in the past thirty years, has come from this source. It is sad, on the other hand, to see how the theory advanced by the most original author in French psychoanalysis only contributes, in this connection, ideas which suggest that, with psychotics, all that the analyst can do is establish the fact of the foreclosure of the paternal metaphor. In this case, one wonders yet again what a Lacanian analyst can hope for from an analytic relationship with a psychotic, or from psychoanalysis with a borderline case. Thus it seems that there is little left except to proclaim loud and clear the virtues of 'beinglessness'. The more beingless one is, the more likely one is to be admitted amongst the elect. Just like Bernini's Saint Theresa: the more one suffers, the greater the joy, and the closer one is to God the Master. One knows that, according to Lacan, it is the slave who experiences enjoyment. As for the Master's joy, it is nullified.[1]

---

[1] Does the Master hold to his masochistic pleasure? Or must one imagine that deciding, judging – this is unsharable pleasure? Even in establishing theory. For this is also to decide what is true and what is false, the truth then being the Master's pronouncement and not that of experience. If experience goes against theory, then one only has to reject experience for the last word to be the Master's word, which is assumed to have depleted experience of its potential truth. The heritage is handed on to the copyist rather than to him who continues to test theory against experience. The battlefield has changed sites. It is no longer in the analytic consulting room, but in the reading room.

What I am saying here is not, as one might suppose, applicable to Lacanism alone, but also to the sects which have developed around the charismatic figures of psychoanalysis. This is directed as much at a certain Freudian orthodoxy upstream, as at Kleinianism and Hartmannism downstream.

Theoretical options have practical consequences. If Lacan, by revoking affect – which Freud does not do –, 'mathematizes' psychoanalysis, it is not only the most interesting sector in psychoanalysis today that cuts itself off from practice, it is perhaps the whole of psychoanalytic practice that suffers: the neuroses that meant so much to Freud, or what is left of them.

One must proceed in the opposite direction: return to the basic model, rethink it in terms of borderline cases to rediscover what Freud excluded from neurosis, namely madness. It is from this starting point, from this new group whose boundaries are indistinct, that we will be able to look in both directions at the same time: in the direction of the neurotic structures and in the direction of the psychotic structures.

One might think, to begin with, that the division between psychosis and madness leads to a new Manichaeism separating good madness from evil psychosis. This would be to under-estimate the complexity of the phenomenon. On the contrary, in each structure one must single out the battle being waged by the forces of madness and those of psychosis fighting each other. This is easy when one finds the two ends of the chain. But it would be impossible to say that the purest neurotic madness contains no psychotic element, as Freud was forced to recognize that masochism has an unlimited field of action. Inversely, madness is still to be found in the most established psychosis. Is it not Freud's greatest originality to have shown that the schizophrenic's delusion, as well as his language, were in fact attempts to restitute (to repair?), to recathect, lost reality?

Thus, we would cease to be obsessed by the appearance, in the course of an analysis that has begun under the favourable auspices of a genuine neurosis, of the sempiternal 'psychotic core' which becomes a kind of trap where the naïve analyst unwittingly allows himself to be snared. Such a 'core', which we would gladly accuse the analysand of having hidden from us, with the same sort of deceit as we used to attribute to the hysteric simulator, would no longer be a trap for the analyst, nor the result of malevolence on the part of the analysand. We should be surprised if such a core does not appear and if the patient takes it away with him, carefully wrapped up in the folds of his unanalyzed transference, at the end of his analysis.

Present day analysts are relatively discrete about successive analyses (second, third . . .); first, because these concern them in the first instance, because they themselves feel the need for them; and secondly, because the analysands of these second or third analyses are analysts. There is a discreet silence – or a white lie – which escapes investigation and a review of what we could learn from this experience. While we may admit that returning to the couch is concomitant with the psychoanalyst's mental hygiene and his professional ethics, we should not confuse the well considered counsel of Freud – whose only analysis was his self-analysis, and who did not take the risk, later on, of lying on the couch of anyone else – with what is currently practised. Re-analysis, as recommended by Freud, was probably intended to take no longer than the military periods served by reserve officers, i.e. a few weeks. Nowadays these analyses last years. Why? The answers are neither very helpful nor very convincing: unresolved transference – is it ever resolved? –, reactivation of conflict due to the events of life – can one avoid it? –, weak defences – are they so 'ailing'? –, the effect of what remains unanalyzed – is the analysable ever exhausted? I shall not take the easy way out by invoking the 'psychotic core' again, this *deus ex machina*. It must nevertheless be asked whether the persisting effects of ill-being, which justify all requests for re-analysis, do not arise on the one hand from the exclusion of the madness on which I am trying to shed light, and on the other, from the relation of this hidden madness to the psychotic part of the personality (Bion).

THE ID AND THE EGO

The future of psychoanalytic theory, clinical practice and technique does not lie in the replacement of Freudian concepts centring around castration with a modern concept concerned with other referents – fragmentation, disintegration, annihilation, etc. – but in the *articulation* of these two approaches to bridge the gap between them. It seems to me essential to re-establish madness in the place where it has been recognized, for all time: at the heart of human desire. *Wo Es war.* For one has not sufficiently measured the leap, the decisive theoretical mutation that Freud made, in replacing the unconscious with the id – while hardly varying the formulations relative to the one and the other. In the 'Metapsychology' – let us return to it – it is stated that the distinction between unconscious/ conscious cannot be applied to instincts: one cannot say that an instinct is unconscious or conscious. This distinction can only apply to its representations. The unconscious is constituted of thing-representations and affects, if one takes into account the rectification in the third chapter of *The Ego and the Id*. In Lecture 31 (1933*a*), when Freud gives a description of the characteristics of the id, there is no reference whatsoever to any content – that is, to a representative inscription; only to instinctual impulses (*Triebregungen*) seeking discharge. In 1932, instinct tips to the side of energy, whereas in 1915 it inclined to the side of information. To say, then, 'ça parle'[1] only makes sense on condition that one assumes the responsibility for this affirmation without attributing it to Freud. Without representation, instinct has become blind. It has also become – a second change – maximally conflictual, because both life and death instincts cohabit the id.

Would this be sufficient to single out the return of passion – to live or to die? Not quite. By blind passion, one means precisely that it is blind. One not only means that passion carries away the ego, like a river leaving its bed and invading the surrounding land, but that the ego itself is blind and is no longer aware that it has lost control. It contains nothing and is no longer contained by anything. Now this second aspect is also one of the innovations of the second topography. And this is clearly stated in the first chapter of *The Ego and the Id* (1923*b*). One of the reasons, and not the least, which led Freud to withdraw the status of a system or agency from the unconscious, is that the ego, the seat of resistance, is itself unconscious of its own resistances. If one removes the blinkers from its eyes, it sees no difference, because it is the blind spot which occupies the whole field of vision. It only sees what it wishes to see, and nothing can force it to see what it refuses to see. And if it is made to admit that it perceives what it does not wish to see, there remains the resort to disavowal or splitting.

Lacan was not wrong to have insisted on the relation of the ego to *méconnaissance*.[2] However, if psychoanalysis is not pure speculation, it is necessary to know how recognition can come about in the course of an analysis. Lacanian theory began by cutting itself off from the image that could have accommodated a space for passion: what is passion if not the affectation of an image? It radically changed orientation, going from narcissism – which is nothing but passion for one's self-image and the forms that are incarnate in it – to narcissistic language. As I must proclaim my passion, which is to say to speak it, I am alienated from my speech. The object has evaporated, and the id has become a grammar.[3] However, as Freud said, no one can escape from himself. Between master and disciples, what is least lacking is passion.

There is no reason to be surprised that the ego, like the id, should be

---

[1] This phrase was coined by Lacan. There is a pun on the word 'ça': it, id; it speaks, id speaks. [Translator's note.]

[2] A term that has no English equivalent. It denotes a 'failure to recognize' or 'misconstruction', and is used by Lacan in relation to the word '*connaissance*' (knowledge). [Translator's note.]

[3] This sentence refers to Lacan's conceptualization of the id, which defines it according to a grammatical structure. [Translator's note.]

blind. There are two reasons, rather than one, why it should be so. Actually it originates in the id, and thus bears the stigmata of passion, like a label of origin. Ego: *made in id*.[1] Besides this, it is blinded by another agency, no less passional: the superego. This could hardly be otherwise, for the superego is born from a split in the ego, and it also takes root in the id. Freudian theory did not leave much room for the interplay of the conscious, the ego, or reality. From experience, one can say that these three concepts only collaborate to optimum effect when they are applied to the non-human world; giving rise to the ideal of the '*mathème*'. At the opposite extreme: the political. We know enough now to understand that passion, be it mad or psychotic, calls the tune.

It is not because we have considerably extended the field of passion and thus of madness, both clinically and theoretically, that we must draw pessimistic conclusions from this. Let us say to begin with that we have taken care to recognize it only where it already exists. We have not introduced it. It is where it has always been. And if it was necessary to recognize it, it is because we undermined its importance. It is by recognizing it that one will be better equipped not to reduce it, but to transform it through analysis; that is to say, to see to it that Eros wins over the destructive instincts. This is probably what Bion meant by differentiating an 'insane psychotic' from a 'sane psychotic'. This requires that the analyst no longer shuts the door to this madness, and that he consents to receive it and to share it by *analyzing* it. To do this (and this already takes place in most cases), one must recognize the true dimension of affect. This means to give free rein to affects in their least usual and least ordinary, or most contrary and most complex, aspects. To take the full force of transference passion is doubtless exhausting, but it is the price to be paid by *the analyst* if the analysis is to succeed. Needless to say, the countertransference comes to the fore here.

Moreover, the acceptance of transference madness, or even transference psychosis, is an initiation for the analyst to the mechanisms of a logic which is not merely the logic of the unconscious, which is implicit in Freud's work; it is to discover other forms of logic (see chapter 1 above). Freud's logic is a logic of hope because it counts on wish fulfilment. Borderline cases open up the horizons of the logic of despair (negative therapeutic reaction) or that of non-commitment (splitting). This implies that we must elaborate our concepts of the mental processes in relation to symbolization. This functioning can no longer be exclusively limited to primary and secondary processes. Tertiary processes (proces-

---

[1] In English in the text. [Translator's note.]

ses of *relation* between primary and secondary processes) become precious tools in the comprehension of material and the formulation of interpretations.

THE THEORETICAL JUSTIFICATION FOR THE DISTINCTION BETWEEN MADNESS AND PSYCHOSIS

What heuristic advantage is there to be gained from substituting the classical terminology – neurosis, perversion, depression, psychosis – with the opposites madness-psychosis? If I propose to rehabilitate the old term of madness, which belongs to the era of pre-scientific psychiatry when authors spoke of '*folie hystérique*', '*folie du doute*', '*folie du toucher*', '*folie morale*'[1] (*moral insanity*), it is perhaps because, by over-stressing wishes and fantasies, we too easily forget, within the protected setting of the analytic session, the unfurling of passion which is the language of the instincts. The restrictions of the analytic setting, the prohibitions which restrain action, the obligation to speak, though they have the merit of revealing the defence mechanisms which give us access to the psychical world of wish and fantasy, make us lose sight, on the other hand, of the way *the enactment of instinct* functions, as well as the impact of passion which accompanies its aberrations. In the matter of madness, the analyst only knows psychical madness, which is revealed by distortions of reality, which bears witness to the ego's mode of functioning. In his article 'Neurosis and psychosis' (1924*b*), Freud describes the distortions to which the ego has to consent by dividing or splitting, to avoid collapse, adding that we may thus understand the eccentricities or follies of men, which would be to the ego what sexual perversion is to sexuality. But if he kept on repeating that the weak point of the ego's organization lies in its behaviour in regard to the sexual instinct, may we not imagine that the eccentricities and follies of men manifested by the ego are only the reflections of what the sexual perversions themselves contain of camouflaged madness – a madness which is in the very nature of human sexuality?

Besides, it seems to me that the opposition between madness and psychosis fits better with the final theory of the instincts. A disturbing coincidence in Freud's work is most noticeable. He realizes, at an equally late stage, that the true antagonist of the sexual instincts is represented by the destructive instincts, and that he has to allow more and more for psychosis, or for the psychical mechanisms – I am thinking of splitting

---

[1] These terms need not be translated into English, but may be referred to as 'doubting mania' and 'touching phobia' – *moral insanity* being written in English by the author. [Translator's note.]

and disavowal – which one finds in psychosis, but which have a far more general influence. One can infer from this coincidence that destructive instincts and psychosis are directly linked together. Thus, when Freud talks of delusion as an attempted recovery or a construction of a neo-reality, one must understand this movement as an attempt to regain lost ground through erotic madness.

The madness at the heart of man is not the prerogative of pathology. But one should not confuse this madness with what we call psychosis. I propose the following formula to distinguish between them: *madness, which is a component of the human being, is linked to the vicissitudes of primordial Eros, which are in constant conflict with the destructive instincts. When Eros prevails, it is because the passions which inhabit it become bound, and psychosis is averted. But when the destructive instincts triumph over Eros, the unbinding process is stronger than binding, and psychosis wins through.*

This is merely a descriptive picture. One must still ask oneself why the destructive forces win in the case of psychosis – a question to which there are as yet no certain answers. I do not believe that Freud ever found the answer. Melanie Klein seems to think that constitutional factors provide the explanation. As for Winnicott, though he attaches more importance to the maternal environment, his optimistic view ascribes a positive value to this destructiveness through the notion of ruthless love. Myself, I incline to the opinion of Harold Searles, or one that is close to his.

Psychosis emerges when the subject is forced to mobilize his destructive instincts as a means of putting an end to a fusional relationship with a primordial object. I do believe that psychosis is a *conjuration of the object*.

We have yet to explain why it is that things happen in this way, by trying to reconstruct the modalities of object-relation functioning.

Unlike the anarchic and disordered mode of id cathexes, the ego has a network of stable cathexes which remain at a constant level. Now how does it acquire this relative independence of the id? It is not sufficient to argue in favour of innate attributes, maturation or experience. We know today the fundamental role that the primary object plays in this evolution. One may suppose that a double mechanism intervenes: on the one side favoured by the role played by the primordial object in maternal care, on the other side favoured by the infant's identification with the primordial object. At the same time, the infant remains subject to a double series of excitation, internal instinctual excitation and external excitation, where what comes from the object carries particular weight. To my mind, it is the relationship with the maternal object which enables the constitution of the ego, from which two consequences arise:

– when, thanks to the object, the ego succeeds in establishing a stable system of cathexes within itself, on a constant level, it will only need to battle against internal instinctual excitement. It can then develop thought mechanisms, although it will not escape from the pressure of instinctual activity. It will be able to elaborate this through the creation of fantasy: the pole of madness attached to the instinct is contained within the limits of fantasy and the vicissitudes of Eros.

– when the ego not only has to fight against instinctual excitement, which is always a carrier of incipient madness on the internal level (though susceptible of being contained), but also has to fight the external source of the object's instinctual madness, which transpires through the object-relationship, then a second front is created to combat the object. It is this struggle against an enemy agent, who should be an ally, that calls for the mobilization of the destructive instincts which are responsible for the outbreak of psychosis.

In this last instance, the ego loses its head, so to speak; at times it is no longer capable of distinguishing between what it perceives of its own instincts and those coming from the object; it panics in confusion and finds no other expedient than to react destructively. It is of little importance to the ego that it has to scuttle itself, as long as it can conjurate the object by destroying it.

THE MOTHER-INFANT RELATIONSHIP VARIATIONS ON A GENETIC MYTH

To understand what happens when this type of relationship is pathogenic, we must first return to a more general situation. Descriptions of the mother-infant relationship have not been taken far enough. Because analysands are the object of our observation, and because contemporary psychoanalytic experience has shown the persistence of mental processes demonstrating the so-called primitive or archaic defences or fantasies of the type described so precisely by Melanie Klein and her successors, many authors willingly adhere to the notion of a psychotic base, still present in the adult, as the vestige of an original infantile 'psychosis' which would be, in a sense, an inevitable condition of very early infancy. Nowadays, even though Kleinian authors seem to moderate their assertions and admit that this terminology is regrettable, I believe they hold to this conception of primitive psychic activity, which has but little to do with neurosis. Personally, I find this conception acceptable but incomplete.

For, in the same way as the Kleinians think that this psychosis, which I prefer to call original madness, is supposedly normal in the infant, I would like to propose that the complementary thesis of 'normal maternal madness' be added to it (cf. Green, 1975). This is neither shocking nor surprising. It suffices to reflect for a moment on pregnancy and maternity, with sufficient perspective and objectivity to grasp that throughout this period, for the woman living through this experience, there is a complete remodelling of her feelings in relation to the world, and the organization of her perceptions, which are entirely centred on the infant. The mother's sensitivity to the most imperceptible signals takes on a quasi-hallucinatory quality for onlookers. Pregnancy and maternity take on a miraculous dimension for the mother; they satisfy wishes of omnipotence and the wish to be, for the infant, all that he is for her, this *unique, incomparable* object, to whom all is owed and all is sacrificed, and this in the normal course of events. It is when this 'madness' does not appear that we have reason to suspect that the matter is disturbing. Freud rightly noted this conjunction between sexuality and love in maternal care. By drawing attention to the fact that the mother does not content herself with simply feeding the child, but also provokes agreeable and disagreeable physical sensations in him, Freud is showing her to be the first seductress. So the activity of care and the erotic activity of seduction are inseparable. And Freud writes in the *Outline*: 'In these two relations lies the root of a mother's importance, unique, without parallel, established unalterably for a whole lifetime as the first and strongest love-object and as the prototype of all other later love relations – for both sexes' (Freud, 1940a, p. 188). Now if these later love relationships show us this short madness in full bloom, one must suppose it to be present from the beginning and primarily in the mother, accompanying all the subsequent vicissitudes of this primordial Eros, in perversion, in neurosis, and even in the most elaborate forms of sublimation.

Were this maternal madness not counterbalanced by another aspect of the mother infant-relationship, it would most probably not have only positive effects. The role that we have assigned to the object, to permit the constitution of the ego, depends on quite different functions. The mother must play the role of an auxiliary ego, a container and a mirror for the infant. However, she can only accomplish this task if she can accept and contain her own instincts at the same time, to be able to awaken the child to instinctual life, which is, after all, life itself. She must enable him to recognize his own instincts in her, to feel that she can be used as a receptacle for them, so that they can be returned to him in a more acceptable form.

So we are faced with a description of maternal love which is totally paradoxical. This does not prevent this love from taking place spontaneously and instinctively. I would sum up this situation in a phrase: after fostering the birth of instinctual life, the only aim of maternal love is to make it tolerable for the infant. Potentially, the mother continually oscillates between the excess of gratification and the excess of frustration. Both have the same effect: that of provoking instinctual excitation which goes beyond the ego's possibilities of elaboration, which is the integration of instincts through a binding activity. When these elaborative possibilities are overwhelmed, the ego has to face the double anxiety of intrusion and separation, which one can observe in borderline cases. Up to this point, everything remains within the limits of what I have called private madness, which only becomes manifest in transference regression.

But one must also take other types of relationship into consideration, and especially that on which the hypothesis of psychosis is founded. In this last case, maternal madness does not show itself so much in the form of love as in intense instinctual activity, which is not contained, either in a direct form or in the disguised form of anxiety or the defences against it. The containing or mirror role of the auxiliary ego can no longer be assumed by the maternal object. In the more favourable instances, the infant, being able to count on the object, has only to defend himself against internal instinctual excitement, as we pointed out; that is to say, against his own madness. It is in relation to this that castration anxiety appears, which I now tend to link with the anxiety of being penetrated. In the more serious instances, as I believe I have shown concerning borderline cases, in addition to this struggle against internal instinctual excitation, the subject has also to struggle against external instinctual excitation which comes from the object. He undertakes this in his endeavour to find a means of adaptation in regard to his limits, which allows him to conserve his object, provided he is continually on guard against threats created by the double anxiety of separation and intrusion. Finally, in psychosis, the help offered by the object – its function as an auxiliary ego, a container and mirror – is far from compensating the instinctual flux (whether direct or in the form of anxiety). A second line of battle is then created against the source of this external instinctual excitement coming from the object, which makes any effective form of defence impossible. Confusion arises as to the internal or external origin of the excitement. It is in these circumstances that the destructive impulses are mobilized, because the ego is not able to constitute itself; it can no longer use its binding capacity. For, besides internal madness with which the ego has to negotiate compromises, it also has to reckon on the object's madness; which is to say, the madness of the object's instincts.

Thus I would say that everything happens as though *it were impossible for the order of the world to appear*; and as though all were chaos, chaos to which the chaos of destruction responds.

Even if this world order were illusory, it would be necessary for it to exist for a while before the ego could become aware of its completely relative nature. It is in these circumstances that the destructive impulses seem to play the role of a final recourse in the endeavour to neutralize the object, engulfing surrounding reality in the same wave of destruction.

Paternal mediation

Hitherto, I have said nothing about the father. This is certainly not because his appearance on the scene comes later. If he is not directly present in the relation, his role is nonetheless fundamental. His presence is either hidden or displaced onto the child. As a matter of fact, it is essential that the maternal madness which is expressed in her love for the infant includes the father; not only because he is the donor, but because he represents a limitation to this madness, inasmuch as the infant's love alone cannot satisfy the mother. He is, so to speak, the guarantee of the transformation of this madness, and of its evolution towards inevitable separation. And because he himself contains the mother's anxiety and is the object of other instinctual satisfactions (particularly sexual), these will not have to be discharged onto the child. But the father is also present in the child himself in the mother's eyes, because, as the product of his parents' union, every child carries in his features the traits of both his father and his mother. The father is thus a mediatory element between mother and infant. I would not like to intimate that the father has the privilege, or misfortune, of being exempt from madness; only he exercises his elsewhere – in the world, in social life, in his preoccupation with power. Perhaps this is just one other demonstration of his attempt to disengage from primitive maternal madness, not because it is redoubtable, but because its delicious benefits are passivating.

Passivation

These genetic hypotheses – less genetic, in fact, than the retracing of the myth of an intelligible genesis on the basis of these disorganizations – have certain implications. I should like to insist on one fact – and here I believe I am in agreement with Freud as well as with Winnicott – and that is the crucial importance of what I call passivation.[1]

Instinctual action, itself active, 'passivates' the subject who is submit-

---

[1] 'The first sexual or sexually coloured experiences which the child has in relation to his mother are naturally of a passive character' (Freud, 1931*b*, p. 236).

ted to it. The role of maternal care passivates the child. If instincts are not to be felt as dangerous and destructive, even though they contain this polarity of madness because of this disquieting effect on the subject, the subject must be able to count on his object, as the child who is passivated by maternal care must be able to count on the mother. Freud already noted this repudiation of feminity present in both sexes as the rock upon which the analytic cure floundered. I prefer to translate this remark by saying that what is in question is the repudiation of the mother's feminity, in both sexes, which is to say, her passivating action. This is for reasons that are not only due to negative characteristics but because the return to maternal fusion is a threat to individuation, especially when it evokes a lost paradise, from which one would never again wish to leave. The mobilization of the destructive instincts in psychosis is the supreme recourse to activity, against passivation by an object in whom it is impossible to put one's trust. Thus, where extreme pathology is concerned, just as much as in normality, it is passivation that is feared – and it is this that must be made tolerable.

Now the psychoanalytic cure is not possible without this confident passivation, where the analysand gives himself up to the analyst's care. Hence it is important to try to connect the hypothesis I have just presented, on the clinical and theoretical level, with the psychoanalytic situation. One should ask oneself what it is that makes this psychoanalytic situation so difficult – whereas it is supposed to be facilitating –, what makes it intolerable. And finally one must study the means by which this analytic situation can be made acceptable, so that it may be fruitful. But this is the subject of another paper (Green, 1979a).

Let us just say that here technique could be reunited with theory. If Freud's final formulations suppose the double equation Eros = binding, destructive instincts = unbinding, one may understand that, as long as one is at grips with madness as with erotic passion, the work of binding is so to speak accomplished in advance; or at least it is sufficiently in the process of being so for the analyst's silence to allow the working through to progress under the auspices of his silent attention. The situation is quite different when psychotic unbinding gets the upper hand of these operations. In this case, the analyst's silence would be collusive with this work of Penelope, where the generative value of silence is turned in to degenerative transformation. It is in these cases that the analytic binding processes – which I call tertiary processes – should come into play, introduced by the analyst's spoken word.

Theorization always obliges us to be somewhat schematic. It is clear, I hope, that we are concerned here with the relations of balance between

Eros and the destructive instinct or relations of unbalance.[1] For binding and unbinding are always at work in madness as in psychosis. It is the resultant that counts, making transformations of the products of creation, or debris, products of disintegration. One must also insist, if one wishes to dot one's i's, on the positive role of unbinding, which produces discontinuity without which the mechanisms of recombination could not take place, for continuity is as much the limitless space of fusion as timelessness. To introduce tertiary processes is to recognize the capital importance of the third party, without whose mediation the subject-object confrontation would be but a closed circuit. This re-establishes a consistency between theory and practice: the structural value of the Oedipus complex and three-factor logic.

Perhaps the whole tragedy of the little boy child, but also all his hope, lies in the fact that, as subject, he always has to deal with two objects.

PASSIONS AND THEIR VICISSITUDES

Now, in conclusion, I am anticipating two objections which are doubtless only one.

– This passion that you see everywhere is not shown up so openly in clinical practice. After all, passional states are easy to recognize when they are manifest, so why extend the field to the more 'apathetic' syndromes?

– Besides, in recommending that we pay so much attention to affect, do you not run risk of reducing psychoanalytic theory to phenomenology, and technique to the cathartic method? On this last point Ferenczi already made a stand without success. Of course, one will understand that these questions, which I have put into the mouth of an imaginary objector, are the questions that I ask myself. It seems to me that I am not proposing any theoretical or technical revolution here, but a readjustment of theory in the light of experience. I am not saying that the work on representations is of little value, or that the analysand's language is contingent, engaging the analyst to go 'beyond' his discourse. I am not so naïve as to believe that affective discharge has, in itself, magical strength. I say that Freudian theory, in spite of having perfectly recognized the implications of analysis, has become lopsided. If one does not wish simply to attribute this to Freud's personality and his personal ideology – a theory which is not without weight; think of what he writes of Michelangelo's Moses and the ideal of the mastery of affect that he upholds as the highest accomplishment of which man is capable – one

---

[1] In fact we are dealing with 'variations of balance' of optimal value which produce what I have called 'efficacious difference', and 'useful distance' (Green, 1979*b*).

must produce an explanation. It seems to me that the attention given to representations comes from the concern for scientific demonstrability. Who is not fascinated by the explanatory figure accompanying Freud's forgetfulness of the name Signorelli? The problem here is that it concerns a matter that can hardly be called a symptom. The painter's name is recalled and all – thanks to the unconscious – falls into place. Schreber's grammar or even his 'fundamental language' throw light on his *text*. It remains to be seen what mobilizing effect this interpretation could have had on him. As for the Wolf Man who has just died – in a pitiful mental condition from what I can gather – it is better to remain charitably silent. No other case has been more discussed, each commentator applying his own theory to it and displaying marvels of ingenuity. One should have put these brilliant constructions to the test of psychoanalytic experience.

So something resists. Searching for it, I propose, in the light of my experience, that what has been obscured should be recognized. For science is not that which is explicable by removing what is embarrassing, but is what can throw light on complexities, even at the risk of appearing impure. In the end what I maintain is that affect is representation. Signifier of the flesh, is what I proposed in *Le discours vivant*. Today I would rather say the *representative of passion*.

Is this a reference to experience? Hardly, for what I have in mind is not conscious experience, but *unconscious* affect and its products of transformation, which I hold responsible for fixation and defences, positive and negative affects, for love and hatred, mad or psychotic. It is in the writings of the English-speaking authors whom I have quoted that I have found something, as in the account of their analyses, which convinced me and which had seemed lacking in my training, influenced as it was by Lacan's teaching. For all that, it is not a question of having been converted, for I still believe that psychoanalysis is a *talking* cure. However, to my mind, this calls for a re-interpretation of Lacan's work, to which I am attached, for most (not all) Lacanians believe themselves to be integrists.

To come back to the first question: the extension of the field of passion. Freud thought – incorrectly, it has been shown, although it matters little in this connection – that perversions were not subject to repression, and he upheld the idea of polymorphous infantile perversion. Natural perversity, so to speak; neurosis becoming a cultural phenomenon, a backlash from the process of civilization. One could thus reproach him for having found perversion everywhere, behind neurosis, depression, psychosis. Even a slightly attentive reader will know that this is not true. And one can say the same for passion.

Passional states exist. They are, we know, the limit of analyzability – as is perversion, for that matter. Freud pointed out that one will never convince a pervert that he could obtain greater pleasure from the exercise of so called normal sexuality than from the satisfactions procured by his perversion. And for a start, why convince him? In presenting him with a table decked with the pleasures of ordinary sexuality, he could always retort that you have no idea of what you miss by disdaining the banquets of perversion. Each does according to his choice, and this is true of passion as well. Resistance to what we call the cure obeys similar mechanisms. Beyond the wish to recover, Freud says, the analysand clings to his illness, and I say that he prefers the object of his passion. But it is clear, surely, that I am speaking of *unconscious* passions and the *vicissitudes* of passions:[1] including passions produced by sublimation, of which I have not spoken. Here there is no need to invoke phenomenology. What is more, I do not believe that affect escapes from symbolization, or from metaphor. In fact I even think that affect is the matrix of symbolization, and not just energy. By designating the *pleasure-unpleasure* principle, Freud shows that, by needing two terms to define it, he has constructed a binary model which is the condition that marks the limits of the statute of the symbol; whereas perhaps the reality principle suffers from being designated by one term alone.[1] Here there is symbolic opposition between the two principles; thus redoubled symbolization – between pleasure and unpleasure, and between pleasure-unpleasure and reality. The logics of theory are coherent.

Logic is not the prerogative of representations. It is also of an affective nature. The oldest authors spoke of the logic of passion. What is more logical or more passional than passionate delusion? Undeconstructible.

Just as perversion does not in effect emerge from repression, whatever Freud might have thought, so '*psychose passionnelle*' is the direct product of passion. On the contrary, it is the expression of the transformation of passion to the highest degree, because forbidden love will lead to the destruction of either the object or the ego. Thus in the diverse clinical pictures where conflicts are forming, one must see them as just so many systems of transformation of unconscious passion, which I have called erotic madness, stemming from the shared madness between mother and infant.

Certain key words are united in significant constellations: life, affect, woman. It is common sense, thus suspect meaning. However, one must

---

[1] I am, of course, referring here to 'Instincts and their vicissitudes' (Freud, 1915c).
[1] Perhaps one could propose the denomination of the reality-truth principle, for they are frequently opposed to each other.

also be careful to mention other negative constellations which behave like a plot hatched by deadly forces. Freud admitted – this is important to note, not as a criticism but as a token of that lucidity of his which few of us today can match – that he had not succeeded in piercing the mystery of feminity ('what do women want?'), that he did not much appreciate occupying the mother's place in the transference, and that he had little taste for psychotics. Could his clinical approach, his technique, his theory come out of this unscathed?

Intellectual impartiality is not without a price.

In spite of not being very fond of passion, Freud nonetheless had a passion for truth; while admitting that it is only attainable through deformations. This does not prevent truth, once discovered, from shaking up a number of them and not just the smallest. However, there is, in spite of its inevitable deformations, a core of truth in Freudian theory, just as there is in delusion. Freud expresses this in the last part of 'Analysis terminable and interminable' (1937c): the *repudiation of feminity in both sexes*. In both sexes: where then is his alleged phallocentrism? The Oedipus complex is the *Vatercomplex*, the paternal complex. But is this not to the advantage of the repudiation, not of woman, but of her most fundamental image: the mother? One is beginning to show interest in the mother tongue, let us be careful not to reduce it too quickly to the tongue of our forefathers. Order would be rapidly re-established, but mothers would hurriedly remind us: 'What you are saying is Greek to me. You say nothing of the smile on waking, of bursts of laughter, of lengthy babbling without an intelligible word, but only of what is understood between these speaking beings; not of piercing cries, of plaintive weeping prolonged to bespeak pain, even when the pain has passed when mother returns; you will say nothing either of the long silences where so much happens while contemplating mother's ear, her breast, or her hand. You will say nothing of pleasure or of suffering; of the joy of childbirth, of being fed from, of cradling in one's arms. You have never seen a mother with her infant. You visit museums to contemplate the Madonnas and Child. You look and you pass on to the next painting . . . a Passion. And you see no link between them. You think that Jesus on the Cross is thinking only of the Father.'

But one no longer paints Passions. Times have changed. What remains is the passion for colour, for form, for volume, the obsession with space and matter. The passion for a look. But whose look?

Freud wrote that the death of one's father was probably the most important event that man had to face. And with cause. He kept his mother for much longer. Re-read his correspondence and see what he writes when death finally takes her from him. It is almost a sigh of relief. And he adds that, with age, the poor lady was no longer what she had been.

So much discretion in the face of this bereavement explains retroactively why he had been so struck by Leonardo's discretion in the same circumstances, when consulting his *writings*.

Repudiation of passion for the mother. Destruction of the Oedipus complex, of the *Muttercomplex*.

Here I am not blowing the trumpets of psychoanalytic modernity. I am not repressing the Father to allow the Mother to surface anew. I do not believe it is useful to replace the Father of the horde with the Great Mother Goddess. I only wonder why analysts persist in this perpetual quarrel of precedence.

Passion for the father is not secondary, in the two senses of the term. It is different. There is a difference of passion, as there is a difference of the sexes. If in this chapter I have been at pains to emphasize the links between passion and erotic madness, and if I have sought the matrix of the one and the other in the mother-infant relationship, I have not forgotten that, without passion between man and woman, the passion between mother and child would be constantly threatened with 'hubris', because of the lack of discovery of the other as other. Capital letters[1] are superfluous here. It is the destiny of passion to affect the other with a capital letter, in erotic madness. In psychosis too, but in this instance he is affected with a negative force.

---

[1] A reference to the Lacanian concept of the Other. [Translator's note.]

10

Negation and Contradiction

> He had spoken the very truth and transformed it
> into the veriest falsehood.
>
> It is a curious subject of observation and inquiry,
> whether hatred and love be not the same thing at
> bottom. Each, in its utmost development, supposes
> a high degree of intimacy and heart-knowledge;
> each one renders one individual dependent for the
> food of his affections and spiritual life upon another;
> each leaves the passionate lover, or the no less
> passionate hater, forlorn and desolate by the with-
> drawal of his object. Philosophically considered,
> therefore, the two passions seem essentially the
> same, except that one happens to be seen in a
> celestial radiance, and the other in a dusky and
> lurid glow.
>
> HAWTHORNE *The Scarlet Letter*

THINGS AND 'NO'

At the meeting of the American Psychoanalytic Association in December
1974 S. Abrams and P. Neubauer presented a paper entitled 'Object-
orientedness: the person or the thing'. Using all the resources of
psychoanalytic egopsychology in the comparison of two children, faith-
fully and regularly observed in minute detail, their paper studied two
types of object-orientedness: toward people and toward things. The
discussion contrasted the child whose object relationship bound him
mainly to persons, and the child whose object-relationship was bound to
things. As I listened I was struck, apparently more than were the authors
of the communication, by one fact. At a given age, each child possessed a
vocabulary of five words. At least on first catching the ear, so to speak,
there was no notable difference as far as four of these words were
concerned. They designated persons who normally were around the
children: Mummy, Daddy, little sister or brother, the maid, etc. But they

First published in *Do I Dare Disturb the Universe? A Memorial to Wilfred R. Bion*, ed. James
Grotstein (Beverly Hills, Caesura Press, 1981).

differed significantly on one point: the child whose object relationships created a bond between him and things said 'This', while the child whose object relationships were oriented toward persons said 'No'. I was struck by this connection between the predominant interpersonal (or inter-subjective) relationship and the use of negation.

Spitz (1957) recognizes – as have many before him – that the concept of negation and the constant use of the semantic 'no' for communication are specifically human patterns. Yet his study of the prototypes of 'no' in the area of motor activity – the infant's rotating and nodding movements of the head – reminded me irresistibly of the difficulties I had in communicating with the Greeks during my vacation: the Greek 'Né', which is phonetically similar to the French 'non', means 'yes', while the voiceless gesture which expresses the negative in Greek is a vertical, down-up movement resembling the up-down movement that accompanies the French 'oui'. It took me a while to get used to it, for I wondered if I was not altogether confusing the messages of these undoubtedly friendly people.

To return to the work of Abrams and Neubauer, it seemed to me that it could be deduced from their study that thing-orientedness (object 'objectivation') was essentially realistic and merely brought about a duplication of presence, just as the 'da' in the cotton reel game only calls attention to the fact that the reel really is there. Person-orientedness, on the other hand, accompanied as it is by the use of negation, made me think of the relations that could be established btween negation and the absence that the child playing with the reel expresses by 'o-o-o'. The reel is not there: *I affirm that I deny*. At this point I could embark on paths of speculation. However, I will abstain from doing so and reflect first on these connections between affirmative and negation in clinical theory (see my remarks on the cotton-reel game in Green (1967, 1970)).

Positivistic Clinical Theory

Clinical theory is positivistic. It translates into metapsychological jargon the results of an observation bearing on the visible, the observable, that which testifies to the responsive mind. Yet psychoanalysis takes as its object the unobservable and the repressed. True, but theoretical language has remained positive in character and I intend to suggest (somewhat arbitrarily) a different formulation of a certain number of clinical clichés based on patients whom I shall imprudently designate by their usual labels, in spite of our natural distrust of such generalization.

The hysteric condenses
But it is because the hysteric, in his repression, strives to create every sort of gap between language and body, that he over-condenses.

The obsessive displaces
But it is because the obsessive cannot resist the temptation to bring in to contact essentially alien elements that he goes on endlessly displacing.

The phobic avoids
But it is because the phobic eroticizes danger that he makes it appear where there is none and projects it onto objects or situations. Space is safe at last when he has become panphobic. Nothing can then arouse his fear unexpectedly since everything has become frightening.

The melancholic is mourning an object
But it is because the melancholic has finally been freed from the object of his passionate hatred that he imprisons its ghost by offering up his ego to restore its life.

The paranoid projects and regards his projection as a reality
But it is really because the world and other people are entirely indifferent to him and because he can believe in nothing that he over-rationalizes external reality and develops a passionate relationship with it.

The schizophrenic splits and disintegrates
But it is really because he is passionately attached, in mutual parasitism, to the mother's oneness that he becomes dissociated.

These are nosological references which describe psychical reality from a distance. Let us put them aside and enter, instead, the analytic situation.

A Clinical Illustration

The patient, whom I shall call Ninon, I considered to be a deeply disturbed hysteric, and she had suffered an ulcerative colitis in the course of her treatment. After ten years of analysis with her I found myself, not for the first time, in a distressing situation. I shall say nothing of this patient's material. I shall say only that I was upset by her responses to my interventions. Three of these, in particular, seemed noteworthy to me. The 'Don't know' every time the associations became sufficiently explicit for her to draw the interpretation that she should have found for herself, and that I was expecting her to find for herself. 'I know!' she would say in an annoyed tone, replying to my interventions, and meaning: 'You haven't told me anything new. I knew that already; it's obvious' – the implication being: 'It's worthless.' Finally, in other instances, she used to say peremptorily 'No!' and accompany this with a veritable body discharge, as if she were lashing out on the couch, which reminded me of what Freud and Bion have said about the evacuation of unpleasant stimuli through motor activity.

One day, however, she related the 'tomato-rice episode'. Due to her mother's ambivalence and complicity, this patient did not attend school until she was nearly seven years of age. She had rationalized her phobia of leaving her mother by her fear of not knowing at school. She would, moreover, be stricken mute in front of strangers (especially the doctor whom her mother patronized assiduously) and suffered from anorexia.

One day her mother had made her a dish of tomato-rice. She made up her mind not to eat it. Furious, her mother began chasing her all over the apartment and trapped her in a corner. she tried to force her daughter to eat. The spoon was pushed against the barrier of her tightly clenched teeth and her mouth was forced open. But, predictably, the rebellious child spat the mouthful out. The enraged mother, determined to win at all costs, then said to her, 'If that's the way you want it, then you'll go to school!' She dragged her there despite screams and tears.

My patient's reaction to the manifest content was to speak of it as a traumatic experience. Of course, it was one. Except that what is missing from this is the secret desire of my patient who, without knowing it, wanted nothing more than to go to school. In fact, it was her mother's ambivalence that prevented her from doing so. The proof is that she came out first in class on the first test, but when she told her mother about it, the mother seemed upset that in the future her daughter might not be happy with anything less than the highest mark. I must admit that, at the time, the tomato-rice story fascinated me to such an extent that I risked falling for the manifest content. It was only later, on a specific occasion, that I understood that here 'no' reproduced her refusal of the tomato-rice and that it was to be taken as a 'yes'. To be more precise, I would say – as I told her later on – that as she was so completely committed to expressing her *negative affirmation*, the apparent expulsion really carried with it, in the opening necessary for the utterance of this 'no', a 'yes' which slipped surreptitiously into her. This was her way of introjecting – the word has now been said – the interpretation. After this intervention, she had the feeling that her analysis had more progress in a few weeks than it had in ten years.

We shouldn't speak too quickly of *defence mechanisms*. Besides, a defence mechanism is, in essence, negative. No matter how strongly one asserts something, it is always a denial of something. That somewhere there is an attack being perpetrated in which one may oneself be both attacker and attacked. Instead, let us go right to the heart of the matter: to the consideration of Freud's article, 'Negation' (1925*h*), which I find both his most remarkable and his leas' satisfactory.

Negation

Negation characterizes a relationship, not an object (Lyotard, 1971). Negation does not have a specific place within language; language as a whole is sustained by negation. 'The negative consists in this: that the terms of the system have no existence other than their value and that this value is conferred upon them entirely by the regulated intervals that they maintain among themselves' (p. 120). My patient, in the tomato-rice episode, was defending her discontinuity with her mother. For what she feared above all – probably because she desired it – was this mastery her mother had over her which made a closed universe of their relationship. It is easy, then, to conclude, with the logicians, that *'there is no negative without affirmation'*.

Lyotard designates three modes of 'no':

1 The grammarian's and the logician's negation (negative propositions).
2. The discontinuity discussed by structuralists and linguists when describing language, its spacing, intervals and invariance.
3. The logician's and the analyst's lack.

When, in chapter 2, I emphasized the complementary anxieties of *separation* and *intrusion*, I was really talking about optimal spacing: about *useful distance* (Bouvet) and *efficient difference*. But what Freud says takes us even further. Marsal, in Lalande's *Vocabulaire de la Philosophie* (1968), observes, in the footnote to the article on the work 'Negative', that 'negative' admits of two opposites: *'affirmative'* and *'positive'*, which are not synonymous. At times, to negate falls into the category of 'assertions'. (Think of what Freud [1925*h*] says: ' "It's *not* my mother', so it *is* his mother.') At other times, to assert and to negate are two members of the category of 'judgement'. This indeed compels Freud to bring in the function of judgement. Nonetheless, he reverses the order in which the two kinds of judgement usually appear: he puts first the judgement of attribution (good/bad) and then the judgement of reality (existence/non-existence), a philosophical feat from which I do not believe we have yet drawn all the consequences.

This article leads us to a system of binary oppositions at every level: good/bad, existence/non-existence. But also suggested are the antithetical pairs Cs/Ucs and self/object. My patient says 'no' to herself and to me simultaneously. *And through this denial she says 'yes' to both of us.* This present emphasis on countertransference (I need hardly point out that I did not enthusiastically welcome her peremptory 'no's' to my interpretations) does not stem from some analytic game of hide-and-seek in which transference and countertransference chase each other around and around. *Counter* (in the sense of 'close to')[1] transference evokes transference and transference countertransference. And does not transference already refer to a place outside that which is taking place? What is going on is the product of what has been *transferred*, displaced, from a place which is only indicated to us by the hypothesis that it is not here alone that the process is going on but that it has already transpired and that, what is more, it will continue to go on elsewhere. *Transference seizes upon that drifting object in the analytic setting which is fed by countertransference.*[2]

But there exists another conception of the negative, as the logicians have seen: the pure concept that has no opposite. Here – to remain within the Freudian framework – no duality is called into play. The Eros-Death instinct opposition is shattered in the aporia of *primary absolute narcissism*, the zero degree of excitation. The commentary this would require is too lengthy to be dealt with now, so let us remain with Freud's 1925*h* article. In other words, let us stay within the bounds of the dual relationship (the relationship of the 2) and leave aside that zero which the human mind has so much trouble in understanding – especially when we listen to our patients, who always *cathect* something – even the aspiration toward Nothingness.

External reality is first denied, rejected and declared alien. It can be regained when the establishment of the reality principle, that is, of the secondary thought processes, recreates an equilibrium between the system of internal relationships and that of external ones. The finding of the object is really a re-finding. If we come to a dead-end because of the paradoxes implied by a proposition of this sort, it is truly because we do not wish to be disturbed by the most troublesome questions. We

---

[1] In French, 'contre' can mean both 'contrary to' and 'close to' (example: 'tout contre moi = 'close to me'). [Translator's note.]

[2] Countertransference is here utilized in the broadest sense: in the reaction of the analyst to the transference of the analysand and for the holding and maintenance of the analytic setting.

analysts understand one another. We understand one another so well that
we no longer understand anything.

Freud's brilliant manoeuvre was in not hesitating to slide the discussion of language (which has its own logic) into that of the one he calls '*the
language of the oldest – the oral-instinctual impulses.*' Do instinctual impulses,
then, have their own language? Or is this merely a metaphor? No, it is a
necessity. It is impossible to deal with instinctual impulses except
through language since, in contrast to orgasmotherapy or primal scream
therapy, psychoanalysis is restricted to verbal communication. It can
conceive of instinct only through language. Nevertheless, the types of
discontinuity are here diametrically opposed to language.

The 'language' of instinctual impulses implies a mental space (an
economy of the space containing instinctual tension-discharge processes) quite different from the mental space involved in language (which
economy is the result of tension-discharge processes of thought).

The essential point with respect to the introjection-expulsion opposition – and this will be my main argument here – is that expulsion (or
rejection; I am not talking about projection) does not do away with the
contradiction. Rather, it duplicates it. Without wishing to provoke, let
me call your attention to Mao Tse-Tung's remarkable essay, 'On
contradiction' (1937). Mao quotes Lenin: 'The two basic (or two
possible? or two historically observable?) conceptions of development
(evolution) are: development as decrease and increase, as repetition, *and*
development as a unity of opposites (the division of a unity into mutually
exclusive opposites and their reciprocal relation).' Mao then adds: 'The
fundamental cause of the development of a thing is not external but
internal: it lies in the contradictoriness within the thing' (p. 313).

In other words, *the original act of expulsion*, which Freud conjectured as
attending the birth of a pleasure ego, opens up within the subject a
pleasure-unpleasure relation which will have to be resolved by repression. In short, there is a vertical splitting inside-outside, immediately
followed by a duplication of the contradiction, within the inside element,
between desirable (to the conscious) and undesirable (to the conscious,
but desirable to the unconscious). Mao says: 'One divides into two.' He
talks in the tradition not only of Hegel but also of Heraclitus.

However, the solipsistic position, which consists in expelling external
reality, is an amputation. External reality will very soon *be missed. The
object of what is missing is in external reality.* That is why the internal
contradiction must be reunited with this external reality from which it
has cut itself off. One way we know of dealing with this amputation is
autoeroticism – the perfect symbol of the turning inwards on the

subject's own self which implies *splitting of the ego* (analogous to that which occurs in mourning) wherein the body replaces the outside world. The body amputates one of its members in order to set it up as a *quasi-object, an analogue of the object, a double of the object.* Then follows a series of couplings: the breast is replaced by the thumb, the reel follows upon the thumb. Language – substituted for the reel – is reduced to its simplest expression, o-o-o-da, two expressions which are not at all synonymous. The logic of binary opposites still retains its prerogatives but the opposites have been infiltrated by dissymmetry. The relations between mouth and breast, between child and mother are characterized by an imbalance – the *difference in potential* which will have to change into a potential difference.

Lyotard is right to emphasize the fact that the introject-expel impulse cannot be simplified into a mere relation of nourishment. Eating and spitting out are mere acts of thought and cognition. If we choose to ignore this concept it is like summoning thought into action, like a deus ex machina, at a point of genetic development. It should be said, though, that in order for the child to have access to *the play of thought (au jeu de la pensée)*, the mother, as in the case of Freud's daughter, must go away. In other words, someone other than the child must be the object of her desire, of which the child will never be more than a symbol. This is an invitation to a shifting of psychic spaces. The absence of the mother has to be linked with her potential reunion with the father.

This system of opposites that Freud traces here through the example of negation continued to obsess him. It makes an appearance in quite unrelated situations. Twenty years before negation it is also in *Jokes and their Relation to the Unconscious* (Freud, 1905c) – it is all there. And even more specifically, it is in the article that linguists have disputed and so misunderstood, 'The antithetical meaning of primal words' (1910e).

Counter-interpretation and Counter-construction

Let us go back to the session, with Freud. In 'Constructions in analysis' (1937d) Freud is still very much involved with his work on negation, which was by then twelve years old. He tells us that the work of analysis 'is carried on in two separate localities, that it involves two people, to each of whom a distinct task is assigned'. For once he is not satisfied with assessing the patient's response in terms of resistance; he analyses it instead. This is worth remembering. In the case of the patient's accepting the construction, says Freud, his 'yes' is by no means *unambiguous* (italics mine). And a little further on he states, 'A "no" from a person in analysis is quite as *ambiguous* as a "yes" ' (italics mine). What, then, should we trust? The formula (already mentioned in the article on negation): ' "I didn't ever think" (or, "I shouldn't ever *have thought*") that' (or, "*of that*").' This is a remarkable formula which allows for the coexistence of past and present (I didn't ever – I shouldn't ever have), of the indicative and the conditional (if you hadn't told me) of intransitive and transitive (that, or of that) wherein thought is at once its own object and the thought of something, namely of an object. *This is a formula which admirably condenses negation and affirmation.*

I propose to talk of *counter-interpretation* and *counter-construction* as the analysand's immediate reaction to the analyst's message. 'Counter', here, means '*juxta*', independent of its positive or negative connotations. But Freud goes further. He adds that what will allow us to go beyond the ambiguity is the train of associations. In other words, the immediate effect of the interpretation or construction in the explicit counter-interpretation or counter-construction will be evaluated by the sequence of associations – that is, the production of the complementary element of the couple born from the interpretation or the construction alone. For truth, as Freud concludes, can be arrived at only through its distortions.

This leads us to a consideration of the function of resistance. Far from being the obstacle to truth, it is its lever. Without resistance there can be no transference. There cannot be any obligation to make *the detour* which is the surest sign of the *return* of the repressed. Respect for resistance is, therefore, not merely an ethical rule of non-intrusion. It is a concern for the preservation of the force of detour, thanks to which the conductive work on the diverted elements will enable us to fully appreciate what has returned, and which had to be diverted by the ego. This conception was already present in the 'Project for a Scientific Psychology' (Freud, 1895), with the notion of side cathexis. This can equally well be applied to the idea of defence, which is often interpreted in a tactical perspective, whereas it is really a matter of *strategy of opposites* in analysis. Is it necessary to insist that the analyst himself is tricked and double-crossed by this strategy when he wants to get directly to the point? He becomes a Cassandra. He tells the truth but is not believed.

Contradiction and Circularity

In short, it is six of one and half-a-dozen of the other. One can perceive the feeling of *malaise* which periodically throws us back into contradiction and periodically demands that we free ourselves from this paralysis in which 'yes' and 'no' reflect one another as if each were mirror of the other. Paradox is a game of the mind, and no human relationship is tolerable if the ambiguity ceases to be more than just a limited condition.

I would like to remind you of a quote from Freud on the Oedipus complex that will bring us back to familiar ground. In *The Ego and the Id* (1923*b*) Freud, for the first time, described the total Oedipus complex, that is, the positive and negative complex whose elements you know. But, in this text, Freud made some passing remarks which appear, to me, to be important. He points out that the simple – that is, the positive – Oedipus complex is described as such for *practical reasons*. This means that he is alluding, with this common term, to a concept found in the 'Project': that of practical thought, the kind that must solve a problem, decide a matter. He illustrates the two-fold structure of the Oedipus complex by bisexuality – that is, by the fact that every individual, whatever his sex – his sexual identity – combines within him the sexuality of *both* of his progenitors, his parents. In other words, the expulsion of the Other's sex returns in Oedipal bisexuality through a dual identification. He goes on to say something more important, namely that, as far as the earliest object-choices and identifications are concerned, it is difficult to have '*a clear view of the facts*' (italics mine). In my opinion, he means that, with respect to the earliest relationships, *object-choices and identifications would not have to be separate and distinct*: they could thus contain within them a basic contradiction. Finally, Freud makes a remark of major importance when he says that 'it is still more difficult to describe *the facts in connection with the earliest object-choices and identifications intelligibly*' (italics mine).

Here we are at the heart of the contradiction. On the one hand, we have these sets of facts and relationships which do not correspond to our standards of *intelligibility* (that is, to those of secondary thought processes) and, on the other hand, we have before us the theoretical task of describing them *intelligibly*. Therein lies the major paradox of Freud's work which speaks of *primary logic in the terms of secondary logic*. This is also the paradox of psychoanalytic practice: *hearing with one's primary ear, speaking with secondary language*. That is why it is sometimes preferable to remain silent rather than artificially inject secondary forms of communication (even if their content aims at primary communication) where primary logic is at work.

This, in my view, explains the shifting of the psychoanalytic referent we find in certain theoretical contributions: the Oedipus and castration complexes are replaced by the primal scene, which is their *primordial double*, the one in which object-choices and identifications are not mutually exclusive but at once contradictory and complementary. However, we have not escaped from the contradiction.

Once again I would like to quote Mao Tse-Tung. Mao writes that

'qualitatively different contradictions can only be resolved by qualitatively different methods' (*op. cit.* p. 321). If it is necessary to have a
thorough knowledge of all the contradictions of a given situation,
nothing could be more mistaken than to treat them all in the same way.
'There are many contradictions in the process of development of a
complex thing and one of them is necessarily the principal contradiction
whose existence and development determine or influence the existence
and development of other contradictions' (p. 331).

Thus, in the dual Oedipus complex, the means of breaking out of the
circularity lies in the feature which makes of the psychically bisexual
child a unisexual being. After elucidating the principal contradiction/
secondary contradiction split, Mao rediscovers the principal and secondary aspects of the principal contradiction within the latter. Citing
Lenin, Mao says, '*Dialectics* is the teaching which shows how *opposites* can
be and how they happen to be (how they become) *identical* – under what
conditions they are identical, transforming themselves into one another,
why the human mind should take these opposites not as dead, rigid, but
as living, conditional, mobile, transforming themselves into one another'
(p. 337).

'No' Does Not Exist in the Unconscious

It would take a certain naïveté to think that, in dealing with these
questions, I could have forgotten that 'no' does not exist for the
unconscious. 'No's' separating force would seem to have no place in this
discussion. As I reflected on this problem I became aware of the reason
behind the epistemological scandal surrounding the death instinct. How
can it be called an instinct? I do not intend to discuss the validity of the
concept of the death instinct now. But I will say that Freud, who
maintained that all drives are active, that is, affirmative and positive,
needed to attribute to this disjunctive tendency, which is the negation of
the tendency to form larger and larger wholes, the status of an instinct,
i.e., an active force. Thus one escapes even less from contradiction
inasmuch as this separating capacity ensures spacing and establishes
discontinuity. That is, it protects against the dissolving powers of
continuity in the fusion with the object and guarantees the existence of
individualising separation.

But let us leave aside the death instinct and return to the unconscious
and to dreams, the 'royal road' that leads to it. Chapter VI, not VII, is
the richest chapter in the book (Freud, 1900*a*). I would like to quote a
passage from it that is worthy of attention. 'The way in which dreams
treat the category of *contraries* and *contradictories* is highly remarkable. It is

simply disregarded. "No" seems not to exist as far as dreams are concerned. They show a particular preference for combining contraries into a unity or for representing them as one and the same thing. Dreams feel themselves at liberty, moreover, to represent any element by its wishful contrary: so there is no way of deciding at a first glance whether any element that admits of a contrary is present in the dream-thoughts as a positive or a negative' (p. 318).

I shall give a clinical illustration of this, taken from Ninon's analysis. After I had given an interpretation that was a little too much of a summary, she made a gesture indicating sharp disapproval and destructive rejection of me which, however, she elaborated better than was her custom. I understood that a tremendous movement of transference, of rapprochement had taken place. At the next session I conveyed to her my feeling that her refusal was linked to a very great closeness against which she was mobilizing all her resources of negation, for fear, I told her, of an acting-out in relation to me. It was as though the words of my interpretation were capable of inducing not only thoughts and desires but also acts that had to be cleared away. She answered, 'Since you're talking about acting out, I'm going to tell you the dream I had. I dreamt I was an analyst, sitting in an armchair like you are [in my interpretation I had mentioned this desire of hers] and I had Serge Gainsbourg* as a patient. On the couch he told me that he wanted to sleep with me [We had also touched on her avoidance of transference by her affair with a man]. I hesitated, then I gave in and in the dream he turned out to be impotent. I wondered: why Serge Gainsbourg?' Then she remembered having recently seen him on TV and thought that this wild man, this indomitable rebel who claimed he wanted to be bound to nothing and nobody, had nevertheless wound up falling for Jane Birkin, whom my patient found pretty and who had also been on the TV show. He had even given her a child [her desire, brought up in the previous session]. The TV show interviewer had asked the singer – and this is a sign of the times – if he ever dreamed. The answer was, 'Never. I take barbiturates' [an illusion which refers back to my patient's own use of tranquillizers]. She then immediately grasped the meaning of this dream as representing *someone who never dreams*. She called it an *anti-dream*.

Before coming back to Freud, I would like to open a parenthesis. Listen to this passage from *Milinda's Questions* (Panha, 1964), a collection of Indian texts dating from approximately the second century BC to the second century AD.

---

¹ Well-known French singer.

'Reverend Nágasena, in regard to him who has a dream as a portent – does his mind, going along of its own accord, seek that portent, or does that portent come into the focus of his mind, or does anyone come and tell him of it?

' "It is not, sire, that his mind, going along of its own accord, seeks for that portent, nor does anyone else come and tell him of it, but that very portent comes into the focus of his mind. As, sire, a mirror does not go anywhere to seek for a reflection, nor does anyone else, bringing a reflection, put it on the mirror, but from wherever the reflection comes, it appears in the mirror." ' (Vol. I, Part IV, Division 8, p. 128).

Contradictions in Dreams

In this same Chapter VI, in the section concerning the means of representation, Freud (1900a) considers logical relations. On the one hand he states that dreams have no means at their disposal of representing the logical relations between the dream-thoughts. But when even they seem to be present, Freud thinks this is *part of the material of the dream-thoughts and is not a representation of intellectual work performed during the dream itself*. 'A contradiction in a dream,' says Freud, 'can only correspond in an exceedingly indirect manner to a contradiction *between* the dream-thoughts' (Freud's italics). This *'between'* clearly indicates that, for Freud, thought is the link between the terms. He goes on to concern himself with trying to find out how dreams can express this link. Very simply, dreams do away with the *'between'* by means of condensation: 'They reproduce *logical connection* by *simultaneity in time*.' (His example is Raphael's painting of the School of Athens.) This observation is extraordinary, for it shows that the non-existence of 'no' is the same as the non-existence of time. *Simultaneity takes the place of successive action in time.* All the same, the causal relation of successive action is not entirely excluded. It comes back into the picture through displacement: the transformation of one image in the dream into another or the transformation of the dream which gives way to another dream.

'*The alternative "either-or" cannot be expressed in dreams in any way whatever.*'

This is the crux of the matter. I quote again: 'One and only one of these logical relations is very highly favoured by the mechanism of dream-formation: namely the relation of similarity, consonance, or approximation – the relation of "just as" ' (pp. 319–20). This is analogical thought at work. 'Similarity, consonance, the possession of common attributes – all these are represented in dreams by unifaction, which may either be present already in the material of the dream-thoughts or may be freshly constructed. The first of these possibilities may be described as "identification" and the second as "composition". Identification is employed where *persons* are concerned: composition where *things* are the material of the unification. Nevertheless, composition may also be applied to persons. Localities are often treated like persons' (p. 320).

All of modern psychoanalysis gets enmeshed in the type of contradiction Freud is referring to: persons–things. It is less an opposition between animate and inanimate than between persons and objects – though I know the difference between thing and object. This juxtaposition refers back to the relation between whole object (person) and part-object. The whole and the part. Identification and composition inter-refer as methods of unification. The series that starts with incorporation and ends with identification will oblige us to return to that mode of composition or alienation represented by possession (in the medieval sense), through the image, the ghost, the double. Here the double comes back with double meaning.

Freud quotes from the Bible – Joseph interpreting Pharaoh's dream: 'This dream, O King, although seen under two forms, signifies one and the same event . . .' Finally, everything can be summed up in one sentence: contradictions are treated like analogies. So, when Freud ends the chapter by asserting that dream-work 'does not think, calculate or judge in any way at all: it restricts itself to giving things a new form', we understand that this exclusion of the function of judgement from the ability to transform is based on the work of analogical thought. This kind of thought neglects differences or, rather, puts to work another kind of difference which takes liberties with the differences of secondary logic. But to what extent does it do so? What is at issue here is interpretation.

This is a dual question: the interpretation that is the dream itself, i.e., the dreamer's interpretation; and, the interpretation of the dream, i.e., the analyst's interpretation.

Analytic Work and Introjection

The dream-work and the interpreter's work complement each other. What strikes me as unusual in Freud's work on dreams is his way of speaking about dreams 'from the inside', like a stowaway. Furthermore, what is astonishing is the way he puts all the resources of his secondary thought processes at the service of the primary thought processes, of the dream. That is, there is a constant to-and-fro in which secondary logic moves into the background to allow primary logic to speak and be heard. For us, Freud, with secondary logic, explains the laws of that universe we visit every night without having fathomed its logic before him. At any rate, the path to dreams, like the path to the unconscious, is the object of the mediation of the ego – of the dreamer who relates the dream afterwards, during his session.

As we are all aware, analysis is only possible in the union of the analysand's free associations and the analyst's evenly-suspended attention, the aim of which is to encourage the analyst's free associations while judgement remains benevolently neutral. *Fluctuat nec mergitur.*[1] But it is not a matter of floating to the point of falling asleep – which, it should be said in passing, does not happen only to analysts. As Bertram Lewin (1950) observed, the patient in analysis is torn between his desire to dream and his desire to sleep. Silence can ensure this function. But silence never disappears. In the analytic couple, one of the two partners is always silent. Thus, the function of silence, while someone is speaking, can always be delegated to the Other. But silence can sometimes speak louder than words, and behind the noise of the words speech can be silent.

We shall try to describe how analytic work is accomplished, with this attenuated but not entirely eradicated presence of contradiction, since, despite our efforts to make contact with the primary processes, the secondary ones are only half-asleep. This is the moment to recall that analytic discourse is a contradiction in terms. Saying everything that comes into one's mind is, as we know, an impossible task. What is more, we are the first to become bored with the productions of certain patients who apply the rule literally and whose omission of essential links reduces their discourse to an unintelligible fragmentation. In fact, the paradox resides in the fact that while the *sequences* (= the train of associations) have broken the links of logical thought, each sequence nonetheless remains under the control of logic. This is what brought me to speak elsewhere of the dual articulation of analytic discourse (*between* the terms of one and the same sequence and *between* the sequences.)

The analysand's discourse is incorporated by the analyst. By this I mean that the discourse is an object. To this incorporation is coupled – I use the term advisedly – an introjection, that is, processes occurring concomitantly with incorporation. Here I agree with Ferenczi's distinction, so usefully recalled by N. Abraham and M. Torok (1972). In my opinion a distinction must be made between different types of *introjection* of the object: the introjection of instincts by the ego (*instinct introjection*); the introjection of affects and representations by the preconscious and the conscious (*imaginary introjection*) and finally the intro-

[1] 'She is tossed by the waves but does not sink': motto of the city of Paris, to which Freud often referred.

jection of verbal and perceptual communications. The latter type of introjection I call *symbolic introjection*, in the modern and, if need be, Lacanian sense of the term. It seems to me that what must be emphasized in this distinction is that *verbal, symbolic introjection* is *limited* and *discontinuous*. It is a type of introjection resembling a chain – a *generative introjection*.

While the analysand speaks, the analyst listens. He is working at listening. Now, the patient's discourse progresses along the unwinding of the verbal chain. The function of associative unlinking which produces silences, intervals, sighs, gaping holes (*béances*) in the discourse and gaps between parts of syllables, words and sentences; *between* the elements of a sequence and *between* the sequences. Now, while the analysand is speaking, the analyst is working on the patient's associations by means of his own associations. This is the original phenomenon of analytic attention. The analyst's associative work, his symbolizing function, consists in making links. But making links is a process of contradictory transformations. That is to say, the analyst, whose most intimate self is being called upon, must refuse in himself the *temptation of the manifest narrative*, its hypnotic effect (in the strict sense of the word). He must consequently implement contradictory operations of thought. There is never a clear-cut answer to 'What is he trying to tell me?' This is ambiguous work. The element must be linked up with some other element, not-A, which can be either -A or A'. This is the ambiguity of analysis. Nobody can come to the aid of the analyst and whisper in his ear the answer, whether not-A is -A (reversal into its opposite) or A' (turning round upon its own self). In other words, the negative not-A (according to the article by Serrus (1968) in Lalande's *Vocabulaire*) is either the product of projection through displacement (for instance: You're behaving with me as you did with your father or mother) or projection through reversal (for instance: You are afraid of it because you desire it). Only the context can decide the matter and the context (that is, the totality of associative sequences) is ambiguous. This leads me to two observations:

1. The model of the psychic structure of the analytic object is the *double reversal*, ending in a double loop.
2. As the introjection of associative communication progresses, a function of oscillating transformations becomes centred in the analyst.

An example: When my patient recounted the tomato-rice episode or her anti-dream, I kept wandering off constantly into associations. I thought in the following order (I am reconstructing this after the fact):

1. Her mother is bad, she is intrusive.
2. Ninon is over-dramatizing with me the way she used to with her mother.
3. It is her mother who over-dramatizes.
4. Ninon has a right not to like tomato-rice.
5. This is already an ulcerative colitis: 'her intestines were shedding tears of blood'.[1]
6. Ninon's aggressiveness cannot tolerate the sight of blood or anything that suggests a comparison with it.
7. In fact, she manipulated her mother the way she is currently manipulating me.
8. What a nasty little squirt she must have been!
9. Yes, but what a mother! She is crazy! Ninon fought for her individuation!
10. What homosexuality there was between the two of them!
11. Luckily there was school to act as a buffer.
12. I understand why she rejects my interpretations.

But, after all that, I was still missing the essential point, which only came to me afterwards, when I gave her the interpretation of her 'no'. That is where the *work of interpretation* was performed. I must confess that when I opened my mouth to begin my interpretation, I did have some vague impression of what I was getting ready to say. But it was in the effort to project it, that is, in the act of formulating my interpretation in the verbal unwinding of my associative chain that the interpretation was forged in my words without my ever having been able to predict what form it might take. But, as I spoke, I said to myself, 'That's it.' I had shut my mouth and could have heaved a sigh of relief when it was over. My interpretation was the fruit of analogical thought: I had counterbalanced what had happened in the past and what was happening between these two series.

In the same way, when I decided to write this article, I knew I wanted to speak about the object. Between my idea then and what you are reading today there exists only an homologous connection. The more

---

[1] I am here making a double reference. On the one hand, this entrance was formulated by her doctor during a very painful and intrusive rectoscopy when she had her ulcerative colitis. This reminded me of the intrusion of the tomato-rice in her mouth. On the other hand, I am comparing the tomato-rice to her bloody faeces.

time went by, the more my first wish seemed to me to have been overtaken by the flow of the theoretical process.

Interpretation is an act of exorcism. It is a means of ridding oneself of what the patient has handed out and giving it back to him so that he may get rid of what has been put in him – or what one has put in him. But in this relation of chronologically successive action that the act of speaking illustrates, due credit must be given to the role of simultaneity in the creation of the interpretation's form and content: simultaneity of the deciphering of what has been heard and of the formulation of attentive thought, in preparation for the interpretation. We surprise ourselves when we interpret.

I would now like to say a word about certain paradoxical forms of introjection of the interpretation, which are the sign of resistance. One type has to do with over-cathecting the interpretation. Just as over-cathecting the patient's discourse has a hypnotic effect, over-cathecting the interpretation amazes and seduces the analysand through the omnipotence projected on the analyst's words. That is one of the dangers of the silent analyst. Everything he says becomes oracular. He is never wrong because he speaks so rarely. On the other hand, what is introjected merely strengthens the patient's narcissism. This voice penetrating you so completely is good, beautiful, marvellous. But it forms a whole that cannot be assimilated.

The second case involves the mascarade of psychic working-out. After I have said something I hear the analysand say, 'Let's see, can we go back over what you just said?' And there is my spontaneous interpretation all sliced up, fallen victim to obsessionalization. There is a strong tendency to react to this counter-interpretation. It is clear that the effect sought by this dissecting isolation wards off any mobilising of affects and immunizes the patient against them.

More or less complete over-cathexis is negation itself. Thus Wisdom (1961) has spoken of the hysteric for whom the penis is itself a penis-symbol. Things become clearer when one realizes that this penis is hollow and is in fact a vagina that is more greatly feared than the penis. In fact, penis and vagina have been condensed in this contradictory logic wherein coupling is non-coupling since fulfilment is always postponed. Inversely, over-cathecting the analysis as an unlinking-fragmenting process shatters the analyst's words and thwarts any *effect of restarting* through the reappropriation of these words by thought.

One can see from the examples that I have just given that symbolic, verbal introjection cannot claim any monopoly on this. The same pairs of opposites can be found, as well, on the level of the imaginary.

Medusa's head can be just as much a mother-figure with penetrating penises as it can be, in Freud's opinion, a figure which wards off danger and has an apotropaic effect on castration. This is an unsolvable question since it depends on whether the matter concerns simple displacement or a reversal into the opposite. Or even a double bind image.

The same holds true for the introjection of instincts. Re-read 'Instincts and their vicissitudes'. That is where we see at work in Freud (1915c), before any mention of repression, before any reference to the representation-affect opposition has been made, the mechanisms of double reversal (turning around upon the subject's own self and reversal into the opposite) in the coupling or pairing of opposites. In the perverted couple, the partner is the exorcist who takes upon himself a share of the pleasure which escapes the pervert, who gets pleasure from it as in a mirror, through identification. And this can be found even in the solitary ritual of the pervert and even in masturbation, as Joyce McDougall (1973) has so neatly shown. As far as the nature itself of the concept of opposite pairs is concerned, Freud clearly saw its characteristic contradiction. The taking inside oneself of pleasure-giving objects via introjection (he quotes Ferenczi) has as its complement projection, which rids the self of unpleasure. We should not forget, however, that this object which is desired for the pleasure it gives will be consumed and consequently destroyed, after incorporation.

Introjection never ceases to be ambivalent. The fiction of the genital personality belongs to psychoanalytic ideology. At best ambivalence becomes ambiguity. This is what we call subtlety. Our genetic model bears the characteristics of both this ambivalence and of the work of the transformation on the model of primordial relationships. Laplanche (1976) has devoted welcome pages to the introjection of the object. Is it the breast, the milk, the lips (or, we could add, the mother's gaze) which is the object? Laplanche condenses the source, the object and the aim. 'It (Id) enters through the mouth.' From primitive anaclisis emerges the specification of the sexual function. So be it. It seems to me, however, that without being inclined to Kleinianism one can suppose that the introjection of the 'it' is a *discontinuous sequence* (the infant's sucking is, in fact, just that: he establishes a rhythm in his ingestion by swallowing). Without indulging in genetic-fiction, we may still imagine the sequence of affects accompanying introjection. The relation to the breast is not uniformly good when it is there and bad when it is not.

During the process of introjection there occur a series of 'thoughts' which I shall translate hypothetically in the following way: 'It's good.

It's still as good as it was. It's better. It's not quite as good. Will there be enough? I don't want any more. I want more. Is that enough? More. It's not as good. It's not coming through as well. It's getting empty. It's filling up. . . .' We see that introjection is concommitant with the process of projection. We must now direct our attention to this question.

Generalized Projection

Projection, which is not the same thing as expulsion, is the putting outside which is paralleled by the putting inside which characterizes introjection. In my view, projection is limitless, as is introjection. All psychic productions are projective. The field of projection covering the opposite is equally true. What becomes of external reality? What becomes of rational thought? They are not any less projective. All we can say is that there are projective spaces and projective moments which are bound up with differently organized primary and secondary systems.

Here again what matters is the *idea of coupled elements*. A projection is dangerous when it prevents the simultaneous formation of an introjection. Tausk (1919) had clearly seen that projection is not oriented only toward the outside but also, but first of all, toward the inside of the body. Consider hypochondria. The fact is that we are once again confronted with another paradox in which the inside of the body has taken the place of the outside world. When the possibilities of exertion have been exhausted, when the systems of bodily fantasies have been overloaded by the burdens that weigh down the psychic body, it is then that projection turns outward. The internal eye of the persecuted-persecuting organ turns around toward external reality – and now seizes upon the latter in its turn. Dreams are projections – a turning inside-out of that external space into the psychic space of the dreamer, the space bounded by the pole of perception and the pole of motor activity, where everything, in fact, happens as it does in external reality. Thoughts are projections. So are art and science. Projection is production. Transference and counter-transference are projections and productions of the setting.

It is because there is transference that the analyst too, can project non-transferential interpretations, which leads the patient to introject the latter as countertransference ones. It is because there is non-transference that the analyst can project transferential interpretations, which leads the patient to start up again the process of transferential projections. Transference is that which is the object of an occultation because between what is experienced and what is projected operates the filter of reversal. Thus a patient made remarks to me in an ostensibly hostile tone. As I interpreted this, I came up against her denial. 'I wasn't hostile.' And I wound up understanding that she truly didn't want to be. But between her wish not only not to be hostile but even to be nice, and its fulfilment through speech, what came out of her at that moment *became* hostile, like the heroines in fairy tales whose mouths give forth only snakes and toads, irrespective of their intentions. The same may happen to the analyst.

The Object and the Circuit

When he distinguished transitional objects, transitional phenomena and transitional space, Winnicott (1971b) took a decisive step in the concept of the object in connection with inside-outside, subjective-objective, non-existing-existing and positive-negative relations. Instead of viewing the object as the stake in play between internal and external reality, he brought into action the notion of the *boundary*. By creating the notion of potential space existing at the point of separation between self and object, by making of this space of separation a space of re-union, by describing the creation of the transitional object within it, he allows us to resolve the dilemma. Psychic reality has been transformed. It no longer remains trapped in the unreality-reality opposition; it now defines itself according to the nature of the potentiality which calls forth infinite transformations. In 1971 Winnicott enriched this description by bringing to light the *negative side of relationships*. For some children the gap is the only real thing. In short, the prolonged absence of the mother has resulted in the child's cathecting a dead object, whether the mother henceforth is present or not.

Here I am in agreement with Winnicott over certain positions that I have defended in the past. This is the case, for example, when he writes that the analyst must understand that there could be a blotting out (what I refer to as a 'radical decathexis') and 'that this blank could be the only fact and the only thing that was real' (1971b, p. 22). Hence, we shall once again have to mention the importance of negative hallucination. Thus *the object is here the non-object*. This negative symbolisation is a contradiction in terms which points out the inevitability of paradox.

The work of the mirror, a product of the logic of opposites, which operates in the analytic setting, is undermined by the realization of this deficiency. It is as though, in these analytic situations, the non-emergence of a living, present object were due to the fact that the interval between the loss of the bad object and its replacement by a good object had been experienced and considered as a fatal desert. Thus, space and time – for it is really a matter of a period of time that was experienced as interminable – are linked. There is no longer any measurable time. There is only infinite waiting, eternal waiting in hopelessness and despair. Whence comes the idea of a '*dead time*', as the suspension of all affective and perceptive experience. The subject does not think he can survive this dead time. Consequently the analyst becomes the object of the negative therapeutic reaction because he is the only reliable object, the only one that survives these destructive periods of which he is the no-object. Any other object would run the risk of never reappearing at the other end of the dead time or of never lasting long enough to be experienced as present. Whence the importance for the patient to assure himself at every session that he has perceived the analyst. And sometimes between sessions as well, with a phone call that assures him, by the voice he hears, that this object is still alive, though it remains a bad one.

If perception is so important it is because it alone can ensure the coupling function. Everything then hinges on the double meaning of absence, which can signify potential presence as well as potential loss. Only perception can guarantee that the potential loss has been warded off. There is only one kind of loss that perception cannot ensure against: loss of love. The constancy of the analytic setting, which the patient perceives, must be complemented by his positive cathexis of it. *Perception is a carnal function.* That is why the analyst lets himself be seen only at the beginning and at the end of each session.

I should like to conclude with the idea that the object is neither a form nor an essence but a *circuit of cathexis with shifting and variable boundaries.* This circuit is basically composed of the introjection-projection pair. Freud was obsessed by the representation-perception opposition, which has remained the criterion by which external reality is tested. This has led to Melanie Klein's teratology of phantasies. Bion (1965) has shown that this generalized phantasy structure can be understood only in terms of the O-K pair, that is, in terms of the relationship between infinite truth and finite knowledge, an absolute-relative pair implying a vertex. External reality will remain our cross and our obsession. Freud has given internal reality its conceptual dignity by not shying away from the ambiguities of the concept of psychic reality. But what trouble he encountered when he had to tackle external reality and the problem of perception!

Let us use Freud's example of *fetishism* again. I would like to emphasize two things. The first comes from the 1927 article on fetishism. '. . . the boy refused to take cognizance of the fact of his having perceived that a woman does not have a penis' (1927*e*). *Denial.* Freud rejected the hypothesis of scotomization. On the contrary, perception persists and brings with it an energetic action to maintain the denial. Consequently, Freud made use of a temporal concept, namely successive action in time, 'the last impression before the uncanny and traumatic one is retained as a fetish . . . pieces of underclothing, which are so often chosen as a fetish, crystallize the moment of undressing, the last moment in which the woman could still be regarded as phallic.' In fact, the regression which reverses the order of events in time 'scotomizes' the simultaneity of the two movements of thought, i.e., the one that has to admit castration and the one that denies it.

Similarly, in 'Splitting of the ego in the process of defence' (Freud 1940*e* [1938]), when Freud treats the conflict between the instinctual demand and the prohibition placed on it by reality, he offers the solution. Rather than decide between them, that is to say, judge, 'the child in fact takes neither course, or rather he takes both simultaneously, which comes to the same thing.' Negation and simultaneity are here bound together. The price – splitting of the ego – will have to be paid.

I propose the working hypothesis that primary repression is inaccessible because the repressed object has not been introjected and then distorted, but rather that repression has taken place during perception. What has been introjected are the alterations effected on the amputated perception. It is the work on these deformed alterations that will enable us to deduce – through construction – primary repression. The function of phantasy is then only a desperate attempt to rediscover this missing fragment of perception. Any work performed on these phantasies without first having made the hypothesis of a mutilated perception is thenceforth phantasmatic, that is, deceptive. Each order (instincts, representations or language) always has a dual aim. On the one hand, it designates to the ego an order other than its own, that is, another system, and invites it to decipher the relevant absent order. On the other hand, it defines itself, that is, it refers to its own mode of individual structuring, which cannot be reduced to the other orders to which it is nevertheless linked. Thus the analyst is neither a real nor an imaginary object. Nor is he even a symbolic one. He is a *potential* object inducing transformations. He is one of the elements awaiting its complement: an inverse or symmetrical one coming from the analysand in order to form the analytic object, which exists only inasmuch as it is an object *between*, an object relation.

I I

Potential Space in Psychoanalysis

The Object in the Setting

THE OBJECT IN ANALYSIS,
THE ANALYSIS OF THE OBJECT,
THE OBJECT OF ANALYSIS

On several occasions, Freud was led to assert that psychoanalytic concepts have chiefly an heuristic value and that only secondarily can they be defined more rigorously or replaced by others. No concept since the founding of psychoanalysis has been more broadly utilized than that of the object. According to Littré, the French Academy Dictionary gives the same illustration in defining the word 'subject' as it does in defining the word 'object': natural bodies are the *subject* of physics; natural bodies are the *object* of physics. Rather than deplore the confusion that arises here, or protest against philosophies which would divide subject and object absolutely, I wish instead to emphasize that their relationship is one of symmetry or of complementarity: no object without a subject, no subject without an object. From Freud's time to ours psychoanalytic theory has not been able to avoid facing up to the truth of this.

Freud completely disrupted the old relation between subject and object. Instead of opposing to the object the subject as it was defined by philosophical tradition, he coupled the object to the drive – the *anti-subject*. For it is quite clear that the drive cannot assume a subjective function. In his theory, drive – and the agency which connotes it, the id – represents for Freud that which is the most impersonal, the least capable of an individual will: both because it is rooted in the body and because it is associated with the radical characteristics of the species as such. Although the drive of Freudian theory is sharply distinguished from the classical notion of instinct, the two remain related by their fundamental-

This chapter, which is translated by Anita Kermode and Michele Sirègar, first appeared in *Between Reality and Fantasy: Transitional Objects and Phenomena*, ed. Simon Grolnick and Leonard Barkin, in collaboration with Werner Muensterberger (New York, Jason Aronson, 1978). An earlier version, 'La psychanalyse, son objet, son avenir', was published in French in *Revue française de Psychanalyse* (1975), 39.

ly improper 'nature' – that is, in their departure from the propriety of self-sameness of the subject. However, with the development of object relations theory, Freud's concept of the ego could no longer provide an adequate theoretical complement to newly emergent formulations of the object. Attempts to supply this deficiency led to the elaboration of such ego-related concepts as the 'self' and the 'I'. Thus the subjectivity of the subject (which Freud had managed, as it were, to bracket off) makes its reappearance in contemporary analytic theory. It returns explicitly in Pasche who gives it an existential dimension, and in Lacan, who, following the structuralist movement, insists on its impersonal character and relates its effects to those of a non-representable set of combinations which he calls the order of the Symbolic. Elsewhere, and from different cultural perspectives, Hartmann, Jacobson, Spitz, Winnicott, Kohut, and Lichtenstein have distinguished, for varying reasons, the ego of Freudian theory from the concept of the self. But the self, which approximates the academic notion of the subject, is unrelated to the function of the subject as viewed from a structuralist perspective.[1]

FREUD'S CONCEPTION OF THE OBJECT

The question of the object must therefore be posed in terms of its historical evolution, since the object in psychoanalysis, the analysis of the psychoanalytic object, and the object of psychoanalysis itself are closely interrelated issues. In Freud (1915c) the object is part of a setting, a *montage*, to which it is simultaneously internal and external. It is internal insofar as it forms a constitutive element of this montage, as one of the components of the drive apparatus. For if there is a psychic apparatus, it is because there is a drive apparatus. The source, the pressure, the aim, and the object of the drive comprise this apparatus. However, the source and the pressure have a physical origin and as such are not displaceable; the displacement or the replacement of one source by another does not eliminate the problem of pressure at the original source. For example, one can try to cheat hunger by masturbating, or sexual desire by eating, but the hunger like the sexual desire will remain unappeased and the illusion can only briefly be sustained. Above all it is crucial to observe that such a displacement of source and such a displacement of pressure can be achieved only through the artifice of a change of aim (e.g., fellatio in the place of coitus) which may also be accompanied by a change of object (e.g., choosing a homoerotic or

---

[1] As used here, the term *structuralist* belongs not to the perspective of Hartmann, Kris, and Loewenstein, but rather to that of F. de Saussure, R. Jakobson, C. Lévi-Strauss, and J. Lacan.

autoerotic object in the place of a heterosexual one). Autoeroticism is an obligatory solution, a replacement dictated by the discontinuity of the object's presence and, in the end, by the more or less belated awareness of its loss. The drive components are sharply separated into two polarities: the source as a somatic, internal element and the object as a non-somatic and external one.

Thus the conceptual framework of the object in Freudian theory includes the following characteristics:

1. The object is part of the drive apparatus: the *included* object.
2. The object is external to the drive: the *excluded* object. At first the object of need, it becomes, by *leaning on* the need, the object of the desire (anaclisis).[1]
3. Of all the components of the drive apparatus, the object is that for which *substitutes* are most easily found. Thus it is eminently an object of transference.
4. The *absent* object can be replaced by another external object or by a part object taken either from the external object (e.g., the breast) or from one's own body (e.g., the thumb).
5. The object can be *incorporated* (as a familiar or as an alien, uncanny thing); it can be *introjected* (as a psychic process); it can be the object of *identification* (as the object which is both identified and identified-with in incorporation or introjection); it can be *internalized* (taken from the outside to the inside).
6. The object is initially *confused* with that which objectifies it and presents it *as* an object, i.e., with that which puts it forth (*ob-ject*). The result may be either a formless chaos where there is neither object nor *anti-object*; or, more often, a state of reversibility pertaining to both the object and the anti-object. (In this context, *anti-object* means *counter-object*, antagonistic yet at the same time close to the object.) Here we have the object of projection.
7. The distinction between object and non-object is made by way of the integration of *object loss*.[2] Its consequence is the creation of an *internal object* distinct from the *external object*. This evolution parallels the distinction between *part object* and *whole object*.
8. Corollary to the formation of the internal object is that of the *fantasied*

---

[1] The German term is *Anlehnung*, which suggests the idea of a supporting function – the sexual instincts as being supported by the instincts of self-preservation. For example, oral pleasure at first *leans upon* hunger (i.e., oral need) and later develops independently from it in the form of pleasure.

[2] This implies that the object exists before it is lost, but that its very loss is what determines its existence as such.

object. Inversely, the fantasy is itself taken, in its turn, as object. Its opposite is the *real object.* The first is governed by the pleasure principle, the second by the reality principle. The fantasied object is located in an extraterritorial position within a psychic apparatus ruled by the reality principle.

9. The choice of object depends on multiple criteria. One of the basic distinctions governing object-choice is that between the *narcissistic object,* formed on the model of the narcissism of the non-object, and the *anaclitic object,* based on the model of the objectal object. This difference is redoubled by the notion of *investment*: the narcissistic investment of the object, the objectal investment of the object — which suggests the importance of the economic transformation.

10. The play of differences which characterize the object may be situated, as we have just seen, along various axes. But two of them have a dominant role: on the one hand, separation of the *good* and the *bad* and, on the other, separation according to the *difference between the sexes* — the phallic versus the castrated object, the masculine versus the feminine object (penis/vagina), and the paternal versus the maternal object (in the Oedipus complex).

11. The object is bound both to *desire* and to *identification* — identification being the primary mode of relationship with the object, leading then to a secondary identification with the object of desire after its renunciation.

12. The object is in a *mediating position* with respect to *narcissism*: at once its agonist and antagonist.

13. The object can be a product of the *constructiveness or the destructiveness of the drives.* It can be either constructive or destructive for the non-object (i.e., for the ego or the self).

14. The *erotic object* (i.e., the object as invested by the constructive qualities of Eros in Freud's final theory of the drives) evolves toward sublimation; whereas the object of destructiveness evolves, not toward objectal chaos, but toward *objectal nothingness* (i.e., the zero point of excitation) because the object is always a source of excitation, whether external or internal, pleasurable or unpleasurable.

15. The study of object relations concerns the relationship to the object or *between* objects. The nature of the link is more important than the action which unites object to non-object or objects amongst themselves. This link is one of conjunction or of disjunction.

Thus the object according to Freud, is by nature polymorphous and polysemous. Here it is vital to point out that in Freud's work the object never depends exclusively on its existence or its essence, its perception or its conception. It should be defined as neither form nor essence but rather as *a network of relationships with shifting boundaries and with variable investments which keeps the anti-object for the anti-subject awake and alive, i.e., in a state of desire.*[1]

THE COHERENCE OF FREUDIAN THEORY

The aim and object of psychoanalysis is, in short, the construction of the *analytic object*, which the analysand can carry away with him from the analysis and can make use of in the absence of the analyst, who is no longer the object of transference. Inversely, the detachment from the analyst of the analysand-as-object implies that the countertransference can be displaced onto another analysand and that the analysand is now capable of becoming another kind of object for the analyst, an *other*.

THE AVATARS OF THE OBJECT IN THE WORK OF FREUD'S DISCIPLES

Freud's disciples went on to tamper with this remarkable theoretical construction, adding on to or else whittling away the main edifice so as to impair, more often than not, the harmony of the whole. The empirical/theoretical gap, i.e., the disparity between facts encountered in practice and the theory which accounts for them, led to an overvaluation of one or another partial aspects of the theory. Thus, with Reich, the problems of character analysis gave rise to an emphasis on the relation to the external object. Then, with Abraham, the true pioneer of object relations theory, the genetic debate led to the specification of the subphases of development, going from the differentiation of the pre-ambivalent part object through to that of the post-ambivalent genital whole object.

One of the consequences was a 'genetic' psychoanalysis whose reduction of the structural dimensions of analytic thought to the merely genetic has seriously impoverished the complex temporal mechanisms of Freudian theory, suppressing, for instance, the crucial concept of deferred action. Psychoanalytic time became psychobiological time, distinguished by mere successiveness, evolutionary and normative (the genital relationship as the Ideal). Linear 'development' replaced tem-

---

[1] This mobility of boundaries is discernible throughout the history of psychoanalysis. After Freud, Melanie Klein curtailed the territory of the external object while extending proportionately that of the internal object. But after Klein, Winnicott in his turn encroached on the domain of internal objects by putting back into the maternal environment – i.e., the external object – what Klein had taken away from it. Nevertheless, this process has not been circular, since the result was to create a third object: the transitional object.

poral dialectic. To be sure, Freud's scheme of libidinal development contributed a good deal to this situation. In consequence, analytic theory began to grow rather less psychoanalytic, rather more psychological. Attention shifted from libidinal development to the development of the ego, whose relationship to reality became (ideally) equivalent to the post-ambivalent genital relationship. (But it is certainly not among psychoanalysts that we will find this ideal illustrated.) Later on, a further step was taken when, with Hartmann, the ego gained a measure of autonomy, allowing the id to become autonomous in its turn (M. Schur). All that remained to complete the process was the introduction into analytic theory of Piaget, whose thought had formerly been entirely antithetical to it.

Given that Freud's work is open to multiple interpretation and thus is susceptible to divergent modes of development, it cannot be said that the orientation adopted by Hartmann and most of North American psychoanalysis is unjustifiable. And, after all, it tallies in many respects with that of Anna Freud. It would seem that psychoanalysis has yielded in large part to the fascinating ascendancy of child analysis. It has been inclined to rely not only on what has been learned from the *psychoanalysis of children*, but also on the *psychoanalytic understanding of the child* (Lebovici and Soulé, 1970), that is, on information gleaned from psychoanalytic applications in fields external to it: direct observation (Spitz); the genetic study of development (Mahler); and the study of the ego through its sensorial or cognitive tools, or through the observation of children brought up under unusual circumstances (D. Burlingham and A. Freud on infants without families). Melanie Klein took an altogether different approach, which has ended in the dissension we are all aware of. But here we must go back again, the better to understand this theoretical lineage.

Groddeck undermined Freud's radical dualism: the object was no longer 'psychic'. It became psychosomatic, and the id was made into a natural divinity. Rank and Ferenczi gave the object, in their turn, quite a different shape. The former emphasized the original separation – birth, which establishes the separation of mother and child and hence that of the object and the non-object. Freud rightly reminded him that this original separation is, at the time, only relative (biological), that it is repaired by the subsequent fusion of mother and child, and that only with the metaphorical loss of the breast does the difference between ego and object get properly established. As for Ferenczi, while calling back into question the split between psyche and soma, his essential contribution was to change the meaning of the transference by understanding it as a process of introjection (as well as of projection), and above all by stressing, in his final years, the significance of the analyst as object, thereby implicitly shifting the emphasis onto the role of the counter-transference.

Abraham and Ferenczi were to influence various independent currents of thought. Balint, the spiritual heir of Ferenczi, emphasized *primary object love*, denying all autonomy to primary narcissism. Later on he gave much importance to the fact that Freud's work dealt essentially with clinical structures which had already achieved a more or less successful internalization of the object, whereas non-neurotic structures are characterized by a failure, more or less, of internalization. *Failure*, in this context, is no more than an approximate term, since what is at stake is rather a *fault*. The basic failure is actually a *basic fault*, a primordial defect giving rise to the fault which then devolves upon the primary love object and which the analyst must, in the course of treatment, replace by a 'new beginning'.

But Melanie Klein (who had undergone analyses with both Ferenczi and Abraham) was already in the process of developing a quite opposed theory of object relations, insofar as she focused on *internal* objects, *fantasied* objects (part or whole), relegating entirely to the background the role of the external object and appealing (like Freud) to the role of constitutional and innate factors, especially the destructive drives. However, she was not able to avoid a misunderstanding. The destructive drives – one should rather say the *instincts* of destruction – are directed onto the object first and foremost by projection. Although she recognized that this projection is not total (in other words, that some internal destructiveness remains in spite of projection), *she behaved as if only this projected part should be taken into consideration*. Note that it matters little whether the object is, in the present case, internal or external, since what counts in Melanie Klein's theory is the *centrifugal* orientation of projection; at all events, a centripetal orientation is never more than the consequence of the return upon himself of the subject's destructive projection (projective identification).

Ferenczi had his disciples, and Klein has hers as well, whether analyzed by her or not. Fairbairn resumes her approach when he deflects the aim of the object. For Freud, the drive sought satisfaction through the object; for Klein, the drive seeks chiefly to cope with destructiveness. For Fairbairn, the drive (but is there still such a thing as drive for Fairbairn?) seeks the object itself (object seeking). Finally Winnicott arrives on the scene. His contribution, derived from the analysis of borderline states, has a number of facets:

a. The baby all by himself does not exist; he is *coupled* with the object of maternal care.

b. Before the inauguration of the paranoid-schizoid phase, we must take into consideration the role of holding – i.e., the change involved in the transition from the intra-uterine to the extra-uterine condition. Nestling within the womb is replaced by nestling in the mother's arms. The phase of *holding* is followed by *handling* and finally by *object-presenting*.

c. The object is at first subjective (or the object subjectively conceived), and then becomes the objective object (or the object objectively perceived). *It is essential that the subjective object precede the objective object.*

d. The object is answered to by the *self*. The self is silent and secret, in a state of permanent non-communication. It shelters the subjective objects and may experience states either of *disintegration* under the influence of anxiety (Winnicott called it 'agony'), or of return to *non-integration* (diffused states going from fusion all the way to non-existence).

e. The mother/object's intolerance of the baby's spontaneity can bring about in the baby a dissociation between psyche and soma, or between the two components of bisexuality, or between one aspect of the drives (e.g., the destructive drives) as against the other. The creation of a *false self*, conforming to the image of the mother's desire, allows protection to the *true self*, which is kept in secrecy. Let us remember that we can communicate only indirectly with the true self.

f. The problem with these states is the problem of dependency. The analyst's attitude in the face of the patient's regression, especially his complicity in preventing regression, may lead to his collusion with the false self; an interminable analysis or a psychotic breakdown is likely to result.

g. The analyst's work consists in a *metaphorical* replacement of the deficiencies of maternal care, either through accepting the analysand's dependence or through accepting his need for fusion within the symbolic interplay – for the analyst does not represent the mother, he *is* the mother. The *analytic setting* represents maternal care. The analyst must also be able to accept his periodic destruction (along with the resultant hatred in the countertransference) as a condition of his periodic resurrection, so that the analysand may be able to *use* the analyst.

h. The *transitional object*, which is neither internal nor external but located in the intermediate area of *potential space*, comes to life and comes into use 'in the beginning' of the separation between mother and baby. The transitional object invokes the idea of *transitional space*, which is extended into the cultural experience of sublimation.

i. The transitional object is coextensive with the category of *playing* and with the *capacity to be alone* (in the presence of the mother or of the analyst).

j. Analytic technique is directed toward bringing about the capacity for play with transitional objects. The essential feature is no longer interpreting, but enabling the subject to live out creative *experiences* of a new category of objects.

k. If the transitional object is a not-me possession, two other possibilities are involved:
1. The non-creation of this object, through being excessively bound to experiences of either fusion or separation.
2. The inversion of the sense of possession by the démarche: 'All I have got is what I have not got.' This suggests a somewhat different concept, which I have formulated as *negative satisfaction*.

It is easy to see that Winnicott has in fact described not so much an object as a space lending itself to the creation of objects. Here the line itself becomes a space; the metaphorical boundary dividing internal from external, that either/or in which the object has traditionally been entrapped, expands into the intermediate area and playground of transitional phenomena. In *Playing and Reality* (1971b) Winnicott gives us glimpses into the private elaboration of this line of thinking: from his early fascination with the image of the seashore where children are playing, to his discovery in talks with Marion Milner of 'the tremendous significance there can be in the interplay of the edges of two curtains', through to an even more personal, and yet thoroughly practical, extension and amplification of the line in his use of the squiggle game.

French analysts have long held themselves aloof from this development, meanwhile splitting up into two main factions. Bouvet's work on object relations grows out of a theoretical blend in which a concept of defensive activity inspired by A. Freud, Reich, Federn, and Fenichel is augmented by Bouvet's own contributions, most significantly his concept of *distance from the object* as illustrated in the variations of the *rapprocher*. The economic dimension, always present in Bouvet, is salient as well in the work of the French psychosomatic school (Marty, Fain, de M'Uzan, David) and in those who stress the role of affect in technique, clinical description, and theory (Green). In opposition to these trends, Lacan has adopted a formalistic approach and has built up theoretical models in which the object (which he calls 'the object (*a*)') is of great importance, especially in relation to the mirror-image. But it would be impossible, within the limits of the present chapter, to give a full account of all the functions of the object (*a*), as this would require an exposition of the whole Lacanian theory, which differs considerably from all those previously discussed (see, however, Green 1966).

Another, although quite different, formalistic approach is that of Bion, who addresses the problem of the object from a perspective unusual to modern psychoanalysis. Adapting to his own ends the Kantian concept of the thing-in-itself, he inserts it into the symbol 'O' standing for that unknowable state of being forever and always inaccessible to being known in itself, and yet at the source of all knowledge, which will never constitute more than an approximation of 'O'. In this he rejoins the formulations of Freud's 'Project for a Scientific Psychology' (Freud, 1895). Note that, just as in Winnicott, it is once again the *space* of thinking that takes precedence over the object. However, it is regrettable that in the work of both Winnicott and Bion the concept of analytic time is less well developed than that of analytic space. We may register our dissatisfaction with the constructions of genetically minded analysts, but we have as yet no theory to offer in their place.

Analytic experience has convinced me that the only way out of the impasse of empiricism versus intellectualism, or 'realism' versus 'abstraction', is through exploiting the technical and theoretical possibilities suggested by Winnicott's work, making all necessary modifications. And so I want now to examine more closely certain of Winnicott's propositions, of interest for the following reasons:

1. They emerge from the study of the analytic setting taken as reference point, which means that theory stays in direct touch with practice.
2. Practice here has to do with borderline patients who, more than classical neurotics, have become the paradigm cases for current analytic practice and theory.
3. The theory deriving from such work is the fruit of an imaginative elaboration deeply rooted in the countertransference feelings of the analyst. Thus the transference gives way to the countertransference as the centre of attention.
4. Winnicott's thought may be open to criticism in many respects, but it reflects, above all, a richly alive experiencing rather than an erudite schematizing.
5. Winnicott's work poses, with remarkable acuteness, the question of the future of psychoanalysis. Rigidly maintaining its classical stance,

psychoanalysis could on the one hand attach itself to an embalmed and stiffened corpse, failing to pursue a critical evaluation of its theories as challenged by present practice. In this case it would be pledged to the mere safeguarding of its acquisitions, without ever calling into question the theory sustaining them. The alternative is a psychoanalysis which, periodically renewing itself, strives to extend its range, to subject its concepts to radical rethinking, to commit itself to self-criticism. In which case it must run the risks entailed by such self-examination, from which the best as well as the worst may emerge.

ANALYTIC PLAY
AND ITS RELATIONSHIP TO THE OBJECT

A great creative thinker – and such Winnicott undoubtedly was, perhaps the greatest of the contemporary analytic epoch – provides endless proof of his gifts, I ought to say even of his genius, throughout his life's work. But often it is during the final stage of his career, struggling it may be against the threat of a fast-approaching death, that he rises to his full stature. I was deeply impressed by feelings of this kind while reading *Playing and Reality* (1971*b*). I should like here to pay tribute to this book, elaborating in my own way what I brought away from it.

Winnicott's name will always be associated with the idea of the transitional object and transitional phenomena, of potential space, of playing and illusion. What has progressively emerged from his initial description of the transitional object – which was constantly being enriched as the years went by – is that Winnicott, in a series of observations which seemed harmless and unassuming enough, had in fact delineated a conceptual field of the highest importance, whose definition was based at one and the same time on child observation and the analytic situation. We must get one thing straight: in his case the observation of the child did not, as one might think, take priority over the observation of the analytic situation. On the contrary: it was because Winnicott was first analyzed, and then went on to become an analyst himself, that he was able, in looking at children, to notice what had been escaping everyone's attention. For we cannot say that the discovery of the transitional object brought to light some recondite and obscure reality. Freud once said that he had done nothing but discover the obvious. The same could be said of Winnicott. The least observant of mothers has always known that her child likes to fall asleep with his teddy bear, or while fondling a bit of cloth or a corner of his blanket. But before Winnicott no one had understood the importance of this, just as no one before Freud had ever been struck by the significance there might be in an eighteen-month-old's game, played during his mother's absence, of throwing away from him and then pulling back again a reel of cotton. Here too it had to be a psychoanalyst, the very first one, who could observe this spectacle with new eyes.

Thus, analytic experience seems to have been the determining factor in the formation of Winnicott's concepts, as it was in those of Freud. Nor is it by accident that it should be Winnicott and his students Khan, Milner, and Little who have provided us with the most fertile reflections on the *analytic setting*.

In chapter 2 I proposed the hypothesis that the analytic situation is characterized by the fact that each of its two partners produces a double of himself. What the analysand communicates is an analogue, a double of his affective and bodily experience; what the analyst communicates is a double of the effect produced on his own bodily, affective, and intellectual experience by the patient's communication. Thus the communication *between* analysand and analyst is an object made up of two parts, one constituted by the double of the analysand, the other by the double of the analyst. What is called the 'therapeutic alliance' or 'working alliance', which I prefer to call the *analytic association*, is, in my belief, founded on the possibility of creating an *analytic object* formed by these two halves. This corresponds precisely to the etymological definition, in Robert's *Dictionary*, of a symbol: 'an object cut in two, constituting a sign of recognition when its bearers can put together the two separate pieces'. In my opinion this is what occurs in the analytic setting. The analytic object is neither internal (to the analysand or to the analyst), nor external (to either the one or the other), but is situated *between* the two. So it corresponds exactly to Winnicott's definition of the transitional object and to its location in the intermediate area of *potential space*, the space of 'overlap' demarcated by the analytic setting. When a patient terminates his analysis, it is not only that he has 'internalized' the analytic interplay, but also that he can take away with him the potential space in order to reconstitute it in the outside world, through cultural experience, through sublimation and, more generally, through the possibility of pairings or (let us rather say) of coupling.

The analytic situation differs from the game of chess (to which Freud was fond of comparing it) in that it is *the analyst who determines the rules of the game*, as Viderman (1970) has rightly observed. In case of disagreement, arbitration is possible only if (in a juridical sense) the rules of law are contravened; but the law governing analysis remains in the hands of the analyst, who exercises both legislative and executive power. These rules which are laid down before the game begins confer a considerable advantage upon the analyst (1) because he has already been analyzed and (2) because usually he has already conducted other analyses. All equality between the two parties is abolished.

But this spatial account of the game needs to be complemented by a temporal one. In analysis it is *always* the analysand who makes the first move. No analysis is conceivable in which, after the statement of the fundamental rule, the analyst speaks first. The analyst can only respond to the first move, which is always played by the patient and only when he decides on it. Similarly, it is always the analysand who makes the last move in the final farewell, the analyst taking leave of his patient only in answer to this farewell (although it may be only temporary).

This structure, which invokes the notion of the double, must also make room for the absent. The absent one in analysis is none other than the analyst's own analyst[1] – which goes to show that analysis always proceeds across generations. As I said before, even if it is his first analysis, the analyst has already been analyzed. In the analytic interplay, the absent metaphorically represented by the analyst's analyst is connected with two other modes of absence: that of past reality, inaccessible as such both to analyst and to analysand, and that of an equally inaccessible present reality. The analyst cannot get to *know* his patient's real life; he can only imagine it. And likewise the analysand can never know the analyst's life; he too can only imagine it. Both are reduced to approximations. Even as the analytic process unfolds, each partner communicates, through verbalization, only a part of his life experience. Here we get back to Winnicott's concept of the silent self, and a memorable sentence comes to mind: 'each individual is an isolate, permanently non-communicating, permanently unknown, in fact unfound' (1963a). From this springs the importance of the capacity to be alone (in the presence of the mother or of the analyst) and its consequence: the analyst is always having to navigate between the risk of separation anxiety and that of anxiety concerning his intrusiveness.

Winnicott has formulated an essential paradox for us, one that, as he says, we must accept as it is and that is not for resolution. If the baby is in health, he 'creates the object, but the object was there waiting to be created and to become a cathected object. I tried to draw attention to this aspect of transitional phenomena by claiming that in the rules of the game we all know we will never challenge the baby to elicit an answer to

---

[1] Hence the inequality and the heterogeneity of the double analytic discourse. The analyst relies upon a discourse with the absent, namely his own analyst, author of his difference from the analysand.

the question: did you create that or did you find it?' (1971*b*, p. 89). This
paradox joins up with another: *the transitional object is and is not the self.*[2]

The qualities peculiar to the transitional object confront us with an
unimpeachable double truth. *The analyst is not a real object; the analyst is not
an imaginary object.* The analytic discourse is not the patient's discourse,
nor is it that of the analyst, nor is it the sum of these two. The analytic
discourse is the *relation* between two discourses which belong neither to
the realm of the real nor to that of the imaginary. This may be described
as a *potential relationship*, or, more precisely, as a *discourse of potential
relationships*, in itself potential. Accordingly, the analytic discourse has, in
regard to past and present alike, only a potential relationship to the
truth. But this does not mean that the analytic discourse may consist in
simply anything at all. It must bear an *homologous* relationship to
imaginary (or psychic) reality; it forms its counterpart. This implies an
approximate correspondence, but an affective approximation, *without
which its effect would be nil.* The homology is one we are obliged to
construct, for lack of positive evidence. Nevertheless, this construction is
not arbitrary, since we cannot help but construct the real, even when it
pleases us to think we are doing no more than perceiving it.

In one of his most fundamental papers, inspired by Lacan's work on
the mirror phase, Winnicott (1966) analyzes the function of the mother's
face as the precursor of the mirror. Here he stresses the importance of the
baby's initial communication not only with the breast but also with the
mother's face. We know that the baby at the breast (or bottle) sucks
while looking not at the breast but at his mother's face. Winnicott rightly
points out that while this is going on the baby may see in the mother's
gaze either himself or herself. If, too precociously, it is the face of the
mother/object that he perceives, he cannot form the subjective object,
but will prematurely evolve the object objectively perceived. The result
is that he must organize a false self, as an image conforming to the
mother's desire. He must then hide away, in secret, his true self, which
cannot and indeed must not be allowed expression. With his false self, he
can achieve only an external identity. But this is a pathological solution.
In the normal progress of events, a compromise is obtained through the
creation of the transitional area of experience.

'If the baby is in health . . .' said Winnicott. Some babies, we know,
are not. And among these some will later impress us with the intensity of
their negative therapeutic reaction. It is striking that Winnicott found it

---

[2] What Winnicott in fact said was that the transitional object is and is not the breast, but
the same formulation may be applied to the self.

necessary to add, in *Playing and Reality*, a supplement to his original paper on the transitional object. The difference between these two pieces of work is considerable, the fruit of twenty years' experience. In the later version Winnicott discusses what he calls the *negative side of relationships*. In certain borderline cases, the absence of the mother is felt as equivalent to her death. Here the time factor must be duly weighed, since it is in terms of temporal accretion $(x + y + z$ quantity of deprivation, expressed as the accumulated moments of the mother's absence) that Winnicott imagines how the baby can move from distress to 'unthinkable anxiety' by way of a traumatic break in life's continuity ('The location of cultural experience'). For such infants *the only real thing is the gap*; that is to say, the death or the absence [in the sense of non-existence] or the amnesia' (1971*b*, p. 22 italics mine). While analyzing a patient of this kind, Winnicott arrived at the conclusion that from the point of view of the child *the mother was dead*, regardless of her absence or presence. It occurred to him that in the transference 'the important communication for me to get was that there could be a blotting out, and that this blank could be the only fact and the only thing that was real' (*ibid*). This remark bears out precisely my own observations about the importance in psychosis of the negative hallucination of the subject. For Winnicott's patient, who had had previous analysis, the negation of the first analyst was more important than the fact of the existence of the second analyst. 'The negative of him is more real than the positive of you.' Such vengefulness is particularly severe with respect to an object which has failed. Here retaliation is a negative response to a negative trauma; in other words, the trauma is not only something which has occurred – in the classical sense of a traumatization (through sexual seduction or an aggressive act) – but that which *did not occur, owing to an absence of response on the part of the mother/object*. 'The real thing is the thing that is not there.' A very true statement, revealing how the thing that is not there, the symbol, is taken as reality; which recalls Hanna Segal's idea of symbolic equation, but in an exactly contrary sense. In Segal's example, violin=penis. But in Winnicott's example, and here he meets up with Bion, *the non-object is the object*. The non-object, in this context, means not the representation of the object but the non-existence of the object. Winnicott speaks of symbols which disappear. Patients in whom structures of this type are found can seem mentally disabled, and in my own initial encounters with such analysands I have come away with a strong impression of their psychic and intellectual poverty. Their motto is: 'All I have got is what I have not got.'

This line of speculation, which Winnicott adds in 1971 to his original hypothesis about transitional objects and not-me possessions, is crucial, as it opens the way to a new conceptual theme, *negative investment*. I have postulated (1967, 1969) the existence of a negative narcissistic structure characterized by the valorization of a state of non-being. Striving for that state of quietude which follows satisfaction with an object, but finding himself in a state where satisfaction has not occurred within limits tolerable for his psychic apparatus, the subject seeks to attain the same state as if satisfaction had been achieved, through the strategy of renouncing all hope of satisfaction, through inducing in himself a state of psychic death not unrelated to Jones's idea of *aphanisis*.

In his paper on the mirror-role of the mother's face, Winnicott uses the illustration of the patient who said to him, 'Wouldn't it be awful if the child looked into the mirror and saw nothing?' The anxiety of the negative hallucination is truly unthinkable. In my opinion, all the defensive manoeuvres described by Melanie Klein's advocates amount to nothing but an awesome strategy for avoiding this fundamental and primordial anxiety.

If 'negative symbolization' can provide an extreme (and very costly) solution, another kind of solution is adopted in borderline cases. In my own experience, what I have most often observed is a need to hold on to and to preserve at all costs a bad internal object. It is as if, when the analyst succeeds in reducing the power of the bad object, the subject has no other recourse than to make it reappear, in fact to resurrect it, in its original or in an analogous form, as if the thing most dreaded were the *interval between the loss of the bad object and its replacement by a good object. This interval is experienced as a dead time, which the subject cannot survive. Hence the value for the patient of the negative therapeutic reaction, which ensures that the analyst will never be replaced, since the object which would succeed him might never appear or might only appear too late.*

In another section of *Playing and Reality*, 'The use of an object and relating through identifications', Winnicott discusses the patient's ability to *use* the analyst. For this to be possible, the analyst must allow himself to be destroyed as frequently as the subject wishes, so that the latter may be reassured that the object has the capacity to survive his destruction of it. Winnicott makes the interesting comment that destructiveness of this kind is not related to aggressiveness. This states yet another paradoxical truth. It must be understood that what is here in question is not the fantasied activity of an experience of mentally acted-out destruction; rather it is a radical decathexis. Hence what we are concerned with is a succession of libidinal or aggressive cathexes and of decathexes which abolish the preceding cathexes and the objects linked to them. When carried to an extreme, such decathexes lead to psychic death, just as anarchic cathexes deeply pervaded by aggressiveness lead to delusion. Thus the fundamental dilemma becomes: delusion or death (physical or psychic). The work of the analyst is aimed at transforming these alternatives into something less extreme, so that delusion may become playing, and death absence. In this context absence does not mean loss, but *potential presence*. For absence, paradoxically, may signify either an imaginary presence, or else an unimaginable non-existence. It is absence in this first sense which leads to the capacity to be alone (in the presence of the object) and to the activity of representation and of creating the imaginary: the transitional object, constructed within that space of illusion never violated by the question. Was the object created or was it found?

Freud, as I remarked above, sometimes compared the analytic situation to chess. If Winnicott is the master-player of psychoanalysis, it is surely not chess that he plays with his patient. It is a game with a cotton reel, with a piece of string, with a doll or teddy bear. Finally, with children Winnicott plays the squiggle game, in which each partner takes a turn drawing a scribble, which is then modified by the other (Winnicott, 1971*a*). The spontaneous movement of a hand which allows itself to be guided by the drive, a hand which does not act but rather expresses itself, traces a more or less insignificant and formless line, submitting it to the scrutiny of the other, who, deliberately, transforms it into a meaningful shape. What else do we do in the analysis of difficult cases? The beautiful clarity of the chess game, unfurling itself under the open light of day, is absent there. Instead we find ourselves in a murky night pierced by flashes of lightning and sudden storms. Meaning does not emerge complete as Aphrodite rising from the waves. It is for us to construct it. Viderman believes that, prior to the analytic situation, the meaning that we seek has never existed; it is the analytic process which constitutes it *as such* for the first time. Meaning is not discovered, it is created. I prefer to describe it as an absent meaning, a virtual sense which awaits its realization through the cuttings and shapings offered by analytic space (and time). It is a potential meaning. It would be wrong to think that like Sleeping Beauty it merely waits there to be aroused. It is constituted in and by the analytic situation; but if the analytic situation reveals it, it does not create it. It brings it from absence to potentiality, and then makes it actual. To actualize it means to call it into existence, not out of nothing (for there is no spontaneous generation), but out of the meeting of two discourses, and by way of that object which is the analyst, in order to construct the *analytic object*.

This theory implies that mental functioning has to be taken into consideration. In chess, there is only one kind of material at stake; the pieces have different *values* and an unchangeable mode of progression. The analytic situation, on the contrary, brings varying materials to light: drives, affects, representations (of things or of words), thoughts, actions. Their specific modes of functioning – to be the plaything of a drive (directed toward the body or toward the world), to feel, to imagine, to say, to think, to act – all these modes are capable of an ultimate exchange of function. The vectorization of drive into language is placed in check here. For speaking could become tantamount to acting, acting to evacuating, imagining to filling up a hole, and thinking could, at the extreme verge, become impossible (cf. 'blank psychosis', Donnet and Green, 1973).

Here we have evidently reached the limits of Freudian practice and theory. There is urgent and growing need for another system of reference which gives pride of place to the countertransference and clarifies its elaborative potentialities. The analyst ought either to use his imagination, or resign, for the unconscious creates its own structure only by way of the Imaginary.

The importance of the analytic setting arises from the fact that it allows the development of a *metaphoric* regression which is a double, an analogue of infantile regression. In the same way, the response of the analyst, comparable to holding, is itself only a double of maternal care. It is as if, out of the totality of physical and psychic maternal care, only the psychic aspect were to be admitted into the analytic situation. The part which is not given play in analysis is the one that is missing when the analytic object is constituted. This object, which takes shape through the communication of psychic maternal care, leaves in abeyance any actual regression to the past on the part of the patient, and any physical care on the part of the analyst.

But we must go yet further. And here my agreement with Winnicott reaches its limit. When Winnicott pointed out that there is no such thing as a baby, reminding us of the couple that it forms together with its cradle or with its mother in the holding situation, his observation, as we know, caused quite a stir.

I would maintain, for my part, that there is no such entity as a baby with his mother. No mother-child couple exists without a father somewhere. For even if the father is hated or banished by the mother, erased from her mind in favour of somebody else, of her own mother or father, the child nevertheless is the product of the union of the father and mother. Of this union he is the *material, living, irrefutable* proof. There are mothers who want to wipe out any trace of the father in the child. And we know the result: a psychotic structure. Thus we can assert that ultimately *there is no dual relationship*. There can be no dual exchanges, but there is always some link establishing the possibility of duality, in the form of areas of reunion and separation within the dual relationships.

In the analytic situation, this third element is supplied by the analytic setting. *The work of the analytic setting is comparable to the mirror-work, without which it is impossible to form an image from an object.* This induces the thought that reflection is a fundamental human property. Probably this attribute is innate, but we do now know that an object is indispensable in order to transform this *innate potentiality into its actual realization, failing which, the potentiality dies out and is lost. The analyst is the object necessary to such a transformation, but he can bring it about only with the help of the work of the not-me, which is the analytic setting defined spatially and temporally. What answers for the setting is the combined discourse of the analysand and the analyst, doubles of their respective experience.* Without affect there is no effective language. Without language there is no effective affect. The unconscious is not structured like a language (Lacan); *it is structured like an affective language, or like an affectivity having the properties of language.*

Winnicott was much blamed, and is still being blamed, for his delight in distorting the classical analytic setting. Since I am not prepared to endorse any and every deformation of the analytic setting, I must distinguish between those I would find acceptable and those I would have to reject. It seems to me that the only acceptable variations of classical analysis are *those whose aim is to facilitate the creation of optimal conditions for symbolization.* For classical neurosis, classical analysis serves this function. With borderline patients (taking this term in its broadest sense), the analyst must preserve in each case the minimum conditions requisite to the maximum development of symbolization. Today the analyst's major difficulty lies in this area. No one can decide for him the modalities or the extent of the variations required by such cases. This predicament has several possible results:

1. The cynicism of the analyst who, exploiting for personal ends his patient's need for dependence, gains a pseudo-independence through such shameless manipulation.
2. The collusion involved in a mutual dependency.
3. Guilt connected with the feeling of having transgressed the implicit analytic law.
4. Freedom in analysis based upon the principle that analysis is the construction of the analytic object.

A protective device is necessary here: the analyst's constant awareness of his countertransference and his full employment of it by way of the transference of the analysand. By the term *countertransference* I mean to take into account not only the affective effects, positive or negative, of the analysand's transference, not only the analyst's capacities for antipathy or for sympathy, but also his total mental functioning, including his reading and his exchanges with colleagues. Having said this, I would still agree with the restrictions that Winnicott imposed upon the countertransference in limiting it to the professional attitude. However far we may wish to extend our identification with the patient, this human identification is still a professional one. Hypocrisy is quite out of place here. We terminate the session and do not yield to the patient who wishes it would go on indefinitely. We leave for vacation without him and are paid for our work. We do our best to listen to him, but we see and hear only what we are prepared to see and hear, just as the patient can only understand what he was already on the verge of understanding, although he could not arrive at it all by himself.

In our activity as analysts, our real work does not lie in a mere receptivity to what the patient is communicating, nor on the other hand is it wholly determined by those preconceptions and presuppositions which are necessarily prior to all communication. The analyst's creativity takes shape within the time and space of the communicative exchange where the analytic object is formed by continuously and discontinuously constructing itself.

Analysts listen more easily to their patients than they can to each other. Doubtless because – and this is the final paradox – a colleague is more an-other than he is an a-like, and a patient is more an a-like than he is an-other. Alter ego.

Surface Analysis,
Deep Analysis

The Role of the Preconscious in
Psychoanalytical Technique

Every analyst knows that his work aims to analyse each patient as an individual, through his most personal self. Can one even talk of single analytical technique when one knows how, in the course of one day, several techniques have been used, each adapted to suit individual patients or even individual types of patient? Nevertheless just as one always uses approximate diagnostic references, so one talks of *a* technique, as some ideal or average practice, even if the facts belie this ideal or this average. One can therefore say that there is an *implicit theoretical model*.

THE IMPLICIT THEORETICAL MODEL

The analytical situation favours transference through regression. This regression is temporal, dynamic, and topographical. If, however, one considers only the temporal (or genetic) regression, one ceases to consider the topographical one. This, as we know, leads to mistakes. Thus the substitution of one content for another (incorporation fantasy) which is attributed to the breast rather than to the penis is neglected in favour of a content-structure equation. In the example I have just given, the oral content refers to oral regression without considering the re-lationship between topographical expression and the method of the presentation. In fact only the structure can tell us if the patient is having an oral or phallic regression. Analysts know that in order to grasp the structure one cannot merely study the content. Freud already knew this. The lack of reliability of the presentation has resulted in more import-ance being attached to the affects. The presentation, therefore, is almost completely ignored in favour of the affects. Consequently the com-

Originally written as a contribution to a symposium on 'The Psychoanalytic Process', this chapter was first published in the *International Review of Psycho-Analysis* (1974) 1.

munication from patient to analyst occurs by means of empathy and therefore the communication from analyst to patient, i.e., the interpretation, is marked by a greater or lesser neglect of the patient's speech and the part language plays in it. Making the unconscious conscious is no longer, as Freud thought, achieved by using links between word-presentations and thing-presentations. The preconscious is less and less used as a mediator, it is short-circuited and communication is almost established between unconscious and unconscious. This is in agreement with Freud's point that affects are capable of becoming unconscious independently of their link with the preconscious (Freud, 1923b). The tendency to use the id derivatives directly may have the consequence that silence is no longer being used as a technical means. Indeed, silence in Freudian theory induces regression. In other words, just as in dreams it is the impediment of discharge activity and therefore the impossibility of obtaining satisfaction which forces thoughts in the dream to change into images by means of regression, so it is the analyst's silence and the supine position which force the patient to express himself in the language of the primary process when censorship, obsessional defences or the most archaic psychotic defences are not too strong. As for hysterical defences, these present themselves through the activity of affects which are restrained because it is not possible to discharge by acting out or conversion.

Ever since analytic technique has been written about, resistance by means of over-understanding (obsessional type) and resistance by means of over-experiencing (hysterical type) have been seen as opposites: this is what Bouvet has called resistance *towards* the transference as opposed to *by* the transference (Bouvet, 1968). It seems that psychoanalytical currents of thought unbalance this opposition since they either favour affect by means of emotional communication between both sides or they favour intellectual communication between both sides. The difficulty is to know how much importance to attach to each alternative and this depends on the needs of the patient and on the *psychoanalytic process*. The major problem is the development of the psychoanalytic process which is, according to Freud, somehow above both persons involved or, according to Winnicott, *between* them.

This brings us to the question of interpreting the transference, which is undoubtedly the driving force of the analytic process. However, it is important to realize that an analysis conducted solely through interpretations of the transference often puts the patient under unbearable pressure. The analysis takes on an aspect of persecution even if these interpretations are designed to help the patient understand what is happening within him. The respect for the patient's resistance is one condition of the *development* of the analytical process. It is sometimes necessary for the patient to project on to the analyst, i.e., to get inside him in order to see what is happening there; but it is also essential that from time to time both look *together* towards a third object.

The concept of *development* we have just mentioned is correlative with the idea of regression which is, paradoxically, progressive. Analysis is not marked merely by regression but rather by a process of regression-progression, a going back and forth, caused by resistance. This process must be respected if the patient is to follow his *own* rhythm. This implies not only silence on the analyst's part, a permissive silence, but also the progressive aspect of interpretations concerning the patient's regression.

One may wonder in this case, what the purpose of analysis is. One can say following the ideologies that psychoanalysis aims at adjusting the patient to reality, promoting his emotional maturity or his personal liberation. *I would prefer to think that the aim of analysis is to prepare the patient for self-analysis.* This view is also in agreement with Winnicott who said that the ability to use an object was closely linked to its survival after its destruction (Winnicott, 1969). In short, one should be able to use the analyst and his interpretations as objects which will serve to establish the capacity to be alone (without the analyst); at first in the presence of the analyst and later without him, as though he were *potentially* present when in fact he is not. Thus silence can at first be seen as an empty space which, as the analytic process progresses, becomes a space to be filled, a space full of fantasy objects: the analysis is not engaged in its destruction but rather in its transformation in a way that is beneficial for the patient.

THE PRECONSCIOUS: MEDIATORY AND TRANSITIONAL

Ever since Freud replaced the first topography by the second one, the role of the preconscious has slowly diminished. The reference to new agencies (id, ego, superego) has not completely obliterated the old ones. But even though one continues to talk in terms of conscious and unconscious, the preconscious is referred to less and less.

Yet, when Freud wrote *An Outline of Psycho-Analysis* (1940*a*) he did not underestimate the part played by the preconscious. In practice the main difference between the preconscious and the unconscious is that the preconscious enters the conscious easily whereas the passage from unconscious to conscious comes up against strong resistances which are, according to Freud, a *sine qua non* of normality. This entails an important technical point. The patient can, by himself, make the preconscious conscious.

Here the analyst's help is negligible. In this situation there are two alternatives: either the analyst uses the preconscious as a mediator and continues the analytical work towards the unconscious by following the route of communications from the preconscious to the conscious, aware of trying to reach the unconscious by this well-worn path, in which case resistances will slowly give way, inflicting the ego with only minor traumas; or else he goes directly from the conscious to the unconscious causing a real narcissistic wound, *due to the method employed for interpreting, rather than to the content of the interpretation.* In this case, needless to say, the patient can react to this intrusion only in an unfavourable way – either by a protective denial of his inner space, or by complacently accepting a false self and without really believing in it, or, again, by building up a masochistic type of therapeutic alliance: 'Give me more interpretations, rape me, hurt me, I like it'. This leads to an erotization of the superego, cheating it of its own nature. The rule that one should *interpret as near as possible to the ego* is justified if one does not wish to foster the establishment of a cement block of resistances which characterizes the beginning of interminable analyses. It is indeed noticeable that analyses which right from the start involve lengthy and frequent interpretations are hardly ever shorter than the others; indeed, it is quite the contrary. It has still to be shown whether they produce better results. The same could be said about analyses where interpretations allow repeated abreactions to arise without allowing time for the ego to assimilate and integrate the new contents. In this case one is back to cathartic treatment and the belief that the provoked upheaval is satisfactory, 'This interpretation really did something to him'. But what?

How can the preconscious be used in analytical work? For Freud language played an essential part in the passage from unconscious to conscious: 'The inside of the ego which comprises above all thought-processes, has the quality of being preconscious. This is a characteristic of the ego and belongs to it alone' (Freud, 1940a). We know that language turns thought into perception, it is therefore language which has this characteristic. Nevertheless Freud adds: 'It would be incorrect, however, to think that the connection with mnemic residues of speech is a necessary condition of the preconscious state. On the contrary that state is independent of a connection with them, though the presence of that connection makes it safe to infer the preconscious nature of a process' (*ibid.*).

Freud is here implicitly referring to the impressions of the senses, to affects as well as to language. Thus language is evidence of the preconscious process but the preconscious state is not entirely made up of

language. Conversely, the affect can be preconscious but is not necessarily so. It can also be conscious or unconscious (Freud, 1923*b*). The
preconscious is a transitional space between the unconscious and the
conscious, a transient space between the id and the ego. The superego is
also involved with the structure of language; this becomes clearer if one
recalls the part played by mnemic residues in the formulation and
introjection of prohibitions. The preconscious is bound to be a transit
space for the verbal translation of thing presentations, but it is a space
which can be short-circuited by the affect. An obsessional defence can be
detected by the fact that language is without affect, the affect itself being
disconnected or repressed. In this situation it is better not to search for
the repressed affect and interpret it directly, in a wild fashion, but rather
to link the repressed affect to the preconscious presentation. This seems to be the
condition for constructive interpretive work. In doing so not only does
one re-establish the broken link, but one can also bring the patient to
realize that the affect had been disconnected or repressed because of its
link with *this same presentation.* Work carried out in this way does not lack
depth but gains in precision and thus reaches the very target the patient
is trying to hide from the transference. That this is so, is best shown by
the fact that the interpretation will be confirmed later when the associative process resumes its course, whether the patient approves of or rejects
the correctness of the interpretation. At this point it often happens that
the patient and the analyst are *thinking of the same thing*; sometimes the
content of the thought is very remote from the preceding material but
throws new light on it. Thus a patient receives the explanation of a fact, a
symptom, a fantasy or a dream which occurred weeks or months before
the session in question.

In brief I have re-stated the fact that the preconscious is a *binding agency*
of mental energy, linking the primary and secondary processes. Indeed
transformation of free energy into bound energy is fundamental to
analytical work as it is to the functioning of the psychical apparatus. This
provides us with a theory about the ego, which attributes to it a role
similar to that which it plays in the therapeutic relationship without
recourse to traditional psychology's theory of the ego. Hartmann's
theory of an autonomous function of the ego with a conflict-free sphere
would imperceptibly bring us back to a pre-Freudian concept of the ego.
It is important to note that the patient is not allowed to act but is asked to
say everything which comes to his mind, thus transmitting the object
relation by means of language; this entails that analytic treatment
necessarily leads to an *instinctualization of language.* This results in language no longer being used for communication as it is in everyday life.

Talking to the analyst involves entering into a very close relationship with him, which is both loving and destructive. There is no equivalent to this in everyday life because, besides language, there are other means of communication such as gestures, actions and face to face relations which vary with the reactions of the recipient.

The same can be said about silence. In analysis, silence is not only an absence of speech as it would be in everyday life, but it is endowed with affect (or is inductive to affect when it is the analyst's). These affects can be representative of either fusion or destruction: that is why the *dosage of silence* is very important. Sometimes silence represents communion, the presence of the analyst, at other times it represents absence, death, or emptiness. It is not so much the quantity of silence that is important as its quality, a feature only the analyst can decide upon. There are no hard and fast rules about silences, each case calls for an appropriate attitude. Relevant to this is Winnicott's idea of 'facilitating environment'. Silence must be judged according to the help it offers to the patient, and should not necessarily be abolished in an attempt to avoid frustration. Language, as opposed to silence, plays an intermediary role between pleasure and displeasure and not only between fusion and destruction.

ASSOCIATING – INTERPRETING – THINKING

One can ask: 'What is associating?' Associating is one of the fundamental activities of analysis and it involves the patient at two levels. At one level associating allows the contents of the unconscious and the id to manifest themselves through the transference and through a reduction of censorship. At the second level the patient is asked *to associate to what he has just associated,* i.e., to find the link which governs the results of the association. The analyst also associates, this being a recognized cause of suspended attention. He associates on the patient's associations, as well as on his own. This countertransference is particularly noticeable when the analyst finds it difficult to associate the patient's associations and also to associate upon the patient's associations. However, for the associations to be revealing as well as meaningful, they must acquire a certain constancy. This is achieved by the compulsion to repeat, which brings to the analyst's attention that which needs interpreting in the transference. Besides the never-ending chain of associations, the compulsion to repeat represents in treatment a sort of artificial labelling of associations, just as in some chemical analyses a particular ion is labelled so that it may be better followed through its transformations. The transference itself is an association in the widest sense of the word, Freud called it a 'false connection'. Transference and compulsion to repeat are linked. The transference can be seen as a resistance or as that to which the resistance is opposed, or again as including the resistance. If it is seen as a manifestation of the attachment to the analyst (whether positive or negative) its essence is its repetitive nature. The analyst offers the patient one object, namely the analyst, on to which he can fix his compulsion to repeat, thereby reducing the number of compulsions to repeat linked with other objects of the outside world. The transference is therefore an association, and rather than talk of a therapeutic alliance I would prefer to call it *analytical association* so as to retain the privileged position and numerous connotations of the former. What is interpreted in the transference (and this is not the whole transference, since the whole transference cannot be interpreted no matter how talented the analyst) is that element which represents an *active* structure, such as repetitive association. It matters little whether this repetitive, active structure is a repetition of the past in the strict sense of the word, or if it is a product of the analysis. In both cases one can only repeat what is already part of oneself and what has established itself against the progressive evolution and control of the ego. But how will the interpretation, resulting from the analyst's associative work, act against the associative repetition of the active structure? The usual answer to this question is that it is achieved by informing the patient of his most intimate and hidden affects. Perhaps this is not enough. The connection between the unconscious content and the formulated content (which results from the interpretation) rests on a logical postulate; i.e., that there is, to a greater or lesser extent, an identity between the two. Thus, by penetrating into the deepest and apparently most irrational layers, we arrive at a certain kind of logic. The primary process, even in its seemingly most primitive aspects, remains governed by logic, not, of course, the logic of the secondary process or that of reason, but nevertheless a form of symbolic logic. Indeed, an analyst does not reason when interpreting, the best interpretations are those which appear spontaneously. But this only means that reasoned and logical (primarily logical) work has taken place outside the realm of the secondary logic of reason.

It is noticeable, in this respect, that – whereas the secondary logic uses language processes (word-presentations in the Freudian theory) only – primary logic employs other means: first thing presentations and also affects, not to mention the acts and bodily states. Here the scale of associations is wider and the associative processes are less limited and more polysemic. The Freudian theory of thought is consequently richer and more comprehensive than non-Freudian theories, since it offers us *several types of thought which are conflicting but occasionally supportive. It is suggested that the phenomenon of association between primary and secondary processes be called the tertiary process.* The quotation from Freud (1940a) on the preconscious acquires its full value when it is interpreted widely. 'The inside of the ego, which comprises above all *thought-processes* has the quality of being preconscious' [my italics]. The preconscious includes therefore phenomena which belong to the conscious state (secondary thought) and to the unconscious state (primary thought) as seen in fantasies. One is therefore justified in using this instrument of thought, i.e., the preconscious, as one of the main tools in the analytical work *towards* the unconscious. It may be the projection of this space towards the outside in the children–mother relationship that accounts for what Winnicott has called the *transitional space* (Winnicott, 1953).

The following clinical example should help to illustrate these points:

A young woman, approximately 35 years of age, started an analysis with me about four months ago because she felt that her emotional and sentimental life was unfulfilled, thus leading to depressive affects. She was married to a man she did not love but with whom she got on reasonably well. However, by mutual consent, she had lived as she pleased since the events in France in 1968. This produced in her a feeling of great liberation. She has had two affairs, since then, neither of which have led anywhere; the first was with a powerful, tyrannical man who was not very understanding about her problems, the second with a colleague who had no intention of becoming seriously involved with her. This second affair came to an end and the man now lives with another colleague, much younger than my patient, towards whom my patient says she feels no jealousy. This then is the background to the session I am going to present.

Patient: They are all mad at the lab [she works in a physiology laboratory]. The least annoying is Kenneth's [a friend and colleague] brother who is schizophrenic and who stands behind you saying nothing, hands you a cigarette when you are looking for one and a light when you need one . . . [this is an indirect allusion to me which stresses her wish for keeping her distance]. I am easily influenced. You told me that for me dreams were a method I could use to convey to you indirectly all the things I cannot tell you about my relationships with people. I had a dream but I resent having it if I am still at that stage [she had been in analysis for four months]. Kenneth came to see me yesterday. We talked and played the flute together; my son Bernard was there [her youngest son who, for reasons I cannot explain, is the father's fantasy-child]. Then Bernard went to work in his room and Kenneth and I worked on an article we were writing together. An article which will be good, rather controversial but good [she complained some time ago that people often used her ideas, depossessing her of her work]. This is the dream: you were in the dream, I was there too and so was

Kenneth. First I was lying on the couch, then Kenneth came and sat down beside me. He was telling you about his problems . . . His mother is terrible and so is his father. And you, you were there. You were coming closer to him and you were being very affectionate to him, you put your hand on his shoulder – the same side, without putting your arm around him. There was some kind of complicity between us. You were asking me without saying so, but with your eyes, if I agreed to let the session go on like this and you were looking after him rather than looking after me. I made a sign to say it was alright. Then as I was facing you, I came closer and closer to hear what was happening [this woman's past was dominated by infantile asthma; she would spend her nights in the bathroom between her parents' bedroom and her's, waiting for the daybreak which would put an end to these attacks. She no longer has asthma but some allergic symptoms still persist]. But in the dream there was someone else sitting on a chair who was visible only in profile. It looked like me, it was me or maybe my son Thomas who resembles me a lot. Yet, this person sitting on a chair and seen from the side must have been the analyst. He had a very disapproving look. But I took no notice of his look of reproach as I came nearer. And then the dream stopped . . . Am I not silly, still letting myself be influenced by reproach. And why do I dream of reproach if I agree? This person is both you and me.

Analyst: It is as though for you there were two people here. The one you know and the one you neither know nor are aware of, the reproachful analyst. You told me a few sessions ago that you didn't have any 'transference feelings' towards me. This situation occurs in the dream with Kenneth, which forbids you to experience it here with me, here it is the analyst who disapproves of it for you.

Patient: Why would you disapprove of it for you? [Integration of the interpretation in echo.]

Analyst: Why did you understand me to say that I disapproved of it for me? It is as though you wanted to tell me that I would not allow you what I don't allow myself. This is what we have said with regard to your mother, who did not allow you any contact with your father and who herself was distant with both him and you.

Patient: So I understand why I put my son Thomas in my place – I am his mother. I am therefore obliged to be twice removed, once from Kenneth and once from my son, in order to represent my mother . . . In short, I cannot really give myself any pleasure, as you have seen, I can only do so through others and I have to be resigned to '*relieve*' [the word comes to her in English; this is a reference to my imagined origins and to an experience of hers in America which she found very liberating] . . . with relief, friendship, understanding – as in the dream.

Analyst: *Relieve* can phonetically be understood another way.

Patient: *Re-live*, that is what I wanted to say . . . I don't feel the energy to live. Pierre [the second friend] came back this morning with presents; he told me that it was wonderful, the place was ideal, the skiing terrific [she lent her mountain studio to Pierre who went there with his new mistress without telling my patient who had guessed nevertheless]. I was very happy that he liked it, I also saw Carole [his new mistress] who was very sun-tanned, I was happy too, then I was irritated.

[*She cried.*]

Analyst: Jealous. You now complete the interpretation of your dream. The link between Pierre and Kenneth is that you allowed them both to borrow your flat [once in the mountains and once in Paris]. It is Pierre who is in your dream and you would have liked him to have asked your permission to take Carole with him. The third meaning of the word 'relive' is *re-leave*, 'to go away'; I had told you that I could not see you Wednesday morning. You would have therefore preferred me to ask for your permission to *re-leave*.

Patient: [Long silence.] I am thinking of things I am trying to make run together. But that goes rather against you.

At the end of the session the patient asked for the alternative session I had previously offered her. She had refused it then, saying it would not be convenient since at the time she was planning to go skiing.

We can see that in this session all the work was done close to the ego, this allowed a constant progress towards regression which manifested itself by the affect of sadness shown in her tears. The unlikely word (*relieve*) was used as a semantic cross-road, opening various routes to what has been suppressed. Other types of interpretation and other interpretations would have been possible, more active and more penetrating by direct impact on the transference. Had I adopted them it would have been along the lines of the fantasy of rape expressed by the patient a few sessions earlier. But rape without pleasure and without profit would have resulted either in a blocking due to resistance or in a masochistic acceptance. I preferred working *stage by stage* in a quasi-archaeological way because of the allergic structure of the patient.

The progressive work of the session illustrates how one can use the preconscious to reach the unconscious. We can formalize what we have just done in the following way:

$$a \rightarrow b \rightarrow c$$
$$a \#\,^{1}b \text{ and } b \# c, \text{ then } a \# c$$

Yet if there is only a slight difference between a and b, and if there is also only a slight difference between b and c, these differences add up and we have an association between a and c which, because of the sum of the two small differences, will result in uniting the two terms which were separated by a large difference.

These same cumulative differences allow one to interpret further into the unconscious, i.e., to go from the conscious to the unconscious (the large difference). One could say that we have relied upon the following model:

Word-presentation 1 # Word-presentation 2
then, Word-presentation 2 # Thing-presentation 1
then, Thing-presentation 1 # Affect
then, Affect   # Thing-presentation 2
finally, Word-presentation 1 ↔ Thing-presentation 2

---

[1] An algebraic symbol meaning 'not very different from'.

Meanwhile, we come across various psychical processes: displacement (or condensation), projection, reversal into the opposite, turning around upon the subject's own self and even sublimation.

What does this distinction between the various materials of psychical organization mean? Why not follow Anglo-Saxon analysts who have abandoned the differences Freud drew between word-presentation, thing-presentation and affect? If it is true that one must account for the direction of the psychical apparatus where verbalization represents the end of a mental elaboration, then, conversely, any replacement of elements which refer to verbalization (word-presentation) by other, non-verbal elements reveals psychical conflict requiring a solution, which in turn demonstrates a certain degree of censorship. Thus, it seems likely that censorship interferes to a minor extent when words are replaced by images, to a greater extent when words are replaced by affects, and to an even greater extent when acting out or bodily states come to the forefront. Of course this needs to be evaluated not as an isolated fact but in relation to longer or shorter chains of association and, other things being equal, to the *patient's associative style*. From a more theoretical standpoint it would seem that the resort to primitive materials of organization in the return of the repressed, is an index of the levels of conflict. Therefore interpreting from the patient's language requires a gradual progress through different levels, starting at the surface and working downwards. It also requires the use of one's ego control, one's powers of inhibition and one's ability to link and integrate the psychical layers which are most distant from the obvious content.

Is there a danger of intellectualization? No doubt there would be if the analyst were to consider only the words. The important thing is not to concentrate one's attention on words but rather to note those occasions when words fail or no longer perform their function. The most telling factor is not language, but its limits. It is, however, by means of language that one realizes the point at which the patient's communication needs an alternative channel, more closely linked with the primary process.

SURFACE ANALYSIS, DEEP ANALYSIS

The analysis of the preconscious and in particular the use of the patient's analytical material (in his own language) has been neglected since Freud. The reason for this appears to be straightforward in that, since the preconscious can be reached by the conscious, the importance of the preconscious is negligible and language is superficial. To me, however, this viewpoint is superficial itself. The preconscious, as we have seen, is a privileged space where *both* the analyst and the patient can meet to share part of the transference and go forward together. There is no point in the analyst running like a hare if the patient moves like a tortoise. A meeting point in depth is more probable if the thread that links the two travellers also serves to keep them sufficiently apart.

This technique seems to be quite the reverse of that of the Kleinians, *as I see it* from their clinical material. These analysts do indeed use the patient's language in his associations, but they use it as a structure which is then directly reduced to the primary language where phonetic syllables are separated, thereby referring to the unconscious. But following Isaacs (in her article on fantasy) it is clear that fantasy does not have any links with the conscious or the preconscious but expresses instinctual activity directly. The work of transforming instinctual activity from its somatic origins into its verbal expression is neglected in this sort of description. This technique has two great disadvantages. On the one hand it causes a continuous forcing of interpretations which leads the patient after some time of resistance either to a therapeutic relationship with a false self, or to a masochistic erotization of this relationship; the patient is never allowed to rest, he must comply. Moreover, the vast quantity of interpretations represents intellectual forced feeding which I think can only lead to either morbid interpretive hunger or to an almost total anorexia towards the analyst's speech.

Furthermore, when interpreting the conscious into unconscious by means of simultaneous translation, the analyst could be interpreting the conscious or the preconscious and *mistake them for the unconscious.* This may lead to regrettable confusions. It is striking how rarely Kleinians interpret the reversal into the opposite: for them anxiety means anxiety – it is never the ego's sign against the forbidden desire; hatred is always hatred – never the defensive reversal of love; the bad mother is never a defensive construction against the interdiction of incest; the terrifying vagina is never a horror of castration, etc. By using the material for simultaneous translation (which is always by reference to displacement on to the analyst and rarely in the sense of reversal); then by repeating interpretations (which hardly vary in extremely long analyses) one risks turning this pseudo-profound interpretive activity into *hypnotic suggestion.* The Kleinians who see themselves as guarantors of interpretive purity, in avoiding extra-transference interpretations or non-interpretive interventions, may in fact, induce a process of suggestion. This does not, as I hope I have made clear, mean that I am an advocate of a type of ego conceived of by Hartmann, autonomous and free of conflicts. I support the Freudian concept of the ego, in which the patient's freedom is respected and which allows one to proceed *according to what the patient is able to understand of what we are saying to him at that point in time of the treatment, i.e., permitting him to elaborate and integrate in a regression-progression process, and so to proceed from the most superficial to the deepest level.* This avoids early and lasting blocks of resistances or – conversely – psychotic, psychosomatic and psychopathic breakdowns.

I have endeavoured to point out in what way my views differ from those of other authors; in addition I should like to point out that the technique adapts itself to the patient. Of course with borderline cases and patients with latent psychosis, the tools one uses are damaged; these structures are particularly fragile and therefore have massive defences which are characterized by a failure of the preconscious. This is a possible explanation of what Balint called the 'basic fault' and Winnicott the 'false self'. Bion insisted on the *thought disorders* one finds in psychotic structures and especially on the fact that words are in such patients equivalent to acts.

Patients sometimes need us to understand what they are experiencing before we interpret it. The important thing for them is that the analyst be capable of experiencing what they experience even before there is any question of understanding it. Here it may be that the technique can only move its focus from the conscious to the unconscious or maybe even from the unconscious to the unconscious. But any generalization about such a technique would, I think, prejudice the rest of the analysis.

Finally, to return to the Freudian view of metapsychology, one should not forget the strength of the dynamic, topographical and economic factors. The relations between free energy and bound energy show us that the most important factor is *mental functioning*, i.e., the mobility and flexibility of the contents (neither static nor unobtainable in the speed of their displacements), this is true for the dynamic factor which makes the conflicts bearable. There is a variety and spreading in the use of different types of communication such as body states, affects, word- and thing-presentations, thoughts and actions, all of which are signs of satisfactory topographical relations. Finally, the system of transformation of desires from the id to the ego should not overwhelm the psychical apparatus by providing it with more than it can cope with, nor force the ego into drastic repression and so become impoverished. Otherwise the sources of energy of psychical activity would be cut off. This is the economical factor. It does not seem necessary to add an adaptive factor (which is inferred in the principles of mental functioning of the psychical apparatus), nor a genetic factor since our idea of the rules of temporal functioning in the unconscious are not yet known well enough. Furthermore, the genesis is implied in the associative process itself, where each element gives rise to the next.

The analytical optimum is defined in terms of distance (Bouvet, 1968), i.e., by the existence of a useful difference between the two associated terms. The relation between the terms a, b, c, must be such that one can deduce a workable interpretation from them. If this distance is too small, the patient learns nothing but takes refuge in a manic defence. If, on the contrary, the distance is too large, the interpretation is useless and the patient cannot make use of the link between the terms because resistances keep them apart. Resistance will also widen the distance between what the patient is experiencing and what the analyst is interpreting, no matter how correct the interpretation may be. The analytical work takes advantage of this *useful difference* while following an interpretation, when the new sequence will be made out of d, e, f, g, where g does not stand for a new content but for the result of a self-interpretation which exists also in the relation between d, e and f. Here what I have called a *tertiary process* will come into action, i.e. there will be a link *between the primary process and the secondary process*. This type of work, which is characteristic of good analysis and which the analyst should encourage in the patient, requires a mediator.

Language is not superficial if it is expressed in a lively speech[1]; a speech where the affect plays a part; where it is neither absent nor overpowering. Language cannot be superficial as we know that it is built upon the deep structures of mental activity. These mental structures, which belong to instinctual activity, have been known to analysts for some time but are still unknown to linguists. This is the reason why Freud placed dualism at the heart of his different theories on instincts. All our activity reflects the incessant agonism and antagonism of fusion and defusion, of conjunction and disjunction, of condensation and displacement, of Eros and the destructive instincts.

In the end, as Freud said: 'God is on the side of the strongest.'

---

[1] *Le discours vivant* (Green, 1973).

13
The Double and the Absent

If it is true that the existence of motion is proved by the act of walking, a similar logic may relieve us of the need to justify applying psychoanalysis to the study of literary texts. There are, in any case, a considerable number of works which argue in favour of just such an approach (Clancier, 1973). The act of walking, however, does not exempt us from posing questions about our course. All the more since, despite authoritative contributions to the field, the efforts of psychoanalytical criticism are greeted with such reticence. Freud himself experienced this. Today, psychoanalytical criticism is even more thoroughly challenged – to begin with, by literary theorists who criticize it for all sorts of reasons. They claim, for example, that it ties the work too closely to an analysis of the author, even though many works of psychoanalytical criticism deal exclusively with the text and leave aside the always conjectural biographical approach. In cases where criticism confines itself to the text, the psychoanalytical critic is blamed for attaching too much importance to one meaning of a work while neglecting the others (social meanings, for example), even though the analyst has always pointed out that his approach in no way claims to be exhaustive. Finally, criticisms will be levelled at the fact that his perspective focuses on the non-literary, and neglects the 'literal' aspect of the work – as though the literal were not a means of gaining access to the non-literal which always underlies and shapes it.

If these complaints issued only from literary sources, we could ascribe them to a very natural reaction against an unpleasant intrusion. Inured as he is to this type of reaction, the psychoanalyst could simply ignore it and count on posterity to vindicate him. Unfortunately, he finds himself at odds with his own peers, his colleagues, who do not tend to approve of such excursions outside [of] the clinical realm. Thus, there seems to be a consensus that the analyst should stay put in his office, with his patients, and not overstep the bounds of his practice. We are told that there is no analysis but that of the transference, and that the transference is only

First published as 'Le double et l'absent', in *Critique* (May 1973), and, in this translation by Jacques F. Houis, in *Psychoanalysis, Creativity and Literature: A French-American Inquiry*, ed. A. Roland (New York, Columbia University Press, 1978). Dedicated to Bernard Pingaud.

found in analysis. Outside [of] these limits, it is said, there is only adventurism and even abuse of power on the part of the analyst. We should not, therefore, be surprised if psychoanalytical criticism, along with every other branch of applied psychoanalysis, is in a state of recession, considering the heights it initially reached during its first analytical generation with Freud, Jones, Rank, Abraham, Ferenczi, and others. But Freud's example alone is not justification enough. His work, from this point of view, is not exempt from criticism. Recently (1972), one of our most brilliant Hellenists, J.-P. Vernant, contested the psychoanalytical interpretation of *Oedipus Rex* and offered instead a sociopolitical one.

This chorus of criticisms does not discourage us. Nothing so stimulates perseverence in an undertaking as to feel oneself the object of such reprobation. But what about concrete experience? Imagine an analyst: he has spent his day listening to a succession of patients, each with his particular neuroses, conflicts, defences and often burdensome transference. When, finally, his workday is over and he returns to his family, he allows himself some distraction – sometimes by going to the theatre or the cinema, or simply by reading a good book which is supposed to allow him to forget his work and his worries. But there is a catch. It is sometimes difficult to stop the psychoanalyzing machine, probably because psychoanalysis isn't just another job. To be a psychoanalyst is to have a psychoanalytical view of any experience. Some deplore this situation because, faced with this professional addiction, there isn't much room left for other things. I am not saying that it *must* be this way; I am saying that it often is.

To set our minds at ease we should note that it isn't *always* so, but only when the analyst is captivated, when the work, whatever it may be, has touched, moved, or even disturbed him. At this point the analyst often feels a need to analyse, to understand why he has reacted in such a way, and this is where his work of criticism, of 'deconstruction' begins. This already limits the scope of his work. It is out of the question that he analyse a text to order; the request can only come from within – that is, if something *has already happened* between the text and the analyst. *The analysis of the text is an analysis after the fact.* However, since the text is not the author, how do we analyze it? Before answering this question we should, perhaps, show how an analyst analyzes not a text, but a patient. The differences and the similarities will then emerge. The first difference between the analysand and the text is that the analysand is subject to a continuous and progressive analysis which precludes any possibility of turning back. During each session he communicates to the analyst what he is living, how he lives it in relation to the analyst, how he lives that part of himself which is shaped by his drives and his defences; all this in the face of his ego, which is more or less organized and more or less related to external reality. Whatever the analyst comes to understand from this communication, he will choose to either keep to himself, or communicate to his patient in order to produce a 'becoming conscious' which involves the analyst himself (interpretation of the transference). This interpretation will supposedly be related to the analysand's past but, even more, it will be based on everything the analyst has learned from the evolution of the patient's analysis. Every analyst knows from experience that what there is to comprehend in the patient's communication amounts to far more than he will be able to grasp. This is not only because, skilled as he may be, his capacity to understand is finite, but also because it is never possible to backtrack. Even if the analyst asks the analysand to repeat such and such a fragment of his communication, this second utterance will always be different from the first. It will always be *another story* and never a repetition. The psychoanalytical process, even if it is based on the patient's regression, always moves forward, even if the repetition compulsion seems to indicate stagnation. Progression is inevitable as long as the patient continues to live and speak. Time flows inexorably, and the analyst, as Heraclitus puts it, never bathes twice in the same stream.

I have just mentioned regression, a major phenomenon that all the conditions of psychoanalysis seek to promote. Because of this regression, the patient's discourse, given its disconnected and rambling style, is sometimes unintelligible to the layman. Besides, the analyst does not listen solely with his ears, but with his entire body. He is sensitive to the words, to the tone of voice, to interruptions in the narrative, to pauses and to the entire emotional make-up of the patient's expression. Without the dimension of affect, analysis is a vain and sterile enterprise. Without a *sharing* of the patient's emotions, the analyst is no more than a robot-interpreter who would be better off changing jobs before it is too late. Today we know that the analyst must be able to bear the chaos of some patients, in order to enable them to emerge and build a certain ordered inner space, without which no kind of social existence is possible.

A recent work (Viderman, 1970) tells us that interpretation is not only the revelation of a hidden meaning but, in a certain sense, the creation of an absent meaning, the veritable invention of a meaning previously left, as it were, in abeyance. A psychoanalytical interpretation relies to a great degree on the hypothetical, because it deals with the patient's internal psychic reality which is shaped by his fantasies. It is not, therefore, an historical interpretation as an historian would define the term, but a conjectural interpretation. Contrary to what Freud thought, the analysand does not contain an image of his past resembling that of a city buried in the sands, like some Pompeii which one could recover almost intact but, rather, a reality warped by his own interpretations, both of reality itself and of the past, whose image does not remain pure but changes according to his own evolution. This does not mean, however, that the interpretations furnished by the analyst are unrelated to what this buried past actually was. Fantasy is also constructed around a core of reality, much in the same way that certain myths and legends, although transforming them considerably, tell of actual historical events. It would, in any case, seem that what is important in analysis is not that the analyst succeed, at any price, in reconstructing a puzzle, but that his interpretations help the patient free himself from the alienating burden he bears and, if possible, help him to utilize his energies in more productive ways. Thus analysis should lead to the *sharing of a truth supposed possible* between the analyst and the analysand, acknowledgement of which aids in their mutual emancipation. A clinical example should allow us to understand better what I have just said.

A patient arrived at her session one morning. She lay down and at first expressed a certain satisfaction, tinged with gratitude, with the preceding session. That session had concerned her dilemma, which was experiencing something with me and having to, at the same time, understand what was going on. She could not accept this dichotomy. Every time she found herself in one of these situations, she felt that she was failing to live up to the other. Thus, if after receiving something from me, she made an effort to understand, she felt as though she were withdrawing from me; on the other hand, she simply enjoyed herself, she would feel guilty for not having made the effort to understand. One could relate this to the difficulties she had in satisfying the two parts of herself: the one requiring an intense relationship with her mother, and the other wanting to obey the wishes of her father, a professor of mathematics. She herself had aspired to become a mathematician.

I had reminded her of her first dream in analysis, where a woman showed her a painting and analysed it. In her dream, she had protested, saying, 'Why bother? You need only to look at it and take it all in!' During the more recent session she told me (probably because the preceding session had been a good one in which she had accomplished analytical work satisfying to both of us, prompting me to furnish more interpretation than is my habit), that she had felt nourished, and that it was as if she still had reserves from the day before and that she needed time to digest them. After this expression of satiety and contentment, she stopped. As for myself, I was lighting my pipe, which she heard me do.

At that point, she began to speak again in an ironic tone, saying, 'It's good, isn't it, that first pipe of the morning!' I should note that this patient was not my first patient of the morning. She knew that there had been someone before her and, therefore, that it was not necessarily my first pipe of the morning. It was apparent, from what she said, that she longed for my pipe, for this pleasure that excluded her, and may even have included someone else. The word 'pipe' suggested two possible meanings: the first involved the fantasy of fellatio which the previous material had brought to mind; the second pointed to nutritional plea-sure. I tended toward the second meaning because it seemed closer to the context of associations – related to the feeling of being nourished by the analyst. I therefore decided on the second meaning, because it seemed more highly cathected by the patient in the transference.

The day before, she had mentioned two occurrences. The first was a comment made by one of her friends, to the effect that her (the friend's) analyst, Dr X, (to whom my patient had almost gone for analysis before deciding on me instead), really gave the impression of being interested in his patient; whereas my patient complained of my reserve and of the fact that, according to her, I had imposed a distance between us by not responding to her wishes. The second occurrence was that, upon hearing that my vacation would interrupt our analysis, she had reacted to my upcoming absence by deciding to join her sister on a trip to America, although her sister had planned to travel alone. In this I detected a displacement upon the sister, of a wish to be with the mother, by denying the disagreeable effect of separation.

I then understood the meaning of 'the first pipe of the morning'. It must have been related to the envy inspired by the first meal that her mother gave to her younger sister – her first feeding – after a night spent with the father. She had to accept losing the satisfaction of the breast and settle for the memory of satisfactions prior to the arrival of her sister (the reserves). Whereupon I told her that it seemed that she felt satisfied and full with the reserves from yesterday's nourishment, but the mere fact of hearing me light my pipe, which proved, to her, that I wasn't really interested in her, had been enough to make her hungry again and resentful. She accepted this interpretation and went on, speaking about her avidity. Among other things she alluded to her difficulties with her husband, to the fact that she reproached him for his lack of affection toward her, even though she was quite intolerant of his virility, demanding sexual relations when he did not desire any and refusing those that he proposed when he did desire them. The allusion to the trip to America – in other words, to the sister – allowed me to follow the momentum of the initial interpretation. I spoke to her about her hunger and the envy she felt toward her sister, as well as towards her friend who, with Dr X, seemed to be better fed and more loved than she. I added that it seemed to me that, although she might have been perfectly sated, the mere fact of witnessing her sister's nourishment had been enough to annul her satisfaction. Rather than feel that she had something extra (the previous day's nourishment), she especially felt what was lacking (the first pipe). By wanting, at any price, to restore the balance, she only succeeded in creating a new imbalance which she then had to correct.

The patient felt very happy: 'That's exactly it. That's extraordinary. I always wanted to equalize things between my sister and myself (to annul the difference, the fact that she was the oldest and her sister the youngest), so that we would be similar. When I gained weight, I wanted my sister to eat and to gain weight too, so that she would be exactly the same as me.' We can see that through this behaviour she defended herself against their respective ranking, and that she wanted them to be like twins in order to deny her sister satisfactions that she herself had to forego, when she couldn't enjoy them through identification. 'If you are like me = not different from me, any pleasure you have, I also have.'

This summary overview of analytical work should allow us to gain some insight into what the analyst does when he analyzes a text. For many reasons, through a curious reversal, it cannot really be said that the analyst analyzes a text. The literary text is the opposite of analytical discourse. It is a highly crafted product, even when it seeks to give an impression of free association. The text is reworked, erased, censored, the product not only of writing (*écriture*) but of one or several re-writes (one never knows how many times a text has been written), overloaded with interpretations, while whatever fails to suit the author has been excised or mutilated. Was this material taboo, or simply bad? Nothing here reminds us of the conditions of analytical work.

Why then even attempt it? All the more since the text, despite the efforts of modern typography, remains wedded to linearity. The text is a succession of phrases which differs from the living discourse of speech. Everything happens as if certain of the conditions of carnal speech, certain transformations (which will always be so many decantations, even if they masquerade as incantations) had produced this succession of grammatical sequences which we find in written language.

These inconveniences would discourage any attempt, if it were not for two circumstances which come to the analyst's rescue. The first of these is that the text is set and one can return to it repeatedly. This is just the opposite of what occurs in analysis where the repetition of a story will always yield another story. To be sure, a re-reading will never repeat a previous reading, but this only applies to the analyst who interprets. The text itself is sealed – and permanent; only within ourselves does it overflow.

The second circumstance is that any text, as crafted as it may be, always bears traces. Thanks to these traces, which always awaken something in the analyst-reader, an interpretation becomes possible, but never urgent as in analysis, never hurried as in the transference with its countertransferential inductions. With the text, there is always time for further reflection. The 'publication' of one's thought does not embarrass the patient.

Moreover, since psychoanalytical interpretation involves a process of deformation of the subject's conscious intentions (on p. 339 below I call it a *delirious deconstruction* of the text, causing it to say irrevocably what it has never said), we must recognize the fact that if someone is to be helped here, it is certainly not the author, who could not care less, but the analyst-interpreter, who helps himself through seeking to comprehend the emotions the text awakens within him. Thus the patient, the potential analysand, is not the author as everyone believes and fears, but the analyst himself.

This extreme subjectivity of psychoanalytical criticism nevertheless aims at a certain objectivity. To be sure, interpretation does not lay claim to absolute truth, but rather to an approximation of truth – but we have seen that the same could be said of analysis itself. The value of this approximation, once more, does not lie in analyzing the author, but rather in seeking to discover what underlies the text's effect on the potential reader. Thus the analyst-interpreter becomes that critic who is the privileged interlocutor, the mediator between reader and author, between the text as writing and its realization as reading. The text is therefore re-written by this reading. There have been many complaints concerning the abusive pretentions of the critic who substitutes himself for the author, but who can believe in the existence of an innocent reading?

Of course, most of the time the analyst has, at his disposal, only the definitive printed version, the one approved by the author, who has consented to furnish this veiled portion of his truth. It happens, however, that circumstances sometimes confirm an interpretation. What follows is a personal experience: While reading Henry James's *The Ambassadors*, the more I read, the more I felt that the key to the story could be found in the vicinity of the character who is not named: the dead father, who is never alluded to. I thought to myself that it was an indication of James's great talent, that he constructed this work around this absent reference which dictates the stylistic efficacy of the literary endeavour. Later on, while reading the *Notebooks*, I learned how James worked. He started with what he called 'the germ' (I think we should read this word in its sexual rather than botanical sense) – an anecdote told in his presence, a news item, a conversation overheard at a dinner party, a trifle around which he spun his tale, like a patient spider.

Now, *The Ambassadors* is a privileged case, in that we possess three versions of this story. The first, a 'germ'; the second, a project of unusual length (forty-five printed pages) sent to his publisher; and finally, the third version, the novel in its completed form. One can envision a very interesting study here, which would involve following the various transformations of the text, in this and other of James's projects, much as has been done in the case of *Jean Santeuil* as it relates to Proust's *Remembrance of Things Past*.

To return to the text, it was with great surprise that I noted the following. In the definitive version, Strether is the ambassador of Chad Newsome's mother, and he has a great stake in his mission. Its success will determine the feasibility of his own plans: to marry the rich widow, mother of the young man, Chad. He will eventually become Chad's ally, losing everything to insure the other's happiness, sacrificing even the love of another woman.

In the second version, the treatment, the character who directs the liberating remarks to the young man tells him, '*You*, you are young. Live! And free yourself from the burdensome duties that your family has heaped upon you.' At first, he is anonymous: a distinguished, older American'. James will later call him Lambert Strether, and give him a double, Waymarsh, who will remain a faithful ally of the mother. The initial title referred to the aged.

What James tells us here about the character reveals the essential fact, about which he will have little to say in the final version: a failed father-son relationship between Strether and his child, left forever unresolved by the boy's death from an accident at the age of sixteen. In the final version, we find only a very discreet allusion to the 'ambassador's' son. It is barely noticeable, whereas, in the *Notebooks*, James treats it as pivotal.

Now, if we go back to the 'germ', 'barely ten words' quoted in the *Notebooks* (p. 225) on October 31, 1895, no more than a short story is being considered, inspired by an anecdote told by a friend, Jonathan Sturge, concerning a common acquaintance (Howell). The anecdote concerns a man who comes to Paris to spend a few days – a brief stay which is interrupted by the announcement of the illness or the death of his own father. The man has come to Paris from his own country to visit his son, a student at the Beaux-Arts. Here, the storyteller tells us how the man in question spoke the very words which are to serve as the keystone of the planned story: 'Oh, you are young, you are young – be glad of it and live.' This, he repeated insistently.

It is obvious that these words, reported to an acquaintance, are those which the father says, or wishes he had said, to his son. The series of transformations which follows becomes clear: the father-son relationship is eliminated; the rather banal initial opposition between a life of duty and conscience on the one hand and, on the other, the regrets inspired by the rediscovery abroad, especially in Paris, of his lost youth, gives way to the relationship between a writer and a wealthy widow whose son (his future stepson) is to be recalled to family duties and financial responsibilities. But the 'germ' already signals the imaginary relationship between father and son. Indeed, James writes: 'He has sacrificed someone, some friend, some son, some younger brother, to his failure to feel . . . the young man is dead. It's all over.' The other young man, who is to be brought back to the fold, will precipitate the *volte-face* (James's term) leading the 'father' to side with the son. We are thus finally confronted with the problem of loss.

The notation from the 'germ' had to be stored in order that, one day (three or four years later), according to James, 'the subject sprang at me one day, out of my notebook'. From then on the subject becomes autonomous, independent of his 'germ', his narrator, and himself. 'He has become impersonal.' Such was the conception, the gestation, and the birth of what was, according to James, 'the best of all my productions'.

How will the text's effectiveness function? We have compared it to the analysand's discourse, with its diversity and, above all, its different registers, from the most carnal to the most spiritual, the most concrete to the most abstract, the most emotional to the most intellectual. We shall retain these distinctions, despite today's tendency to get rid of them, because they function on the level of experience. We noted that the analysand's discourse calls upon a variety of materials in order to express itself: word-, thing- and affect-presentation, states of the body, acting out. This has enabled us to speak of a *polygraphy of the unconscious* as if it were using several writing systems to express itself (Green, 1970*a*). However, just as, in the end, there exists a vectorization which, through a series of transformations, leads to verbalization, the text of life changes into the written text through the final transformation that is written language. Everything is resolved into sentences. In *The Pleasure of the Text*, R. Barthes (1975, p. 49) recounts an interesting experience:

One evening, half asleep on a banquette in a bar, just for fun I tried to enumerate all the languages within earshot: music, conversations, the sounds of chairs, glasses, a whole stereophony of which a square in Tangiers (as described by Severo Sarduy) is the exemplary site. That too spoke within me, and this so-called 'interior' speech was very like the noise of the square, like that amassing of minor voices coming to me from the outside: I myself was a public square, a *sook*; through me passed words, tiny syntagms, bits of formulae, and *no sentence formed*, as though that were the law of such a language. This speech, at once very cultural and very savage, was above all lexical, sporadic; it set up in me, through its apparent flow, a definitive discontinuity: this *non-sentence* was in no way something that could not have acceded to the sentence, that might have been *before* the sentence; it was: what is eternally, splendidly, *outside the sentence*. Then, potentially, all linguistics fell, linguistics which believes only in the sentence and has always attributed an exorbitant dignity to predicative syntax (as the form of a logic, of a rationality); I recalled this scientific scandal: there exists no locutive grammar (a grammar of what is spoken and not of what is written; and to begin with: a grammar of spoken French). We are delivered to the sentence, to the *phrase*, as we call it in French (and hence: to phraseology).

The function of the text, reduced to the linearity of written language, is to resuscitate all that has been killed by the process of writing. In a letter to Strakhov, dated June 26, 1876, Tolstoy writes: 'In everything, in almost everything that I have written, I have been led by the need to gather my ideas, each connected to the next, in order to express myself; but each idea expressed in words loses its meaning . . . the connections themselves are made, it seems, not by thought, but by another process; to directly reveal the principle of these connections is impossible . . . we can only indirectly . . . through words, describe types of activity, situations. . . .' Types of activity, situations, transformed by the process of writing where the unconscious plays a part, become words, connected and locked into sentences. 'Locked in' and 'connected' well express what is involved: a process of imprisonment, of containment – lodging a content in a container, W. Bion would say – and a concatenation involving only the resources of language.

It is here that we see the effective power of writing to promote affects of writing which undermine and compete with the affects of life. So great becomes our fascination with the affects of writing, that we sometimes prefer them to those of life. Writing and reading are passions. Structuralist criticism, inspired by linguistics, in an unprecedented experiment in formalization, attempted to bypass these effects of textual affect. The text shrivelled up under this analysis which yielded nothing but a lifeless skeleton. Its flesh melted away. After taking a long detour, Barthes, who has had a great impact on contemporary French criticism, realized that these efforts were leading to a dead end. This is why textual analysis returns, like the repressed, to an analysis of the pleasure of the text. The psychoanalyst finds himself more comfortable with this manner of interpreting, where the pleasure of interpretation merges with the pleasure of reading and writing.

The most important question has yet to be answered. Why does one write? Why does one read? From where does this pleasure, which we call intellectual, come?

Writing (as Derrida, in his own way, has eloquently demonstrated) is, according to Freud, communication with the absent, the reverse of speech, which is rooted in presence. In psychoanalysis, the contrived conditions of the analytical situation seek to create a kind of present absence or absent presence. The analysand does not see the analyst; at times he may feel a loneliness bordering on despair because of the analyst's non-visibility. The analyst, in turn, is made to feel like a parent who abandons his child. But he also knows that there is someone else, someone who is at the same time himself and yet not entirely himself, ready to assume any role the analysand attributes to him: father, mother, brother, sister or any other important figure of the past or present.

In writing, no one is present. To be more precise, the potential and anonymous reader is absent by definition. He might even be dead. This situation of absence is a prerequisite for all written communication. But here, absence is compounded by the fact that writing is *not* the transcribed speech of simple communication. Writing fashions this dimension of absence while it re-presents, while (in a certain sense) it renders present. In another sense, writing deepens this dimension of absence which endows it with its specificity.

Conversely, for the reader, the author is always absent. The text alone creates this quasi-presence or quasi-absence, much as the analyst does for the analysand. Even when we read a text whose author is known to us, he remains absent. Because as well as we may know him, the author never resembles the living being whom we meet and with whom we exchange, from close range or from a distance, banal or profound words. The author is a secret character. But is he, strictly speaking, a character? He is unknown to all, to such an extent that one sometimes wonders how this person with whom we are dining, or playing cards or chess, could

322 ON PRIVATE MADNESS

possibly be the same one who wrote such and such a book. This makes me sceptical of psychobiographical studies when they are considered more than a simple element of information meant to compliment our actual contact with the text. Even if he writes for me – if the work is dedicated to me – I will learn nothing about the work by quizzing its author. This is why the author, who values his double identity, is so often irritated by our analyses and, when he is interviewed, always leaves us perplexed. The demon of writing does not show himself to those for whom the writing is intended.

By the same token, the reader is never the same individual with whom I dine or play cards. He is, even when I witness his reading, absent, in a private space, out of reach. The work, as I said in the previous chapter, is in this no-man's-land, this potential, transitional space (Winnicott), this site of a trans-narcissistic communication where the author's and reader's doubles – ghosts which never reveal themselves – communicate through the writing.

Ghost means death. And absence means potential death. What then does this pleasure have to do with death?

The act of writing is a strange act, as unnecessary as it is unpredictable, but for the writer it is also as tyrannical as it is inevitable. It may be that attempts at psychoanalytical interpretations have remained for too long on the level of preconscious meanings, by emphasizing the role of creation and even self-creation fantasies. Freud blazed a trail but did not follow it to the end. Melanie Klein, after him, saw in the act of writing a desire for repairs in the wake of the destructive instincts – if only because of the negation of the real world, which coexists with the desire to write. Winnicott, finally, placed the work in that potential space where it has the status of a transitional object, that arena of play and illusion between ego and object.

To this, we would like to add the notion that the work of writing presupposes a wound and a loss, a work of mourning, of which the text is the transformation into a fictitious positivity. No creation can occur without exertion, without a painful effort over which it is the pseudo-victory. Pseudo, because this victory can only last for a limited time, because it is always contested by the author himself, who constantly wishes to start over, and thus to deny what he has already done, to deny in any case that the result, satisfying as it might seem, should be taken as the final product.

As Blanchot has shown us in *L'espace littéraire*, the farther along in the process of creation, the closer the work draws to that point of inescapable silence, the 'vanishing point' where the temptation to become silent lies.

The work is bound by two silences: the one from which it emerges, and the one towards which it tends. Writing is suspended in the provisional space, which is the space of reading writing. This is why we feel not only that the text always says something since it breaks that silence, but also that what it chooses not to say is even more essential. We become conscious of it only when the last word has been read and we have closed the book. And we will then have to begin anew with another work by the same author or by another. Reading and writing constitute an uninterrupted work of mourning. If there is a pleasure of the text, we should bear in mind that it is a substitute for a lost satisfaction that we are seeking to regain in indirect ways.

It is said that there are writers who write joyously; we know that some works are read jubilantly. Does this invalidate our theory? No, because what we witness is a victory over a loss, a victory which may manifest itself as sacred fury, as dionysiac dance, as mystical ecstasy. We need only scratch the surface to discover, beneath the denial by triumph, anxiety; beneath the negation of loss, the work of mourning. This is not to say that the author's anxiety or loss are what is involved, at least not exclusively and, in any case, not directly. We are talking about the text's anxiety and loss, about something which inhabits the text's space and emerges from within it; like a stream, with a distant source, which travels underground over a long distance before reaching the surface. Between anxiety and loss on the one hand, and the text on the other, there is something else: the unconscious. The author's unconscious, of course, but especially the text's unconscious. But how to prove it?

Structuralist literary critics, even those who have the most reservations concerning psychoanalysis, admit that a text possesses formal unconscious structures. The analysis of Baudelaire's 'Les Chats', due to the combined efforts of R. Jakobson and C. Lévi-Strauss, was greeted with admiration. But where the Freudian unconscious is involved, there is a manifest reticence. This unconscious can be detected – I dare not say that it can be proven – and this, without necessarily referring to the author. This textual unconscious is present in the text's thematic articulations, its brutal silences, its shifts of tone, and especially in the blemishes, incongruities, and neglected details which only interest the psychoanalyst. Traditionalist critics dissect a text with incredible care; philology holds no secrets for them; their erudition is overwhelming. There comes, nevertheless, a time, a moment of truth, when one has to ask, 'But, what does this mean to me? How, why does this do something for me?'

Here is where ideology enters the picture. No matter how prudent the traditionalist critic, he will eventually reveal the implicit system of thought to which he adheres. His ideology can remain camouflaged only if he has recourse to the ruse of 'paraphrase criticism', which involves relating the contents of a work using other terms. We should remember, however, that the work is not a tissue of intentions, that nothing can replace the study of the writing itself. Still, we cannot proceed without questioning the work, the text of writing, in terms of the text of life – not only in terms of an author's life, but also of life as a common space shared by human beings, in which the work takes root or circulates, if only in order to reach its audience. This whirlwind or commotion of life which Freud ascribed entirely to Eros, also includes a core of silence, a neutral navel which life makes us forget as it winds itself around it.

I will hazard an example. It concerns, once again, one of those details which often go unnoticed: a note to Proust's *The Fugitive*. The captive has just escaped. Marcel desires her intensely and wants desperately to recapture her. The intensity with which he pursues her leaves him no alternative other than to transform this escapade into the death of the desired object. Anything goes: Saint Loups embassy offering a 'reward' in the search for Albertine, the stratagem of replacing her with Andrée, or of waiting for her to show willingness to return and then feigning indifference, etc. But, at the beginning there is, above all, the intense fantasy of seducing and winning her back with sumptuous gifts:

I was going to buy, in addition to the motor-cars, the finest yacht which then existed. It was for sale, but at so high a price that no buyer could be found. Moreover, once bought, even if we confined ourselves to four-month cruises, it would cost two hundred thousand francs a year in upkeep. We should be living at the rate of half a million francs a year. Would I be able to sustain it for more than seven or eight years? But never mind; when I had only an income of fifty thousand francs left, I could leave it to Albertine and kill myself. This was the decision I made. It made me think of *myself*. Now, since one's ego lives by thinking incessantly of all sorts of things, since it is no more than the thought of those things, if by chance, instead of being preoccupied with those things, it suddenly thinks of itself, it finds only an empty apparatus, something which is does not recognize and to which, in order to give it some reality, it adds the memory of a face seen in a mirror. That peculiar smile, that untidy moustache – they are what would disappear from the face of the earth. When I killed myself five years hence, I would no longer be able to think all those things which passed through my mind unceasingly, I would no longer exist on the face of the earth and would never come back to it; my thought would stop forever. And my ego seemed to me even more null when I saw it as something that no longer exists. How could it be difficult to sacrifice, for the sake of the person to whom one's thought is constantly straining (the person we love), that other person of whom we never think: ourselves? Accordingly, this thought of my death, like the notion of my ego, seemed to me most strange, but I did not find it at all disagreeable.

Then suddenly it struck me as being terribly sad; this was because, reflecting that if I did not have more money at my disposal it was because my parents were still alive, I suddenly thought of my mother. And I could not bear the idea of what she would suffer after my death.[1]

Albertine has therefore left. And not in just any fashion – she leaves *during Marcel's sleep*. Already, in *The Captive* (pp. 409/10), it is clear that Marcel has made the connection with the good-night kiss in Combray. The presentiment of Albertine's departure comes to him one evening when she refuses to return his good-night kiss before they part. Marcel then suggests that she stay at his side. The two lovers talk throughout the night, Albertine having rebuffed Marcel's advances. One evening, Albertine breaks her promise to Marcel, who fears drafts, and opens a window. He interprets this as a fatal sign. 'Filled with an agitation such as I had not perhaps felt since the evening at Combray when Swann had been dining downstairs, I paced the corridor all night long, hoping, by the noise that I made, to attract Albertine's attention, hoping that she would take pity on me and would call me to her, but I heard no sound from her room. At Combray, I had asked my mother to come.' Here, Marcel does nothing. Perhaps he is paralyzed by waiting for sounds to come from a forbidden room. The rest of the passage shows Marcel identifying with his bedridden and dying grandmother.

Finally, Albertine's disappearance is noticed by Françoise, who informs Marcel of it when he awakens. His response is extraordinary: 'Ah! very good, Françoise, you were of course quite right not to wake me. Leave me now for a moment, I shall ring for you presently' (*The Captive*, p. 422).

The author does not react much to it. But how can the serious reader not grant to this disappearance all the attention it deserves? In Combray, little Marcel feared, more than anything else, the separation from his mother at bedtime. A mother who, in the scene of the good-night kiss, seems to have no desire to join the father in the conjugal bed. Henceforth, sleep is the essential question for Marcel. *Remembrance* begins with: 'For a long time, I used to go to bed early'. Here night takes on two meanings. It is a space/time of loss, the possible disappearance of the love object. Albertine's example confirms this. It is also a space/time of pleasure

---

[1] *Remembrance of Things Past*, vol. 3, pp. 1115–6. It is worth noting that this passage relates to the text of *The Fugitive* on p. 475 (according to the editors of the Pléiade edition), whereas Proust had originally inserted this addition to the manuscript three pages further on – where Marcel announces to Albertine his desire to replace her with Andrée. Thus the object (Albertine) is caught between the empty structure of the subject on the one hand, and, on the other, the object which succeeds it by replacing it. She is caught between two deaths, the not-yet and the no-longer.

shared with another, from which Marcel, little or big, is always excluded.

During that memorable night in Combray when the object is won, that is to say when its disappearance is warded off, the mother is united with the child *in reading*. (Proust always knew that his mother desired not Professor Adrien Proust, in whose presence she never failed to express the feelings of a perfect wife, but literature – to such an extent that she delayed the progress of her son's work, which only started, we should note, after her death. But I err, since I seem to confuse Marcel Proust and the Marcel who has no surname, a significant fact.) In view of this, what does *The Fugitive* reveal? It is that Albertine will be mourned via the second meaning of sleep, to the detriment of the first: namely, the curiosity concerning the pleasure the object takes in the hidden space/time of night. The dream, grounded in the void of sleep, repairs the wound, as Marcel confesses (*Time Regained*, p. 953), because it allows him to be the beneficiary of pleasures bestowed on another. Hence, the dream is the genuine past recaptured, since Marcel is sensitive to the power of condensation, to the speed with which he attains wish fulfilment. In the work, this becomes the mad search for proof of Albertine's infidelity, of her supposed homosexuality. No, Albertine is not Albert; she is a double of the mother, a homosexual mother. This indicates, whereas it has always been underestimated, Marcel's (not Proust's) love for his father.

But only one side of the truth speaks here. The other remains silent. It involves the 'empty structure' in which we see the expression of *negative narcissism*: the invisible shadow of the subject's image. Proust is concerned with the image in the mirror. What concerns us, now, is the exact counterpart of this situation. On one side is the subject and his image in the mirror – in other words, his double; on the other, a mirror without reflection, where the self-contemplative subject sees no image. This is the absent. The suffering of mourning is preferable to forgetting the loss. The whole of *Remembrance of Things Past* is centred around not memory, but the invincible power of oblivion. The writer is caught between the double and the absent: the double that he is, as a writer who produces another image of himself, exists in another world, and he is absent, he who emerges from silence and returns to silence. His absence is as essential to the constitution of the work as is his duality.

James, in a little-known story called *The Private Life*, expresses this opposition in terms of two artists. One is an author who has a private life but no public life (because, in society, he is a failure), while the other, a painter, shines in public but has no private life (because his paintings are drab and uninteresting). James concretizes these metaphors. The writer is actually two characters; one has a social life and the other writes. As for the painter, when he is alone, without an audience, he literally disappears.

The story is about creating, about the division of the subject which occurs therein, and about the need to erase images of the world creating out of a void. It also involves manifesting this void in the created product. In fact, the text's very positivity carves out this void. These two characters, Clarence Wauwdrey (the writer), and Lord Mellifont (the painter), must be joined if we wish to shed some light on the problem of creation. Writing, and reading – for what is reading-writing if not 'the capacity to be alone in someone's presence' (Winnicott, 1958)? – show us their two sides: that of the image which fascinates us, and of that of the invisible which serves as the image's backdrop; that of the voice which captivates us, and that of the silence without which we could not hear it. The analyst searches for both.

A third example confirms this opposition. It is borrowed from Russian literature – a literature which, incidentally, is not particularly well endowed from this point of view. (We could probably find even better examples among German authors: Hoffmann, for instance, to whom Freud (1919h) referred in his work on the Uncanny). I mention what follows in passing, keeping in mind that it deserves to be developed further, a possibility we will discuss later. Two works complement each other: Gogol's *The Nose* and Dostoyevsky's *The Double*. In the first, the *negative hallucination* (of the partial object) is explicit. The hero looks at himself in the mirror and discovers that he has lost his nose; he searches for it until he finds it in the form of a whole object (a civil servant). In the other, Dostoyevsky describes not a mourning over the lost object, but persecution by the double who, through his intrusive positivity, replaces, *doubles*, the subject everywhere, always arriving at the subject's destinations before him, preceding him at all times.

These three examples are illustrations; we are not seeking to limit our argument to its explicit expressions. Rather, we should conceive of this as an ever-present structure, which certain writers of genius have made visible. But this structure is also at work *in* literary production, caught between persecution and mourning, between the double and the absent.

Psychoanalytical interpretation of reading-writing leaves many problems unsolved. Once its legitimacy has been established, one is still left wondering what gives a text its literary merit – because here the method is found lacking in discriminatory power. Must we conclude that this problem arises from an exclusively 'literal' approach – not to say literary? Poetry offers us extreme examples of this situation. But in poetry, far more than in prose, condensation and displacement are explicitly at work. Everything happens as if the work tended toward a constantly shifting relationship between *veiling* and *unveiling*. Enough has to be said to preserve a *cell of intelligibility*, yet not so much for the language to become utilitarian and banal. *The text must follow the path of a difference constantly seeking its measure by imposing a detour on its message.*

We should specify that the text sustains two forces. For simplicity's sake, we will call 'vertical' the one which springs from the body, from its depths, urging, 'driving' the text; the other, which we will call 'horizontal', is *the pressure that comes from language* – words, sentences and style receiving, through the very irradiation they provoke, recoil effects, caused by the very production of the text. But this pressure of language is neither abstract nor deserted. Not only do language and writing populate this space, but also all the writings which haunt the author: those of his masters, his rivals, his peers, and his potential successors. There remains, like a residue that cannot be eliminated, the radically retrenched space of writing; a space which functions as a limit, as a border which Lacan would term 'littoral'. Without this double perspective, something is always overlooked. If language alone is considered, affect becomes negativity and we cease to understand why Flaubert vomited while writing *Madame Bovary*; why Proust became more asthmatic as his work progressed; or why Kafka's anxiety hastened his death. If affect alone counts, we are left to ask, why does it occur in written form? Why doesn't the symptom suffice? Why this morbid obsession with writing?

There has been much discussion of the split in the subject, and no doubt our theory of the subject contributes to this point of view. But we must also concern ourselves with other forms of this split: the split of body and thought; and that of affect and idea, of which fetishism is the illustration. Yet, whether it is one or the other, both have the same function: filling the empty structure. Reading-writing, once the structure is filled, inhabits the interstice of this split, this potential space.

It is a space in which the problem of the Real is abolished (no one questions the reality of literary beings), at the juncture of outer and inner (it is a transitional space). It is a solitary space – furnished, however, with the presence-absence of the object: a space of the maybe (*neither yes nor no, but that* may *be*). For those who enter it, it is a space endowed with a power of fascination which can lead to a veritable descent into hell or ascent to heaven. The space of reading-writing is a purgatory.

The 'genetic' relationship we have just established between the absent and the double (the 0 and the 2) contests any unitary theory of the subject. It reiterates the heuristic value of the split, but it grounds it in negativity. This succession, however, does not imply a chronological process. A retroactive reversal functions here, because while the double seems to succeed the absent, it is also possible to say that the double is erased by the absent. Sometimes this 'erasure' will only affect one of the double's parts. (In mythology, when one twin is immortal, the other often is not.) Sometimes the suppression is radical, sparing neither partner. This reversal, which challenges the succession, can be regarded in terms of simultaneity, as if the double and the absent were produced in one stroke. The 'Uncanny', Hoffmann's *Unheimlichkeit*, but also Poe's, Nerval's, and many others', bears witness to this. Today, no doubt, science-fiction continues to develop this theme. Beyond these particulars, however, all writing is at stake: splits between author (person) and author (producer of text): between the author and the narrator; the author and his text; a given text and others (of the same or different authors). . . .

These remarks apply to non-contemporary texts. Contemporary texts (influenced, to some extent, by psychoanalysis), have, in so little time, so transformed the written language, that they require new techniques on the part of psychoanalytical criticism. This will be the work of the future. But we can already see, in some contemporary literature, that anxiety and loss are compounded on the level of the writing. This loss mourned now seems to be that of the act. One writes to question the death of writing. One enters into the impossible situation of writing about the death of writing not to postpone it, but to hasten it. It is as if one believed this death inevitable, and that the only way of surmounting it were to submit to it and to contribute to it (much in the same way that one can control a scientific law by obeying it). To cite one more ruse employed by the double and the absent, I take as an example René Laporte's *Fugue*. This book is no more than an essay on 'Why write? Why write this rather than that? Why use these signs rather than others?' This remarkable essay is subtitled 'Biography', which we could tendentiously translate as: the writing of life or the life of writing.

Dismantling something can never account for its existence as a whole. What I gain from a certain perspective necessarily causes me to lose sight of what another perspective might reveal. We must accept the fact that the literary problematic denies us any total access to the literary object. The analyst will never deny that there is a space peculiar to literature, created by writing. The literary critic is, no doubt, chiefly interested in the question of writing creating itself. But the analyst will always question the constitution of this literary space, because it isn't writing, so much as what makes it possible, that interests him.

Concerning tragedy, Freud once commented that it is one of the pleasure principle's most remarkable triumphs to be able to extract pleasure from a show of pain. By virtue of this, we could say that any writing is tragedy, since from its pains, it manages to create pleasure, for the author himself – if not, where would he find the energy to write? – and for the reader, who prefers the company of books to any other and who finds great joy in reading sad stories. But why, then, do so many masterpieces lack joy?

We have seen that the work, as elaboration of anxiety and loss, is, in its very relation to death, the opposite of death. It opts for life's illusory clamour, as against the certainty of death; it prefers masochistic pleasure to brutal joy. In these times of a Dionysian revival, we are told to burn all books and all of culture, too, in order to rediscover some vital new human contact which would restore our lost eroticism. I would not be surprised if, in the middle of some dazzling Dionysia, a participant stands on the fringes of the crowd, keeping to himself, forgetting the others and forgotten by them, inscribing a sign on a surface, for an absent person.

And everything will start over again.

14
The Unbinding Process

THE LITERARY TRIANGLE

The question of the relationship between literature and psychoanalysis has already been abundantly documented, and yet there seems to be plenty more to say about it, since fresh testimony is continually being called to the witness stand. Whether it be a mere coincidence or a meaningful correlation, the literature-and-psychoanalysis theme has never received such lavish attention as it does today precisely at a time when another surreptitious theme keeps cropping up with strange obstinacy: the theme of the death of literature. While some will mourn over literature's demise, others, in spite of their desire to be seen as avant-garde participants in this battle (indeed, one wonders what battle!), wish it would come about sooner. No doubt they look forward to its corpse serving as fertilizer for a new culture. In this respect, one could argue that psychoanalysis may be one of the signs of the imminent death of a senescent culture characterized among other things by the decay of literature, which, to put it optimistically, may herald the appearance of the yet-unborn thoughts on which tomorrow's culture may be founded. For that matter, one can argue just as easily that the death of literature would inevitably bring in its wake the death of psychoanalysis, for despite the profound changes the latter has wrought in the movement of ideas, it belongs to the same culture. While we cannot endorse such judgments without further examination, neither is it possible to dismiss as purely fortuitous this simultaneous emergence of studies bringing psychoanalysis to bear on literature, and of this peculiar sense of literature's decline – be it temporary or definitive.

Rather than write on the death of literature, since we are not called upon to testify to its decease, let us consider that a literary mutation has taken place, leaving it for the future to decide whether or not it has been fatal to literature. This mutation is contemporaneous with the birth and development of psychoanalysis. Furthermore, it should be noted that the great majority of literary works which have been the object of psycho-

This article is a translation of 'La déliaison', first published in *Littérature*, No. 3 (October 1971), pp. 33–52. It appeared in *New Literary History* (A journal of theory and interpretation), 1980, Vol. XXI, No. 1. The translation is by Lionel Duisit.

analytic studies were written before this mutation took place. It is therefore legitimate to explore – the scope of the inquiry being thereby more
clearly defined – the meaning of this curious phenomenon whereby
psychoanalysis turns toward the works of the past rather than toward
contemporary works, as if shying away from the latter, or even declaring
its incompetence to deal with the literature of its own age.

There seems then to be a sort of *avoidance* on the part of psychoanalysis
with regard to contemporary literature, even though their common
ground is so obvious, psychoanalysis being so demonstrably present on
all three sides of the literary triangle: the writer's side, the reader's side,
the critic's side. One ought indeed to inquire into the two-way effect of
relations between literature and psychoanalysis: the effect of
psychoanalysis on literature on the one hand, and that of literature on
psychoanalysis on the other. From Freud to Lacan, literature has left an
imprint on works of psychoanalytical thinking, a formal framework
encompassing both language and the phenomenon of writing [*écriture*]
which would justify a study of its own. We shall confine ourselves,
however, to the examination of the one-way effect of psychoanalysis on
literature, leaving the other task to the more literarily inclined scholar.

Before we begin, we ought to make one preliminary distinction. The
effect of psychoanalysis on literature (writers, readers, or critics) may be
the result either of knowledge or truth, i.e., the actual experience of
undergoing analysis. To set up such a dichotomy may arouse suspicion.
Any division of the literary world into two classes, the initiate and the
noninitiate, tends to produce ambivalent effects. The legitimacy of such
a distinction will no sooner be adopted than criticized. For instance, one
could contrast a notoriously weak literary study by an analyst with a
brilliant essay authored by one with no previous psychoanalytic experience. Our brash ostracism of the non-initiate does not entail any *de facto*
or *de jure* prohibition. Our contention is merely that if one intends to
claim ultimate authority on the subject, theoretical knowledge is no
substitute for the appropriate training in the practical field of
psychoanalysis. Of course, to have undergone psychoanalysis or even to
be a psychoanalyst does not necessarily guarantee the validity of one's
scholarly production.

In order to practice psychoanalysis, even the psychoanalysis of texts –
it is mandatory, in our opinion, that one undergo the *experience* of
psychoanalysis. Clearly, however, such a prerequisite does not affect all
the characters in the literary triangle equally. Although reading and
writing have been considered as a single activity seen from two different
sides, for our purposes they need to be distinguished. As far as the writer

is concerned, the experience of psychoanalysis only affects him insofar as he chooses to write on psychoanalysis or to impart a deliberately psychoanalytical orientation to a literary work, a rare occurrence. But contemporary literature is glutted with writings full of heavy-handed knowledge *about* psychoanalysis, which does not always improve literary production. Such knowledge, which the writer absorbs in spite of himself, cannot be ignored, and must constantly be reckoned with in the course of the writing process. The writer can be made self-conscious by this peculiar way of looking at his own writings, and it may increase his self-imposed censorship rather than help release its grip on him. Any challenge the writer might make to this knowledge – whether self-consciously to reject it or to overstep its boundaries – will unfailingly become a stumbling block. Yet if the writer opts to assume the implications of this knowledge as he writes, it turns out to be no more than it is, a knowledge devoid of truth.

As far as the reader is concerned, this prerequisite is also no more than marginally relevant at best. It applies only to the reader whose goal is deliberately to achieve a psychoanalytical reading. Actually, however, the spread of psychoanalytical knowledge affects an ever-growing mass of readers, whose knowledge has been achieved through reading. Yet it is surprising how fragile this knowledge turns out to be when put to the test, as for instance when it is the *effect* of a reading itself that is subjected to analysis, even self-analysis. So it can be said without exaggeration that neither the writer nor the reader comes clearly under what seemed to us a requirement – a requirement that may indeed have seemed too rigorous to some.

It becomes apparent that the only one that is truly concerned is the critic who wants to use the psychoanalytical method. It is in this tertiary position, whereby the critic becomes a reader-writer and a writer-reader, that the collusion between knowledge and truth becomes inevitable. The critical activity of the last few years has produced essays that have drawn widely on psychoanalysis, none of them lacking in sparkling brilliance. Upon close examination, however, those gems exhibit, in the eye of the psychoanalyst, all the flaws characteristically spawned by a display of knowledge unsupported by experience. The highly abstract quality of such works enables them to free themselves quite blithely from the minimum constraints by which all experience is bound. But psychoanalytical criticism is a theoretically oriented practice; that is to say, it is based on a practice and a theory that illuminate one another. It cannot limit itself to pure theory.

This cautionary remark is all the more appropriate at this time and place because psychoanalytical practice, on whatever plane it may be called upon to operate, is primarily underpinned by a critical activity which goes back, after the fact, over the field of what one might call provisionally, for lack of a better term, a subjective epistemology.

It seems just to require, by virtue of reciprocity, that the psychoanalytical critic be also a literary man, that is to say, a practitioner of literature. But what does it mean to practise literature? On the strength of the preceding remarks, it can only mean to possess a knowledge of literature. Could practising literature be described as being oneself a literary author? Yes, if the distinction between writer and critic is absorbed into an extended definition of the writing process; no, if the distinction is allowed to stand. In any case, the psychoanalytical critic stands at the intersection between two fields: the psychoanalyst's and the critic's. As a critic, he can be looked upon as an *écrivant*, to use Roland Barthes's term.[1] Only after recognizing such limitations could one claim that he practises literature. The psychoanalytical critic would be an *écrivant* on literature. The literary practice of the psychoanalytical critic would have as its aim the study and interpretation of the relations between the literary text and the unconscious (in the sense that psychoanalytical theory gives to this term),[2] whether it is a question of the text's unconscious organization, or of the part played by the unconscious in the production (and consumption) of texts, or any other aspect. Once this sector is circumscribed in this way, it becomes apparent that the psychoanalytical critic claims only a part of the field of criticism. The segmentation of his object enables the psychoanalyst to reach an aspect of the text which other approaches are unable to reveal, but on the other hand, it is this aspect and this aspect alone which he will bring to light, handing over to the other sectors of criticism the assignment of unveiling the other aspects. But, in order to uncover the hidden treasures, it is imperative for him to have previously travelled, *in vivo*, the path which will have put him in touch with something of which his consciousness is unaware but which may open up the sphere of the unconscious – above all, *his own* unconscious. To have travelled such a path is an essential condition for the possibility of writing about the unconscious of others, even that of literary texts.

---

[1] This does not preclude his being a literary writer in addition to that. Let's keep in mind that Freud was the recipient of the Goethe prize.

[2] There are others, for instance, the meaning used by Lévi-Strauss and Foucault.

THE INTERPRETATIVE POWER

In the conduct of a cure, it is not uncommon for the psychoanalyst to run into a particular form of resistance, as the analysand reacts to the interpretation that has been proposed, not so much by showing the effect it had on him (pleasure or displeasure, acceptance or refusal, recognition or misapprehensions, etc.), but mainly by challenging the interpretative authority of the analyst: 'I wonder,' he says, 'what permits you to say that. How did you manage to derive this interpretation from what I told you? What route did you follow? On what basis did you select such and such a trait? How did you go about establishing connections between the elements of my discourse and then merge them into your interpretation? That's what I am interested in, rather than what you have said to me.' The analyst does not pause to consider these questions. He does not accommodate this desire to know, because it is not cognition that is at stake in an analysis, no more than the confirmation or invalidation of the interpretation. Any interpretation is marked by the risk taken by the one who offers it, which can turn his words into empty or meaningful speech. But the measure of its success does not depend solely upon the analyst, his particular gift, or the perceptive nature of his insights. The analysand must be reckoned with. The all-important consideration will be the ongoing vitality of the analytical process, for which the best testimony is the associative sequence provoked by the proposed interpretative construction.

The literary critic who is not an analyst often reacts to the interpretations of his psychoanalytical counterpart as does the analysand we have just mentioned: 'Your method, that's what we are interested in. Show us how you proceed. Tell us what enables you to transfer the technique used with your patients to a field that lies outside its frame of reference, in order to apply it to texts.' Since this question does not emanate from the couch but arises out of an exchange, one might be tempted to answer it. But then it seems that the mere description of the material and its analysis is not sufficient to quench the thirst of the question. Or, alternatively, that the analyst is more or less suspected of keeping surreptitiously to himself a secret process of which he would give only the results, refusing to reveal the nature of the recipe. The question's thirst cannot be quenched, because the question lies elsewhere.

What the analysand we mentioned earlier was asking for, under the influence of transference, was to gain access to a power he would like to appropriate for himself, which, once internalized, would solve all his problems at one stroke. On the one hand, he will elude the unpleasant feeling aroused by certain interpretations unpalatable to his narcissism.

Availing himself of the power to interpret – the only power in the possession of the analyst – the analysand will select for himself the least truthful interpretations, confining himself to those he can accept without overstepping the threshold of his tolerance. On the other hand, he will use this interpretative power as a weapon in the service of a 'wild' (i.e., unschooled) analysis of others. For that will certainly be his pleasure. An extra twist of refinement will enable him to invert this pleasure – a pleasure nonetheless – into the exquisite delights of a purely intellectual masochism.

Today, with information flowing freely, psychoanalytical writings get a lot of exposure – in some cases the number of printed copies of a psychoanalytic work seems amazing considering how little of this information can be assimilated. Such exposure encourages the expansion of psychoanalytical knowledge, which in turn must find its place among competing fields that cannot be ignored by anyone who wishes to be in touch with his times.

The aforementioned analysand was seeking a swift and efficient acquisition of the analyst's interpretative power, thus sparing himself the trouble of plodding through the dark forests or quagmires of the unconscious. The consumer of psychoanalytical knowledge, if he is a reader and writer – that is, a critic – seeks to expand his tool kit by acquiring an instrument he can use skillfully after a few practice sessions. As far as the theory of writing is concerned, psychoanalysis will answer the call, but it will be absorbed into a larger system. Psychoanalysis merges into psychosynthesis. If we seemed to be on the dogmatic side a minute ago when we insisted that whoever ventures into text analysis must have had the experience of psychoanalysis, it was not as a result of bias, but because such a requirement – which does not extend beyond a pious wish – seemed justified by the recent developments of criticism and literary history. Using psychoanalysis as it is done today, serving it up with diverse sauces, is not really taking it properly into account. Why not leave it alone altogether, if one hesitates to take the decisive step of testing it on oneself first, as any analyst will do? One may try to elude the point and argue that we are not concerned here with psychoanalysis proper, but with an interpretation which taps the lessons derived from psychoanalysis without, in so doing, declaring itself psychoanalytical. But this sort of casuistry will only convince those who seek verbal guarantees. Who would deny that this is intellectual distortion, since the thesis upheld makes use of the terminology, concepts, and thinking modes of psychoanalysis, as if those could have any validity outside the experience from which they spring?

As we have readily acknowledged, psychoanalytical interpretation is not exhaustive; it is specific. It goes without saying that other segmentations could lead to other interpretations. But let each man follow his working hypotheses, handle them uncompromisingly, and extract from them all they can yield. The psychoanalytical critic is sometimes charged with being intransigent. Yet all he is fighting for is the rigour inherent in any discipline – a strange word to be sure, yet how true – that does not accommodate amateurism, be it enlightened or not. The necessity of articulating psychoanalysis with other sciences – not all of which are 'human sciences' – is unquestionable. But this cannot be achieved from the outside, and specifically not by those with a book-based knowledge of psychoanalysis, even if it is part of their profession to read books, think about them, and write down the result of this thinking. Sooner or later bridges will be built, their foundation laid by those who qualify as craftsmen in their own discipline, who know its resources as well as its limits. Is this an encomium of technique? If the psychoanalyst were only a technician, he would be content with the psychoanalysis he practices on analysands and would not feel the urge to go wandering off into the world of books, like Don Quixote.

THE UNBINDING PROCESS

What does a psychoanalyst do when confronted with a text? He performs a transformation – actually he does not do it deliberately; it is a transformation that is imposed on him – whereby he does not read the text but listens to it. This does not mean, of course, that he has someone read it to him or that he reads it aloud, but that he listens to it according to specifications that pertain to the psychoanalytical process. Herein lies the paradox: alongside the rigorous reading, a loose, free-floating reading is taking place. Free-floating does not mean careless – far from it. It pays attention to everything that is out to mislead the reader. It follows the threads of the text (the text as 'textile' is an accepted concept nowadays), but in so doing it ignores the Ariadne's thread the text offers to the reader. Such a thread stretches the text toward its goal, has the last word, represents the end point of its ostensible meaning. Thus the psychoanalyst applies to the text the same treatment he applies to conscious discourse which covers up unconscious discourse, except that, in the case of a literary text, he must do without the advantages he has when he confronts the manifest text of a dream, since he cannot evaluate the dream-work by scanning the associations which reveal the day's residues and working his way back from the thoughts generated by the dream to the desire underlying the dream. The literary text and the text of the dream have but one feature in common: they are both presented through secondary elaboration. That is why the literary text may be more aptly compared to a (conscious) fantasy to the extent that the fantasy features both primary and secondary processes closely intermingled, the latter reshaping the former by endowing them with a great many attributes pertaining to secondarity. Of all those attributes, the most striking is perhaps the binding process [*la liaison*]: free (unbound) energy seeking to be released, making use of the condensation and displacement compromises, forcing the coexistence of opposites while remaining unresponsive to temporalization, manages to transform itself into bound energy whose release is postponed, restrained, and limited in conformity with the laws of logic and temporal succession.[1]

But the fantasy, like the text, even when it strives to adorn itself with features of secondarity, will leave behind, due to the very fact that it is a work of fiction – hence governed by desire – scattered traces of the primary processes on which it is constructed. Those traces always give themselves away, behind the logic-bound construction of the text, because of their accessory, subsidiary, and contingent nature. The eye skims over them fleetingly, but the reader's unconscious perceives and registers them. Whence the fact that the effect of every literary text – and the stronger the text, the more marked (in both senses of the word) the effect – is to awaken both an idea and an affect in the reader. The idea is one of enigma, and the affect involves the fascination of the text as an emotional source. Both invite questioning and both prompt the analyst to take up that questioning and analyze the fascination. In brief, the analyst reacts to the text as if it were a product of the unconscious. The analyst then becomes the *analyzed* of the text. It is within himself-as-text that he must find an answer to this questioning, all the more in the case of a literary text, since he can only rely on his own associations. The interpretation of the text becomes the interpretation which the analyst must provide for the text but when all is said and done, it is the interpretation that he must give *himself* of the effects of the text in his own unconscious. That is why it matters so much that this exercise in self-analysis be preceded by an analysis performed by another or, if one prefers, by an analysis of the Other. The analyst puts this interpretation to the test by communicating it. It is an ordeal in a quite real sense that we are talking about, for he exposes in broad daylight the flaws of his reading and the limits of his self-analysis. The risk incurred then is of course the risk of missing the unconscious meaning of the text, but even

[1] I am excluding here the case of poetry, which poses special problems in this respect.

more it is the risk of laying bare his own resistance to the unveiling of his own unconscious. In some instances, an overtly superficial interpretation will give away the analyst's rationalizations; in other instances, a specious construction will indicate that he is 'off the plate', which means, in psychoanalytical jargon, a 'plated-on' interpretation. To interpret is always to assume this interpretative risk.

The credibility of the interpretation is not at stake. Acceptance or rejection are of no use at all in assessing the value of the interpretation. If delirium [*délire*] itself is an interpretative construct, then one must in turn accept the idea that the psychoanalyst's interpretation is also a delirium in the eyes of others. But the strength of response ignited by the interpretation testifies to its fecundity or to its barrenness. The analyst, working with the cues that have been picked up by his viewing-listening process, does not 'read' [*lire*] the text, he 'unbinds' [*délier*] it. He breaks open the secondarity in order to retrieve, upstream from the binding process, the state of bondlessness [*déliaison*] which the binding process has covered up. The psychoanalytical interpretation jerks the text out of its groove (*délirer* means 'to lift out of the groove'). The analyst unbinds the text and frees its 'delirium'. Hence the hue and cry of the tradition-bound critics who echo the protest of the beginning analysand: 'You're delirious!'

Freud was not content with unraveling the meaning of the neurotic symptom, which partakes more or less of madness but differs from it in that its 'abnormal' nature is acknowledged by the patient. Indeed, he pursued the analysis to the farthest confines of alienated thought, reaching out to the psychotic symptom where delirium reigns supreme. That dreams have hidden meaning had been known since the remotest antiquity. Freud gave this meaning a new structure and related it to desire. But what about delirium? Desire and delirium are now seen to refer back and forth to each other. What Freud found out about delirium is the fact that it is built around a nucleus of truth. The psychoanalytical interpretation as delirium – which some will prefer to call delirious psychoanalytical interpretation – uncovers in the text a nucleus of truth. Today we should be saying, less ambitiously, a nucleus of truths:

(1) The truth of desire, since the text implies for the writer the desire to write, and the desire to be read, and for the reader to desire to read, a remote substitute for the desire to see and to know which is an integral part of all sexual curiosity;

(2) The truth of fantasy, which dwells in the text, makes of the text a *pre*text for the fantasy (and vice versa); the *pre*text of the fantasy shared

by the one who writes and the one who reads in a mutually narcissistic relationship, the text being a *trans-narcissistic object*;

(3) The truth of illusion, which bestows upon the fictitious entity we called the literary text a value one may substitute for reality or for the desire to live;

(4) The historical truth finally, which makes the text a product of its creator's life history, and relates meaningfully to the life history of its consumer. For no psychoanalyst can renounce the study of the relationships between the history of an author's life (not to be confused with his biography, not even with his psychobiography) and the history of a work. Similarly, the effect of this work on the reader is going to interrelate with something that pertains to the history of his life.

The nucleus of truth (in the singular or in the plural) gains consistency, undergoes transformations, and culminates in binding processes which structure the fabric of the delirium for the madman, the fabric of the text for the writer, and the fabric of the interpretation for the psychoanalyst. The similarity we have tentatively drawn among those three cases – needless to say – is not self-evident. The elaboration process of delirium, that of the text, and that of interpretation are by no means reducible to each other. What justifies the work of interpretation does not consist merely in unveiling the effects of the text, or even in revealing its latent organization. The delirium and the text both construct something, but, one must admit, without being aware of what they construct. It is true that the writer operates on the conscious level, but the process which falls within the purview of his consciousness (and is part of his craft) has to do with the secondarity of the text, that is to say, the level of the text whose function it is to obliterate the unconscious as it tries to cover it up. Or, to be more precise, the elaboration process has to do with the chiaroscuro effect in which the dual function of veiling versus unveiling the unconscious always manages to leave in the shadow the dynamic effectiveness of the text in order to enhance its literary effectiveness. Everyone knows how aggravated writers are when faced with interpretations performed on their texts, whatever feeling of pride may accrue to them from public recognition. This irritation is noticeable with all types of interpretations, not only those pertaining to psychoanalysis, but it reaches its highest pitch with the latter. Just as the madman 'hangs on' to his delirium and claims non-interpretability by any other individual who might question the closed meaning he bestows upon it, so the writer insists on the literality of his text, which must not be made to say anything but what it says. Like the madman, the writer 'doesn't want to know anything about it'. It looks as though a splitting must necessarily exist to ensure a watertight separation between the constructed text and its foundation, especially when we are dealing with a non-literary foundation. Some critics, defending the mystery of creation, go as far as to allege profanation when confronted with a psychoanalytical interpretation.

The analyst, for his part, goes on with his deconstruction-construction, often ruthlessly, sometimes – rather rarely one must admit – hitting it just right, when the censuring process does not thwart his own anlysis. For this unbinding of the text is the necessary step toward a new binding, different from the one that occurs in the literary work. This new binding corresponds to the logic of the primary process, a logic which articulates the relation between the text and the nucleus of truth. So the analyst, in turn, produces a 'text', that of his construction. The writer is assigned the task of 'making visible'. In fact, even as he reveals, he is covering up something in order to show something else through the writing process. The writing process is at once a *conversion* of and a *diversion* from the effectiveness of the text. The psychoanalytical critic proposes in turn his construction. But what the writer has produced is an object of captivating fascination at once dazzling and blinding when the text operates at full efficiency. What the critic has spread out before our eyes, through his interpretation, breaks that spell, even as it reveals the hidden riches of the text. It 'unbinds' the reader from the spell cast upon him by the text. However marginal psychoanalytical interpretation may be, it is received with a certain regret because it generates a sense of disillusionment, of 'offended majesty'. The consolation one may derive from a better understanding of the text is scant compensation for the loss of its mystery. The light provided by the interpretation illuminates the text too harshly; it strips the text of the halo of its original reading. One resents the psychoanalyst for having dispelled the hallowed penumbra of the text ideally suited to the hatching of fantasies that used to accompany the reading.

Any truth-oriented knowledge is accompanied by an irretrievable loss; a narcissistic wound is inflicted upon whoever wants to lift the veil of illusion. In like fashion the analysand, after the cure has been successfully conducted, sometimes misses his neurosis, for it gave him the impression that he was unique as a person, even if the price to be paid was anguish and suffering.

TO READ AND TO WRITE

In unbinding the text, the psychoanalytical critic does not merely set it off-centre – as it is fashionable to say. He makes it skip its groove and in so doing transfers it to another field which people claim is no longer literature. And that is partially true. If in the process of unveiling the interrelations between the text and the unconscious another reality comes into view, it is indeed a nonliterary reality. That is what the writer and the non-analytical critic are loath to accept. They would rather see this 'skipping out of the groove' occur within the field of literature, and yet a literary work must of necessity refer to an extra-literary reality, since it can legitimately be argued that the role of literature is precisely to convert a sector of reality (whether psychic or external) into a literary reality. This neo-reality – Freud uses the very same word to designate delirium – is precisely known for its claim to be self-sufficient and every bit as important as the reality from which it is derived in the transformation process. Under the circumstances it is more appropriate to use the word *reality* in the plural rather than the singular. Thus literary criticism today takes on multiple dimensions, one of which is psychoanalysis.

Rather than try to find out which themes of desire are the most frequently treated by literature, let us move toward a psychoanalytical interpretation of the reading-writing activity. That way we shall proceed toward the most general and at the same time the most sharply focused goal. Reading and writing, in terms of psychoanalysis, are not primary processes, but complex activities acquired relatively late; they come as a result of training, making use of partial drives tamed by education and the 'civilizing' process. Reading and writing are sublimations, which means that the underlying partial drives are inhibited from attaining their goals, displaced, and desexualized. Once broken down into their constituent parts, those partial drives have to do with scopophilia [voyeurism]. The desire to see is patent in the act of reading. The book cover, the binding, function as garments. They display a name, a title, a shared identity (the publishing firm) which offer themselves fascinatingly to the eye. When the book lies on a shelf in the library, it is easily accessible to the eye in its quest for pleasure; when it is displayed in a bookstore window, the transparent obstacle increases our curiosity. We enter the store to 'take a look around'. Except in cases when we know what we are looking for and ask the clerk for it, we don't like to be disturbed in our inspection. We keep browsing until, responding to some indeterminate cue, we pick up a book. Here the pleasure starts, as we open it, finger it, thumb through its pages, probing it in various places. If its pages are as yet uncut, we may have to peep acrobatically between two pages that have been folded from the top or from the side, for, as it happens, it's that particular passage we are interested in. Finally, a choice has to be made. If the promise of pleasure seems likely to be kept, we pay for the book and leave the store arm-in-arm with it. Whether we are looking forward to being seen in its company, or some shyness moves us to hide its identity, we'll introduce it naked or wrapped. In order to read, we'll need to lock ourselves up with the book – in a public place or in more confined quarters – sometimes in the most unlikely or, shall we say, the least propitious places for this kind of exercise.[1]

What is it then that draws us toward reading? The drive toward pleasure through a visual introjection which satisfies a certain type of curiosity. The pleasure is, of course, more disguised if our reading is motivated by study, work, or need, i.e., the need to acquaint ourselves with useful, perhaps indispensable, texts. But this falls outside the purview of literature. One may even wonder whether the criterion for literature does not precisely lie in the production of writings which cannot elude their relation to pleasure. We are thus talking here about a kind of pleasure experienced by means of the eyes. Of course we can have texts read to us, but this is only a derivative practice, for listening to a text (in the non-psychoanalytical sense) is not reading it. In the latter case, the listener relies through identification on the person reading. Reading is related to the pleasure of seeing, which implies that the reader is moved by a certain curiosity. But this type of curiosity, even though it would seem that the act of reading entails some form of abstraction, remains quite far from what we call 'intellectual curiosity', because it is much more sensuous than the latter. The discrepancy between the two is precisely that between scopophilia and epistemophilia. Epistemophilia is more akin to the search for an explanatory 'theory', as exemplified by the sexual theories put together by children to explain how babies come into this world. Scopophilia is a drive toward a much less inhibited, displaced, or desexualized pleasure. It involves the affect more than the intellect. A literary work is appreciated according to the emotional effect it induces in the reader, much more than through the understanding that emanates from it, even if it takes a great deal of intelligence on the part of the writer to produce this effect.[2] Hence it is a question of scopophilia rather than epistemology, which means that we ought to develop some sort of scopology in the face of today's overriding concern with epistemology. To put it bluntly, reading has a great deal to do with voyeurism.

[1] We need not insist on the bathroom radiators which, through a tacit family consensus, are converted into a real library, making reading a scatological ritual.

[2] On a secondary level, the desire to see which underlies reading is reinforced by a desire to know, to know what other books contain, literary or not, to increase one's literary and intellectual baggage all the way to erudition. Such a path often leads the book lover to a professional level: educator, critic, writer, etc.

Let us then concern ourselves with what is characteristic of literary voyeurism. The pleasure of reading is different from that experienced while looking at a collection of reproductions, a photo album, a film, a picture exhibition, a naked body. The specificity of the reading pleasure lies in the fact that it is experienced through the mediation of the written word.

Now the writing process presupposes the absence of any representation. To be sure, a form of representation not directly present in the text, may redirect the impact of the written text. The craftsmanship that goes into the making of a book will make use of all the resources of the printer's art, even in texts which do not carry illustrations of the type found in children's books or luxury editions. The printing process will exploit all the available techniques to make an *impression*. This is another derivative practice of the scriptural process. Basically, the written word is a (graphic) representation of the absence of representation (i.e., the imaginary). The perception of the written word as such refers only to itself: the deciphering process alone will open the way to representation.

To read a text is to translate a systematic set of symbols which represent nothing by themselves. In other words, writing does not show anything beyond the combination of symbols: that's the experience we go through when confronted with a book written in a totally foreign language: if the reader is a voyeur, what he sees in a book are signs that represent no object directly. In order to see it, it will be necessary to read, that is to say, bind symbols together,[1] respect the intervals between words, recognize punctuation, and finally set the tone which indicates that the recognition has moved away from the elements into the configuration of meaning. The articulation of words, syntagms, and text is dependent on an intense consumption of visual and intellectual energy. Yet as the reading goes on, the reader 'sees', that is to say, he works out a representation of what the text is about. So that it is the text which now 'regards' the reader – in both senses of the term – since what he sees in this *secondary vision*, he sees within himself, not in the text. He has switched, in his voyeurism, from an active position to a passive one. One may blush at the reading of a text as if someone were looking at you, guessing at your feelings. The intermediary voice[2] combines those two

---

[1] Everyone knows that the main difficulty in the apprenticeship of reading is to get a child to admit that *b*, followed by *a*, without interval, comes out as *ba* – a difficulty which the global reading method tries to bypass, sparing the child an intellectual effort that is indeed necessary.

[2] The reference here is obviously to a 'grammatical' voice, or mood, which is 'intermediary' in that it hesitates between 'passive' and 'active'. [Translator's note.]

positions where the seer-seen is found in the same person, the text functioning like a mirror held to the reader. The text's lack of representation has then induced the reader, even as he binds together the symbols in the deciphering process, to bind, within himself, a chain of representation which is his own, not that of the text. Such a simple statement as 'the marchioness left home at five o'clock', in spite of the most explicit indications of the text, conjures up a marchioness who is only, and can only be, the creation of the reader. To what extent do the reader's representation and the writer's original representation coincide? The question cannot be resolved. First, because the writer, in most cases, will never answer it; second, because even if he answers it, there is no guarantee that he'll be telling the truth; finally, because even if he insists that he is telling the truth, in an attempt to cross the boundary of preconscious censorship, the censorship of the unconscious will remain intact. Actually, one would be better advised to think that he cannot say anything about it precisely because he knows nothing about it. As he writes, the writer converts certain representations into the written word. But he hides the point from which those representations originate, and delivers only those he is willing to transmit through the scriptural process. So there are several levels to be considered: the writing process seen as an absence of representation, the (preconscious) representations conjured up by the written transcription and to which that transcription refers more or less implicitly, the (unconscious) representations that are suppressed and erased by the writing process. The representations proper (preconscious), to which all writing refers, are then located between two nonrepresentations: those of the written text and those of the unconscious.[3]

In the last analysis, if the writer exhibits anything at all as he writes, it will be writing pure and simple: that is to say, literary specificity. It is therefore partially correct to say that he shows nothing through the writing process; as a matter of fact, he offers to view the scriptural construction, a display confined to the text. The scriptural sleight-of-hand involved here consists in removing from sight the preconscious representations, which the writer can always ascribe to the reader, and in showing nothing more than the scriptural construction, namely, a form. To Polonius, who inquires about what Hamlet is reading, the latter answers: 'words, words, words'.

[3] Indeed, one can establish a homologous scheme for the reader but with this difference: the reader consumes a written text produced by another person who plays an inductor's role on the other two levels, whereas it is those other two levels that induce the writing process in the writer.

In voyeurism and exhibitionism, the object of the drive is usually the penis. But partial drives are transformed in the reading and writing processes, and the object is no longer the original object. The representations we discussed do not remain inactive: they form into groups, become condensed, distorted, develop into a phantasmic organization. Thus preconscious representations organize into preconscious fantasies, since any text, regardless of how realistic it is intended to be, remains a fictive entity, which confirms its kinship to fantasy. Similarly, the unconscious representations, blocked from view as they are, remain active nonetheless and develop into unconscious fantasies. It is mainly at the communication level between the unconscious fantasies of the writer and the unconscious fantasies of the reader that their complicity as a couple is established. At the level of the unconscious fantasy, the object is not representable, or to be more precise, it is only representable on that other stage from which it must be retrieved by a deductive process, that is, by stripping it of its Fregolian trappings. It is at the preconscious level that the object assumes the form of a disguised representation that can be included in the series of objects: child–faeces–penis – which are all 'little things separable from the body', to quote Freud, who articulated them in this sequence. The literary work will have to be important, noted, admired, fraught with potential for infinite development, etc. At the conscious level, the object becomes the actual text in its written form. It carries with it the same wishes as those mentioned before. But those wishes are silent, and that for which the object (or text) claims our attention is no longer located at the representational level but at the scriptural level. It is only as such that it can achieve value. The written word has become an invisible fetish, as indispensable to pleasure as the fetish is to the fetishist. It is a Janus-faced fetish, one face looking at the writer, the other at the reader. The reader says to the writer, 'Show yourself', at the very moment the latter calls out to him, 'Look at me', a proposition which can probably be reversed without entailing any fundamental change, as the reader can be made to say, 'Expose me', at the moment when he responds to the writer's call, 'Look at *yourself*', full use being made of the polysemic resources of this inversion.

However, the object shown by the writer is not present on his body – it is a created object. A new transformation must be taken into account at this point. What the writer shows is the result of a creative process, somewhat like the royal child shown to the people as proof that birth has really occurred.

It has thus become clearer why it is not only the penis that is involved here, but the series penis-faeces-child – a child that the writer has brought into the world by himself, without anybody's help, for even though he may be indebted to his precursors, he is its sole creator, the only father – both the father and the mother, for that matter. It becomes apparent that both aspects of sexual curiosity are fused into one, the desire to show-see a penis and the desire to find an explanation for the mystery of birth. The writer bypasses any sexual theory involving the parents, since he is at the same time both parents joined for the procreation of the child he has produced.[1]

As far as this is concerned, he can again enlist the reader's complicity. For every reader dreams of having written the book he has loved and which has stirred him to pleasure, as every writer derives strong satisfaction from identification with the pleasure he has aroused. A metaphorical locus, a *potential space*, to use Winnicott's expression, has come to exist between writer and reader, within which the field of illusion is constituted as the celebration of a transitional trans-narcissistic object. This metaphorical locus is one of the loci inhabited by the nonrepresented and nonrepresentable unconscious fantasy. This nonrepresentability of the unconscious fantasy has its counterpart in the non-representability of the writing process.[2] Thus at both ends of the writing process (unconscious fantasy and text) representation is abolished. But the most difficult task, according to Freud, is to erase the traces of this abolition. At the level of the unconscious fantasy, the traces are made manifest by an empty space, a blank, an 'absence', whenever the revealing disguise, in spite of its distorting influence, is too much of a telltale. At the scriptural level, this trace is none other than the trace left by the written word when the unconscious signified finds its way into the signifier. But literature, like any form of creation, undergoes mutations. Because it is alive, it changes, even at the risk of being led to its death as a result of mutations. It is the destiny of representation which will again engage our attention when we examine the ordeal imposed upon it by the scriptural processes of modernity.

[1] Marthe Robert has shown the links between the family romance and the creation of novels in 'Telling Stories', *L'Éphémère*, No. 13 (1970). The psychoanalytical critic analyzes this self-creation fantasy and thus commits a crime of high treason. Sarah Kofman has treated this theme in *L'Enfance de l'art* (Paris, 1970).

[2] The concept of *unconscious fantasy* presents such complexity that analysis hesitates to tackle it. We have held the view, elsewhere, that if unconscious fantasies are inaccessible to consciousness, and as such must be traced back through their offspring, their structure is only partially relevant to representation at the unconscious level. The most unconscious portion of the unconscious fantasy is not susceptible to representation because it is welded to the instinctual motion that causes it to exist. Cf. Green (1970).

inherent in the scriptural act, as if thinking and writing had become one and the same process. Particularly in the latter case, the action of writing becomes its own object, its own representation. One could say that we have passed from the scriptural process of representation to the representation of the scriptural process.

This distinction between classical and modern writing styles is probably too clear-cut. Yet it is nonetheless rooted in reality. These styles could be opposed by describing them as figurative and non-figurative. We are not denying the fact that chiasmi may exist between the two, even in one writer and within one text. One could even claim that there is no such thing as figurative writing, since the writing process is intrinsically nonfigurative, its literary specificity not representable. Yet one is forced to admit that it would be difficult, in that respect, to abolish all distinctions between, say, the writings of Chateaubriand or Flaubert, or those of Malraux or Camus, on the one hand, and those of Artaud or Beckett, of Blanchot or Laporte, to limit ourselves to examples chosen for their illustrative value. Marthe Robert has managed to show eloquently that *Don Quixote* is a book on books, on literature, an exemplary work that cannot be read in any other way except through the eyes of representation. The reason for this is that *Don Quixote* organizes the adventures of the main hero or secondary characters in 'tableaux', which the narrative flashes on and off to bring them to life 'on paper'.[1]

In figurative writing, literary specificity fulfilled one function among others. It served at once as a buffer, a filter, and a converter. The literality of the text would drink up the blood, the sweat, the tears that fed the text, only to give it another face in the creation of its written form. The signified became absorbed partly into the literary signified (the preconscious representations conjured up by the text) and partly into the written signifier. The functional and economic value of the signifier was this veiling-unveiling relationship, this surreptitious obscuring of the thing shown, scintillating yet evanescent, which imagination sets out to capture. The writing process was this switching back and forth, while the reading process was the retracing of the itinerary by which this switching came to exist. However explicit the text may have intended to be outwardly, it always left internal gaps. The closer it came, supposedly, to being explicit, the wider the distance between the explicit and the implicit grew, because the more urgently the question was being asked how a written work, a fictitious entity, can become life-inspiring. To understand to the full a written work where everything is explicit, where

---

[1] This is a reference to Marthe's Robert's title *Sur le papier*. [Translator's note.]

representation is rendered integrally, one must leave the field of literature and open an anatomy treatise. Yet this treatise, even though its goal
is to describe living bodies, has originated in the description of the
corpse. And for that matter, a corpse which has been 'treated' in a
solution designed to arrest the decaying process after death. 'To write' is
the contrary of 'to describe'. Describing is predicated on total unveiling,
on the absolute nakedness of death. To the death of the object of
description corresponds symmetrically the death of the writing process
in the description.

A rift then always lies between text and representation. Freud had
good reason to propose a characterization of the unconscious in which
only 'thing representation' could be accommodated, whereas he had the
conscious and preconscious include both 'thing representation' and
'word representation'. We must add, however, that the unconscious
nucleus is inaccessible, that is to say, some representations will forever
remain unconscious, non-representable; there will always remain a gap
between thing-representation and word-representation. If the rise to
consciousness consists in establishing a relation between thing-
representation and word-representation, there is an order peculiar to
word-representation, the manifestation of which is the writing process.
In the written text, the relation between thing-representation and
word-representation is tipped, on the side of word-representation. While
the text may refer to thing representations, it comes alive mainly through
the relations among word-representations, which adds to the imbalance
of this relation already present in language. In the written text the
articulation between the sphere of things and the sphere of words
becomes modified in topical, dynamic, and economic terms. The writing
process creates its own space, its own autonomous movement, its specific
economy. Even though the relation between thing-representation and
word-representation has not been dissolved, the vectorization of their
equilibrium has changed. The relation keeps edging towards an ideality
(or a materiality) where thing-representation decreases in favour of
word-representation, to the point where word-representation replaces
thing-representation. What is noteworthy here is the peculiar status of
thing-representation. It is positioned as a hinge, since it is the transit
vehicle toward word-representation in the writing process. But it is itself
a mediator toward the body and, as such, tightly interwoven with the
instinctual motion which is the most elementary form of a drive, or what
Freud calls the psychic representative of the drive, not to be mistaken for
the representational representative (of things or words). Similarly,
word-representation is the medium through which thought becomes

manifest. Thus representations (thing or word) are mediating terms between body and thought. They are products *already* transformed (in relation to the body) and calling for *further* transformations (in relation to thought). Here lies the usefulness of the concept of drive as a crossroads concept between the somatic and the psychic; we realize its structure as a delegation of the body (the body with its drives is not the body pure and simple), endowed nevertheless with a certain thinking power (the logic of the primary process). In this contradiction lies the very fruitfulness of the concept, since it blends within itself an absence of organization in relation to thought, and an embryonic organization in relation to the body.

It is between the two poles of this dichotomy that the modern writing process is becoming disjointed. That is to say, it is tending to split between a writing of the body and a writing of the thought. On the body-writing side, representation no longer lays the foundation of a structured fantasy; it becomes fragmented into short-lived, evanescent bodily states, the writer failing repeatedly to communicate through the writing process this uncommunicable reality because neither the spoken nor the written word can yield a rendering of it. The affect is not even any longer the object of the writing process, or at least not in the subtle form that Proust imparted to it. The new object is the state of the body proper in its most violent manifestation. Incidentally, it is to be noted that a short circuit occurs between body and thought, which makes thought a corporal organ. Artaud and Beckett are to be read in that perspective. As far as the former is concerned, he has insisted repeatedly that he was indifferent to 'literature', that the only thing that mattered was the extraliterary reality which he accounted for when he wrote. If all his life Artaud maintained relationships with psychiatrists, thaumaturgists, clairvoyants, it is because he wanted to expose to them his body, teeming with miasmas that he did his very best to summon, for his thinking process was a body, and, of course, a sex-oriented body. From the beginning of his writing years, he insisted on having 'testicular liquid' injections. To him, the most important thing was to maintain contact with the 'powers of the mind', but the only way he could conceive of them was as the powers of bodily sex. When Artaud described the many phenomena that impeded his thinking, his writing mode was redolent of Gaetan Gatian de Clérambault's, the most brilliant representative of organicism in psychiatry, whom, unless I am mistaken, he never met. When his would-be followers or his friends recommended an occasional revision in his writings, he would refuse any modifications, alleging that he could not care less about the literary value of this text, but only about the transmission of a corporal state, of a tension-packed moment admitting no 'corrections'. One can easily imagine him roaring with protest at the use currently being made of his works. If we have dwelled on this example at some length, it is only because it seemed a particularly good documentation of the case. A whole literature has developed in his wake, with less felicitous results, because few authors have been as determined to pay the price for the experimental thrust which guided both Artaud and Daumal, a price which turned out to be quite high.

There is no such thing as an 'imitation' of Artaud: only a few ravens of contemporary literary criticism have tried to meet his gaze – after making sure they did not take any chances with their own sanity – a gaze unable to stand the contemplation of works painted by Van Gogh and a mind that eventually sank into psychosis.

At the opposite pole we are witnessing the advent of a literature which I shall call that of the sublimated text – a text devoid of any representation or meaning, a text which strives to say nothing beyond the mere statement of the writing process. This writing style is non-figurative in the same respect as the preceding one, which was not so much concerned with representing the body as in making it come alive in chips, in fragmented form and piecemeal. Here the absence of figurability makes the script the only representation. The script is unto itself its own opacity and its own transparency: indeed, its own cause. Its ultimate goal is, through the eradication of all representation, to reach a state of total blankness. It deletes the very lines it forms as it moves along. The drifting of a traditional literary text, its progressive lag away from unconscious representation which makes it a transformation product of fantasy, has been eliminated to make way for an absent text. The text celebrating absence has become the absence of any text. All such text is absolutely, integrally, pointing toward its own silence.[1] Everything that is not the text is off-text, nontext.

It is easy enough to understand that what one is trying to evacuate through this type of writing mode is the relation to the signified for the sole benefit of the signifier. The pure script, unfettered by the signified,

---

[1] We owe it to Blanchot to have shown how any production of the literary space tends, without ever reaching it, toward that silent point which constitutes its origin and its end at the same time. It remains to be proved whether this point was only detectable through the cover-up of a hidden silence. But from the very moment Blanchot names that silent point for our benefit, the literary cover-up exerts itself in vain to make it speak. The result is not so much that the silence shifts away 'a little further', but rather that being 'named' affects it deeply: thanks to this 'naming', or in spite of it, it becomes absolute dumbness under the anonymous disguise of silence. What we mean by that is not that the result does not say anything, surely not, but that it exhausts itself saying that something.

set free from representation, has severed its moorings to the object; it has become its own object. To use a comparison which, like most comparisons, is imperfect, we propose that the hallucinatory fulfilment of desire which conjures up the absent object has yielded to a negative hallucination. The purpose is not only to kill representation in the egg, but also him for whom an object exists as object of desire. The only desire left is the desire to write without object. In the preceding writing procedure, the important thing was to stop holding back any of the most recondite recesses of the body; in this one, there is nothing more to see, because there is nothing to be shown except the writing process. Nothing is left except writing-thinking and thinking-writing. The work is a blank book.

Those two procedures have in common the abolishing of the figurative dimension. By so doing, they have broken the chain of operations peculiar to the classical writing mode. As a result, psychoanalytical criticism itself undergoes transformations. It can no longer resort to the same criteria that used to guide its proceedings and corresponded to an application of the Freudian method. If it is to approach these works, it must modify its analytical procedures. Psychoanalytical criticism must use different metapsychological landmarks, which it will find in post-Freudian authors, in Melanie Klein or Lacan, for instance. Practically nothing has yet been done in that field, but certain breakthroughs can be expected that will alleviate current frustrations. Such initiatives are adventurous, yet it is quite possible that Bion's theorizing, for instance, may turn out to be very helpful, to the extent that it expresses concern for a theory that might control the most elementary, along with the most differentiated, aspects of psychism.[1]

We would then have at our disposal a reliable 'key' to probe texts that illustrate the process whereby the alpha function has been transformed. This alpha function purports to elaborate the primitive material of psychic activity into material usable by the unconscious, and also to elaborate preconceptions into conceptions and concepts.

THE RETURN TO REPRESENTATION

Thus, one way or another, modern writing modes are no longer willing to be trapped into representation. Whether it leans toward the concrete or the abstract, the writing process is deliberately non-figurative, but, as a result, it always finds itself in a position where it fails to perform its function. For the writing mode 'of the body', the text is never sufficiently alive; it always falls short of what it is supposed to transmit, and as a

[1] Bion is the author who has extended the Freudian notion of binding to its furthest point (cf. Bion, 1963).

consequence the thinking process is overburdened. For the thought-oriented writing mode, the text tells too much; it is still too closely bound to the materiality through which it must pass; it does not 'think' enough. But the significant weakness of modern writing in its fight against representation lies rather in an implicit contradiction, for to write, due to the very fact that all writing is a visible trace – visible because legible, and indeed it is destined to be read – is still, one way or another, to represent. Writing is caught between the non-representability of the writing process and the inevitability of its representation. A blank book is still a book, be it an authorless, titleless, and typeless book; it is an object which has its appointed place in a library or bookstore. It is not at all easy to break completely loose from representation; representation sees to it that a minimal participatory fee shall be paid, short of which it ceases to be a writing mode. Indeed, the less anchored in representation a text is, the more it lets the reader in on the representing, if not the visual, process. The vaguest of texts are those that challenge our imaginations most. The whole effort exerted in literature lies in alternating motions toward and way from its focal point. Even in the body-oriented writing mode, the mode that spurns literature in order to attain a certain living reality, one is bounced back to the writing act, since it is through the writing act that one has chosen to attain it. Ironically, those who were intent on reaching out beyond the literary have become models for literature. In the intellectual writing mode, the bid toward identification between thinking and writing ends up leaving an unavoidable hiatus between one and the other, due to the very specificity of the writing process, which is thus enhanced. In this switching back and forth of the writing process, we find the same motion, pointing in opposite directions, to eliminate representation. Pointing toward the body, the writing mode would very much like to transcribe the corporal in raw terms, but it can only represent it, just as corporal activity must be transcribed in the language of representation if it is to communicate. In the last analysis, Artaud's writing mode, when he speaks about his body or his states of mind, is most representation-oriented. The succession of metaphors plays a prominent part. There is no way to make the body speak or to 'write' it without resorting to modes of representation. Affects can be communicated through silence; they can be hinted at by non-linguistic signs. Amorous or aggressive emotions, pleasure, displeasure, do not need language to be mutually guessed, shared, or thwarted. But as soon as one decides to communicate by means of the spoken or written word, recourse must inevitably be made to representation, especially if the transcribing function of that representation is to remain unobtrusive.

Even the disengagement from representation which accompanies anguish (said to be without any object) will have to convert pure affect into representation when the need to communicate comes to be felt. Granted that any representations meant to convey the affect are likely to be invested with such a charge that the chances are slim that they might be confused with other, less affective representations – which incidentally proves that a purely distributional concept of representations is clearly inadequate – yet the communication process demands that whoever wishes to transmit bodily states simply must metaphorize them.

Where the opposite writing mode is concerned, the transmission of thought follows a similar process. Freud maintained that the role of language is to impart to thought processes, which are by nature devoid of any sensuous qualities since they consist of relations, a perceptual reinvestment which makes them communicable. This is pretty obvious when it comes to transcribing thoughts into spoken words, that is, by emitting significant sounds through the channel of language. But for thought to pass from the unconscious state to the conscious state, a new investment must of necessity intervene, whereby thought switches from an abstract to a concrete set of relations through the use of language, which secures consciousness for it. If in relation to thing-representation, word-representation can be considered a transformation where the thing becomes 'absent' for the benefit of language, in the relation of thought to language, on the contrary, language imparts presence to thought. Writing institutes a new relation. Jacques Derrida has shown the solidarity between language and presence on the one hand, and between writing and absence on the other. To speak and to write are different things, and everyone knows how weak a text seems when it is written in 'spoken' style. Yet, whatever degree of absence one may wish to achieve in the scriptural process, the fact remains that one must resort to representation, at least in the form of traces through which the text comes to exist.

Perceiving those traces is all-important for the transcribing process to be understood. The collusion between writing and thinking cannot evade the transformation from the invisible to the visible. Thus, if the scriptural process aims at the most sparing use of representation, writing nevertheless remains unavoidably linked to representation, for not only the materiality of signs is involved, but also the representation of meaning through those signs. Maybe that is what differentiates a literary text from a philosophical text. If the concept of 'trace' tries to reach beyond the dichotomy of signifier/signified, it is because it purports to subsume their effect under one symbolization. As a result, composing traces or deciphering them is still making use of representations, even as one is trying to do without them.

What happens then when the writing process decides upon this double evacuation of representation – that is, of content? It seems to us that, far from conferring an autonomous status on the scriptural process, which would somehow help focus interest exclusively on the literal, such a program is more likely to be heading toward a massive return to representation, not only at the level of the text, but also because it is easy for an ideology crowded with innumerable non-literary referents to graft itself onto literature. The revolution in writing is one aspect among many of an impending cultural revolution which, while signalling the death of literature, is expected to usher in a new form which goes beyond it. Classical literature, even though we continue to pay the tribute of our sentimental attachment to it, remains the expression of a past now gone forever. One could interpret this revolutionary call as a contradictory effort to claim the specific character of the literary act as a revolutionary act, while at the same time recasting the objectives of the literary revolution to fit the cultural revolution. By embracing the expectations of revolutionary masses, one renews contact with a whole mass of readers, few of whom are really concerned with literary evolution. In fact, the question still to be answered, whatever literary specificity may turn out to be, is whether literature can be self-sufficient and invoke literary values as its sole justification. Is not the nature of literature precisely to express that relation to an extraliterary reality, which the scriptural process must forever transform to make it 'speak' a different language, without ceasing to refer to it?

Literature is a machine designed to elaborate the relation of writing to external reality and to psychic reality and to retrieve those realities after they have been interpreted and necessarily distorted. Should it fail to allow this exchange to take place, literature becomes a dead letter. Now in this two-way communication, representation is a sort of nucleus liable to be developed into a variety of formulae, some referring to the body, others to the thinking process. Through this double reference, it embodies the interplay between psychic reality and external reality. It has its locus in the 'potential space' of their mutual chiasmi: the field of illusion. The struggle toward the demystification of literature is marred by a faulty identification claim. Literature cannot be scientific or philosophical. It is founded upon illusion, because literary writings are simulacra, fictitious entities. But they are in a way so 'true' that men can become passionately involved in them, do battle, and even risk their own lives to defend them or to justify their love or hatred toward the writings of others. Nothing is more revolting to the real book-lover than the *auto-da-fé* which closely precedes extermination camps. The life of the text and the text of Life are so inextricably mated that any onslaught upon either of them endangers the other. Sartre once said, I believe: 'What is literature next to the death of a child?' Yet what is a child's life in a world without literature?

All that's left to do is to formulate a wish, leaving it up to the future to decide whether it is a mere illusion: namely, that the cultural revolution allow the literary revolution to continue making its pitch in the field of literary illusion and not force it to dissipate itself into the subservient role of feeding the illusions of the cultural revolution. But who knows what the future will bring?

As we move to our final remarks, we have to wonder what role psychoanalysis may have played in the death of literature. True enough, there is no lack of justification for arguing that this death – which seems just around the corner, if indeed it has not already occurred – is only one among many others. Agonizing victims abound in what we call the current crisis of civilization. But we may well wonder if psychoanalysis has not, on its own, contributed indirectly to this death. It seems as if the unveiling of the unconscious through the use of analysis has driven literature into an even more radical veiling process, which has resulted in an out-and-out foreclosure of representation. This is a mere hypothesis, which perhaps overestimates the influence of psychoanalysis on an evolution reaching beyond the scope of psychoanalysis to many other factors.

There may be substance in the suggestion of an analogy between contemporary writing modes and psychotic language. If so, these modes are truly consonant with the current era, just as the period which saw the advent of psychoanalysis was perhaps mostly the era of neurosis. There is no dearth of voices to proclaim emphatically that it is today's world that is psychotic and, by way of consequence, psychosis-inducing. Under the circumstances, wracked between the writing mode of the body and that of the mind, literature struggles in a world from which the mediation of representation has been excluded. The language of the body invades the thinking process, overflows it, and in·the long run prevents it from affirming itself as thought. The language of the mind cuts itself off completely from the body, to deploy itself in a barren space. It could be said that in both cases the unbinding process has taken place once again. In corporal language, it is the breaking open of the scriptural act that caused the binding to disintegrate, leaving only dispersed or fragmented elements open to view. In intellectual language, the ever-tightening grip of the binding process, at the secondary level, which gave this sort of literature its compact texture and frigid appearance, has broken its mooring to the primary process, the traces of which it did its best to erase. In the former case, the visible unbinding was 'horizontal'; in the latter it was 'vertical'. By contrast, classical writing strove to impose an order stringent enough to make the surface meaning respond to the binding, yet allowing traces of the depths,[1] which the text suppressed, to escape from time to time. Should we yield then to the nostalgia of those 'good old days', gone forever? Indeed we should not. Nor should we fall prey to fatalistic pessimism either. Perhaps literature will die, or perhaps a mutation, which imagination cannot now conceive, will occur and give it another face. Our present horizon is confined by our modes of thought. After all, why should we be more capable of imagining what will come after psychoanalysis than people were in 1880 of imagining what Freud was about to reveal, which had been there, under their noses, since time immemorial? One adventurer is enough to change the face of everything.

---

[1] Contemporary texts, according to literary avant-garde opinion, must be 'spoken' in their shallow dimension. One does not explore them in the 'verticality' any longer; one sets them en abyme. The term is a felicitous condensation of abîme ['chasm'] and abyss [English for 'chasm'], which refers to the deepest oceanic rifts. How does lateral intertextuality come to communicate with the abyss in question? This seems difficult for us to conceive without going through the mediation of the unconscious (the reader's and the writer's), unless we lapse into a mystical philosophy of language or history.

References

Abraham, N. (1978) 'Le crime de l'introjection', in *L'écorce et le noyau* (Paris, Aubier)
Abraham, N., and Torok, M. (1972) 'Introjecter-incorporer: Deuil *ou* melancolie', *Nouv. Rev. Psychanal.* 6
Abrams, S., and Neubauer, P. (1974) 'Object-orientedness: the person or the thing'. A paper presented at the winter meeting of the American Psychoanalytic Association
Anzieu, D. (1986) *Freud's Self-Analysis* (London, Hogarth Press; New York, Int. Univ. Press). Translation of *L'auto-analyse de Freud* (Paris, Presses Univ. de France, 1959, 2nd ed. 1975)
Arlow, J. A. (ed.) (1973) *Selected Writings of Bertram D. Lewin* (New York, Psychoanal. Quart. Inc.)

Bak, R. C. (1946) 'Masochism in paranoia', *Psychoanal. Quart.* 15
Balint, M. (1950) 'Changing therapeutical aims and techniques in psycho-analysis', *Int. J. Psycho-Anal.* 31
– (1960) 'The regressed patient and his analyst', *Psychiatry* 23
– (1962) 'The theory of the parent-infant relationship', *Int. J. Psycho-Anal.* 43
– (1968) *The Basic Fault: Therapeutic Aspects of Regression* (London, Tavistock Publications)
Barnett, M. C. (1966) 'Vaginal awareness in the infancy and childhood of girls', *J. Am. psychoanal. Ass.* 14
Barthes, R. (1975) *The Pleasure of the Text* (New York, Hill & Wang)
Bataille, G. (1957) *Erotism*, trans. M. Dalwood (London, Calder, 1965)
Bergeret, J. (1970) 'Les états limites', *Rev. franc. Psychanal.* 34
– (1974a) *La personnalité normale et pathologique* (Paris, Dunod)
– (1974b) *La dépression et les états-limites* (Paris, Payot)
Bion, W. (1957) 'Differentiation of the psychotic from the non-psychotic personalities', in Bion (1967)
– (1959) 'Attacks on linking', in Bion (1967)
– (1962) *Learning from Experience* (London, Heinemann; New York, Basic Books)
– (1963) *Elements of Psychoanalysis* (London, Heinemann; New York, Basic Books)
– (1965) *Transformations* (London, Heinemann; New York, Basic Books)
– (1967) *Second Thoughts* (London, Heinemann; New York, Jason Aronson)
– (1970) *Attention and Interpretation* (London, Tavistock Publications)
Bleger, J. (1967) 'Psycho-analysis and the psycho-analytic frame', *Int. J. Psycho-Anal.* 48
Bonaparte, M. (1953) *Female Sexuality* (London, Imago; New York, Int. Univ. Press)
Bouvet, M. (1954) 'La cure type', in Bouvet (1968, II)
– (1956) 'La clinique psychanalytique: la relation d'objet', in Bouvet (1967, I)
– (1958) 'Technical variations and the concept of distance', *Int. J. Psycho-Anal.* 39
– (1960) 'Depersonnalisation et relations d'objet', in Bouvet (1967, I)
– (1967/68) *Oeuvres psychanalytiques*, Vols. I and II (Paris, Payot)
Braunschweig, D. (1971) 'Psychanalyse et réalité', *Rev. franç. Psychanal.* 35
Brenner, C. (1974) 'On the nature and development of affects', *Psychoanal. Quart.* 43
Brierley, M. (1937) 'Affects in theory and practice', in *Trends in Psycho-Analysis* (London, Hogarth Press)

Burchfield, R. W. (ed.) (1972) *Supplement to the Oxford English Dictionary* (Oxford, Clarendon Press)

Castelnuovo-Tedesco, P. (1974a) 'Affects, sensory experience, and time'. Unpublished paper summarized in Castelnuovo-Tedesco (1974b)
– (1974b) (reporter) Panel on 'Toward a theory of affects', *J. Am. psychoanal. Ass.* 22
Castoriadis-Aulagnier, P. (1975) *La violence de l'interprétation* (Paris, Presses Univ. de France)
Chomsky, N. (1968) *Language and Mind* (New York, Harcourt Brace)
Clancier, A. (1973) *Psychanalyse et critique littéraire* (Paris, Privat)
Clérambault, G. de (1942) *Oeuvres psychiatriques* (Paris, Presses Univ. de France)
Codet, H., and Laforgue, R. (1925) 'Les arriérations affectives: la schizonia', *L'évolution psychiatrique* 1

David, C. (1966) 'Représentation, affect, fantasmes'. Roneotyped manuscript (Enseignement de l'Institut de Psychanalyse)
– (1967a) Discussion of J. Rouart, 'Les notions d'investissement et contre-investissement', *Rev. franç. Psychanal.* 31
– (1967b) 'L'hétérogénéité de l'inconscient et les continuités psychiques', *L'Inconscient* 4
– (1972) 'La perversion affective', in *La sexualité perverse* (Paris, Payot)
– (1971) *L'état amoureux* (Paris, Payot)
Delcourt, M. (1955) *L'oracle de Delphes* (Paris, Payot)
Deutsch, F. (1957) 'A footnote to Freud's "Fragment of an analysis of a case of hysteria"', *Psychoanal. Quart.* 26
Deutsch, H. (1942) 'Some forms of emotional disturbances and their relationship to schizophrenia', in *Neuroses and Character Types* (New York, Int. Univ. Press, 1965; London, Hogarth Press)
Diatkine, R., and Simon, J. (1972) *La psychanalyse précoce* (Paris, Presses Univ. de France)
Dodds, E. (1951) *The Greeks and the Irrational* (Berekeley, Univ. of California Press)
Donnet, J. L. (1973) 'Le divan bien tempéré, *Nouv. Rev. Psychanal.* 8
Donnet, J. L., and Green, A. (1973) *L'enfant de ça. La psychose blanche* (Paris, Editions de Minuit)

Eissler, K. R. (1953) 'The effect of the structure of the ego on psychoanalytic technique', *J. Am. psychoanal. Ass.* 1
– (1958) 'Remarks on some variations in psychoanalytic technique', *Int. J. Psycho-Anal.* 39
Engel, G. (1962) 'Anxiety and depression-withdrawal', *Int. J. Psycho-Anal.* 43
Erikson, E. H. (1959) *Identity and the Life Cycle* (New York, Int. Univ. Press)

Fain, M. (1966) 'Regression et psychosomatique', *Rev. franç. Psychanal.* 30
Fain, M., and Braunschweig, D. (1971) *Eros et Anteros* (Paris, Payot)
Fairbairn, W. R. D. (1940) 'Schizoid factors in the personality', in Fairbairn (1952)
– (1952) *Psycho-Analytic Studies of the Personality* (London, Tavistock Publications)
Fenichel, O. (1941) *The Problems of Psychoanalytic Technique* (New York, Psychoanal. Quart. Inc.)
– (1941a) 'The ego and the affects', in *Collected Papers*, 2nd series (New York, Norton, 1954)
Ferenczi, S. (1909) 'Introjection and transference', in Ferenczi (1952)
– (1928) 'The elasticity of psycho-analytic technique', in Ferenczi (1955)
– (1929) 'The unwelcome child and his death instinct' in Ferenczi (1955)
– (1930) 'The principle of relaxation and neo-catharsis', in Ferenczi (1955)
– (1931) 'Child analysis in the analysis of adults', in Ferenczi (1955)
– (1933) 'Confusion of tongues between adults and the child', in Ferenczi (1955)
– (1952) *First Contributions to Psycho-Analysis* (London, Hogarth Press)

– (1955) *Final Contributions to the Problems and Methods of Psycho-Analysis* (London, Hogarth Press; New York, Basic Books)

Foucault, M. (1965) *Madness and Civilisation: A History of Insanity in the Age of Reason* (London, Tavistock Publications)

Freud, A. (1936) *The Ego and the Mechanisms of Defence*. Revised edition, *The Writings of Anna Freud*, Vol. II (New York, Int. Univ. Press; London, Hogarth Press)

– (1954) 'The widening scope of indications for psychoanalysis', in A. Freud (1968)

– (1968) *Indications for Child Analysis and Other Papers. The Writings of Anna Freud*, Vol. IV (New York, Int. Univ. Press; London, Hogarth Press)

– (1969) 'Difficulties in the path of psychoanalysis', in A. Freud (1971)

– (1971) *Problems of Psychoanalytic Training, Diagnosis, and the Technique of Therapy. The Writings of Anna Freud*, Vol. VII (New York, Int. Univ. Press; London, Hogarth Press)

Freud, S. (1893c) 'Some points for a comparative study of organic and hysterical motor paralyses, *SE*[1] 1

– (1894a) 'The neuro-psychoses of defence', *SE* 3

– (1895) 'Project for a scientific psychology', *SE* 1

– (1895b) 'On the grounds for detaching a particular syndrome from neurasthenia under the description "anxiety neurosis"', *SE* 3

– (1895d) With Breuer, J., *Studies on Hysteria*, *SE* 3

– (1900a) *The Interpretation of Dreams*, *SE* 4 and 5

– (1901b) *The Psychopathology of Everyday Life*, *SE* 6

– (1904a) 'Freud's psycho-analytic procedure', *SE* 7

– (1905a) 'On psychotherapy', *SE* 7

– (1905c) *Jokes and their Relation to the Unconscious*, *SE* 8

– (1905d) *Three Essays on the Theory of Sexuality*, *SE* 7

– (1905e) 'Fragment of an analysis of a case of hysteria', *SE* 7

– (1909b) 'Analysis of a phobia in a five-year-old boy', *SE* 10

– (1909d) 'Notes upon a case of obsessional neurosis', *SE* 10

– (1910d) 'The future prospects of psycho-analytic therapy', *SE* 11

– (1910e) '"The antithetical meaning of primary words"', *SE* 11

– (1910h) 'A special type of object choice made by men', *SE* 11

– (1910k) '"Wild psycho-analysis"', *SE* 11

– (1911b) 'Formulations on two principles of mental functioning', *SE* 12

– (1911c) 'Psycho-analytic notes on an autobiographical account of a case of paranoia', *SE* 12

– (1912b) 'The dynamics of transference', *SE* 12

– (1912e) 'Recommendations to physicians practising psycho-analysis', *SE* 12

– (1912–13) *Totem and Taboo*, *SE* 13

– (1913c) 'On beginning the treatment (further recommendations on the technique of psycho-analysis, I)' *SE* 12

– (1913f) 'The theme of the three caskets', *SE* 12

– (1913j) 'The claims of psycho-analysis to scientific interest', *SE* 13

– (1914g) 'Remembering, repeating and working-through (further recommendations on the technique of psycho-analysis, II)', *SE* 12

– (1915a) 'Observations on transference love (further recommendations on the technique of psycho-analysis, III)', *SE* 12

– (1915c) 'Instincts and their vicissitudes', *SE* 14

– (1915d) 'Repression', *SE* 14

– (1915e) 'The unconscious', *SE* 14

– (1916–17) *Introductory Lectures on Psycho-Analysis*, *SE* 15 and 16

---

[1] *The Standard Edition of the Complete Psychological Works of Sigmund Freud*, translated from the German in 24 volumes under the general editorship of James Strachey (London, Hogarth Press, 1953–74; New York, Norton).

– (1917c) 'On transformations of instinct as exemplified in anal erotism', *SE* 17
– (1917d) 'A metapsychological supplement to the theory of dreams', *SE* 14
– (1917e) 'Mourning and melancholia', *SE* 14
– (1918b) 'From the history of an infantile neurosis', *SE* 17
– (1919a) 'Lines of advance in psycho-analytic therapy', *SE* 17
– (1919h) 'The "uncanny" ', *SE* 17
– (1920g) *Beyond the Pleasure Principle*, *SE* 18
– (1922b) 'Some neurotic mechanisms in jealousy, paranoia, and homosexuality', *SE* 18
– (1923b) *The Ego and the Id*, *SE* 19
– (1924b) 'Neurosis and psychosis', *SE* 19
– (1924c) 'The economic problem of masochism', *SE* 19
– (1924d) 'The dissolution of the Oedipus complex', *SE* 19
– (1924e) 'The loss of reality in neurosis and psychosis', *SE* 19
– (1925h) 'Negation', *SE* 19
– (1926d) *Inhibitions, Symptoms and Anxiety*, *SE* 20
– (1927e) 'Fetishism', *SE* 21
– (1930a) *Civilization and Its Discontents*, *SE* 21
– (1931b) 'Female sexuality', *SE* 21
– (1933a) *New Introductory Lectures on Psycho-Analysis*, *SE* 22
– (1937c) 'Analysis terminable and interminable', *SE* 23
– (1937d) 'Constructions in analysis', *SE* 23
– (1939a) *Moses and Monotheism*, *SE* 23
– (1940a) *An Outline of Psycho-Analysis*, *SE* 23
– (1940b) 'Some elementary lessons in psycho-analysis', *SE* 23
– (1940e) 'Splitting of the ego in the process of defence', *SE* 23
Gillespie, W. H. (1969) 'Concepts of vaginal orgasm', *Int. J. Psycho-Anal.* 50
Giovacchini, P. L. (1972a) 'Interpretation and definition of the analytical setting', in
    Giovacchini (1972d)
– (1972b) 'The blank self', in Giovacchini (1972d)
– (1972c) 'Summing up, in Giovacchini (1972d)
– (1972d) *Tactics and Techniques in Psychoanalytic Therapy* (New York, Science House;
    London, Hogarth Press)
– (1973) 'Character disorders', *Int. J. Psycho-Anal.* 54
Gitelson, M. (1958) 'On ego distortion' (panel discussion), *Int. J. Psycho-Anal.* 39
Glover, E. (1939) 'The psycho-analysis of affects', *Int. J. Psycho-Anal.* 20
Green, A. (1962) 'L'inconscient freudien et la psychanalyse française contemporaine',
    Temps Modernes 195 or *L'Inconscient*, ed. H. Ey (Desclée de Brouwer)
– (1963) 'Une variante de la position phallique-narcissique', *Rev. franç. Psychanal.* 27
– (1966) 'L'objet (a) de J. Lacan, sa logique et la théorie freudienne' *Cahiers pour l'analyse* 3;
    translated as 'The logic of Lacan's *objet a* and Freudian theory: convergences and
    questions', in *Interpreting Lacan*, ed. J. H. Smith and W. Kerrigan, *Psychiatry and the
    Humanities* 6 (Yale Univ. Press)
– (1967b) 'Le narcissisme primaire: structure ou état', *L'Inconscient* 1, 2
– (1968) 'Sur la mère phallique', *Rev. franç. Psychanal.* 32
– (1969a) 'Le narcissisme moral', *Rev. franç. Psychanal.* 33
– (1969b) 'La nosographie psychanalytique des psychoses', in Laurin & Doucet (1969)
– (1970) 'Répétition, différence, réplication', *Rev. franç. Psychanal.* 34
– (1970a) 'L'affect', *Rev. franç. Psychanal.* 34
– (1971) 'Lear ou les voi(es)x de la nature' (Lear or the voices/ways of nature), *Critique* 284
– (1972) 'Note sur les processus tertiaires', *Rev. franç. Psychanal.* 36
– (1973) *Le discours vivant. La conception psychanalytique de l'affect* (Paris, Presses Univ. de
    France)
– (1975) 'La sexualisation et son économie', *Rev. franç. Psychanal.* 39. Translated as
    'Sexualization and its economy' in *Psychoanalysis in France*.

- (1976) 'Un, Autre, Neutre: valeurs narcissiques du Même', *Nouv. Rev. Psychanal.*, Narcisses 13. In Green (1983)
- (1979) *The Tragic Effect: The Oedipus Complex in Tragedy* (Cambridge, Cambridge Univ. Press)
- (1979a) 'Le silence du psychanalyste', *Topique* 23
- (1979b) 'L'angoisse et le narcissisme', *Rev. franç. Psychanal.* 43. See Green (1983)
- (1983) *Narcissisme de vie. Narcissisme de mort* (Paris, Minuit)
- (1984) 'Le langage dans la psychanalyse', in *Langages* (Acts of 2nd Symposium of Aix-en-Provence, Editions Les Belles Lettres)
Greenson, R. R. (1967) *The Technique and Practice of Psychoanalysis* (New York, Int. Univ. Press; London, Hogarth Press)
Gressot, M. (1960) 'L'idée de composante psychotique dans les cas limites accessible à la psychothérapie', *L'Encéphale* 49
Grinker, R. R. Sr. (1977) 'The borderline syndrome: a phenomenological view', in Hartocollis (1977)
Grinstein, A. (1972) 'Un rêve de Freud: les trois Parques' (Freud's dream of the three Fates), *Nouv. Rev. Psychanal.* 5
Grumberger, B. (1971) Le *narcissisme* (Paris, Payot)
Guiraud, P. (1950) *Psychiatrie Générale* (Paris: Ed. Le Francois)

Hartmann, H. (1950) 'Comments on the psychoanalytic theory of the ego', *Psychoanal. Study Child* 5
- (1951) 'Technical implications of ego psychology', *Psychoanal. Quart.* 20
- (1964) *Essays on Ego Psychology* (New York, Int. Univ. Press; London, Hogarth Press)
Hartocollis, P. (ed.) (1977) *Borderline Personality Disorders* (New York, Int. Univ. Press)
Heimann, P. (1950) 'On counter-transference', *Int. J. Psycho-Anal.* 31
Holt, R. (ed.) (1967) *Motives and Thoughts* (New York, Int. Univ. Press)

Jacobson, E. (1953) 'The affects and their pleasure-unpleasure qualities in relation to the psychic discharge processes', in Loewenstein (1953)
- (1964) *The Self and the Object World* (New York, Int. Univ. Press; London, Hogarth Press)
Joffe, W. G., and Sandler, J. (1968) 'Comments on the psychoanalytic psychology of adaptation, with special reference to the role of affects and the representational world', *Int. J. Psycho-Anal.* 49
Jones, E. (1927) 'The early development of female sexuality', *Int. J. Psycho-Anal.* 8
- (1929) 'Fear, guilt and hate', *Int. J. Psycho-Anal.* 10

Kernberg, O. (1970) 'Factors in the psychoanalytic treatment of narcissistic personalities', *J. Am. psychoanal. Ass.*
- (1971) 'Prognostic considerations regarding borderline personality organization', *J. Am. psychoanal. Ass.* 19
- (1972) 'Treatment of borderline patients', in Giovacchini (1972d)
- (1974) 'Further contributions to the treatment of narcissistic personalities', *Int. J. Psycho-Anal.* 55
- (1975) *Borderline Conditions and Pathological Narcissism* (New York, Jason Aronson)
Khan, M. M. R. (1962) 'Dream psychology of the evolution of the psychoanalytic situation', in Khan (1974)
- (1969) 'Vicissitudes of being, knowing and experiencing in the therapeutic situation', in Khan (1974)
- (1971) 'To hear with eyes', in Khan (1974)
- (1972) 'The use and abuse of dreams in psychic experience', in Khan (1974)
- (1974) *The Privacy of the Self* (London, Hogarth Press; New York, Int. Univ. Press)
- (1978) 'Secret as potential space', in Khan (1983)

– (1983) *Hidden Selves: Between Theory and Practice in Psychoanalysis* (London, Hogarth Press; New York, Int. Univ. Press)

Klauber, J. (1972) 'On the relationship of transference and interpretation in psychoanalytic therapy', *Int. J. Psycho-Anal.* 53

Klein, G. (1967) 'Peremptory ideation structure and force in motivation', in Holt (1967)

Klein, M. (1940) 'Mourning and its relation to manic depressive states', in Klein (1975*a*)

– (1946) 'Notes on some schizoid mechanisms', in Klein (1975*b*)

– (1957) *Envy and Gratitude*, in Klein (1975*b*)

– (1975*a*) *Love, Guilt and Reparation and Other Papers, 1921–45. The Writings of Melanie Klein*, Vol. I (London, Hogarth Press; New York, The Free Press, 1984)

– (1975*b*) *Envy and Gratitude and Other Papers, 1946–63. The Writings of Melanie Klein*, Vol. III (London, Hogarth Press; New York, The Free Press, 1984)

Knight, R. P. (1953) 'Borderline states', *Bull. Menninger Clinic* 17

Kohut, H. (1971) *The Analysis of the Self* (New York, Int. Univ. Press; London, Hogarth Press)

Lacan, J. (1956) 'Réponse au commentaire de Jean Hippolyte sur la *Verneinung* de Freud', *La Psychanalyse* 1. In Lacan (1966)

– (1956*a*) 'Fonction et champ de la parole et du langage en psychanalyse', *La Psychanalyse* 1. Also in Lacan (1966). Translated as 'The function and field of speech and language in psychoanalysis', in Lacan (1977)

– (1966) *Ecrits* (Paris, Le Seuil). See also Lacan (1977)

– (1973) *Télévision* (Paris, Le Seuil)

– (1975) *Séminaire XX, Encore* (Paris, Le Seuil)

– (1977) *Ecrits: A Selection*, translated by A. Sheridan (London, Tavistock Publications; New York, Norton)

Lagache, D. (1947) *La jalousie amoureuse* (Paris, Presses Univ. de France)

– (1952) 'Le problème du transfert, *Rev. franç. Psychanal.* 16

Lalande, A. (1968) *Vocabulaire technique et critique de la philosophie*, 10th ed. (Paris, Presses Univ. de France)

Lampl-de-Groot, J. (1967) 'On obstacles standing in the way of psychoanalytic cure', *Psychoanal. Study Child* 22

Laplanche, J. (1976) *Life and Death in Psychoanalysis* (Baltimore, Johns Hopkins Press)

Laplanche, J., and Pontalis, J.-B. (1967) *Vocabulaire de la psychanalyse* (Paris, Presses Univ. de France)

– (1973) *The Language of Psycho-Analysis*, a translation of Laplanche and Pontalis (1967) by D. Nicholson Smith (London, Hogarth Press; New York, Norton)

Laporte, R. (1970) *Fugue* (Paris, Gallimard)

Laurin, C., and Doucet, P. (eds.) (1969) *Problems of Psychosis*, Vol. 1 (Amsterdam, Excerpta Medica Foundation)

Lazar, N. D. (1973) 'Nature and significance of changes in patients in a psychoanalytic clinic', *Psychoanal. Quart.* 42

Lebovici, S., and Soulé, M. (1970) *La connaissance de l'enfant par la psychanalyse* (Paris, Presses Univ. de France)

Lewin, B. D. (1950) *The Psychoanalysis of Elation* (New York, Norton)

– (1954) 'Sleep, narcissistic neurosis, and the analytic situation', in Arlow (1973)

– (1964) 'Reflections on affect', in M. Schur (ed.) (1964)

Lichtenstein, H. (1964) 'The role of narcissism in the emergence and maintenance of a primary identity', *Int. J. Psycho-Anal.* 45

– (1965) 'Towards a metapsychological definition of the concept of the self', *Int. J. Psycho-Anal.* 46

Limentani, A. (1972) 'The assessment of analyzability', *Int. J. Psycho-Anal.* 53

Little, M. (1958) 'On defusional transference', *Int. J. Psycho-Anal.* 39

Little, M., and Flarsheim, A. (1972) 'Early mothering care and borderline psychotic states', in Giovacchini (1972d)

Loewenstein, R. M. (1958) 'Variations in classical technique', Int. J. Psycho-Anal. 39

Loewenstein, R. M. (ed.) (1953) Drives, Affects, Behavior, Vol. I (New York, Int. Univ. Press)

Löfgren, L. B. (reporter) (1968) Panel on 'Psychoanalytic theory of affects', J. Am. psychoanal. Ass. 16

Luquet-Parat, C. J. (1964) 'Le changement d'objet', in J. Chassequet-Smirgel (ed.) Recherches nouvelles sur la sexualité féminine (Paris, Payot)

Lyotard, J. F. (1971) Discours, Figure (Paris, Klincksieck)

McDougall, J. (1972) 'L'antianalysant en analyse', Rev. franç. Psychanal. 36

– (1936) 'Primal scene and sexual perversion', Int. J. Psycho-Anal. 53

– (1974) 'The psycho-soma and the psychoanalytic process', Int. Rev. Psycho-Anal. 1

Mâle, P. (1956) 'Etude psychanalytique de l'adolescence', in S. Nacht (ed.) (1967)

Mallet, J. (1966) 'Une théorie de la paranoia', Rev. franç. Psychanal. 30

– (1969) 'Formation et devenir des affects', in La théorie psychanalytique (Paris, Presses Univ. de France)

Mao, T. (1937) 'On contradiction', in Mao (1967)

– (1967) Selected Works of Mao Tse-Tung (Peking, Foreign Languages Press)

Marshall, M. (1968) 'Note on article negat', in Lalande (1968)

Marty, P., and M'Uzan, M. de (1963) 'La pensée opératoire', Rev. franç. Psychanal. 27

Marty, P., M'Uzan, M. de, and David, C. (1963) L'investigation psychosomatique. Sept observations cliniques (Paris, Presses Univ. de France)

Masson, J. M. (ed.) (1985) The Complete Letters of Sigmund Freud to Wilhelm Fliess, 1887–1904 (Cambridge, Mass., and London, The Belknap Press of Harvard Univ. Press)

Meltzer, D. (1967) The Psycho-Analytical Process (London, Heinemann)

Milner, M. (1952) 'Aspects of symbolism in the comprehension of the not-self', Int. J. Psycho-Anal. 33

– (1968) The Hands of the Living God (London, Hogarth Press; New York, Int. Univ. Press)

Modell, A. H. (1969) Object Love and Reality (New York, Int. Univ. Press; London, Hogarth Press)

– (1971) 'The origin of certain forms of pre-oedipal guilt and the implications for a psychoanalytic theory of affects', Int. J. Psycho-Anal. 52

Moore, B. E. (1968) 'Some genetic and developmental considerations in regard to affects', unpublished paper summarized in Löfgren (1968)

– (1974) 'Toward a theory of affects', unpublished paper summarized in Castelnuovo-Tedesco (1974b)

Moore, B. E., and Fine, B. D. (1967) A Glossary of Psychoanalytic Terms and Concepts (New York, American Psychoanalytic Association)

Morin, E., and Piatelli-Palmarini, M. (1974) L'unité de l'homme (Paris, Le Seuil)

Morel, B. A. (1852) Etudes cliniques (Paris, Baillère)

M'Uzan, M. de (1967a) Discussion of J. Rouart, 'Les notions d'investissement et contre-investissement', Rev. franç. Psychanal. 31

– (1967b) 'Expérience de l'inconscient', L'Inconscient 4. In M'Uzan (1977)

– (1968) 'Acting out "direct" et acting out "indirect"', Rev. franç. Psychanal. 32. In M'Uzan (1977)

– (1970) 'Affect et processus d'affectation', Rev. franç. Psychanal. 34. In M'Uzan (1977)

– (1977) De l'art à la mort (Paris, Gallimard)

Nacht, S. (1963) La présence du psychanalyste (Paris, Presses Univ. de France)

Nacht, S., and Lebovici, S. (1955) 'Indications et contre-indications de la psychanalyse', in S. Nacht (ed.) (1967)

Nacht, S. (ed.) (1967) *La psychanalyse d'aujourd'hui*, 2nd. ed. (Paris, Presses Univ. de France)
Neyraut, M. (1974) *Le transfert* (Paris, Presses Univ. de France)

Panha, M. (1964) *Milinda's Questions* (London, Luzac)
Pasche, F. (1969) 'De la dépression, in *A partir de Freud* (Paris, Payot)
Peto, A. (1967) 'On affect control', *Psychoanal. Study Child* 22
Pontalis, J.-B (1974) 'Dream as an object', *Int. Rev. Psycho-Anal.* 1. Also in *Frontiers in Psychoanalysis* (London, Hogarth Press, 1981; New York, Int. Univ. Press)
Pulver, S. E. (1971) 'Can affects be unconscious?', *Int. J. Psycho-Anal.* 52

Racker, H. (1968) *Transference and Countertransference* (London, Hogarth Press; New York, Int. Univ. Press)
Rangell, L. (1967) 'Psychoanalysis, affects and the "human core"', *Psychoanal. Quart.* 36
– (1969) 'The intrapsychic process and its analysis', *Int. J. Psycho-Anal.* 50
– (1974) 'Affects and the signal process', unpublished paper summarized in Castelnuovo-Tedesco (1974*b*)
Rapaport, D. (1953) 'On the psychoanalytic theory of affects', *Int. J. Psycho-Anal.* 34
Rosenfeld, H. A. (1965) *Psychotic States* (London, Hogarth Press; New York, Int. Univ. Press)
– (1969) 'Contribution to the psychopathology of psychotic states', in Laurin and Doucet (eds.) (1969)
– (1971) 'A clinical approach to the psychoanalytic theory of the life and death instincts', *Int. J. Psycho-Anal.* 52
Rosolato, G. (1975) 'The narcissistic axis of depression', *Nouv. Rev. Psychanal.* 11. In *Relation d'inconnu* (Paris, Gallimard, 1978)
Rycroft, C. (1968) *A Critical Dictionary of Psychoanalysis* (London, Nelson; New York, Basic Books)
– (1968*a*) *Imagination and Reality* (London, Hogarth Press; New York, Int. Univ. Press)

Sandler, J. (1972) 'The role of affects in psychoanalytic theory', in *Physiology, Emotion and Psychosomatic Illness* (Amsterdam, Elsevier)
Sandler, J., Dare, C., and Holder, A. (1973) *The Patient and the Analyst* (London, Allen & Unwin)
Sauguet, H. (1969) 'Le processus psychanalytique', *Rev. franç. Psychanal.* 38
Saussure, F. de (1916) *Cours de linguistique générale*, 5th ed. (Paris, Payot)
Schafer, R. (1964) 'The clinical analysis of affects', *J. Am. psychoanal. Ass.* 12
Schur, M. (1968) 'Comments on unconscious affects and the signal function', unpublished paper summarized in Löfgren (1968)
Schur, M. (ed.) (1964) *Drives, Affects, Behavior*, Vol. 2 (New York, Int. Univ. Press)
Searles, H. F. (1965) *Collected Papers on Schizophrenia and Related Subjects* (London, Hogarth Press; New York, Int. Univ. Press)
Segal, H. (1957) 'Notes on symbol formation', *Int. J. Psycho-Anal.* 38
– (1972) 'A delusional system as a defence against the re-emergence of a catastrophic situation', *Int. J. Psycho-Anal.* 53
– (1973) *Introduction to the Work of Melanie Klein*, 2nd ed. (London, Hogarth Press; New York, Basic Books)
Serrus, R. (1968) 'Article negat', in Lalande (1968)
Shapiro, E. R., Zinner, J., Shapiro, R. L., and Berkovitz, D. (1975) 'The influence of family experience on borderline personality development', *Int. Rev. Psycho-Anal.* 2
Sherfey, M. J. (1966) 'The evolution and nature of female sexuality in relation to psychoanalytic theory', *J. Am. psychoanal. Ass.* 14
Spitz, R. A. (1956) 'Transference: the analytic setting and its prototype', *Int. J. Psycho-Anal.* 37
– (1957) *No and Yes* (New York, Int. Univ. Press)

– (1958) *The First Year of Life. A Psychoanalytic Study of Normal and Deviant Development Object Relations* (New York, Int. Univ. Press, 1965)

Stern, A. (1938) 'Psychoanalytic investigation of and therapy in the borderline group of neuroses', *Psychoanal. Quart.* 7

Stoller, R. (1975) *Perversion* (New York, Pantheon Books)

Stone, L. (1961) *The Psychoanalytic Situation* (New York, Int. Univ. Press)

– (1971) 'Reflections on the psychoanalytic concept of aggression', *Psychoanal. Quart.* 40

Tausk, V. (1919) 'On the origin of the "influencing machine", in schizophrenia', in *Psychoanal. Quart.* 2 (1933); also in R. Fliess (ed.) *Psychoanalytic Reader* (New York, Int. Univ. Press, 1948)

Torok, M. (1978) 'Maladie du deuil et fantasme du cadavre exquis', in N. Abraham (1978)

Valenstein, A. F. (1962) 'Affects, emotional reliving, and insight into the psychoanalytic process', *Int. J. Psycho-Anal.* 43

Vernant, J.-P. (1972) 'Oedipe sans complexe', in *Mythe et tragédie en Grèce ancienne* (Paris, Maspero)

Viderman, S. (1967) 'Remarques sur la castration et la revendication phallique', *L'Inconscient* 3

– (1970) *La construction de l'espace analytique* (Paris, Denoël)

Winnicott, D. W. (1945) 'Primitive emotional development', in Winnicott (1975)

– (1949) 'Hate in the counter-transference', in Winnicott (1975)

– (1953) 'Transitional objects and transitional phenomena', in Winnicott (1975)

– (1955) 'Metapsychological and clinical aspects of regression within the psycho-analytical set-up', in Winnicott (1975)

– (1956) 'Clinical varieties of transference', in Winnicott (1975)

– (1958) 'The capacity to be alone', in Winnicott (1965)

– (1960a) 'Ego distortion in terms of true and false self', in Winnicott (1965)

– (1960b) 'Counter-transference', in Winnicott (1965)

– (1963) 'Communicating and not communicating leading to a study of certain opposites', in Winnicott (1965)

– (1965) *The Maturational Processes and the Facilitating Environment* (London, Hogarth Press; New York, Int. Univ. Press)

– (1966) 'The mirror-role of mother and family in child development', in Winnicott (1971b)

– (1967) 'The location of cultural experience', in Winnicott (1971b)

– (1969) 'The use of an object and relating through identifications', in Winnicott (1971b)

– (1971a) *Therapeutic Consultations in Child Psychiatry* (London, Hogarth Press; New York, Basic Books)

– (1971b) *Playing and Reality* (London, Tavistock Publications; New York, Basic Books)

– (1974) 'Fear of breakdown', *Int. Rev. Psycho-Anal.* 1

– (1975) *Through Paediatrics to Psycho-Analysis* (London, Hogarth Press; New York, Basic Books)

Wisdom, J. O. (1961) 'A methodological approach to the problems of hysteria', *Int. J. Psycho-Anal.* 42

Zetzel, E. R. (1956) 'Current concepts of transference', *Int. J. Psycho-Anal.* 37

Index

Compiled by Diana LeCore